NEW PERSPECTIVES ON THE SOUTH
Charles P. Roland, General Editor

Twentieth-Century Southern Literature

J. A. BRYANT JR.

THE UNIVERSITY PRESS OF KENTUCKY

Publication of this volume was made possible in part by a grant
from the National Endowment for the Humanities.

Editorial and Sales Offices: The University Press of Kentucky
663 South Limestone Street, Lexington, Kentucky 40508-4008

01   00   99   98   97   1   2   3   4   5

Library of Congress Cataloging-in-Publication Data

Bryant, J. A. (Joseph Allen), 1919–
     Twentieth-century southern literature / J.A. Bryant, Jr.
          p.   cm. — (New perspectives on the South)
     Includes bibliographical references and index.
     ISBN 0–8131–2040–3 (cloth : alk. paper). — ISBN 0–8131–0937–X
(pbk. : alk. paper)
     1. American literature—Southern States—History and criticism.
2. Southern States—In literature.   3. American literature—20th
century—History and criticism.   4. Southern States—Intellectual
life—20th century.   I. Title.   II. Series.
PS261.B79   1997
810.9´975´0904—D21   97–10495

For Sara

Contents

Editor's Preface

Words, whether spoken or written, have given the South its most distinctive form of cultural expression. Oratory was the Old South's most flourishing means of address; writing eclipsed oratory in the twentieth century. Hardly had the celebrated critic H.L. Mencken coined his arid epithet on the region, dubbing it "the Sahara of the Bozart" (a cultural desert), when it flowered into what was to become known as the "Southern Renaissance." Southern literature continues to blossom.

The author of the present work, Professor Joseph A. Bryant Jr., has enjoyed a long career of studying and teaching American and English literature, and has gained from it an extraordinary breadth of knowledge, acuteness of perception, and a maturity of judgment in his fields. He concisely and brilliantly captures here the essence of his subject.

This book is, therefore, ideally suited for inclusion in the New Perspectives on the South series, which is designed to give a fresh and comprehensive view of the defining aspects of the regional experience. Each volume is expected to be a complete essay representing both a synthesis of the best scholarship on its topic and an interpretive analysis drawn from the author's own reflections.

CHARLES P. ROLAND

Preface

The present book is best thought of as an overview—one observer's account, more or less in sequence, of the significant literary achievements of southerners during the twentieth century. A friendly observer has called it a "primer," a designation that is probably as accurate as any. To some extent, moreover, it is an idiosyncratic primer, with a selection and emphasis which, though intended to be fair, are the author's alone. Inevitably the scholarship in it is in large part a compilation and assessment of the discoveries and insights of others, hundreds of researchers and critics who have patiently studied one or more aspects or parts of a field that, as fields go, is bewildering and sometimes baffling in its diversity and complexity.

Many of these workers' contributions have been recorded in two valuable bibliographies, Louis D. Rubin Jr.'s *A Bibliographical Guide to the Study of Southern Literature* (Baton Rouge, La., 1969), and Jerry T. Williams's *Southern Literature, 1968–1975* (Boston, 1978). Listings of more recent work may be found in the annual bibliographies of the Modern Language Association and in the newsletter published by the Society for the Study of Southern Literature. Much of that activity is reflected in the most recent comprehensive account, *The History of Southern Literature* (Baton Rouge, La., 1985), prepared by a group of established scholars under the general editorship of Louis Rubin Jr. For students at all levels this work is an indispensable starting point and resource. The present writer gratefully acknowledges that it has been so for him.

Finally, for valuable criticism and encouragement I am indebted to the members of my family and to several friends of long standing. Among the latter I am especially grateful to two former colleagues, Jerome Meckier and John Cawelti of the University of Kentucky, to George Core of the *Sewanee Review*, to George Garrett of the University of Virginia, whose scrutiny of an earlier draft and suggestions for improvement have put me deeply in his debt, to Armando Prats, who came to the rescue when my computer faltered, and to Walter C. Foreman, without whose knowledge of computer strategies completion of this book might have been postponed indefinitely.

Introduction

At the beginning of the twentieth century, even the most ardent chauvinist would have hesitated to make a case for the existence of a southern literature. The South, in the years before and immediately after the Civil War, had produced competent writers, among them a few whose works continue to bear the scrutiny of discerning readers. Poe was one of these, but for the most part he had ignored the region in his writing. Sidney Lanier had written knowledgeably and sympathetically about the South, but Lanier considered its intellectual climate stultifying and sought for a time to leave. Mark Twain, born on the fringes of the South, disparaged its manners and mores. The rest, with one or two exceptions, had been content to turn out either a succession of plantation narratives, sentimental stories rich mainly in spurious nostalgia, or local-color sketches of varying degrees of authenticity.

No one at the time could have foreseen that within fifty years critics both in the region and outside it would begin pointing to a "Southern Renaissance" and speculate about its causes and its future. Nevertheless, at midcentury the evidence that something of the sort had happened was plain to see. It was also clear that no one city or region, no single movement or coterie, could take credit for more than a fraction of the large body of literature that southerners had managed to produce almost while no one was looking, and that publishers, mainly in the North, had been willing and sometimes eager to publish—this abundance, moreover, in spite of decades of economic depression and a dearth of cultural amenities so severe that one of its critics, Baltimore's H.L. Mencken, himself at least technically a southerner, had referred to the area as a "Sahara of the Bozart."

The body of material, which effectively gave the lie to Mencken's epithet, was remarkable both for its diversity and for its coherence. The sentimental romance was still there (*Gone with the Wind* was a best-seller in the late 1930s), as was the tale of local color, although happily the device of dialectal spelling had all but disappeared; but these old standbys were now overshadowed in the eyes of discriminating readers by a wide variety of novels and specimens of short fiction, a poetry of genuine sophistication, essays on a multitude of topics, and a respectable body of literary criticism that was commanding attention, international as well as national, beyond any that had been produced in America since Poe. The coherence in southern writing was

1

traceable, at least in large part, to a sense of place that after the Civil War had become a major informing principle in virtually everything that southerners produced.

Frequently that sense of place was twofold, manifesting itself first as consciousness of a specific location—Middle Tennessee, Southern Appalachia, the Mississippi Delta, the Virginia Piedmont, or perhaps even a city, Charleston or New Orleans. But as a rule, the reader could usually detect, lurking somewhere above or behind a writer's particular regional consciousness, unmistakable intimations of a transcendent and controlling awareness of the South as a whole and of his or her identity with it. Undoubtedly the sharpness of that comprehensive sense of place derived from the polarization between South and North that had precipitated the Civil War in the first place and then increased in intensity as the result of circumstances that came afterward: specifically, a decade of Reconstruction that impoverished and embittered the populace, followed by half a century of political and economic discrimination and finally a worldwide depression.

During these long and troubled years the process of reconciliation between the two parts of the country remained almost at a standstill; meanwhile, presses, mainly in the North, where the presses were, continued to turn out idealized versions in song and story of what life in the South had been like before the war. Earlier some of the most memorable of these had come from the pen of Thomas Nelson Page, whose sentimental tales, sketches, and poems were popular throughout both the South and the North. At first these productions were cherished uncritically by a southern readership that had felt the sting of defeat; later they were cherished and taken as reliable portraiture by those generations whose memory was necessarily secondhand at best. For northern readers, of course, they had the appeal of exotica and provided an interesting contrast with Mrs. Stowe's picture in *Uncle Tom's Cabin*, which continued to be read there. In any event, for the better part of a century after the war, being southern remained a source of pride that Virginians, Texans, Georgians, and Tennesseans could share, and did so all the more readily as images of plantation life, benevolent whites, and happy darkies became standard fictional fare and the blood and pain of actual war receded into a safe and comfortable past.

Not that other common bonds were lacking. Most people in the South were still agrarian in outlook if not in fact and felt the rhythm of the seasons in their bones, and most maintained the fierce sense of personal independence that had translated into the southerner's political doctrine of state's rights. Other bonds were more down-to-earth: for example, the frontiersman's taste in foods—corn pone, aged ham, greens cooked with hog jowl, buttermilk, beans, and squash. Women maintained their pride in domestic skills, which they demonstrated in direct application if circumstances required or in managerial roles where the establishments were more affluent. Men of all stations kept alive the frontier passion for blood sports—hunting deer, squirrel, dove, and quail; listening to dogs run the fox on crisp winter nights; fishing in all seasons, alone or in company with friends. If the old customs of play parties, church socials, or simply calling on friends on a Sunday afternoon had begun to disappear from all but the most isolated rural communities, the passion for talk, not intellectual exchange but gossip and friendly disputation, remained.

One perennially popular subject for conversation, among women whenever and wherever they gathered and on occasion between women and men, was that of the ever-changing family relationships, one's own family and those of friends and neighbors; for among southerners, of whatever section, one of the most common characteristics was a sense of family, and propriety required that one know not only his or her genealogical derivation to the fourth and fifth generation but also that of everyone else in the community. Actually, people in the community were frequently related to some degree, and it was sometimes useful to know the degree precisely. For detailed information of this kind, one frequently relied on the mental charts of some self-appointed family genealogist (never actually so named), usually an elderly matriarch or bachelor, who dutifully noted the shifting relationships with every new birth or betrothal; but all southerners were expected to have at least a rough working knowledge of such matters.

Closely related to the business of family relationships, and often inseparable from it, was the matter of religion. Most, of course, regarded themselves as Christian, not counting the occasional freethinker, but even among freethinkers most were prepared to declare a church preference—Presbyterian, Episcopalian, Methodist, Baptist, or Disciples of Christ (sometimes referred to disparagingly as Campbellites)—and discuss or debate its merits. Catholics were rare, except in those sections where Catholicism was the rule or well established—Louisiana, Maryland, parts of southern Georgia, the Kentucky Bluegrass region—but Catholics, being a minority in most places, were inclined to keep to themselves. Among Protestants church preferences tended to run in families and constituted a secondary family designation. Wives, as they did with regional political preferences and other such matters, normally took their husband's church preference along with his name. Protestant families of differing denominations, however, mixed freely with one another and on social occasions sometimes fell back on religion to provide additional material for lively conversation.

Political orientation tended to follow a pattern that had been established before the Civil War and confirmed as a consequence of it. People in the more prosperous agricultural areas tended to declare themselves Democrats. Most of those in poorer areas tended to be adherents of factions that coalesced to form the party of Lincoln and vote Republican. Blacks after the war usually voted with them, when they were allowed to vote. The presidential election of 1928, when the Democratic candidate was a Catholic, confronted Protestant southern Democrats with a dilemma from which they never fully recovered. In that year many either abstained or voted Republican, and although Roosevelt managed to bring most of them back into the fold in 1932, the spell had been broken and the possibility of straying established.

Up to and including the years of World War II, however, patterns of allegiance in the South were not greatly different from those that had prevailed since the end of the Civil War. The network of families, religious denominations, and political alliances were much the same. The cuisine had not changed. Pastimes remained the same. Dialectal variations persisted. Veterans returning from the First World War nourished exotic memories of France, Belgium, and England, and moving pictures and radio had given currency to paler versions of those images among those who had remained at home and those who had been too young to go abroad, but the homogenization that was to transform southern life in the wake of TVA, with the advent of rural electrification, better roads, better schools, and chain stores, had only begun. For all practical purposes the Old South was recognizable as the Old South through the years of World War II. Slave or free, black was black, and white was white. Appalachian, upland farmer, and denizens of the plantation South retained their respective identities. The tightly knit family and social units remained identifiably southern, and the Protestantism of both, except in southern Louisiana, more often than not, could be taken for granted.

In general such was the picture of the South reflected in much of the work that up until 1950 southerners wrote about themselves—but only in general. From the turn of the century on, there were perceptible changes. For almost two decades, through World War I and its aftermath, those changes were minimal; but thereafter southern writers, almost as if intent on reinventing themselves, began to refract and disperse the conventional image. Preparation for this greater change had started with the Spanish-American War of 1898, when southerners were given an opportunity to join hands with northerners in a common military enterprise. Fortunately, the opportunity was one that required no backing down on the South's part, no overt demonstration of a willingness to rejoin the Union. To see that, one need only keep in mind that the Mexican War (1846–48), in which southerners had been star performers at all levels, including the presidency, had given substantial expression to a frontier and slaveholding South's motives for expansion. As a result of that war, the addition of Texas to their brotherhood had been validated, and an entire southwest territory had been added to the vast acquisition of the Louisiana Purchase, thereby affirming their deep belief in what a Yankee newspaperman had called the nation's "Manifest Destiny." The lesser war half a century later seemed to many southerners at the time to confer a blessing upon at least one impulse that had been uniquely theirs almost from the beginning: Cuba, it seemed, was once more in view.

World War I, however, was another matter, there the southerners' willing cooperation in a European war that had no special connection with their identity as southerners almost automatically involved a degree of reconciliation—at the least a first step toward ending the chill that had characterized North-South relationships since the days of Reconstruction. It also gave a new generation of authors and would-be authors a contact with a sophistication in art and manners that had been lacking in much of their prevailingly agrarian world. At any rate, in the first decade after that war a new generation of authors rose to take their places in the southern literary landscape: in fiction, Cabell, Stribling, Roberts, Wolfe, and Faulkner; in poetry, Ransom, Tate, Warren, and others of the Fugitive group at Vanderbilt University. By the end of that decade these and others like them had engendered a momentum that would turn the region from the literary Sahara, which with rare exceptions it was, into a land of green fields and running water.

A first stage of the greening came in the 1930s with all but the first of the books that Wolfe was to write in the course of his short life, several of Faulkner's best novels, novels and short stories by K.A. Porter, Caroline Gordon, Allen Tate, Stark Young, Erskine Caldwell, Andrew Lytle, and a score of others whose writings were noteworthy in their time and memorable in ours. These were the years in which R.P. Warren published his first book of poems and his first novel, and in collaboration with Cleanth Brooks founded the *Southern Review* and produced the first of several textbooks that would revolutionize the teaching of literature. These were also the years in which the Vanderbilt poets, stung into defensiveness by the continuing disparagement of northern critics and by the implications of the reforming zeal of New South advocates, launched the Agrarian movement with a view to defining and maintaining the true quality of southern culture. Predictably their efforts provoked ridicule as well as more disparagement, mainly from those in both sections of the country who neglected to attend closely to what these men were saying, and in the end they had little effect on the course of events in the South. Their views, however, made an impression on thoughtful people everywhere and gave young southern writers courage to put aside sentimental images that for half a century had beclouded understanding of their heritage. Black writers also began to be conspicuous during this period. In the 1920s, Jean Toomer had published his memorable *Cane*, though Toomer made no point of his African blood. Richard Wright, Zora Neale Hurston, and Arna Bontemps, on the other hand, openly proclaimed their color as they wrote authoritatively about the black experience.

As World War II approached, activity began to slacken. Wolfe died, and public interest in Faulkner's work all but came to an end. Even so the war years of the 1940s saw some of the South's best work to date: novels and short fiction by R.P. Warren, Eudora Welty, Marjorie Kinnan Rawlings, Andrew Lytle, James Still, and Jesse Stuart, new volumes of poems by Ransom, Tate, and Warren, new critical essays by Ransom and Tate, and more textbooks by Warren in collaboration with Brooks. Faulkner, in spite of declining popularity, published two of his better works in the early part of the decade, *The Hamlet* in 1940 and *Go Down, Moses* in 1942. Then in 1946 the New York critic Malcolm Cowley brought out *The Portable Faulkner* with a brilliant introductory essay and a superb selection from the works. Among the eastern literati this kind of recognition by one of their most respected critics was tantamount to a nomination for canonization, and almost immediately the reading public began demanding Faulkner's works, practically all of which had gone out of print. The result of this shift in popularity was a tremendous success for his next novel, *Intruder in the Dust* (1948), which was subsequently made into a movie. In 1950 he received the Nobel Prize for Literature, the first—and only—southerner to be so honored.

In a very real sense, Faulkner's good fortune, however, became the good fortune of all southern writers. With Cowley's recognition of one of their number and the conferring of the Nobel Prize, attention suddenly turned to their part of the world, and readers everywhere began their discovery of a new field of American literature. The term "Southern Renaissance," which a few southerners had been using cautiously, sometimes with more hope than confidence, began to be heard among critics and reviewers elsewhere, and editors and publishers moved to adjust their sights to include not only those talented southerners who predictably had sought better opportunities in the North but a still undetermined number who inexplicably had chosen to remain where they were. For the first time in literary history, being southern and a writer was beginning to have its advantages.

The story of Southern literature since World War II consists in part of a continuing renaissance, at least during the 1950s and early 1960s, but increasingly it has included writers with little real knowledge of the older South, the living traces of which were still available to nourish people such as Faulkner,

Wolfe, Eudora Welty, and the Vanderbilt poets and novelists. Thus it may be said—as it frequently has been said—that the Southern Renaissance came to an end some years ago, with little fanfare, well before the end of the century itself. Nevertheless, southern writing, the true legacy of that renaissance, has continued—alive, if numbers tell us anything, and well, to judge by the vigor and quality of some of the recent work. It has also remained distinctively southern, certainly in subject matter and frequently also in idiom, suggesting that the region still retains something of its unique identity and that aspects of it remain to be explored recreatively in poetry and fiction. The potential for more—even for another renaissance—is not lacking. Luckily, for the moment at least, the tradition of writing survives in the South, although there as elsewhere the habit of reading may well be in jeopardy. At any rate, the following is an overview of what led up to the South's extraordinary flowering, the flowering itself, and what came after. The last, though not in any sense a renaissance, is in its way almost as remarkable as what went before. We can be thankful for that and, where the future is concerned, hope for the best.

PART ONE

The Making of a Southern Literature

1
The Development of
Modern Southern Fiction

In the difficult years following the Civil War, literature produced in the South continued, as before, to be mainly fiction. Much of that followed the pattern that had been established, or at least anticipated, by John Pendleton Kennedy in his ambivalent celebration of Virginia plantation life, *Swallow Barn* (1832). Kennedy, writing three decades before the outbreak of war, had portrayed the Virginia planter as the heir to such cavalier virtues as pride in family and land, love of honor, respect for bravery, and courtesy toward women, but Kennedy was also prepared to acknowledge that the planter's pastoral existence rested upon the indefensible evil of chattel slavery, for which, he believed, some permanent remedy should be sought. His postwar successors felt less free to be so openly ambivalent.

A notable example was the Atlanta journalist Joel Chandler Harris (1848–1908), who limited his observations about the disparity between the races to symbolic representation in a series of folk tales told by an aging black narrator to the child of his widowed mistress. Harris had found a model for his character in the plantation darkie of poet Irwin Russell's "Christmas Night in the Quarters" (1878), and he began his own variation on that figure by creating a stereotyped black street character to enliven his series of newspaper sketches. When these proved locally popular, he gave his creation a young child for an audience, moved both to a plantation, and through the old man's mouth delivered in convincing dialect the now familiar tales of Brer Rabbit and his animal friends. The result was Harris's first book, *Uncle Remus: His Songs and Sayings* (1880), the immense popularity of which led him to produce a number of others centered on black characters, including three more collections of Uncle Remus's stories (1883, 1892, and 1905). Historians have since debated whether Harris himself realized fully what he had done in elevating his early conventional portrait of the black man to a position of dignity, especially whether he sensed the iconoclasm implicit in making a slave character the narrator of stories in which a normally defenseless rabbit managed repeatedly to subvert the authority of the bear, the fox, and the wolf, all of whom

11

regarded themselves as his superior by virtue of position and natural endowment; readers at the time seem not to have given the matter much thought.

If Harris led the way, however, credit for establishing the conventions of plantation fiction that would provide succeeding generations of chauvinistic southern writers with an easy model must go to Thomas Nelson Page (1853–1922), who used the form to give popular currency to the now familiar romantic myth of an Edenic South in which the young men were invariably gallant, the young women beautiful, and their black retainers happy darkies, content in their service to benevolent masters. This same myth provided the context for his first short story, "Marse Chan" (1884), which was an immediate success in both the North and the South and subsequently became the first story in his most popular book, *In Ole Virginia* (1887). The narrator in the story was an ancient black man, Sam, who told a passing traveler the sad story of his beloved master's unhappy courtship and subsequent death in the war just as the young lady was at last prepared to grant his suit. Page embellished his sentimental tale with all the trappings of the southern myth and provided in his black man's melancholy pronouncement, "Dem wuz good ole times, marster—de bes' Sam ever see! Dey wuz, in fac'!" a theme for plantation fiction as a whole. After this initial success Page wrote prolifically—essays, sketches, short stories, and novels—always promulgating the theme in which he himself seems to have believed, that "befo' de war" an idyllic South had existed which the northern invader had neither appreciated nor understood. Several generations of southern readers were more than ready to believe with him; and apparently many northern readers also took pleasure in doing so, as witnessed by the widespread popularity of Margaret Mitchell's *Gone With the Wind* in 1936, which, though with qualifications scarcely noted at the time, perpetuated the same myth.

As the nineteenth century drew to a close, however, the taste that had fostered the sentimental romanticism of antebellum fiction began to give way, slowly at first and never completely, to a preference for realism that would prevail throughout much of the twentieth century. An interesting development in the use of the black narrator came near the turn of the century with Charles W. Chesnutt's collection of realistic tales, *The Conjure Woman* (1899). Chesnutt (1858–1932) was born in Cleveland, the son of slaves who had sought refuge from oppression they had endured in North Carolina. He returned to North Carolina shortly after the end of the war, grew up in Fayetteville, and taught school there and in other towns in the area for several years before he returned north in 1883 to begin what became a long and successful career as a court reporter, lawyer, and advocate of better race relations. Chesnutt began his career as a serious writer in 1885 with a story published by the McClure newspaper syndicate and wrote prolifically for twenty years thereafter. In *The Conjure Woman*, his first and best book, he allowed a black narrator to present honestly and dramatically the insensitivity of antebellum white overseers and the sadness of black slaves driven to emulate the strategies of Brer Rabbit as a means of preserving their dignity and ensuring their survival. Within the space of six years, Chesnutt produced a second collection of stories, this time without the use of a black narrator, and after that three novels, but none of the later works achieved the success of his first collection. After 1905 he ceased to write, and the public forgot him. It was more than two decades after his death, in 1922, before he again became a factor in the development of southern literature.

A more serious challenge to the authenticity of the southern myth had appeared before Chesnutt, and even before Page with his "Marse Chan" began to elevate it to a position of orthodoxy. This challenge came from George Washington Cable (1844–1925), a native of New Orleans, whose early fiction, especially *Old Creole Days* (1879) and *The Grandissimes* (1880), skillfully portrayed a doomed Creole community incapable of reconciling its proud patrimony with the evils of slavery and racism which that patrimony had generated and fostered. Thereafter Cable's work, as Chesnutt's last novels were to do, became increasingly polemical. His outspoken criticism of southern attitudes and practices so disenchanted southern readers that in 1885 he felt compelled to leave the region and settle in Northampton, Massachusetts, where he continued to write about New Orleans and Louisiana until a few years before his death. Unfortunately, in his northern exile Cable as a writer became increasingly romantic and sentimental, and his later work, though popular nationally at the time, failed to fulfill the promise of his first short stories and his one distinguished novel.

Another native of New Orleans, Grace Elizabeth King (1852–1932), incensed by what she considered Cable's disparagement of his region, at age thirty-three took up writing and produced a short story, "Monsieur Motte," which three years later she expanded into a book. For some years thereafter, King continued her writing. She traveled widely, both in the North and in Europe, and achieved a measure of distinction for perceptive portrayals of the difficulties encountered by Creole families during the period of Reconstruction. Her best work, *The Pleasant Ways of St. Medard* (1916), drew upon the experiences of her own family during that time, but it appeared well after the popular taste for regional fiction had declined and added little to her reputation. At her death King was all but forgotten and like her contemporary Kate Chopin was destined to find her most receptive readers among later generations.

Chopin (1851–1904), whose reputation in the latter half of the twentieth century has exceeded that of all the foregoing, was born Kate O'Flaherty in St. Louis, offspring of an Irish father and a French Creole mother. She moved south as a newlywed in 1870 and lived there comfortably for thirteen years, first in New Orleans and later at Cloutierville in Nachitoches Parish, near her husband's family plantation. For two years after her husband's death in 1883, she continued in the role of plantation manager; then in 1885 she returned with her six children to St. Louis, where she remained for the last nineteen years of her life. Her entire career as a writer took place within the first fourteen of these years.

Chopin's initial attempt at a novel, *At Fault* (1890), was undistinguished, but it contained a treatment, controversial for the time, of alcoholism and divorce as well as some remarkable sketches of plantation life. Favorable reception of the latter, however, led to further sketches and stories, which, when published in 1894 as *Bayou Folk*, established her reputation as a local colorist. Several of the stories in Chopin's second collection the following year, *A Night in Arcadie*, with its sympathetic portrayals of a nineteenth-century woman ill at ease with the restraints society had imposed upon her, disturbed conventionally minded readers. Her second published novel, *The Awakening* in 1899, with its skillfully written story of a woman who for a time actually breaks through those restraints, created a scandal. The admirable sketches of life in New Orleans which graced that work went all but unnoticed in the furor that completely eclipsed her brief popularity. Chopin died five years later, still attempting to write but virtually forgotten by her contemporaries. Ironically, her reputation, now reestablished, rests on an aspect of her work that once condemned her to obscurity.

Several local colorists flourishing in Tennessee and Kentucky fared better. One of these was Mary Noailles Murfree (1850–1922), better known (for a time even to her publisher) by the pseudonym Charles Egbert Craddock. During her youth Murfree had spent summer months at a resort on the Cumberland Plateau, where she came to know the Tennessee mountain people at first hand, and the stories about them that she later published in the *Atlantic Monthly* ensured the success of her first collection, *In the Tennessee Mountains* (1884). Murfree continued to publish prolifically throughout most of her life, but her best works came early, when the public's appetite for her brand of realism was at its peak. Among these were two volumes, a novel, *The Prophet of the Great Smoky Mountains* (1885), and *In the "Stranger People's" Country* (1891). As fashions changed, she changed with them and during her later years wrote historical novels and romances; but her posthumous reputation, mainly among literary historians, rests upon her first works in which she displayed a talent for the delineation of character and an ability to portray the speech and mores of an isolated group of southerners, untouched by the Edenic myth, who might otherwise have been ignored.

Murfree's Kentucky counterpart was John William Fox, Jr. (1863?–1919), whose involvement in his father's mining and timber enterprises brought him into intimate contact with the mountain people of eastern Kentucky and western Virginia. The result was a series of collections, among them *A Cumberland Vendetta and Other Stories* (1896), *"Hell fer Sartin" and Other Stories* (1897), and *Christmas Eve on Lonesome and Other Stories* (1904). Fox's skill in portraying these mountain people would have been sufficient to guarantee him a place in the story of southern literature; but like Murfree he also had a talent for constructing longer works, though not her talent for character delineation. Half a century after his death Fox is best remembered for two of his sentimental novels, *The Little Shepherd of Kingdom Come* (1903) and *The Trail of the Lonesome Pine* (1908).

These were some of the southern writers whose view of their region diverted and to some extent edified readers at the turn of the century. All these, together with a score of others scarcely remembered at all, each in his or her way, helped to prepare the ground for the major southern fiction of twentieth-century writers such as Stark Young, Elizabeth Madox Roberts, William Faulkner, Robert Penn Warren, Eudora Welty, and Andrew Lytle. For the most part they were primarily regionalists, but one or two—notably Cable and Chopin—continue to command respect for talents and insights unnoted or unappreciated in their own time.

One writer, older than any of these and vastly more gifted, could by virtue of derivation alone justly claim a place in the story of southern literature. His best work belongs to the nineteenth century, but without it twentieth-century southern literature, to say nothing of the rest of American literature, would be unthinkable. Samuel Langhorne Clemens (1835–1910), universally known as Mark Twain, although born in Missouri when it was still western frontier, derived substance and style from antebellum southern humorists and wrote masterpieces about life on the Mississippi. The first of Clemens's southern works began as a memoir in seven installments, "Old Times on the Mississippi," published in the *Atlantic Monthly* in 1875. Later he expanded these into a book, which he published in 1883 as *Life on the Mississippi*. The finished work was still a memoir, ostensibly in the manner of his *Innocents Abroad* (1869) and *Roughing It* (1872), but as the historian Louis Rubin has noted, it is the memoir of a mature novelist of genius and presents a coherent narrative suggestive of the maturation of a literary artist who has learned to look beneath the kinds of surface that local colorists were depicting and beyond to the timeless realities that can make the picturesque meaningful.

Two other narratives of life along the river followed, *The Adventures of Tom Sawyer* (1876) and *Adventures of Huckleberry Finn* (1885), both widely recognized as classics of American literature. The first of these, which Clemens called "a hymn to boyhood," was a hymn replete with discords, realistic images of the darker aspects of the Edenic world that other accounts had discreetly omitted. The second was a masterwork symbolizing in the inexorable course of the river and Huck's encounters along its way paradoxes that have manifested themselves throughout Western humanity's long progress toward domination of the globe. Clemens's use of Huck as narrator also enabled him to focus the story on all mankind's perilous advance toward self-realization and made of the innocent boy's account, whether he realized it or not, a universal paradigm. *Huckleberry Finn* remains, beyond doubt, the greatest single achievement in southern fiction. Still, Clemens by choice was only incidentally southern, and he made his contribution as an American author, without reference to regional provenance. Like Hawthorne and Melville before him and his contemporary Henry James, he opened doors for all the American novelists who should come after; his work, like theirs, belongs in the end to no region but stands on its own unique ground.

RICHMOND: THE FIRST MAJOR SOUTHERN NOVELS

As the old century came to an end, an outside observer might have said that if a renaissance was to happen in the South, it most likely would take place in Virginia, and if there, in Richmond. Long before the Civil War Richmond had served as the cultural center of the southern states. William Byrd, a scholar and author as well as a landowner, had established the city in 1737 and given it its name. It had been the site of the Virginia Convention in 1775, the roster of which included such names as George Washington, Thomas Jefferson, Richard Henry Lee, Peyton Randolph, and Patrick Henry. In 1779 it became the state capital and in 1861 the capital of the Confederacy. Throughout the nineteenth century Richmond, with its industries, book firms, and newspapers, competed with New Orleans for the right to be called the most cosmopolitan city in the South. Even the devastation that followed the evacuation of the city by Confederate troops in 1864 failed to dim its luster or diminish the vigor of its people. By 1900 several writers either born in Richmond or closely associated with it were beginning to attract national attention. Among these were three women, all novelists.

The oldest was Amelie Louise Rives (1863–1945), who in 1886 began writing a series of romantic tales, some told in dialect, which she collected in a volume entitled *Brother to Dragons and Other Old-Time Tales* and published with considerable success in 1888. Over the next forty years Rives was to write and publish some twenty-three novels, now largely forgotten; but with her third, *The Quick or the Dead?*, also published in 1888, she introduced an element of psychological realism into her work that marked a departure from the popular romances and local-color stories of the day and earned for her a small but secure place in southern literary history.

The historical novels of her younger contemporary, Mary Johnston (1870–1936), born in Buchanan, just west of the Blue Ridge Mountains, were more memorable. Johnston's second novel, *To Have and to Hold* (1900), a skillfully written tale of early Jamestown, has continued to be read and, in recent years, applauded by critics. In 1905 she moved to Richmond and remained there for seven years. Afterward she lived with her sisters in the mountainous setting of Warm Springs but maintained the friendship she had formed in Richmond with another novelist, Ellen Glasgow (1873–1945), and participated with Glasgow in the suffragist movement and other feminist causes. Two Civil War novels, *The Long Roll* (1911) and *Cease Firing* (1912), marked the beginning of Johnston's maturation as a novelist. The first volume deals with the war as Virginia knew it and presents authentic portraits of persons—Robert E. Lee, Jeb Stuart, A.P. Hill, and Jefferson Davis—who figured prominently in the events there. The most striking of these figures, and central to the development of the novel, is the enigmatic genius who still dominates southern memory of the war, Stonewall Jackson. The second deals with the last days of the war in Richmond, when events took on a life of their own and proceeded to an inexorable conclusion in devastation and temporary despair. Both exhibit a neat blend of fiction and documentable history which, as the novelist-critic George Garrett has observed, made a breach in the wall that had long separated fiction from nonfiction, through which such later practitioners as Shelby Foote, Mary Lee Settle, and Norman Mailer would pass with relative ease. They also initiated a series of works, some sixteen novels in all, in which Johnston's own intellectual questing gave new substance to explorations of the southern past. In this respect at least, her fiction resembles that of Ellen Glasgow, who replaced her, at least in her own time, in the eyes of northern critics.

The work of Ellen Glasgow has continued to hold its position as the most significant body of fiction produced in the South before the advent of Wolfe and Faulkner. Glasgow, like Rives, was born in Richmond and with the exception of some five years in New York maintained a home there until she died in 1945. Almost from the first, however, she manifested many of the characteristics of the independent women she would write about in her novels. By choice she had little formal education, preferring to read widely on her own. She early rejected her father's Presbyterianism and, at the suggestion of a friend, immersed herself instead in a variety of philosophical works, those of Herbert Spencer, J.S. Mill, and Charles Darwin, especially the last of these, whose emphasis on the instinct for survival in all creatures, regardless of category or sex, impressed her profoundly.

In early womanhood Glasgow engaged in several protracted affairs but never married, and although bound sentimentally by ties of affection to her native region, she nevertheless deplored its reverence for antiquated mores and the institutions that had perpetuated them. Above all, she resented and resisted the secondary role that it imposed upon women of her station. Her first published novel, *The Descendant* (1897), actually one of two that she had for some time struggled to complete, was a commercial and critical success and set the thematic direction for the first phase of her work. In it an illegitimate poor-white girl from Virginia with radical inclinations escapes to New York and finds there a congenial companion in a well-bred young southern woman, a fellow escapee, who has defected to the North to study painting. In both characters Glasgow projected her own impulse to nonconformity in a world she described succinctly in the first chapter of *Barren Ground* (1925): "The good families of the state have preserved, among other things, custom, history, tradition, romantic fiction, and the Episcopal Church. The good people, according to the records of clergymen, which are the only surviving records, have preserved nothing except themselves." She continued the same projection in her second novel, *Phases of an Inferior Planet* (1898), and in her third, *The Voice of the People* (1900), she carried it back to a Richmond setting. Adding social criticism in that work to her celebration of nonconformity, Glasgow worked into her narrative a comparison of the aristocratic pretensions of Virginia's colonial capital, Williamsburg, which she found tolerable, with the less tolerable pretensions of her native city. At some point in her early development as a novelist, she took an even more significant step. "As a young girl, thinking over my first book," she explained in 1933, "I . . . resolved that I would write of the South not sentimentally, as a conquered province, but dispassionately, as a part of the larger world. I . . . resolved that I would write not of southern characteristics, but of human nature." And for Glasgow emphasizing human nature meant taking into account that instinct for survival and self-realization in both sexes that had impressed her in her reading of Darwin.

The shift was apparent in several of the novels that she wrote during the next two decades: *The Battle-Ground* (1902), in which the wife of the hero returns with her husband to a devastated Richmond in 1864 and takes sober satisfaction in the prospect of rebuilding, this time as an equal partner in their enterprise of living; *The Deliverance* (1904), in which a brother and sister, destitute after the war but still proud, indulge a senile parent in her inability, or unwillingness, to recognize that she is no longer living in the imagined Eden of antebellum Virginia; and in *Virginia* (1913), the story of the self-emancipation of a young woman instructed both at home and in a proper finishing school about the behavior expected of her in a male-dominated society.

The next few years constituted an unfortunate interval for Glasgow. In 1911 she had taken an apartment in New York, where she lived and wrote *Life and Gabriella*, one of her weaker novels. At her father's death in 1916 she returned to Richmond and soon found herself involved in an affair with one Henry Anderson, a politically ambitious man of the New South, and collaborated with him on an uninspired novel, *The Builders* (1919), which promptly failed. Then a series of misfortunes—the decision of an earlier lover, with whom she had remained on good terms, to marry another woman, the death of her early publisher, Walter Hines Page, and Henry Anderson's much publicized flirtation with Queen Marie of Romania—all compelled her to take stock of herself. Meanwhile, she hastened her recovery by writing another novel, *One Man in His Time* (1922), and by bringing out a collection of short stories, *The Shadowy Third and Other Stories* (1923).

In 1925 Glasgow completed and published the novel by which she is best known, *Barren Ground*. Skillfully written, rich in meaningful detail, it presents the story of Dorinda Oakley, one of the "good people" of the exhausted southern Virginia farm country, who finds within herself the fortitude to rise above circumstances that had reduced many like her to submission: a shiftless family, a weakling for a lover, and the broomsedge that repeatedly has claimed dominion over their worn-out land. The compassion in her triumph over all these obstacles is the measure of her strength, which renders her independent of them and enables her at the end to dismiss the prize of a socially approved marriage with a smiling, "Oh, I've finished with all that. . . . I am thankful to have finished with all that." The popular and critical success of *Barren Ground* had a therapeutic effect for Glasgow that her two previous novels had failed to achieve, and within the next decade she turned out three more novels that secured for her the permanent place she holds in American fiction.

Two of these works were satirical comedies, *The Romantic Comedians* (1926) and *They Stooped to Folly* (1929), both of which dealt amusingly with the disintegration of codes that had long denied women of "good families" the full range of human needs and responses. The third, *The Sheltered Life* (1932), which some consider technically her masterpiece, was a sober piece with contrasting portraits of the women in Richmond society: Mrs. Archbold, who presides over the family establishment and preserves its illusions about men and women; neurotic Aunt Etta, unmarried and unloved; strong-willed Aunt Isabel, loved but unmarried, whose union with an attractive carpenter of lower station prompts some ingenious but transparent justification; young Jenny Blair, bewildered by contradictions between the illusions she has been taught to cherish and the reality that in the end she is unable to avoid; and at the center of the story, Eva Birdsong, beautiful and admired, who successfully denies the existence of the double standard allowed to even the better sort of men until truth forces her to prove the validity of her compromised ideal by shooting her philandering husband. However one may rate it, *The Sheltered Life* was both the climax of Glasgow's achievement as a novelist and a summing up of those themes that she had dealt with separately in her other major novels. In her remaining years she published two more, *Vein of Iron* (1935), set in the days of the Great Depression of the early 1930s, and *In This Our Life* (1941), for which she belatedly received a Pulitzer Prize. In 1943 she published a collection of prefaces to her novels, *A Certain Measure*, and at her death in 1945 left in manuscript format an autobiography and a sequel to her prize-winning novel, both of which were published posthumously.

Although critics almost unanimously have noted the unevenness of Glasgow's collective performance, most concede that the best of her work amply justifies her prominent place in the development of southern fiction and a somewhat more modest position in American letters as a whole. At her best she enhanced the realistic mode that she inherited, enriching it with superior characterization and a degree of irony far surpassing that of any of her predecessors. Granted that she sometimes allowed the vagaries of personal life to dictate the direction and tone of her work, she early found her most congenial literary role to be that of a satirist, a knowledgeable critic of the manners and mores of a proud but moribund establishment just beginning to confront the disconcerting task of self-redefinition. As her career advanced, she made the most of that role, deploying to the full, usually with compassion, her intelligence, extraordinary powers of perception, native talent for writing, and a sense of history in at least half a dozen books.

Glasgow was never the reclusive writer. As a citizen of Richmond she participated in a variety of communal efforts to confirm the city's place as a cultural center in the New South of the twentieth century. She extended her hospitality to a host of well-known writers and other dignitaries, who discovered a congenial literary climate in Richmond's vigorous Virginia Writers Club. She was one of the movers in establishing the *Reviewer*, which, although it survived for only four years in Richmond (1921–24), could name among its contributors John Galsworthy, Allen Tate, Julia Peterkin, Robert Nathan, DuBose Heyward, and Paul Green. In 1931 she joined with historian Douglass Southall Freeman in sponsoring a memorable conference of southern writers at the University of Virginia, one of the first of its kind, which brought together a remarkable assembly of literary figures, among them, in addition to Heyward, Tate, and Green, Donald Davidson, Caroline Gordon, James Boyd, Laurence Stallings, Thomas Wolfe, and William Faulkner. In short, Glasgow became both in public and private life a one-woman response to H.L. Mencken's notorious and not wholly unjustified characterization of the South as a "Sahara of the Bozart," and Mencken himself acknowledged the salutary effect of her example and influence.

An even more conspicuous exception noted in Mencken's sweeping denunciation of the southern Sahara was Richmond's James Branch Cabell (1879–1958). Cabell conformed neatly to one of the stereotypes of the Virginia aristocrat. By nature shy but proud of his ancestry and endowed by circumstances of birth with good manners to supplement a native intelligence and latent talent, he grew up with visions of heroism in his head. Almost from the first these were visions tempered and humanized by a wealth of gossipy stories about Civil War heroes, several of whom his elders had known intimately, and this bounty served to leaven the store of classical myth and Arthurian legend that he had begun to amass almost before he learned to read. His parents sent him to the College of William and Mary, Virginia's oldest, where he played the dandy and distinguished himself in composition and languages, so much so in the latter that as an upperclassman he was allowed to teach French and Greek to undergraduates. There in his senior year, however, Cabell's age of innocence came to an abrupt end.

Rumor, soon proved to be unfounded, that he was involved in a college homosexual affair delayed his graduation and caused temporary embarrassment. A more lasting shock came at his return to Richmond in 1898 to find that his parents had separated, and still another when, after three years in newspaper work he was suspected of involvement in the murder of a cousin, reportedly his mother's lover. Cabell's response to this succession of setbacks was to plunge into work as a professional genealogist, his principal occupation for the next ten years. During this period, however, he continued to write, publishing stories and sketches in national magazines, among them Mencken's *Smart Set*. In 1903 his mother took the manuscript of his first novel, *The Eagle's Shadow*, to a New York publisher, who brought it out the following year.

From that point on until his death Cabell published steadily, sometimes two books in a single year. At first he found his most congenial mode to be that of satirical social comedy, after the manner of his friend Ellen Glasgow, and for such comedies he drew heavily upon his experiences in Richmond (Lichfield in the novels) and Williamsburg (Fairhaven). His notable successes in this semiautobiographical mode during his early years as a writer were *Cords of Vanity* (1909) and *The Rivet in Grandfather's Neck* (1915); in later years, *Something about Eve* (1927). In 1913 at age thirty-three his life took a happier turn with marriage to a charming widow, Rebecca Priscilla Bradley, more than four years his senior and the mother of five children. From that point on, vicissitudes, both public and private, seemed to bother Cabell less, and as he later testified, he found in the course of writing *The Cream of the Jest*, published in 1917, that his best subject was his role as an artist in the world of changing manners and morals. The works of the next decade are the ones by which he is most likely to be remembered: *Jurgen* (1919), *Figures of Earth* (1921), *The High Place* (1923), *Straws and Prayerbooks* (1924), *The Silver Stallion* (1926), and the aforementioned *Something about Eve.*

It was *Jurgen*, however, that made Cabell famous and, for the time being, notorious. Sexual play, discreetly presented, had enlivened several of his early novels for sophisticated readers, but *Jurgen* was more explicit and proceeded on the assumption that the same sexual drives characterized both sexes. Authorities in New York charged that the book had violated the state's antipornography laws and took the publisher to court. The combative Mencken, who had published short stories by Cabell and professed great admiration for his work, came quickly to the defense and prompted other literary figures to do likewise. The publisher was exonerated after two years, but by that time the sales of *Jurgen* had skyrocketed and Cabell himself had become in the eyes of the reading public a symbol of sophistication and, at least in the eyes of the literary world, a champion of an author's right to proceed as his gifts dictated without fear of censorship.

In retrospect one is impressed more by the imaginative skill of the work than by its power to shake the sensibilities. The story, detached from time and place and reminiscent of Rabelais, is that of a middle-aged composite of Faust, Don Juan, and Odysseus, who, having bargained with the devil for the body of a twenty-year-old, enjoys a progress from passionate youth through several stages of indulgence and commitment, only to return at the end to the relative repose of home and a shrewish wife. In the course of his philanderings, he encounters three queens of mythology, Guenevere (chivalry), Anaitis (gallantry), and Helen (vision), the last symbolizing the sublimation of physical love in poetry, and arrives at last at a celebration of marriage—the whole presumably an allegory of Cabell's own maturation, from innocence through stages of experimentation to a realization of peace in art and the companionship of a woman on more or less equal terms.

Midway in this his most fruitful period, Cabell announced that he had intended all his previous work to fit into a comprehensive epic plan, a universal biography of man. Accordingly he set to work recasting and revising everything he had done up to that point to form what he called "The Biography of the Life of Manuel," which he published as the Storisende Edition of *The Works of James Branch Cabell* in twenty (actually eighteen) volumes (1927–30). Thereafter for more than fifteen years he published fiction, essays, and allegorized biography under the name Branch Cabell, resuming the "James" only with *Let Me Lie* in 1947. In the last ten years of his life he produced four more books, but his fame and reputation had declined steadily since the Storisende Edition, and he died virtually forgotten. Most agree that Cabell's achievement, taken as a whole, is an anomaly in the development of southern fiction. His best work has no predecessors and no successors of note; but it stands securely in the niche he himself created, and it contributed, more perhaps than he realized, to the demolition of provincial barriers that had restricted southern authors to American models of romantic fiction, historical and otherwise, and to regionalism that had guided them for almost half a century. With Cabell and several other adventurous writers who in the 1920s and 1930s were beginning to explore the possibilities of fiction, it became increasingly common for writers in the South to venture farther afield and try their hand at the themes and devices exploited by European authors, on the continent as well as in the British Isles, who in their time had been among the avant-garde.

CONTRIBUTIONS FROM THE MID-SOUTH

During this period half a dozen other writers in Georgia, South Carolina, Tennessee, and Kentucky—all but one of them noticed and encouraged by Mencken—contributed in varying degrees to the widening scope of southern fiction. One, whom Cabell also had encouraged, was an Atlanta librarian, Frances Newman (1883–1928). Newman's career as a writer of fiction began late and ended abruptly, just as she was beginning to show promise. Before 1924 most of her writing had been limited to reviews and work on a critical anthology, *The Short Story's Mutations*, which she completed and published in that year. At Cabell's insistence, however, she had begun to try her hand at fiction; and the result was a superior story, "Rachel and Her Children," which won an O. Henry Memorial Prize, also in 1924. Then in 1926 she published the first of her two novels, *The Hard-Boiled Virgin*. The second, *Dead Lovers Are Faithful Lovers*, followed in 1928, the year of her death. The titles of both novels point to the cynicism that was often the fate of southern women of her generation, who, even if they managed to ignore the limitations of their upbringing, still had to deal with the consequences of asserting their human needs and drives in a male-dominated world that denied them full status as equals. Several of Ellen Glasgow's heroines faced the same predicament, but Newman's well-bred women did more than demand equal status. They indulged in erotic thoughts and fantasies that well-bred white women were not expected to have, and well-bred readers, in the North and the South alike, were offended and alarmed.

In South Carolina two writers were emerging who asserted something like full human status for black people, but both kept their characters safely within the confines of black society and so avoided disturbing the composure of their reading public. One of these was Julia Peterkin (1880–1961), who in her early forties had begun writing stories and sketches for Mencken's *Smart Set* and Richmond's *Reviewer* about the Gullah people on the coastal plantation where she lived. In 1924 she published *Green Thursday*, a collection of twelve stories, and three years later her first novel, *Black April*, with the black foreman of a plantation as its central figure. Peterkin's first book, had she done nothing else, might have passed simply as another better-than-average contribution to the South's continuing output of local color. The second, however was different, and Vanderbilt's reactionary Agrarian, Donald Davidson, who was as perceptive as he was conservative, recognized the significance of what she had done, suggesting it also might well be the first genuine novel in English of the Negro as a human being. He might have said something of the sort about her next novel, *Scarlet Sister Mary* (1928), the story of a black woman who lived by her wits. For that Peterkin won a Pulitzer Prize, but her last novel, *Bright Skin* (1932), dealt with the special problem of being mulatto in a black community and sparked little interest. Peterkin's contemporary DuBose Heyward (1885–1940) was luckier with his two novels about Charleston's blacks, *Porgy* (1925) and *Mamba's Daughters* (1925). Both were popular and critical successes, and Heyward with the assistance of his wife turned both into equally successful plays. *Porgy* was ensured an even longer life when George and Ira Gershwin converted it into a folk opera that played as musical theater on Broadway and later found its way to legitimate opera stages in Europe and eventually into the repertory of New York's Metropolitan Opera.

It was the Tennessee writer T.S. Stribling (1881–1965), however, who opened the way for the full-scale literary treatment of blacks that reached maturity in the novels of William Faulkner. His *Birthright* (1922) with its account of the unsuccessful efforts of a Harvard-educated black to improve the status of black people in his native town won the enthusiastic approval of the iconoclastic Mencken and encouraged Stribling to write a series of didactic novels satirizing the bigotry and materialism of small-town life in the mid-South. *Teeftallow* (1926) and *Bright Metal* (1928) dealt with that life in Tennessee; *Backwater* (1930), in neighboring Arkansas. Then in the early 1930s he produced a memorable trilogy—*The Forge* (1931), *The Store* (1932), and *The Unfinished Cathedral* (1934)—which chronicled the rise of a poor-white family and anticipated superior performances by Faulkner in his depiction of Sutpen's rise and the insidious progress of a proliferation of Snopeses from shiftless poverty to domination of Yoknapatawpha County. As Stribling might have expected, his work met with suspicion on the part of southern critics, but nationally his work was generally acclaimed until Faulkner's began to eclipse it.

Another Tennesseean of the period who attracted Mencken's attention concentrated in her best work on the pitfalls of the tradition-bound male-female relationship that Frances Newman was satirizing. This was Evelyn Scott (1893–1963), who almost from the start exemplified in private life the developing revolution in southern attitudes that she depicted in her best work. Scott was born Elsie Dunn in Clarksville, Tennessee, to parents of means who had provided an atmosphere of gentility for her childhood and sent her for finishing to respectable Sophie Newcomb College and the Newcomb College of Art in New Orleans. She responded to this modest measure of liberation by running off to Brazil with a married man, a dean at Tulane, and sealing her break with Tennessee, family, and tradition by taking the name that she kept for the rest of her life. While there she contributed verse to *Poetry*, *Dial*, and other little magazines and on her return to the States in 1919 published a small volume of poems, *Precipitations* (1920).

The following year she found her proper medium with a successful novel, *The Narrow House*, which became the first in a trilogy that included *Narcissus* (1922) and *The Golden Door* (1925). In these she traced a southern family through three generations, placing emphasis on the tension created in their marriages by the conflict between inherited social mores and the demands of their natural sexual impulses. In 1923 Scott published the explicitly autobiographical *Escapade*, an account of her own attempt to resolve the same conflict during her years in Brazil, material that ten years later she would transmute into *Eva Gay: A Romantic Novel* (1933), there giving prominence to the part that writing can play in such a resolution. Meanwhile, she had turned to historical material for a second trilogy: *Migrations* (1927), which dealt with the country's westward expansion; *The Wave* (1929), a sweeping account of the Civil War; and the most ambitious of the three, the two-volume *A Calendar of Sin, American Melodramas* (1933), covering events from the end of the

Civil War to the outbreak of World War I and once more stressing the damaging effect of traditional notions about sex and marriage.

From that point on public interest in Scott's work declined. In 1930 she had married the English novelist John Metcalf and from 1939 until 1952 lived in London, but she was never able to find a publisher for any of the work she produced there or during the years after her return. The causes she had espoused in her happier years no longer needed a champion, at least among the readers her books could be expected to have, and she died in 1963 virtually forgotten. Those few who remembered, mainly scholars, recognized the advance she had fostered in fiction's freedom to treat frankly the role of sex in human relations and her willingness to put to the test techniques of narration that another generation of southern writers would exploit with profit.

In Kentucky another woman, twelve years older than Scott, having begun late in life and concluded her career more than twenty years earlier than she, produced a modest body of fiction that would meet the test of time more successfully. Elizabeth Madox Roberts (1881–1941) neither confirmed nor seriously challenged the lingering archaic mores and perhaps for that reason was passed over by Mencken and his friends. She was born in Perryville, Kentucky, the site of one of the crucial battles of the Civil War, and spent most of her life in nearby Springfield. Her father, a one-time schoolteacher, surveyor, merchant, and farmer, supplemented her early training with an exposure to the classics and philosophy, especially the idealism of Bishop Berkeley, and thus provided the base for much of the writing she was to do. For several years Roberts taught school in Springfield and in neighboring communities but finding that occupation physically taxing, at age thirty-six enrolled for graduate work at the University of Chicago. There her fellow graduate students, among them Yvor Winters and Glenway Wescott, introduced her to the poetry of Yeats, Eliot, Pound, H.D., and Wallace Stevens and prompted her to begin writing verse of her own in the new mode. Roberts had already published a small volume of poems about Rocky Mountain flowers, *In the Great Steep's Garden* (1915), the result of a protracted visit in Colorado. The book of children's poems that grew out of the Chicago experience, however, *Under the Tree* (1922), established her credentials as a minor modern poet and encouraged her to try her hand at novels.

With her first, *The Time of Man* (1926), she emerged on the literary scene as an important novelist. *The Time of Man* became a Book of the Month Club selection and almost immediately established her national and international reputation. During the next twelve years she published seven more: *My Heart and My Flesh* (1927), *Jingling in the Wind* (1928), *The Great Meadow* (1930), *A Buried Treasure* (1931), *The Haunted Mirror* (1932), *He Sent Forth a Raven* (1935), and in 1938 *Black Is My True Love's Hair*. By that time, however, public interest in her work had sharply diminished, and in the remaining three years of her life her work consisted only of a third book of poems, *Song in the Meadow* (1940), and a collection of short stories, *Not by Strange Gods*, which appeared in 1941, the year of her death.

In subject matter, style, and vision, Roberts's novels were unlike those of any of her contemporaries, and her moments of popularity were probably accidental, coming as they did when her two most successful books coincided with waves of fashion. *The Time of Man* in 1926 was the story of shiftless tenant farmers and appealed to much the same audience that had applauded Glasgow's *Barren Ground* the year before. Four years later, *The Great Meadow*, set in the context of the settling of Kentucky, appeared just as the taste for historical fiction that would persist throughout the 1930s had begun to gain momentum. Moreover, both of these dealt with characters who, although untutored, underprivileged, and born to hardship, managed to endure adversity and achieve, as R.P. Warren later put it, "the strength to deal with life."

A few perceptive friends, critics, and fellow novelists, however, among them her former classmates Winters and Wescott, T.S. Stribling, Sherwood Anderson, and Ford Madox Ford, had a better idea than her public of what Roberts had really done. They saw that her stories were reflections of a congenital inclination (perhaps reinforced by the early exposure to Berkeley) to create a unique world out of whatever she saw, heard, and touched in her rural Kentucky milieu, and she accepted that world, the only one she knew, without demur or condescension. At their best, the adult characters in her novels are like the child whose poems we hear in *Under the Tree*, Wordsworthian innocents who construct their dreams of life, or fictions, out of sensible things most sophisticated adults have learned to disregard, and thus they remain immune to fatal disappointment. Most important, as an artist Roberts instinctively grasped the Jamesian principle of narrative focus and the need to render in language, to use Ford's term, the action of her story rather than merely relate it. The result was poetry in fiction, the like of which had not appeared before in southern writing: a series of novels that to be appreciated demanded the sustained attention required by the best modern verse. Some have suggested that her decision to write principally about women should make all her works attractive in an age of feminist activity. Perhaps so, but the sensibility she gave to Ellen Chesser and Diony Jarvis in her two popular successes, though her own, is not exclusively feminine. It is also the sensibility that distinguishes Yeats, Synge, and Pound, to say nothing of Emily Dickinson, Keats, and Shakespeare. Roberts may or may not be the equal of any of these, but she is comfortable in their company.

The Emergence of the Black Writer

Another development in southern fiction during the years following World War I took place, in part, outside the South. In 1933 the black scholar Sterling Brown (1901–89) published in the *Journal of Negro Education* a memorable essay, "Negro Character as Seen by White Authors." In it he reviewed the stereotypic molds used by whites, even before the time of Thomas Nelson Page, to present black people to their reading public. In his concluding section Brown noted the handful of writers who had avoided stereotyping and singled out for special approval the southern novelists Stribling, Heyward, and Scott. At the time of his writing, however, somewhat more than a handful of southern black authors in the preceding decade, expatriates in their way, had begun to speak for themselves in poetry, drama, and fiction that foreshadowed the major work their younger contemporaries would produce in the years following World War II.

Even before that time southern blacks had not been altogether silent. Charles W. Chesnutt, writing around the turn of the century, was a notable example, but Chesnutt had spoken briefly and quietly and made a point of avoiding a display of his color. Another was the poet James Weldon Johnson (1871–1938), who in 1912 published anonymously *The Autobiography of an Ex-Coloured Man*, a novel that gave a frank account of the expedient of "passing" resorted to by those blacks who could manage it as a means of coping with the discrimination they inevitably faced in white society. Johnson's novel received little attention when it first appeared. No one then could foresee that it had anticipated the awakening shortly to occur among aspiring black writers in many parts of the South and elsewhere that would enable them to begin to assume their place in the mainstream of American letters.

One impediment for black authors in the years preceding World War I was the scarcity of outlets for any work they might produce. From time to time black writers had managed to publish in such national magazines as *Smart Set*, *Atlantic Monthly*, and *Harper's*, but there were no magazines receptive by policy to black authors. Suddenly by 1920, or soon thereafter, there were three: the NAACP's *Crisis*, the National Urban League's *Opportunity: A Journal of Negro Life*, and *Messenger*, the official organ of the Brotherhood of Sleeping Car Porters. At the same time large numbers of blacks, drawn north to meet labor shortages during the war, had congregated in urban centers, notably in New York's Harlem, where they formed an intellectual community prepared to take advantage of the opportunities that were opening for black artists of all kinds. Many of these were either southern or had strong ties with the South, and as might have been expected most were primarily poets. Two who would continue to be prominent long after the so-called Harlem Renaissance had run its course were James Weldon Johnson, whose novel was reissued, this time with more success, in 1927 with a preface by Carl Van Vechten, and Langston Hughes (1902–67), Missouri-born but with strong ancestral ties to the deep South, whose early fiction would include a novel about growing up black, *Not without Laughter* (1930), and a collection of short stories, *Ways of White Folks* (1934).

Three novelists of at least minor stature, however, all southern, emerged from the Harlem center of the black awakening: Jean Toomer (1894–1967), Zora Neale Hurston (1891–1960), and Arna Bontemps (1902–73). Toomer's connection with the Harlem Renaissance was tangential, but it produced a novel of sorts, *Cane* (1922), one of two books that he published during his lifetime and commonly acknowledged to be the work most representative of the spirit of the new black awakening. He was born in Washington, D.C., and reared in the household of a grandfather, P.B.S. Pinchback, who had served as lieutenant governor of Louisiana during Reconstruction. As a child Toomer went by the name Eugene Pinchback. Thereafter he lived at various times in the New York area, Chicago, Philadelphia, Georgia, Wisconsin, Massachusetts, and France. His changes in residence were paralleled by even more changes in job, vocational direction, religion, and politics, but throughout the changes he read widely, wrote steadily, and continued to search for a philosophical pattern that would enable him to establish his identity in some larger comprehensive unity. The writing of *Cane* came about as the result of three weeks spent in Sparta, Georgia, where he served temporarily as the principal of a black school. One of the sketches that he produced there was accepted for publication by the NAACP's *Crisis*, and on returning to New York Toomer found himself involved in the activities of Harlem's community of artists. Not long after, Boni and Liveright accepted the entire collection, and although like Charles Chesnutt before him he requested that he not be identified as black, his editor Waldo Frank had already written an introduction for *Cane* proclaiming its author's color. Thus Toomer, in spite of his wish to be simply an American author, came before his larger public as a newly liberated black.

The tenuous unity of *Cane*, which contained poetry and drama as well as prose, was maintained principally by the controlling vision of an unnamed narrator. It consisted of three parts. The first section contained six sketches illustrative of the black woman's difficulties in maintaining her natural sexual identity in the face of taboos, traditions repressive of females, and male lust. The second presented blacks transported from the benefits and dangers of their rural setting to urban Washington, where they encounter a new set of difficulties: the materialism and greed of white society, the demand that they develop something like white ambition to ensure their survival in that society, and the ever-present threat of racism in its many forms. The last section introduced a character, Ralph Kabnis, who returns to his roots after adjusting to the demands of an alien white society only to discover that he no longer belongs to either.

The beauty of *Cane*, unlike anything else in black writing up to that point, lies in a sophisticated prose that approaches poetry in its working, presenting in recurring images—pine, cotton, and cane fields—the instinctual life of black people. It might have served as an impressive beginning to the career of a major artist had not Toomer, ever the vacillator, elected to deploy his talents in other ways. For the next forty-five years he wrote plays, lyrics, a long philosophical poem, autobiographical narratives, didactic aphorisms (a collection of which he published privately), lectures, and essays (some of these appeared in little magazines and other journals). The bulk of Toomer's work, however, ultimately found its way unpublished to a special collection at Fisk University in Nashville. Fortunately, in 1980 his admirer the scholar Darwin T. Turner published *The Wayward and the Seeking: A Collection of Writings*, which has served in part to preserve the memory and reputation of a writer who but for an unwillingness to compromise his freedom to pursue understanding by all available means might have satisfied his aim and achieved real distinction in pursuit of art alone.

Zora Neale Hurston, less talented perhaps than Toomer but endowed with a greater capacity for single-minded perseverance and the beneficiary of good luck when she needed it, achieved considerably more. Contrary to her own statements, she was born in 1891 (not 1901 or 1903) in the all-black town of Eatonville, Florida, to respectable middle-class parents. Between the death of her mother in 1912 and her arrival in New York in 1925, she lived for a time with relatives in Jacksonville, left there to join a traveling repertory company as mistress of the wardrobe, stopped off at Morgan Academy in Maryland long enough to complete her high-school studies, and after that worked at various jobs in Washington, D.C., while taking college work at Howard University. At Howard her early attempts at fiction attracted the notice of the university's professor of philosophy, Alain Locke, who recommended her short stories to Charles Johnson, the editor of *Opportunity*. Fired with the notion of becoming a writer, Hurston set out for New York just as the Harlem Renaissance was getting into full swing.

There for a time her good luck continued. Johnson conducted *Opportunity* contests for his young writers, with awards dinners following; and at one of these Hurston met a patron who arranged for her to go to Barnard, where she received her A.B. degree in 1928. Meanwhile she mixed easily with the literati in nearby Harlem, amused them with her good humor and talent as a raconteur, and, stimulated by their company, continued her writing. During her years at Barnard she also met the Columbia anthropologist Franz Boas and so impressed him with her instinct for folklore that he made it possible for her to return to the South to collect materials, twice to Eatonville and once to New Orleans. In 1934 she published as *Mules and Men* an account of these expeditions along with seventy folktale texts she had collected. In 1934, however, she had already published her first novel, *Jonah's Gourd Vine.* Then in the fourteen years following, in addition to *Mules and Men*, she produced an account of a trip she made to Haiti, *Tell My Horse* (1938), an autobiography, *Dust Tracks on a Road* (1942), and three more novels, *Their Eyes Were Watching God* (1937), *Moses, Man of the Mountain* (1938), and *Seraph on the Suwanee* (1948). After that Hurston returned to Florida to teach and work as a maid, publishing only magazine articles in her last years and writing a novel that was still incomplete at the time of her death.

At that time, 1960, Hurston the novelist was all but forgotten, and she remained so for a decade thereafter. Readers with an interest in folklore have found the greatest contribution of her career to be the material she had presented in her autobiography and the two books that preserve the memory of a transplanted African culture in the Deep South and Haiti. Even these readers are frequently put off by her easy acceptance without accompanying protest of the status quo that in her time still relegated black people to the back seat of Western society. Moreover, by 1960 most of the participants in the Harlem Renaissance were gone and with them the memory of a Zora whose good humor and high spirits had once helped to make palpable the vigor that transformed the Harlem of the 1920s into a point of light in America's evolving culture. Luckily that evolution eventually produced the civil rights movement of the sixties and seventies and brought Hurston the novelist back into view.

Clearly Hurston's first two novels were her best, grounded as they were in the life she had known best, that of Florida's Eatonville, where southern blacks were able to proceed on their own in native dignity and without the interference of whites defensively mindful that they had once been masters. *Jonah's Gourd Vine* tells the story of a couple, reminiscent of Hurston's parents, whose relationship is strengthened when the promiscuity of the husband, a minister, brings him into conflict with his congregation. Hurston's understanding of the man's predicament and, more important, her portrayal of the wife's ability to understand move the novel beyond sentimentality and give it power. Some critics have found its context of black speech and folkways distracting and noted Hurston's inability to give it a strong narrative line, but Hurston remedied both faults, at least partially, in her second novel and masterpiece, *Their Eyes Were Watching God.*

In that work she presents Janie Crawford, a young black woman who escapes the servitude that might have been her lot and, in spite of two husbands who one after the other try to force her to conform to socially acceptable stereotypes, finds in the end both love and self-realization. Her first husband is an old man who wants only a household drudge for a wife; her second, an ambitious young man who becomes mayor of his town and expects her to serve as a decorous adjunct to his position. At last she meets and marries an even younger Tea Cake Woods, who respects her right to be herself and become what she will. The novel thus takes its place in the succession of explorations of the dilemma confronting southern females, the difference being that this female is black and her adversary is the black community, brilliantly rendered, rather than the white.

Hurston's third novel, *Moses, Man of the Mountain*, had a special appeal for white readers who had been amused by Roark Bradford's *Ol' Man Adam an' His Chillun* (1928) and Marc Connelly's Pulitzer Prize–winning adaptation, *Green Pastures* (1930). It also had a special appeal for blacks, who were accustomed to seeing in the legend of Moses a parallel to their own painful liberation from slavery. Hurston's Moses is a hoodoo man, and her Hebrews speak authentic black dialect and exhibit black folkways, but she treats them all with a dignity and good humor characteristic of Hurston herself throughout the course of her own escape from the bondage of oppressive custom, black as well as white. Her fourth novel, *Seraph on the Suwanee* (1948), was a disappointment commercially and artistically. Like her first two, it dealt with self-realization, but the characters were white, and Hurston for all her imagination could not bring them to life. She set to work on a fifth, about Herod the Great, but never finished it.

As has been noted, Hurston displeased some readers in her time—and some in the generation that revived her work—by a steadfast refusal in her most active years to strike a vigorous militant note. In the eyes of those given to protesting, her good-humored willingness to shrug off the discriminations that continued to embarrass and restrict blacks smacked of a passivity they abhorred, but protesting was low on Hurston's list of priorities. Her delight was in the ways, manners, and speech that had characterized black people from the days of slavery to the present and had given them an identity worth preserving. She took pride in that identity and confidently made it the basis of her art. No black writer before her had done that—certainly no novelist—with anything like her authority and skill; and those who would come after, conspicuously among them Alice Walker, would take courage from her example and profit by it.

The third novelist, Arna Bontemps, was born in Alexandria, Louisiana, but reared and educated, far removed from his roots, in California, where for a time he thought seriously of becoming a doctor. To test an abiding interest in writing, however, he came to New York and, as Blyden Jackson put it, "landed in the vortex of the Harlem Renaissance." Bontemps's first love had been poetry; consequently, he quickly struck up what was to become a lifelong friendship with Langston Hughes and for five years mainly wrote and published poems, won prizes, and eventually established a reputation as the most promising poet of the Harlem group. Then suddenly he turned to fiction and in 1931 published a novel, *God Sends Sunday*, the story of Augie, the son of a former slave, who managed to escape the hard existence of life on a Louisiana plantation by becoming a jockey. Bontemps was able to give a lively account of Augie's adventures, but for the moment he lacked the experience, and perhaps the insight, to provide a context with the authority that Hurston regularly brought to her work and that Toomer, after only three months in Georgia, was able to give to the first section of *Cane*.

He did considerably better with *Black Thunder* five years later, a respectable historical novel about Virginia's Prosser rebellion in 1800, with a more authentic background of folkways and speech. There, however, his signal achievement was the characterization of Gabriel Prosser as both a heroic figure and a human being with human weaknesses as well as strengths and, above all, human dignity. In that accomplishment he provided black novelists to come with a model for similar protagonists. Bontemps's third novel, *Drums at Dusk* (1939), dealing with the Haitian revolution, showed a marked advance in narrative technique, but Bontemps had no ready means of identification with blacks in Haiti, and his vision faltered. After that he passed on to other projects, in poetry, history, and short fiction, and readers and critics alike tended to forget that one black author had successfully invaded the white domain of historical fiction and in the process left to his successors an example of technical finish and control by which their works would be measured.

NEW AND REVISED VIEWS OF THE SOUTH

Just when the movement in Harlem ended is impossible to determine. Most agree that by 1935 it was over, and the artistic impulses released by blacks there had begun to lend their force to the mainstream of twentieth-century American culture. More important, for the first time a significant number of black people, the majority of them with southern backgrounds and ties, had begun to speak for themselves, and whites, or at least some of them, had begun to listen. Moreover, the acknowledgment among the white reading public, however passive, that a black minority could produce worthy representatives inevitably suggested that other minorities in the South might also have undiscovered talents and potential for dignity. Thus as the Great Depression of the 1920s and 1930s worsened, writers with proletarian inclinations began to call attention to the neglected citizens of Appalachia, anonymous mill workers, and white sharecroppers in the South. Among these were two women, Olive Tilford Dargan (1869–1968) and Grace Lumpkin (1892–1980), whose *Call Home the Heart* (1932) and *To Make My Bread* (1932) respectively both dealt with the demoralization of mountain people drawn to work in the textile mills at Gastonia, North Carolina, and with the strike that took place there in 1928. At about the same time, Henry Harrison Kroll (1888–1967), himself the son of a sharecropper, produced two novels, *Cabin in the Cotton* (1932) and *I Was a Sharecropper* (1936), depicting the exploitation of poor whites by unscrupulous southern landowners.

By far the most memorable among the works of proletarian fiction during the 1930s were those by Georgia-born Erskine Caldwell (1902–87): *American Earth* (1931), a collection of short stories; *Tobacco Road* (1932), at first only a moderately successful novel, which the following year became a phenomenally successful Broadway play; *God's Little Acre* (1933), a novel that achieved notoriety when the New York Society for the Suppression of Vice unsuccessfully sought to have it banned; two more collections of short stories, *We Are the Living* (1933) and *Kneel to the Rising Sun* (1935); and a third novel, *Jackpot* (1935). Caldwell, after five years spent in sporadic attendance at one college and two universities (he never graduated from any of them), work at a variety of odd jobs, and intervals of boxcar hopping, had decided during a one-year stint at the *Atlanta Journal* to become a professional writer. Thereafter for sixty-five years he did nothing else, turning out more than sixty books of short stories, essays, novels, travelogues, and reminiscences.

His work was usually marked by a journalist's eye for a good story and salient detail, sometimes by a personal fondness for the bizarre, and always by a cavalier disregard for those considerations of style and form dear to academic critics. Southerners, put off by what they took to be a disparagement of the region, frequently attempted to disown him, but though he never again lived in the part of the South he had presumably disparaged, he visited there frequently and repeatedly declared himself to be a southerner. He was a caricaturist among writers, painting life as he saw it with broad strokes, and southern critics came in time to treat his work with limited respect, noting that it was rooted in that same fund of antebellum southwest humor from which Mark Twain had drawn much of his strength. Caldwell was no Mark Twain, but in his most distinctive works, *Tobacco Road* and *God's Little Acre*, both early, with their outrageous characterizations of Jeeter Lester and family and Ty Ty Walden he played an important role in stimulating the reform he insisted he had had no intention to advocate. These works were translated into more than forty languages and to the embarrassment of some and the amusement of many projected an international image of the South that persisted until the works of Faulkner began to modify it two decades later.

Another view of the South that emerged during the thirties and captured at least the national imagination was more palatable. Most southerners knew instinctively if in no other way that their identity as a region was a product of the Civil War. The old image purveyed by Thomas Nelson Page and his kind, now only feebly reinforced by living memories, had never been able to bear close scrutiny, and reevaluation was long overdue. A native Pennsylvanian, James Boyd, began it with his novel *Marching On* in 1927, followed by T.S. Stribling's Civil War trilogy, *The Forge* in 1931, *The Store* in 1932, and *The Unfinished Cathedral* in 1934. In 1936, a banner year, Faulkner published *Absalom, Absalom!*, Andrew Lytle *The Long Night*, and Margaret Mitchell *Gone with the Wind*, which won a Pulitzer Prize. The year 1937 saw two novels about the war in national bookstores, Clifford Dowdy's *Bugles Blow No More* and Caroline Gordon's *None Shall Look Back*; and 1938 two more, Allen Tate's *The Fathers* and Faulkner's *The Unvanquished*. This selective roster is that of the Mississippi scholar John Pilkington, whose all too brief chapter in *The History of Southern Literature* (1985) called attention to America's maturing attitude toward its formative war. Few would disagree with Pilkington's list or the thesis that it supports. In those years before World War II, the South had finally begun to see the Civil War as something more than an ancient culture's finest hour.

Several of the works on the list—those by Faulkner, Lytle, Gordon, and Tate—for other reasons are quite as important as any of those already noted in this brief survey of southern fiction in the 1920s and 1930s and will be dealt with in more appropriate places, but two of them and their authors should be given brief mention here. The first is Stark Young's *So Red the Rose*, the last and best of his four novels. Young (1881–1963) was a Mississippian who after almost twenty years of teaching at colleges and universities had decided at age forty to try his hand at freelance writing in New York. Within five years he became a leading drama critic and saw two of his plays produced on Broadway. He had also found time to write essays, short stories, and novels dealing with Mississippi, past and present, as he understood it. In 1930 he contributed an essay to the Nashville Agrarians' *I'll Take My Stand*, appropriately titled "Not in Memoriam but in Defense." Most of Young's writing about the South was defensive of those antebellum attitudes and mores that in his view justified the southern attempt to dissociate itself from the values of the industrial North.

In *Heaven Trees* (1926), his first novel, he drew upon the characters and characteristics of his own Mississippi families, the McGehees and the Starks, to produce an anatomy of the advantages and dangers of the older southern way of plantation living. In the next two novels, *The Torches Flare* (1928) and *River House* (1929), he presented a contrast between contemporary life in the North and that in the South and took note of the erosion of southern values since 1865. None of these three novels, however, could have secured for Young the place he achieved in the history of southern fiction with *So Red the Rose* (1934), which traces the fortunes of two Mississippi plantation families from 1860 to the beginning of Reconstruction. In a manner reminiscent of Tolstoy, throughout the work he touches major events and personages of the Civil War, sometimes giving the reader glimpses of them at first or second hand but always drawing attention back to the principal actors, the Bedfords and McGehees, their friends and relatives, their children, their servants, their houses and land, and the response of all these to the omnipresent conflict. As the fighting proceeds, Malcolm Bedford, too old for combat, comes home to die of typhoid; the McGehees lose their son at Shiloh, and later when Vicksburg falls, their home, Montrose, to fire. Again and again, however, the figure at center stage is that of Agnes Bedford McGehee, the mainstay of her family as the world dissolves about them. It is she who goes under cover of night to recover her son's body from the field at Shiloh, and it is she who in the end recognizes the tragedy that has befallen both sides and attempts to transmit her compassionate understanding to a five-year-old nephew.

The one novel by Atlanta's Margaret Mitchell (1900–49), set beside the rich account of plantation life during the war in *So Red the Rose*, seems more popular romance than historical novel. Mitchell wrote her *Gone with the Wind* during the late 1920s and, having previously failed to get novels published, put the work aside. Finally in 1935, she sent her manuscript to Macmillan, who published it in 1936. It immediately became a best-seller, and three years later David O. Selznick produced a lavish film version that broke all attendance records. The astonishing popular reception of *Gone with the Wind* as a film, however, which would continue undiminished for decades, was due in part to an emphasis on aspects of the story that Mitchell herself had taken pains to qualify. Consequently, to many the novel itself seemed little more than a variation on the popular plantation romance of older generations, a latter-day version of Page's Edenic myth. Sentimentalists responded accordingly; and critics, who otherwise might have taken the novel seriously, either condemned or simply ignored it.

In recent years apologists have noted that Mitchell replaced the conventional Virginia cavaliers and southern belles with more authentic North Georgia types, descended from yeomen and adventurers turned landowners, now newly ascended to bourgeois status and more concerned with acquiring wealth than preserving a traditional culture. Her heroine, who would be applauded by feminists of the succeeding generation, was cut from the same cloth, with a superficial gentility that scarcely concealed an unscrupulous acquisitiveness and capacity for self-reliance. Thus what was "gone with the wind" after the war was not an old order but one only lately wrested from the frontier wilderness. Nevertheless, regardless of how one takes Mitchell's skillfully constructed and highly readable novel, it did more perhaps than any other single work to redirect the attention of the reading public to a South that in the years following World War II would confirm its place as the most concentrated field of literary activity in the nation. Meanwhile activity elsewhere, still unassessed, that would achieve that confirmation in the eyes of the world of serious writers and writing was already well under way.

2
Poetry and Politics at Vanderbilt, 1920–40

The most significant preparation for the South's assumption of a permanent place in American letters at midcentury occurred during the interval between the two world wars at Vanderbilt University, a place where almost no one at the time would have predicted extraordinary literary activity. The catalyst for much of that activity was a single person, John Crowe Ransom, a man of powerful but inconspicuous charisma, who sparked the imagination of a group of slightly younger men and prompted three developments that were to have a shaping effect on the course of southern writing and arguably on the course of American letters as a whole.

The earliest of these developments began as informal discussions among a group of faculty, students, and one or two outsiders, who after a time, for reasons not entirely clear, elected to call themselves Fugitives. These young men soon turned their attention to poetry, produced a little magazine of distinction that ran for almost four years (1922–25), and brought their formal association to a close with the publication of *Fugitives: An Anthology of Verse* in 1928. The second development, commonly known as the Agrarian movement, grew in part out of the first but concentrated from the start on economic and social issues confronting the contemporary South. It achieved national visibility (at the time some said notoriety) with the publication in 1930 of a collection of essays by twelve southerners, *I'll Take My Stand: The South and the Agrarian Tradition,* but the group soon began to fall into disarray and ceased to exist as a coherent movement around 1937. The third development, which came to be known as the New Criticism, was in part a product of the first two, although it was never formally organized and in its flowering not distinctively southern. It achieved visibility only after the Vanderbilt participants had left for careers in other parts of the country, and in time it coalesced with similar trends in literary criticism that were manifesting themselves elsewhere in America and in England. In this form it continued to have an impact on literary studies, in and out of academia, well after most of its southern founders had turned to other pursuits.

In the public mind only the first two of these developments were associated exclusively with Vanderbilt, yet all three bore the school's indelible mark, sometimes to the discomfort of university officials. In addition to Ransom, both Allen Tate and Robert Penn Warren were conspicuously involved in all three of the developments, and Donald Davidson, who remained at Vanderbilt for his entire career, played a leading and sometimes dominant role in the first two. Other noteworthy Vanderbilt members participated in at least one: Merrill Moore, who was active in the Fugitive movement and remained a tireless writer of sonnets even after he had moved to Massachusetts and established himself there as a leading psychiatrist; Andrew Lytle, later best known as a novelist and essayist, who had contributed a poem to one of the issues of the Fugitives' magazine but took an important part in the Agrarian movement and remained faithful to Agrarian principles long after most of the other members had faltered; and Cleanth Brooks, younger than the others, who midway in the Agrarian movement had contributed to one of its publications and then gone on to achieve distinction first as an editor, teacher, and writer of influential textbooks and subsequently as an ardent champion of southern literature in general, interpreter of the works of William Faulkner, and leading American apologist for the New Criticism. In time Vanderbilt University came to recognize that its wayward sons had conferred upon the school honors that it now welcomed but had never merited and with reunions, symposiums, and visiting professorships tried to make amends.

THE FUGITIVES

The Vanderbilt circle that eventually came to be known as the Fugitive group began to assemble off campus for philosophical discussion shortly before America's entry into World War I. The course of that group's development and demise is by now a familiar one. The members first met at the home of Sidney Mttron Hirsch, a brilliant Jewish eccentric—mystic, theosophist, "half guru and half clown," as a later historian characterized him—who had traveled widely and was largely self-educated. Davidson, then a senior at Vanderbilt, was an original participant in the discussions, and Ransom, a fledgling instructor in the English Department, whose interests were primarily philosophical, joined soon after the group's establishment. Meetings resumed after the war was over, with Hirsch again as the focal member and three new members, all undergraduates—Allen Tate, a junior, then Merrill Moore in 1922, and Robert Penn Warren in 1923. Even before the interruption by war, however, the interests of the group had begun to turn toward poetry, and Ransom, by now the author of a published collection of verse, *Poems about*

God (1919), quietly assumed a position of leadership. Nevertheless, it was Hirsch who first suggested that the group produce its own magazine, the first issue of which appeared in April 1922. They named it *The Fugitive* after one of Hirsch's poems, apparently without much forethought. Subsequently they agreed that their flight was from the conventionalism that had marked popular American poetry, including most of the poetry that had been written previously in the South.

Three issues of *The Fugitive* came out in that year and eighteen more in the three years following. At first, members were the only contributors, but the December 1922 issue contained poems by Robert Graves, Wytter Bynner, William Alexander Percy, and David Morton, and all the issues thereafter included poems by outside contributors, among them, in addition to the foregoing, Laura Riding, Hart Crane, John Gould Fletcher, Joseph Auslander, and Louis Untermeyer. Ransom wrote a brief foreword for the first issue and contributed essays and editorials to many of the others. Then beginning with the October 1922 edition, most of the issues contained book reviews, written principally by Davidson and Ransom.

The Fugitives had no illusion that the kind of magazine they were undertaking would survive for much longer than it did. Their primary aim was simply to write good poetry. They had no intention to make their work distinctively southern, but they did expect it to demonstrate that a group of southerners could produce important work in the medium, devoid of sentimentality and carefully crafted, with special attention to the logical coherence of substance and trope—poetry, in short, that could be taken seriously and would demand as much attention from the reader as had gone into the making of it. In general, they succeeded. Vanderbilt officials tended to be either suspicious of these goings-on or indifferent to them, but students sensed the element of rebellion involved and expressed enthusiasm. Southern reviewers, in Nashville and elsewhere, though they frequently complained that some of the poems were too much "tainted with thought," found in the project a welcome challenge to the prevailing notion that the American South was a cultural wasteland. Readers and reviewers in New York and England for the most part treated *The Fugitive* with respect and gave the new southern poetry qualified praise.

Unfortunately, some also referred to Ransom as *The Fugitive*'s editor, thereby irritating several members who had taken pride in the "democracy" that characterized their editorial policy. Editor or not, Ransom by the quality of his work alone would have appeared to detached viewers to be the dominant member of the group. Three others, Alec B. Stevenson, Stanley Johnson, and Jesse Wills, had all from time to time produced individual works of merit, and Merrill Moore, the most prolific of them all, would continue for years to come to produce publishable sonnets at the same rate and same level of quality. For three of the younger Fugitives, however, the four years of publication had been apprentice years. Davidson, five years Ransom's junior, though he had been at the craft longer than any of the others, had contributed poems that gave at best intimations of the kind of work he would be able to produce, and the contributions of Tate and Warren gave only oblique hints of their later distinguished work. Ransom's work apparently had undergone a transformation almost at the outset. His *Poems about God* (1919), interesting but technically rough, had given almost no indication of the prosodic skill, subtle irony, and satirical contrast of formal literary language with the colloquial idiom that characterized his "Necrological" in the second issue and those poems that thereafter would constitute a significant part of his best work: "Bells for John Whiteside's Daughter," "Captain Carpenter," "Philomela," "Piazza Piece," "Janet Waking," "Blue Girls," and (under a different title) "Equilibrists." Thus it is not surprising that readers and reviewers far removed from Nashville tended to think of *The Fugitive* as Ransom's magazine.

Ransom appeared only slightly less dominant in *Fugitives: An Anthology of Verse*, which the group brought out two years after their magazine had ceased publication. This book-length collection contained forty-nine poems previously published in *The Fugitive* but almost as many more that the members had written during the interval, including two of Tate's best, "Death of Little Boys" and "Ode to the Confederate Dead." Meanwhile, Ransom had published *Chills and Fever* (1924) and *Two Gentlemen in Bonds* (1927), Davidson had written and published two volumes of his own, *An Outland Piper* (1924) and *The Tall Men* (1927), and Tate was preparing to publish *Stonewall Jackson, The Good Soldier: A Narrative* and his first book of poetry, *Mr. Pope and Other Poems*. For Davidson and Tate, their period of apprenticeship, if it may be called that, was over, and the period of maturation was already well under way.

For Ransom as poet, the years of *The Fugitive* constituted his period of maturity. He continued to write memorable poems for a time, but the poetry that sustains his reputation as the leading Fugitive appeared in his second and third volumes (1924 and 1927). The three volumes of selected poetry that followed (1945, 1963, and 1969) contained revised versions of earlier pieces but little new work of enduring significance. One sometimes hears it said that Ransom's preoccupation with other matters—agrarianism in the 1930s and critical theory thereafter—diverted his interest or even killed the poet in

him. It seems more likely that the idea of poetry that directed his early accomplishment reached fulfillment more quickly that it might have done in
one of lesser genius, leaving little more for him to do. His early insistence
upon form and craft betrayed a fundamental view of the poem as artifact,
something to be brought as close as possible to a perfect union of idea and
medium, in which the two should stand as one. In the view of many his strategies came astonishingly, perhaps for him dangerously, close to success in a
handful of poems, so that thereafter he deployed his poetic energy in revising, with varying degrees of success, the remainder that in his view had come
short. Even so, it would be wrong to think of Ransom simply as a supreme
master of his craft. The ironies that give his poems much of their pungency
derive from dichotomies in his thinking—between the ideal and the real, mind
and body, intellect and feeling, the spirit and the flesh—that in the end proved
for him to be unresolvable. The better part of wisdom, his poems imply, is to
accept the contradictions that arrive from such oppositions, if possible with
good humor, and to let them lie, like the equilibrists in his poem, "perilous
and beautiful."

Allen Tate, Ransom's junior by eleven years and his onetime student,
shared some of the older man's dedication to form; but he avoided, at least
partially, the temptation to see poems as perfectible objects and throughout
most of his career used the crafting of poetry as a device for self-scrutiny and,
by extension, for exploring the human situation—in short, as a means to knowledge. The result was a more varied body of work than Ransom's and one that
in its succession of revisions reflected the tortuous course of a restlessly questing mind. The successive versions of Tate's best-known poem, "Ode to the
Confederate Dead," which he worked at for a decade (1927–37) before letting it go, provide a notable illustration of the use he made of poetic activity.
In all the versions of it he dramatized the plight of contemporary man—in the
poem symbolized by a southerner like himself—as he attempts to come to
terms with his realization that all human dreams of permanence, order, and
meaning in the world are at best illusive fictions in a Heraclitean universe in
which death is the only certainty.

His best poems, and his work as a whole, do much the same thing, as Tate
himself seems to have realized when two years before his death he put
together his work in poetry in *Collected Poems 1919–1976* with all the
items carefully dated. The first three sections of the volume contain, in
chronological order, the sixty-three poems by which he is most likely to be
remembered, among them "Death of Little Boys," "Mr. Pope," "The Last
Days of Alice," "The Mediterranean," "To the Lacedemonians," "Ode to
the Confederate Dead," "Seasons of the Soul" (perhaps his masterpiece),

three parts of a long poem (never finished) in terza rima, and two moving tributes to the wife and children of his old age, all but the last five written between 1925 and 1950. These are followed by his six translations from Latin and French verse (not in chronological order) and a concluding section of forty-six early poems, again chronologically arranged, most of them previously unpublished.

Tate's production of poems waned after 1950, but with this last comprehensive collection he demonstrated his consistent commitment to modernism, his mastery, and eventual transcendence, of techniques learned early from the work of T.S. Eliot, his respect for form in the face of a chaotic world that he never repudiated, and his abiding belief in the superior power of symbolic language to reflect and explore the complexity of human existence. Above all, he showed that poetry had been the medium in which his deepest convictions—about history, the American South, literature, and religion—had been generated. For the average reader, Tate's larger body of work in prose is more accessible: biographies of Stonewall Jackson and Jefferson Davis, a major novel, *The Fathers*, written in the wake of his passing engagement with agrarianism, and a succession of essays that contain some of the finest literary criticism written in America. He remained a poet and a southerner to the end, but the vision of the human situation that he developed in his career as a "man of letters" transcended its regional beginning to a degree unequaled by any other southerner of his time, save perhaps Robert Penn Warren, Tate's youthful roommate at Vanderbilt.

Warren shared his friend's admiration for the poetry of T.S. Eliot and talent for language; but the promise manifest in poems he wrote for *The Fugitive* and during the two decades thereafter was overshadowed by early successes in prose fiction and by the textbook anthologies that he produced with Cleanth Brooks, which revolutionized the teaching of poetry and fiction in America. In 1935 Warren published his first volume of verse, *Thirty-Six Poems*, and in 1942 a second, *Eleven Poems on the Same Theme*. Most of these were reprinted in *Selected Poems, 1923–1943*, together with several new pieces, notably "Mexico Is a Foreign Country: Five Studies in Naturalism" and "The Ballad of Billie Potts." Had Warren written no poetry after 1950, American letters would still be indebted to him for these poems and several others, including "Pursuit," "Original Sin," "Bearded Oaks," and "Picnic Remembered." In all of them "the Kentucky voice of Warren," to borrow Davidson's phrase, is like no other, but before midcentury it was not yet a major one. That voice began to be heard only in Warren's first version of *Brother to Dragons: A Tale in Verse and Voices*, published in 1953. Thereafter in poetry as well as prose fiction he surpassed his teachers.

THE AGRARIANS

The year that saw the end of *The Fugitive*, 1925, was also the year of the Scopes trial in Dayton, Tennessee, in which a state law forbidding the teaching of evolution in public schools was pitted against a young teacher who had dared to defy it. The setting was one of the countless bastions of religious fundamentalism in the region, and the trial that took place there quickly developed into a spectacle that attracted national attention, with an ill and aging William Jennings Bryan defending the law on religious grounds and the criminal lawyer Clarence Darrow challenging it as an affront to intellectual sophistication and common sense. Eastern reporters covering the affair, among them H.L. Mencken and Joseph Wood Krutch, used the occasion to disparage a backward Tennessee and by extension the South as a whole, and their success in doing so served as a catalyst that brought all four of the leading Fugitives— Ransom, Davidson, Tate, and ultimately Warren—to the defense.

Their inclination for a shift in that direction had been implicit in the Fugitive movement almost from the beginning. Their intention as Fugitives, the members consistently maintained, had been to produce not a new kind of southern poetry but simply good poetry in the South, and their original enemy, if they may be said to have had one, was the sentimental image of an Old South, promulgated by writers such as Thomas Nelson Page and widely received in the South as well as in the North and East. In the course of their development, however, the more perceptive among the Fugitives had begun to recognize the importance of the regional context that had produced them— one that for various reasons had been spared the worst aspects of the nation's advance toward an industrial economy which seemed destined to erase sectional individuality and render irrelevant the South's long-standing claim to distinctiveness. They recognized the benefits of such an economic and social advance but were sensitive to the possible losses; and Ransom had begun to suggest what those losses might be in one poem, "Old Mansion," that he published in *The Fugitive* in 1924 and to make them explicit in another, "Antique Harvesters," which appeared in the *Southwest Review* for April 1925. Similarly, Davidson, whose earliest poetry had been romantic in a manner vaguely reminiscent of the early Yeats, had turned suddenly to regional subject matter in poems that anticipated his major work, and Tate, although absent from Nashville after 1923, had begun work soon after his departure on a version of his "Ode to the Confederate Dead" that he contributed to the Fugitive anthology of 1927. After that he proceeded to write his biographies of Stonewall Jackson (1928) and Jefferson Davis (1929). Warren, who graduated from Vanderbilt in 1925, undertook a round of advanced studies, first at Berkeley, then at Yale, and finally at Oxford; but while at Yale he manifested an abiding interest in things southern with a biography of his own, *John Brown: The Making of a Martyr*, published in 1929. To what degree latent inclination combined with these activities to make the three self-consciously southern at this point is difficult to tell. Suffice it to say that public opinion—local, national, and even international—had declared them all southern, and they accepted the label with fairly good grace.

For Donald Davidson, however, regional bias was clearly bone-deep. When Harriet Monroe in a *Poetry* review of a work by DuBose Heyward and Hervey Allen urged the South's new poets to capitalize upon the limitations implicit in the commonly accepted romantic image of their situation, Davidson quickly drafted a sarcastic reply for the June–July 1923 issue of *The Fugitive*. The broader assault upon southern attitudes and mores that followed two years later in the wake of the Scopes trial put him openly on the defensive, where he remained for the rest of his life. Although Davidson tempered his initial responses to that event—perhaps out of deference to his superiors at Vanderbilt, several of whom were sympathetic with the progressivism of the New South movement—he began almost immediately to consider the possibility of making a general response to detractors of the South and advocates for progress alike, one that would make clear the basis for his group's common loyalties. The result, after protracted correspondence with Tate and negotiations with Ransom, was *I'll Take My Stand: The South and the Agrarian Tradition*, by Twelve Southerners, published by Harper and Brothers in 1930.

Ransom contributed the lead essay, "Reconstructed but Unregenerate," an expanded version of a piece he had already published elsewhere, and wrote a statement of principles to serve as an introduction. Davidson's "A Mirror for Artists" declared his conviction that a harmonious agrarian society, such as he believed the antebellum South to have been, was essential to the production of great art. Tate, whose interest in religion was second only to Ransom's, argued that the South's deficiencies in the arts were due principally to the region's lack of a doctrinally adequate religious base, one that could integrate all aspects of its communal life. Warren from Oxford sent his view of the social situation in an essay that anticipated his eventual espousal of integration, maintaining that the Negro, though destined to remain in a separate status, should be given opportunities and rights under the law equal to those enjoyed by whites. The piece alarmed Davidson, who only at Tate's urging allowed it to remain. Of the other contributors, four were from Vanderbilt: Frank Owsley, historian; John Donald Wade, a member of the English Department; Lyle Lanier, psychologist; and Henry Blue Kline, graduate student in English. Two others had Vanderbilt connections: H.C. Nixon, formerly of the History Department but recently moved to Tulane, and Tennesseean Andrew Lytle, Vanderbilt graduate, who like Davidson would remain faithful to the cause of agrarianism throughout his life. Two more contributors, John Gould Fletcher, already an established poet, and the New York drama critic Stark Young, both southerners, gave national visibility to the project. As might have been expected, the contributions of these twelve men varied in quality and significance, but with minor reservations they all subscribed to the principles set forth in Ransom's introduction. Predictably, the sale of their book was disappointing, appearing as it did during a major depression, but it was widely reviewed—praised by a few, deplored by others, and ridiculed by many who found the economic assumptions naive and the nostalgia for old times intolerably sentimental.

With various defections and additions the Agrarian brethren, as they came to call themselves, continued as a group for the next six years. By the fall of 1931, however, the euphoria that had accompanied the achievement of a book in print dissipated, and they were compelled to acknowledge that *I'll Take My Stand* had been at best a shaky beginning for what the more ardent among them had hoped might be a crusade. Two of the members went their separate ways. Henry Blue Kline, who had earned an M.A. in English at Vanderbilt, continued to teach at the University of Tennessee; later he became an industrial economist and worked with several government agencies. Stark Young remained in New York, where in addition to writing distinguished dramatic criticism he produced even more distinguished fiction and translations of the plays of Chekhov. The others, particularly the Nashville seven—Ransom, Davidson, Tate (though frequently absent), Owsley, Lytle, Warren, and Wade—continued to meet irregularly and plot strategy for an enterprise that in their minds had become a movement.

Ransom proceeded to immerse himself in the study of economics. Both Ransom and Davidson engaged in public debates, and Davidson expressed his ever-increasing enthusiasm in repeated bursts of literary activity, some of which eventually found its way into his two collections of social criticism. Their talk of publishing a journal came to nothing until Tate in 1933 arranged for a more permanent outlet with the editor Seward Collins, who in 1934 converted his faltering periodical *Bookman* into the *American Review*, which for two years served as the principal vehicle for the Agrarians' essays and reviews. In 1935 and 1936, the Nashville brethren sent delegates to meetings of Francis Pickett Miller's Conference of Southern Policy Groups. At about this time Nixon and Fletcher also severed their ties, but the others found an unanticipated opportunity for a second symposium in *Who Owns America?*, coedited by Tate and his friend the Louisville journalist Herbert Agar. This volume contained short pieces by twenty contributors, including eight by members of the Nashville group and one by Cleanth Brooks, recently joined with Warren in the editorship of the *Southern Review* at Louisiana State. But the essays were uncoordinated and sometimes representative of conflicting points of view; and by Christmas of that year it was clear to the brethren in Nashville that their movement, such as it was, had run its course.

In the decades following, *Who Owns America?* quickly faded from view, but *I'll Take My Stand* stood, and continues to stand, as one of the significant literary and historical documents of the twentieth century. Contrary to the assumption of many readers at the time, it was not a call for a revival of the pre–Civil War South, nor did it offer specific remedies for the region's manifest deficiencies. Rather, as literary historian Louis Rubin has insisted repeatedly and eloquently, it constituted a protest against the dehumanizing potentialities of a burgeoning industrialism that had already homogenized many communities, large and small, in the North and was beginning to threaten the distinctive social units of the South. As such, it also constituted a challenge to the widely respected champions of a New South, who were urging participation in what they considered the social and economic progress that had characterized the nation since the beginning of the century and with accelerated pace since the end of World War I. Notable among these was Edwin Mims, chairman of the Vanderbilt English Department, whose *The Advancing South* (1926) had angered Ransom, Davidson, and Tate and led to strained relations that seemed likely to threaten their professional futures. In ways troubling at the time that threat proved to be real enough, but hindsight makes it clear that involvement in *I'll Take My Stand* confirmed for all three, as it did for Andrew Lytle, the direction that their divergent careers as literary artists were beginning to take.

For two of the contributors, John Gould Fletcher and Stark Young, participation in the symposium had made little difference. Both men were already set in their professional ways. Fletcher, though an Arkansas native recently returned home to live out the rest of his days, was essentially an expatriate. He had done his memorable work years before, as an Imagist in association with Pound, Amy Lowell, and others gathered in London, and during the 1920s had contributed respectable poems to *The Fugitive*. After his Agrarian interval he returned to poetry, received a deserved Pulitzer Prize for his *Selected Poems* in 1938, and published in 1937 a remarkable autobiography, *Life Is My Song*, rich in its reminiscences of the Imagists and those Fugitives he had known best, Ransom, Davidson, and Tate.

By contrast, Stark Young was a displaced Mississippian who never ceased to be a southerner at heart. He had earned his undergraduate degree at the

University of Mississippi and his M.A. degree at Columbia, where he studied theater under Brander Matthews. For more than a decade thereafter he taught at schools in Texas and Mississippi before going to Amherst, where he remained for six years. In 1922 he took a position as drama critic with the *New Republic*, a post that he held until his retirement, all the while writing and translating plays and contributing essays and reviews to various other periodicals, including *Theatre Arts Magazine*, where he also served as editor. In the midst of this busy career he maintained his southern identity by writing novels reflective of the Mississippi in which he had grown up: *Heaven Trees* in 1926, *The Torches Flare* in 1928, and *River House* in 1929, the year in which he wrote his position paper for *I'll Take My Stand*. The title he chose, "Not in Memoriam, But in Defense," might well have served for the whole collection, reflecting as it does what is arguably the most defensible aspect of the Agrarian movement. At any rate, Stark Young was an ideal spokesman for the high degree of civility achieved among certain of the antebellum Mississippi planters and perpetuated by their nineteenth- and twentieth-century descendants in spite of war, reconstruction, and depression. His fourth and final novel, *So Red the Rose*, completed in 1934, is a brilliant representation of the life achieved by Young's Mississippi forebears and the response they made to the cataclysm that befell them—a work widely recognized after more than half a century as a minor masterpiece of historical fiction. Nevertheless, Young could, and probably would, have written *So Red the Rose* just as it stands, even without an Agrarian symposium and the invitation to contribute to it.

Something of the sort is also true of the work of Andrew Lytle. Lytle's birth and upbringing in Murfreesboro, Tennessee, his education at Vanderbilt, where he studied under Ransom and became friends with Davidson and Warren, and the experience gained in managing his father's farm in northern Alabama, all combined to make an Agrarian of him, even before he had a name for it. A brief, abortive sojourn at Yale disabused him of a transient whim to become a playwright and confirmed a latent conviction that his future lay in the South; visits with Tate in New York set him to work on a biography of the military genius and archetypal southern farmer-general, Nathan Bedford Forrest. Thus he was prepared when the invitation came to write something for the Vanderbilt brethren's forthcoming symposium. His contribution was "The Hind Tit," a spirited defense of the South's upland farmer and the farmer's way of life that has scarcely been equaled either by Lytle himself or by anyone else. It was the perfect companion piece to *Bedford Forrest and His Critter Company*, which came out on the heels of *I'll Take My Stand* in 1931. In the years that followed, Lytle proved second only to

Davidson and Owsley in defining and maintaining the soul and character of agrarianism, and agrarianism's fundamental premise—the virtue of disinterested love of land and its children—undergirded most and the best of what he would write thereafter, including a succession of finely crafted stories and novels, all written between 1932 and 1957, followed by a masterpiece of reminiscence, *A Wake for the Living: A Family Chronicle*, in 1957.

For John Ransom, however, Vanderbilt agrarianism provided a crucial occasion for changing direction. When the Fugitives disbanded, Ransom had already achieved a stature as poet that was sufficient, at least in the eyes of many critics, to ensure a ranking by posterity superior to that of all his compeers, with the possible exception of Warren. Retrospection suggests that his achievement may have been due in part to a talent for speculation that was more fundamental to his nature than the talent for crafting poems. Suddenly he found himself returning to the subject of his first published work, *Poems about God* (1919), working out with great pains a rationale for the Methodist version of Christianity that had nourished him. The result was *God without Thunder*, published in the same year as *I'll Take My Stand*. In that work Ransom's basic concerns, derived from his dualistic view of natural man's sensibility and only faintly visible in his first book of poems, began to come clear.

In his view, human beings were endowed at birth with a capacity for perceiving things in their particularity and an ability to make such abstractions as might be necessary for controlling the world about them. He considered both capabilities, when kept in balance or at least in tolerable tension, essential to a complete humanity. But even with such a balance Ransom remained suspicious of the human tendency to let pride in abstraction gain an upper hand. The Agrarian episode presented him with an opportunity to do battle with a manifestation of that tendency on a field close to home—specifically, the attempt by science or technology to reduce an older holistic agricultural society to one narrowly focused on productivity. Thus at the end of that episode when he found himself free to turn again to poetry, he remained embattled and deployed his energy not to the creation of more poems but to an examination of poetry as the best means of perceiving and presenting the world's body whole and undiminished. He now began to write essays in critical theory, describing and defending the kind of poetry that he believed could best fulfill the true function of the medium, which was to present reality more comprehensively, as experience, in both its structure and its texture. In this enterprise he became one of the founders of the New Criticism, to which he gave, perhaps inadvertently, a name as well as a direction.

Allen Tate, a Kentuckian, had many of Ransom's capabilities and tendencies, but there were important differences. He shared Ransom's concern for wholeness ("whole horse and . . . nothing less," as he put it in *I'll Take My Stand*), and like Ransom he was preoccupied with religion throughout most of his career. But whereas Ransom for all his professed distrust of abstractions had indulged in abstraction freely, Tate even in his most theoretical essays managed to keep particularity in the foreground. Moreover, Tate like Ransom was only theoretically an Agrarian. He knew nothing of farming, and he had no taste for gardening. His admiration for the agrarian South was essentially patrician, something he inherited from his Virginia-born mother. He had little of Ransom's feeling for the situation of the upland farmers of Tennessee and Alabama. Like Lytle his self-conscious southernness had been fueled by exposure to an unsympathetic Northeast—in Tate's case, one of much greater intensity and longer duration—but being patrician, he adjusted more readily to alien northern ways, particularly to the residue he found there of European customs and modes of behavior.

His ideal even at the beginning had been that of a man of letters in the modern world, a world that included England, France, and Italy as well as the American South. Still, Tate's instinct for the particular led him to establish his permanent posture in the region in which he was born. The two biographies he published (on Stonewall Jackson and Jefferson Davis) were early manifestations of that direction in his development, as was the projected biography of Robert E. Lee, never finished. So was his protracted examination of the dilemma facing the sensitive modern, which took the form of a contemporary southerner desperately trying to wrest an identity from a past he had been taught to revere as heroic; when he saw that past repeatedly disregarded by forces at work to replace it with something crassly materialistic, he leaped to the defense. Characteristically, once there he found himself more often than not leading a charge.

When in 1933 it became clear that the Agrarian brethren would never focus upon a practicable strategy, Tate abruptly turned to fiction, at first writing sketches modeled after the two main branches of his family and then a full-length novel, *The Fathers*. As with the "Ode to the Confederate Dead," the setting was southern, Virginia and Georgetown at the beginning of the war, and the dilemma posed there was one that many southerners faced, then and increasingly in the years to come. It was also a universal dilemma that recurs among thoughtful people whenever an established society enters into its last stage of decadence, and the past, however appealing, seems no longer able to sustain its younger, hopeful members. Tate had become an indelible southerner, and agrarianism had helped to make him so, but he remained a southerner in the modern world, keenly aware both of his heritage and of his need to adapt it for survival in a world of communities understandably indifferent.

Of all the Agrarian brethren Warren was the first to achieve national prominence as a writer of fiction, and that by virtue of his third novel, published in 1946, *All the King's Men* (actually his fifth, counting two that he completed but never published in their entirety). Like Tate and Lytle, Warren had first demonstrated his talent for prose narrative with a biography, *John Brown: The Making of a Martyr* (1929). Then during the next ten years he had written diligently, occasionally turning out poems but more often fiction, aiming always at the well-crafted work that would satisfy his Jamesian ideal. His first publication in the mode was "Prime Leaf," a respectable novella of some sixty pages that appeared in *American Caravan* in 1931. In time this shorter piece served as the basis for *Night Rider* (1939), his first published novel and, according to subsequent critics, the best of his ten in point of construction. Meanwhile, from one of his unpublished manuscripts he extracted the story "Christmas Gift" (1937) and from the other, three more, including one of his best, "When the Light Gets Green" (1936). Eventually, however, he concluded that short fiction was not his forte, and having completed his masterpiece "Blackberry Winter" (1946), he abandoned the form and never wrote another.

Donald Davidson's path after 1933 diverged radically from those taken by Ransom, Tate, Warren, and Lytle, each of whom in different ways and at different stages of their respective careers would incorporate a portion of the spirit of southern agrarianism in works of criticism, poetry, and fiction. Only Davidson, with a fierce single-mindedness and unwavering fidelity, remained committed to what he conceived to be the pure form of the movement, long after it had ceased to exist as an active cause anywhere except in his own mind. Earlier Davidson had declared himself committed to poetry, and some would attribute his new allegiance to a suppressed fear that the modernism in poetry which Ransom and Tate were championing might in fact be the real essence of all poetry, in all times and places. Others would attribute the change to his incorrigible inability to outgrow an attachment to the agricultural milieu of Middle Tennessee, in whose communities as a child he had found his greatest happiness. Undoubtedly, both characteristics had something to do with it. At any rate, the abortive Agrarian movement provided Davidson with a comfortable focus for his life and justified a deep-seated inclination to let rhetoric, at which he was a master, substitute for poetry. More important, it charted for him a satisfying course of political advocacy that provided the context for everything he would write thereafter.

That course, still uncharted, had been set by the time he published *The Tall Men* in 1927. There in a set of nine related sections of dramatic verse he displayed recollections that he would not, or could not, let go: romanticized tales of the tall men who had wrested the wilderness from the Red Man and tamed it to civilized uses; old recounted memories of the tall men's successors who fought the Yankee invader unsuccessfully but unyieldingly; accounts learned from books of the tall men's predecessors, who had worked their way across northern Europe, spawning children whose children's children would one day cross the Atlantic to bequeath their heroic patrimony to a new world; and his own recollections of those Tennessee tall men who in modern times had returned to brothers in a threatened old world and helped preserve their common heritage. All these he placed dramatically in the context of a southern city (unnamed but clearly Nashville) in which the same race of men, still tall but spiritually diminished, had not yet fully awakened to the dangers of urbanization and industrialism that were threatening to emasculate them.

Meanwhile, he was already at work writing essays in defense of the region's "poetic supernaturalism" that was defying "the encroachments of cold logic" and preserving an ancient culture against the advance of industrialism and science. Davidson's contribution to *I'll Take My Stand*, "A Mirror for Artists," had set forth eloquently his convictions that art could flourish best in a stable and religious society and that the role of the artist in that society was to support as well as to adorn it. Everything that he wrote thereafter, in prose and in verse, served to reaffirm these convictions—in the 1930s alone more than forty articles in defense of agrarianism; a book of essays on the same subject, *The Attack on Leviathan: Regionalism and Nationalism in the United States* (1938); a new book of poems, *Lee in the Mountains and Other Poems* (1938); and the first edition of his textbook *American Composition and Rhetoric* (1939).

Of his new poems the best, and certainly the most memorable, was the title piece, in which he spoke for an aging General Lee, reduced to the presidency of tiny Washington College and declaring at the end that God himself would in time bring to flower the temporarily discredited dream and vindicate the patience of "all generations of the faithful heart." The same faith, which the general himself may or may not have held, sustained Davidson throughout the rest of his career, at least until the final years, when his disappointments threatened to turn into despair.

In 1961 he brought out another volume of poems, *The Long Street: Poems*, and prepared a collected edition, *Poems: 1922–1961*, which was published by the University of Minnesota Press in 1966, two years before his death. In 1946 and 1948 he had published what is probably his best work, a two-volume contribution to the Rivers of America Series, *The Tennessee*, still widely recognized as a major piece of historical writing in spite of some unabashed slanting against the TVA in volume 2. Then in 1957 Davidson collected his social and literary criticism in *Still Rebels, Still Yankees*, and in 1963 an old student, John Tyree Fain, brought out a collection of his book reviews,

The Spyglass: Views and Reviews, 1922–1961. During the last two decades of his life, however, he turned to new forms, first drama and then the novel, to display his continuing dedication to the agrarian way of life and to celebrate the South's treasury of ballad lore that he believed the agrarian way, given a chance, could have preserved as a part of a living culture. The dramatic work, produced at Vanderbilt in 1952, was called *Singin' Billy*, a folk opera with music by his friend Charles F. Bryan of George Peabody College for Teachers. It was published in 1985, seventeen years after his death. The novel, *The Big Ballad Jamboree*, remained in manuscript form until the University Press of Mississippi published it in 1996. It too is a celebration of that ballad tradition which in later years he taught with missionary zeal to Vanderbilt's graduate students, fearful that it would be forever corrupted beyond recognition by the commercialism of Nashville's music industry.

Davidson's last important prose work published during his lifetime was a series of lectures, *Southern Writers in the Modern World* (1958), in which he reviewed and reflected upon the events of his long career but voiced no opinions that he could not have voiced forty years before. In his view the South was still a continuation of the best that Western European culture had to offer, while the North was a deviation. This was the message that he had given to several generations of students at Vanderbilt and in his summer seminars at the Bread Loaf School in Vermont: the enemies were still "the dominance of industrial economics to the exclusion of all other considerations, and after that . . . the dominance of the modern Leviathan state as the manager of the total economic system." The place of the poet, he believed, was in the vanguard of battle. Unfortunately, the New South that Davidson had spent most of his life opposing still seemed unstoppable, and he would die ten years later still pressing the challenge, although by that time even he was almost convinced of the futility of it.

THE NEW CRITICISM

Of the three movements that developed at Vanderbilt, the one that came to be called the New Criticism proved the least troubling to campus demeanor. The Fugitives had appeared and disappeared within a space of five years. Agrarianism lingered longer, in the fierce dedication of Frank Owsley and Donald Davidson. The New Criticism lasted longest of all, but it achieved public notice only after its Nashville participants had taken positions in other parts of the country, where it neither disturbed nor influenced the Vanderbilt climate. Actually, none of the three movements had its primary source there. The distinctive character of the Fugitives' best poetry was traceable to literary currents already flowing in England, and the Agrarian movement, for all its provincial bias, was soon identifiable to impartial observers with impulses initiated by such groups as the American Transcendentalists, John Ruskin and other social critics in nineteenth-century England, and the English Distributists in the Agrarians' own time.

Similarly, the creation of the New Criticism, in part a natural response to the long-standing domination of serious critical activity by academic specialists in literary and cultural history, took place in England, where its proponents included the American expatriates Ezra Pound and T.S. Eliot and the psychologist I.A. Richards. Vanderbilt's participants, who gave the movement its focus and perhaps its greatest strength, were John Crowe Ransom, after 1937 a professor at Kenyon College in Ohio, Allen Tate, variously situated in North Carolina, New Jersey, and New York, and Robert Penn Warren and his colleague Cleanth Brooks, both of whom had accepted positions at Louisiana State University in Baton Rouge and founded there a quarterly of international distinction, *The Southern Review*.

As he had in the other two movements, John Ransom took the lead. When it became evident in 1933 that the Agrarian movement was going nowhere, Ransom had turned his attention to criticism and within five years produced a series of purely literary essays, fifteen of which he published in 1938 as *The World's Body*, a collection that was subsequently recognized as one of the major documents in twentieth-century critical writing. Among the essays were two perceptive pieces on Milton, one on "Lycidas" and one on Milton the man; an appreciative essay on writers of the unappreciated new poetry; strictures on the sentimental poetry then in fashion (with Edna St. Vincent Millay's as an example); an intelligent appraisal of the aesthetics of George Santayana, to which Ransom himself was indebted; comments on the aesthetics of I.A. Richards that he would later reconsider and deal with more dispassionately in a second volume (*The New Criticism*, published in 1941); and disparaging remarks on T.S. Eliot's *Murder in the Cathedral* and Shakespeare's sonnets. These last he would afterward recant and try to make amends for in still another essay added as a postscript to the second edition of *The World's Body*, published in 1968. In six of the essays, however, the ones most closely scrutinized by later aestheticians and critics of criticism, Ransom set forth in deceptively simple and unpretentious terms his views about poems and poetry and the strategy appropriate for those who would be critics of it.

With the publication of these essays in 1938, many admirers of Ransom's poetry began suggesting openly that his preoccupation with other matters had effectively killed the poet in the man. The suggestion was premature but understandable. By 1925 he had all but stopped writing poems, at that time turning his combination of analytical power and creative urgency to the task of giving agrarianism as much shape and permanence as it was capable of achieving. Now with that diversion out of the way, he assumed a dual role of analyst and editor, seemingly putting creativity even farther behind than before. Ransom, however, was still Ransom. As with Coleridge, whom he admired and whose total achievement in many ways resembled his own, his life's work eventually proved to be all of a piece.

Ransom's preparation for his role as critic began early. In the waning months of the Fugitive episode, he laid plans for a book, never finished, to be called *The Third Moment*, and for this he worked out a scheme depicting how primitive human beings had progressed from an initial period of childlike perceptions to one in which they could reduce those perceptions to useful abstractions or concepts. At this second stage of the race's development, infant sciences had begun to emerge, ultimately producing enormous gifts for the benefit of mankind's welfare but at the same time eroding mankind's respect for the uniqueness of individual objects. A third moment in human development—one not yet fully attained by the race as a whole—involved a merging of the first two moments, with innocent perceptions innocently accepted, combining with the orderly structures discovered, or devised, by abstract science. At this stage, he believed, art in its various formal manifestations could begin to appear—music, painting, and poetry—and with the forms of art, a superior knowledge of the world in the fullness that only an art completely realized can provide. By this its most important function, art might yet rescue humanity from its desperate alternatives—an innocent but limited bestiality on the one hand and a monotonous existence forced upon it by advancing science on the other.

The working out of such a scheme would have required more technical expertise than Ransom possessed at the time, but he never aspired to be a professional philosopher. His work in aesthetics and criticism was Coleridgean in its deliberate amateurishness, though it manifested frequent marks of indebtedness to philosophers, ancient and modern, whom he had read with admiration—Aristotle, Kant, Whitehead, Bergson, and Santayana. Like the last of these his manner of writing was always that of the nonprofessional civilized observer—easy but controlled, urbane, often witty, with a gentle irony that concealed, sometimes barely, the deep earnestness that characterized everything he did. Throughout he maintained his distrust of the abstraction that scientists were resorting to and insisted that the knowledge of reality which poetry alone can provide is the acme of human wisdom. In the complete world that poetry at its best reveals (his term for such poetry was "metaphysical"), individual objects—in which he included all coherent units of human experience, things, events, fictions, characters, and even moral principles—are constantly dissolving in the eternal flux. Ransom considered it the proper business of a poet to achieve by "a desperate ontological or metaphysical manoeuvre" the preservation in words of whatever among the world's objects interested him, in an indissoluble union of the texture that presents itself to our senses and the structural core inferred by scientists. Poems elusively imprecise in the manifold reference of their terms but controlled by the poet with devices of meter, metaphor, and rhyme were themselves valid objects in their own right, but they were the objects that most readily reveal the complex nature of all other objects, and they teach us by their being the respect due to objects of all kinds, made or found. "[Poetry] suggests to us," he concluded in the essay "Poetry: A Note in Ontology," "that the object is perceptually or physically remarkable, and we had better attend to it."

In the final essay of *The World's Body* Ransom turned his attention to the fate of poetry on the academic scene. Literature, he said in effect, had hitherto been almost exclusively in the guardianship of those with no real understanding of it—specialists who had devoted their academic careers to linguistics, historical scholars who had amassed vast stores of useful but nonessential background data, and humanists and other moralists zealous to spread the "messages" they found in literary documents. The need now, he said, was for teacher-critics, in and out of the academy, who could attend to the works themselves and encourage others to look to poems, plays, and works of fiction for intense experiences of reality, permanently available.

A tentative answer to that declaration of need was already at hand in a textbook anthology that had been compiled at Louisiana State by John T. Purser and two of Ransom's Vanderbilt pupils, Cleanth Brooks and Robert Penn Warren: *An Approach to Literature: A Collection of Prose and Verse*. It came out first in 1936 and was reissued repeatedly thereafter in revised editions for the next forty years. A more effective response appeared in the same year as Ransom's *The World's Body*—Brooks and Warren's *Understanding Poetry*, which eventually became a standard text in colleges and universities throughout the country, tending to redirect the teaching of poetry wherever it was adopted and making the names of Brooks and Warren virtually synonymous with the New Criticism in American academic circles. Their equally successful *Understanding Fiction* in 1943 continued the redirecting and extended its scope, paving the way for a third text, *Understanding Drama*, by Brooks and his colleague Robert B. Heilman, in 1945. Predictably, these textbooks, popularizations only in the best sense of the term, invited imitations, but with a single exception none of their competitors quite reached the level of quality or effectiveness of the texts produced by the men who had transferred the fire kindled at Vanderbilt to a more hospitable climate at Louisiana State. The exception was yet another result of the same fire, *The House of Fiction*, produced by Allen Tate and his wife Caroline Gordon in 1951, the year in which Tate left a temporary residence in New York to accept a tenured position at the University of Minnesota.

While at Louisiana State, Brooks had joined with Warren and others to found *The Southern Review*, which in its years under their joint editorship (1934–44) was widely recognized as the most distinguished literary quarterly in America. Brooks's work at Louisiana State, however, was only the beginning of a productive career devoted to critical writing. In 1947 he transferred to Yale and there set to work with W.K. Wimsatt on the two-volume *Literary Criticism: A Short History*, which the two dedicated to the critic and theorist René Wellek and published in 1957. Thereafter in a series of remarkable studies of Faulkner's fiction Brooks produced what most scholar-critics regard as the most comprehensive account to date of that author's work. His other books of criticism include the early *Modern Poetry and the Tradition* (1939) and *The Well-Wrought Urn* (1947), the second of which prompted Ransom to declare Brooks "the best living 'reader' or interpreter of difficult verse."

Warren during his years at Louisiana State was too much preoccupied with his own fiction and poetry to produce similar independent works of criticism. The literary critic in his makeup, even then, was fully integrated with the artist, whose proper objective, as he declared in "Pure and Impure Poetry" (delivered as a lecture in 1942 and published a year later), was "to remain faithful [within the limits of that artist's gifts] to the complexities of the problems with which [he is] dealing." This declaration, inconspicuous in context, signaled the only important difference between the views of Warren and those of his Vanderbilt cohorts, and it was a difference in emphasis rather than substance: in their minds the perfected poem stood as the epitome of knowledge; in Warren's, the poem (whether cast as verse or prose) was always secondary, a means of knowing the object of his attention. The object—a physical entity, an event, an idea, a principle—took precedence in Warren's scale of values and he produced his own poetry, fiction, and such theorizing as he did with that priority in view.

He published two collections of critical work during his lifetime, the last, released in 1989, the year of his death, containing those pieces by which he set most store. Included in this volume were three major items from the *Selected Essays* of 1958, "Pure and Impure Poetry" and his comprehensive scholarly studies of Conrad's *Nostromo* and Coleridge's *Rime of the Ancient Mariner*. Four others from the earlier collection were important but less noteworthy: essays on Melville, Hemingway, Faulkner, and Frost. One of the new items was "Notes on the Poetry of John Crowe Ransom at His Eightieth Birthday," a tribute to the mentor he valued above all others, which he had published in the *Kenyon Review* in 1968. In that essay he encapsulated the essence of poetry in the phrase "a celebration of life" and described his own view of the essential characteristic of honest criticism as "a dramatic art . . . which implies the human context of the subject discussed and, too, the human context of the discussion itself."

Three other essays in the 1989 volume are traceable to work Warren had done in preparation for an anthology of American literature that he edited with R.W.B. Lewis and Cleanth Brooks. Of these the study of Whittier, given that author's stance as Quaker moralist and abolitionist, was probably the most remarkable, but in it Warren—for many unthinking readers still the quintessential New Critic—obliquely reiterated his belief in a "deeper truth" about poetry: "By repudiating poetry Whittier became a poet. . . . By getting rid of the 'poetical' notion of poetry, he was able, eventually, to ground his poetry on experience." This ability to take a broader view had also been the basis for the appreciation Warren gave to a somewhat older novelist—one ignored by the sophisticated critics then in fashion—in *Homage to Theodore Dreiser* (1971), and it helped to explain the readiness with which Warren throughout his career deployed significant amounts of energy in extraliterary explorations of the status of American blacks, the meaning of the Civil War, and the role of literature in a democratic society.

As for Ransom, his important writing after *The World's Body* was mainly in criticism. In 1941 he published a second collection of essays, *The New Criticism*, honoring and examining critically the work of those practitioners who had preceded and influenced him: I.A. Richards, William Empson, T.S. Eliot, and Yvor Winters, with a complimentary nod to R.P. Blackmur. Ransom's title for that work is generally, and justly, credited with giving a name and an identity to the movement in which he was, if not the founder, one of the most distinguished participants. By the end of his career he had succeeded in giving literary criticism a definition, stature, and visibility that it had never before enjoyed in America.

In some accounts of the New Criticism, the role of Allen Tate has tended to be undervalued, but time may well correct that. Granted that Tate was Ransom's pupil and his junior by eleven years, it was Tate who as one of the youngest Fugitives first nudged his mentor in the direction of modernism and thereafter by conversation, correspondence, and close association in their Agrarian enterprise provided the whetstone of intelligence on which Ransom during the Vanderbilt years sharpened and shaped his own views of literature and criticism. Their personalities and mode of life could hardly have been more different. To most observers Ransom's life, private as well as professional, was orderly and conducted within the bounds of received convention; Tate's by contrast was chaotic, combative, and marked by passionate pursuits that the pragmatic Ransom must have regarded as unfortunate distractions. Nevertheless, in full maturity both men were committed to the same view of literature and the same view of the poet's role in society. Wherever these matters were concerned they stood on the same ground, but Tate explored that ground more thoroughly than Ransom and extended his scrutiny to the surrounding terrain with a skill and vivacity that guarantees the best examples of his critical writing a permanent place in American letters as creative works in their own right.

Tate published eight books of essays during his lifetime. The first six of these were *Reactionary Essays on Poetry and Ideas* (1936), *Reason in Madness: Critical Essays* (1941), *On the Limits of Poetry* (1948), *The Hovering Fly* (1949), *The Forlorn Demon: Didactic and Critical Essays* (1953), and *The Man of Letters in the Modern World* (1955). In 1959 the publisher Alan Swallow brought out Tate's *Collected Essays*; but that volume, gratifying to Tate though it may have been, was for his purposes inadequate both in comprehensiveness and form. Accordingly he prepared a second volume, *Essays of Four Decades*, published in 1968, which presented all the critical writing that he considered worth preserving, with the various items grouped to suggest such coherence as collectively they might possess but, as in the collection of poems that he would publish nine years later, with dates for each to enable historically minded readers to see more readily the progressive development and interaction of his views.

On reading these essays, in whatever order, the figure of Montaigne almost automatically comes to mind. Like the compositions of his French predecessor, Tate's are registers of a personal pursuit of knowledge rather than strategic reports of previous reflection. "I published my first essay twenty-five years ago," he wrote in 1953. "Since then, year after year, I have been conducting an unfinished education in public." Then in the brief preface that he provided for the 1968 collection, he confessed that his primary reason for writing had always been to find out what he could about the topic at hand, "the enlightenment of a possible reader always being the secondary reason." In range Tate's curiosity was minuscular compared with that of Montaigne, but within its limits, it was remarkably broad.

His main concern was language, and in particular the language of poetry, which he believed had been threatened, all but fatally, by a "dissociation of sensibility" that had begun in the late Renaissance as mathematics and empirical science assumed their domination over men's minds. The phrase and the diagnosis it implied had been Eliot's originally, but Tate quickly adopted the latter, as did Ransom. Eliot had noted that some seventeenth-century poets resisted the trend, notably Donne, Marvell, and the lesser known Bishop Henry King. Thereafter, he said, poets had fallen into the habit of thinking and feeling by turns and increasingly disregarded their primary function, which was that of "amalgamating disparate experience." Tate in the discursive manner of a zealous amateur went on for forty years exploring the evidences of that continuing dissociation in the broad fields of history, politics, and religion, especially the last of these. In dealing with any particular period, he almost invariably focused on the poetry, noting that even in the worst of times one or two reactionaries had usually managed to resist the trend and keep alive the poetic function of language.

Among the British authors he examined at some length were Samuel Johnson, Donne, Keats, Hardy, Yeats, T.S. Eliot, and Herbert Read; among the Americans, Poe, Emily Dickinson, Hart Crane, Ezra Pound, Archibald MacLeish, E.A. Robinson, and his own friend John Peale Bishop. At one point he also took a careful look at Longinus, and more than once he called attention to the exemplary poetry of Dante's *Commedia*. A single conviction dominated and guided all his explorations. For him as for Ransom, any literature worthy of the name of poetry, whether in verse or prose, exhibited a use of language in which the tangible and the intangible, the sensible and the abstract modes of perception, were presented as one, undivided and indivisible. In modern times the fragmentation that had multiplied in the wake of the original split made reconciliation of these two modes all but impossible. The solution, he believed, if there was to be a solution, would lie in the preservation of language with all its communicative and creative functions intact: the one communicative device by which the human race as a whole can articulate its manifold perceptions and symbolize the synthesis that is reality. Unlike Ransom, Tate maintained a lingering hope that religion might somehow perform the same trick. He lamented the absence of an effective religion in southern culture, which in spite of the protests of his colleagues at Vanderbilt had continued to disintegrate along with the rest of contemporary society. For a time he looked back nostalgically to the illusive unity of medieval Christendom and midway in life joined the Catholic Church, but in the end he concluded that the language of poetry, broadly conceived and produced in full awareness of its complex function, provided the only real hope. "The end of social man," he wrote in the essay that he placed first in his final collection, "is communion in time through love, which is beyond time"; to the preservation of that communion, he declared, the man of letters in the modern world must dedicate himself.

3

The New Emphasis
on Craftsmanship

If the influence of the Vanderbilt men was important for the future of poetry and criticism in America, it was at least equally so for the future of fiction, especially in the South, where for the rest of the century it would continue to be the field of choice for aspiring writers. Where fiction was concerned, there was virtual unanimity among the writers at Vanderbilt, and they spoke with one voice to a generation of university students in their classrooms. Five of the Agrarians went on to edit literary quarterlies: Brooks and Warren founded the *Southern Review* at Louisiana State and served as its editors until the magazine's demise in 1942; Lytle served as interim editor of the *Sewanee Review* in 1942 and returned in 1961 to begin a formal tenure there of twelve years; Tate in his brief editorship of the *Sewanee* (1944–46) redesigned its format, redirected its policy, and thereafter maintained an active interest in its selection of contributors; and Ransom after leaving Vanderbilt founded the *Kenyon Review* and edited it for twenty years (1939–59). Four of them also participated in the production of influential textbook anthologies. In 1943 Brooks and Warren brought out their *Understanding Fiction*, which extended the revolution in teaching they had begun with *Understanding Poetry* five years before; and in 1950 Tate and his wife, Caroline Gordon (1895–1981), published a similar but more sophisticated text, *The House of Fiction*.

Inevitably these talented author-critics differed in the evaluation of individual works and in placing emphasis on one strategy as opposed to another, but their fundamental criteria for fiction were the same. Fiction of integrity and value, they believed, should be essentially anonymous, projecting no intention of the author save that of achieving its perfection and independence and requiring nothing extraneous to facilitate the comprehension or judgment of it. That is, a story or novel should be totally self-contained and capable, as the Irishman Frank O'Connor put it, of standing on its own two feet and telling the author to go to hell. Above all, it should have the dignity of any other legitimate art and constitute an extension of reality rather than a reflection of it. Their strategies for meeting these criteria were derived for the most part from the obiter dicta and practice of formal masters of the craft: Flaubert, Maupassant, Henry James, Chekhov, Joyce, and Ford Madox Ford. Most of these strategies had as their objectives the use of precise and meaningful detail, coherence in action, and consistency in narrative point of view (focus of narration, some called it) and in tone (attitude toward the material presented).

By such measurements most of the fiction that had been produced by southern writers up to that time left much to be desired. Among authors of an older generation, Poe and occasionally Mark Twain had produced work that stood up well; among established contemporaries, William Faulkner had often done so, and even more consistently Katherine Anne Porter. To the academic critics at Vanderbilt and elsewhere, the phenomenon of Thomas Wolfe was puzzling. No one could doubt the man's talent and energy, especially the latter; his *Look Homeward, Angel* in 1929 had electrified readers at all levels of sophistication. Nevertheless Wolfe's work, they felt, was best characterized as an outpouring of dithyrambic prose that would always require editorial discipline to give it form and purpose. Among the other newer writers those who came closest to meeting critics' criteria were Eudora Welty and Peter Taylor. To these Warren, Gordon, and Tate, had they been making a list, might with propriety have added their own names as well as that of their friend, Andrew Lytle, since all four tried assiduously to practice what they preached—and usually did both with considerable skill.

The Tates' intelligent dedication to craftsmanship, moreover, had been reinforced at a crucial stage in their development by a close association with Ford Madox Ford, whose best practice they imitated. In time both turned in performances that won Ford's approval, whereupon Tate turned aside to concentrate on poetry and criticism. For Caroline Gordon, however, fiction was to be a lifelong preoccupation, and except for her one book of criticism, *How to Read a Novel* (1957), and her part in *The House of Fiction* (1950), she worked at very little else. Gordon was a member of a prosperous and proud farm family, the Meriwethers, in Todd County, Kentucky. Her father had come west from Virginia to serve as tutor to the Meriwether children, married one of them, Caroline's mother, and remained in Tennessee to establish a small Latin grammar school in nearby Clarksville. There and at tiny Bethany College in West Virginia, Gordon had all her formal education. Afterward she taught school for three years and then went to work as a reporter for the *Chattanooga News*. An article she wrote about Nashville's Fugitive poets resulted in an acquaintance with several members of the group, including Allen Tate, whom she married shortly thereafter, in November 1924.

For the next four years the two lived in New York, where their circle of friends included Hart Crane, Katherine Anne Porter, Malcolm Cowley, John

Peale Bishop, and Ford Madox Ford, whom Gordon served as secretary. When in 1928 a Guggenheim award took Tate to France, Ford was there also to acquaint the young couple with life in Paris and introduce them to a new set of friends, principally the circle of expatriates that included Gertrude Stein and Ernest Hemingway. Toward the end of the Fugitive interlude Tate's interest had turned temporarily to biographies, and during the residence in New York he had completed one of these, *Stonewall Jackson: The Good Soldier* (1928), and begun work on a second, *Jefferson Davis: His Rise and Fall*, which he finished in France and published in 1928. Gordon by contrast, with Ford on hand to serve as mentor, spent her time working on her first novel, *Penhally*, which was published with moderate success in 1931. Soon thereafter she too received a Guggenheim, and the couple returned to Paris, Tate to work fitfully and fruitlessly at a biography of Robert E. Lee and Gordon to make a careful study of the techniques of Henry James and begin a novel about the contemporary South. Soon, however, she put that project aside to write the memoir of her father that resulted in *Aleck Maury, Sportsman*, published in 1934. The projected novel on the contemporary South, which she called *The Garden of Adonis*, became her third and appeared in the same year as a fourth, *None Shall Look Back* (1937), a novel about the Civil War. Her final historical novel, *Green Centuries*, which dealt with the advance of white settlers into Indian country beyond the Appalachians, came out in 1941.

By almost any accounting, *Penhally*, *Aleck Maury, Sportsman*, and *None Shall Look Back* were Gordon's best novels. In these three she managed to keep in check a tendency to let extraliterary preoccupations take precedence over the techniques she had learned from her reading of Flaubert, Turgenev, and James and from her association with Ford. Undoubtedly, she understood the craft of fiction better than any other southern novelist of her generation, and in her view she always gave craft priority in her practice. Nevertheless, her convictions about southern history and, in later years, about the Catholic religion were the inflexible priorities in her life, and these rather than art became the ultimate determinants in almost everything that she did. The novels that she wrote during the 1930s all supported in one way or another her views about the South's unique role as the preserver of Western culture as she understood it, and thereafter her writing tended to serve as an apologetic for the Catholicism that she embraced formally in the late forties. By 1950 these two preoccupations had become inseparable in her mind.

Penhally, Gordon's version of the plantation novel, was written under Ford's watchful eye and avoided being overtly partisan. It was the story in three parts of one rural Kentucky establishment (roughly modeled after Merry Mont, the Todd County estate of the Meriwethers) and the several generations of the Lewellyn family who lived there. On the eve of war, internal divisions were already threatening family unity, as one Lewellyn brother left to fight for the South, and another, zealous to protect his inheritance, stubbornly exercised his right as the citizen of a nonbelligerent state to stay with his land. Both brothers acquitted themselves respectably during the time of conflict, but afterward temporary division between them became permanent discord. In Part 2 a new generation of Lewellyns, weakened and disoriented by the aftermath of the conflict, proved unable to exercise the responsibility their inheritance entailed, making it inevitable that in part 3 still another generation would fall victim to the deadly materialism and spiritual erosion that rapidly began to overwhelm North and South alike. Public response to *Penhally* was lukewarm. The time span that Gordon had elected to cover in a work of less than three hundred pages limited her opportunity for character development, and her focus on the house itself, rather than on one or more human figures, was scarcely enough to sustain the average reader's interest. Still, critics' praise of individual episodes was enough to set Gordon to work on a new novel, this time one that would demonstrate at length the challenges agricultural life in the South must meet if it were to survive as a cultural force in the twentieth century.

A novel that intervened, however, *Aleck Maury, Sportsman*, published in 1934, was by almost any measure Gordon's best and certainly the one for which she is principally remembered. Although dedicated to Ford Madox Ford, it was actually a tribute to her father, who had given her a lifelong devotion to the Greek and Latin classics and who taught by his unpretentious example the reverence for the natural world that formed her base for the Agrarian sympathies she shared with her husband and his Vanderbilt colleagues. She presented the story as a reminiscence, a form well-suited for the exhibition of her special talents: the first-person narrative of a retired teacher of the classics, who in retrospect has come to see his life as an unacknowledged pursuit of opportunities to indulge his ruling passions, hunting and fishing. Now too old for the field, Maury has settled with the patience of a dedicated sportsman for the joys of such streams as he can make his way to and knows that these will be more than enough to sustain him for as many years as he may have left. Several of the episodes that make up the plot reflect events in which Gordon herself had participated—in particular, those portraying the daughter's concern for an aging father who refuses to submit to an existence in protective custody. In these episodes the central character, fully rendered, gives a unity to the work that more than compensates for the episodic nature of the parts, which in themselves, again expertly done, suggest that Gordon's real talent was for the shorter forms of fiction. At any rate, it was clear that in the smaller units she most effectively presented her understanding of the daily exchanges that perpetuate the solidity of clanlike southern family life and could there deploy her genius for unifying a composition of manageable length with symbolic detail. The germ for *Aleck Maury, Sportsman,* in fact, had been a superior short story, "Old Red," which she wrote during her first stay in Paris and which, along with "One More Time" and "The Last Day in the Field" (also stories about Aleck Maury), would form the centerpieces for her two collections of stories, *The Forest of the South* (1945) and *Old Red and Other Stories* (1965). Like the novels, her short stories were uneven in quality, but the best of them were jewels of their kind, equal to any that had been written in America up to that time, including the handful of superlatively crafted short pieces by her contemporary, Katherine Anne Porter.

With *Aleck Maury, Sportsman* behind her, Gordon returned to *The Garden of Adonis* and worked on it simultaneously with another novel about the Civil War. The second of these was successful, financially as well as critically, in the way she had hoped *Penhally* might be. Called *None Shall Look Back* after a passage in the biblical Book of Nahum, it told as one action the story of the Civil War's western theater and three people involved in it: Rives Allard, Georgia cousin of a prominent family of Kentucky tobacco planters; Lucy Churchill, his Kentucky cousin and young wife; and the one undoubted military genius in that theater, Gen. Nathan Bedford Forrest. Gordon's model here was nothing less than Tolstoy's *War and Peace,* and like Tolstoy she assumed for most of her narrative the risky position of omniscient author, but she deftly narrowed her focus from time to time to give the three principals a credibility that her characters in *Penhally* never quite achieved.

In particular her characterization of Forrest, with his zealous dedication to the southern cause, his brilliant performances in the field, his frustrations with lesser leaders whose blunders and indecision negated much of what he attempted to do, and his fury and grief at the death of his brother in battle, provided a core of strength that gave the novel a power unequaled by other novels about the war that were then crowding the bookstalls. In addition, Gordon's Forrest served as the principal bearer of the novel's theme, this time one to which readers of most persuasions could respond, of death as the ultimate reality of all warfare. For readers attuned to Gordon's way of thinking about the South, the agrarian theme was there too, though not insisted upon. In the course of the story Rives Allard, agrarian to his finger tips, dies gloriously in defense of Georgia's way of life, and Lucy, on hearing the news, turns her thoughts toward a more genial Kentucky version of that same way; but precisely what constitutes this unique way of life is left for the reader to infer.

By contrast in *The Garden of Adonis*, which came out in the same year (1937), Gordon attempted to develop at length the theme that had emerged unobtrusively in the third section of *Penhally*: the threat of northern mercantilism to a way of life that, like the Agrarians, she believed the South had been in the process of consolidating when war intervened to arrest it. As in *Penhally*, however, she chose a canvas too broad to display adequately her special talents. Her plan here involved describing the fate of not one but four farm families of differing economic and social status as they attempted to cope with the Great Depression of the 1930s. The central figure, Ben Allard, an ineffectual descendant of the Allards of *None Shall Look Back*, retains something of the love of land and family that motivated his forebears, but he proves unable to communicate that love to the poor-white families who share the land with him; these families, rootless and motivated mainly by sexual passion and greed, have neither the imagination nor the will to withstand exploitation by the shopkeepers, bankers, and developers who dominate their environment in a hostile new age. For most readers this cautionary message was stronger than the messenger, and even the most sympathetic of them could recognize that in spite of well-developed episodes and a few examples of superior characterization, Gordon's third historical novel lacked a central figure with enough strength to give coherence to the whole. The result was failure, both critically and financially.

Disappointed but still encouraged by the success of *None Shall Look Back*, Gordon set to work on a fourth novel, this time one that might avoid all suspicion of special pleading. The result was *Green Centuries*, published in 1941, a carefully researched account of the restless pioneers who had followed a less-than-heroic Boone into the new territory beyond the Blue Ridge Mountains and begun the displacement of that region's ancient Indian cultures. She made it the story of two innocents, Orion Outlaw and Cassy Dawson, who abandoned the restrictive codes of European civilization that persisted even in their frontier environment and plunged into the western wilderness, there unwittingly to reenact the fall of humankind.

In the eyes of a few friendly critics in later years, this work was Gordon's best performance. They applauded her honesty in avoiding the currently fashionable view of the pioneers as bearers of Western culture and democracy and her shrewd appraisal of the Indians' social order, stable but flawed by an inherent cruelty. Moreover, they noted that in the process of composition she had displayed as never before the full range of her talents, native and acquired: her eye for significant detail, her ear for the subtle nuances of conversational speech, and her comprehension of the strategies necessary for turning segments of narrative into episodes comparable in intensity with the best of her short stories. Unfortunately, in so doing she had also demonstrated once more that her real gift was for short fiction rather than the broad canvas of a novel. Less sympathetic readers at all levels in 1941 saw in *Green Centuries* mainly another unwieldy "baggy monster," to use Henry James's term, that refused to hang together for easy comprehension. Moreover, in those years of impending global war many apparently found it difficult to generate an interest in problems faced by early frontiersmen in western North Carolina.

Thus for both Tate and Gordon, who during the enterprise had generated expectations of financial success, the reception accorded *Green Centuries* was a profound disappointment. Tate, whose novel *The Fathers* had received a similar response from the reading public in 1938 though for different reasons, abandoned fiction entirely. Gordon after a time persisted but with little more success. The novels that she wrote after 1941, technically as impressive as anything she had written previously, fared poorly on publication and have attracted scant notice since. All but one were romans à clef, and all witnessed aggressively to the efficacy of Catholic Christianity, which after the midforties had become the ruling passion of her life.

Women on the Porch (1944), the first of these so-called Christian comedies, tells of a couple, separated but not quite estranged, who like Orpheus and Eurydice rescue one another from their respective hells by capacities for charity that they discover in themselves. He is able to turn her aside from a futile attempt to find stability in what remains of her decaying family establishment; she with a wife's love and a spirituality like that of her namesake (St. Catherine) manages to save him from the vacuity of life in the city. Thus mutually sustained, both manage to rise from a relationship grounded in purely physical attraction to one of transcendent love. Inevitably commentators at the time noted that the novel came out on the eve of an estrangement between Gordon and Tate that for the moment, at least, also proved to be temporary; but there was clearly a connection between the couple's private lives and Gordon's next novel published in 1951.

From 1930 until 1938, the two had lived in an unprepossessing farmhouse near Clarksville, Tennessee, which they named Benfolly after Tate's brother Ben, who had provided the money to pay for it. Their hope was that they could do a minimum of simple housekeeping and gardening and spend most of their time writing, but a fairly steady succession of visitors, from Nashville, New York, and elsewhere frustrated their good intentions. In any case, the eight years at Benfolly provided a store of material that Gordon exploited in *The Strange Children*, her sixth novel and the first in which she made use of a Jamesian central intelligence. Benfolly clearly provided the setting for the story, which is that of a young couple, the scholarly lapsed poet Stephen Lewis and his wife Sarah of the Aleck Maury series (representatives there also of Gordon and Tate), who in the end come to a realization that the world of intellectuals they have aspired to be a part of is in reality a spiritual wasteland. The focus of the narration is that of their daughter, nine-year-old Lucy Lewis, and it is she who first responds to the one Christian, a Catholic, among the Lewises' sophisticated guests and so precedes her parents in spiritual enlightenment.

In her third Christian comedy, *The Malefactors* (1956), Gordon leaned even more heavily both on her personal situation and the Christian theme. There she made another lapsed poet, Tom Claiborne, her central intelligence and built her story on details of her years with Tate—his infidelities, his preoccupation with dreams, and their onetime friendship with the unfortunate Hart Crane, whose disorderly life she saw as an unfulfilled quest for transcendental love. That love comes at last to her hero Claiborne through the ministrations of a saintly Catharine Pollard, reminiscent of the Catholic philanthropist Dorothy Day, who teaches him the meaning of human relationships and guides him to a reconciliation with his wife.

All three of these novels established Gordon in the minds of knowledgeable critics, among them the novelists Flannery O'Connor and Walker Percy, as a master of the craft of fiction, but her unfortunate propensity for making what should have been an independent work of art a vehicle for extraliterary biases limited her general audience and delayed the appreciation of her contribution to the development of southern fiction. By 1959, the year of her final divorce from Tate, Catholicism had become the central fact of Gordon's life. She set to work on an ambitious two-part novel dealing with her own life and that of her ancestors. The first part, designed as a prologue to the second, was an account of the Greek hero Heracles, anciently recognized as a prototype of Christ and, in her mind, of the Kentucky pioneer as well. This she published in 1972 as *The Glory of Hera*. Nine years later, however, she was dead and the second part still unwritten.

Ironically in 1938 Tate in a single novel, *The Fathers*, had accomplished what Gordon attempted to do in nine. He modeled his work on Ford Madox Ford's masterpiece, *The Good Soldier*, and astonishingly managed to produce in one effort something worthy to stand beside its distinguished predecessor. Like Ford he used a first-person narrator, presenting his story as a reminiscence of a sixty-year-old physician, Lacy Buchan, bent on coming to terms with events that had shaped his youth. Two families are involved: the Virginia Buchans, representative of a once-flourishing planter aristocracy, and the Poseys, formerly landed but now settled in urban Georgetown. The central figure in Lacy Buchan's narrative is a young George Posey, who shortly before the outbreak of the Civil War marries Lacy's sister, Susan, and brings her to live in his moribund Georgetown establishment. George is uncommitted to either side in the conflict and seeks by largely clandestine means to preserve the integrity of his two families, but Susan, desperately unhappy in her strange situation and bewildered by her husband's unexplained absences, precipitates a series of events that ensures the destruction of both.

The crisis comes as she lets it appear that a black servant in the Posey household, actually George's half-brother, has attempted to rape George's younger sister, recently betrothed to her brother Semmes. When Semmes Buchan, following accepted custom, summarily kills the black man, George impulsively kills Semmes. Lacy Buchan is a witness to this double killing and a near-witness to the events that follow—the madness of Susan, the destruction of the Buchan family home as northern troops sweep into Virginia, and the suicide of his father. Years later he tries, never quite successfully, to make sense of those terrible times but finds at least one rock of certainty in his abiding admiration for George Posey, branded an opportunist by some for his disregard for loyalties to region and principle that others held sacred but who nevertheless remained steadfastly loyal to his human commitments.

At the time *The Fathers* was published, few were prepared to recognize that Tate had written a novel transcending his own publicly proclaimed loyalties. Some assumed that it must be read as the apologetic of an unreconstructed southerner; others, that it constituted a subtle defense of agrarianism. Actually it was neither. Whatever his intentions may have been at the outset, Tate the artist, once engaged, let the work have its way; the result was a Civil War novel in which the war serves mainly as a context for a fresh examination of the human condition and situation. One may justly point out that his characterization of Posey falls well short of the achievements of such masters as James, Conrad, and Ford, but it is one that asks to be judged by their measure; and it stands virtually alone in the examples of longer fiction produced by southern writers in the thirties and forties.

By 1938, however, another southern writer had demonstrated an ability to produce at least shorter pieces comparable in craftsmanship to the best of their kind in the language. That writer was Katherine Anne Porter (1890–1980), whose *Flowering Judas and Other Stories*, published in 1930, were masterpieces of technical control and raised, prematurely as it turned out, expectations of a novel. Except for *Ship of Fools*, the novel that finally appeared in 1962, all of Porter's works are relatively short. Her second collection, in 1939, was entitled *Pale Horse, Pale Rider: Three Short Novels*, but these may be more accurately characterized as novellas. A third and last collection of new work appeared in 1944, *The Leaning Tower and Other Stories*.

For a writer of formalist fiction in the manner of Flaubert and James, Porter had an unlikely beginning, at least in her own view, and she managed to obscure it throughout most of her life with enigmatic hints, misdirections, and sometimes outright falsehoods. More than once she claimed to be a member of that "guilt-ridden, white pillar crowd" of southern aristocracy, but actually she was born Callie Russell Porter to poor parents of no aristocratic pretensions whatever in Indian Creek, Texas. Her father early proved to be incapable of supporting a family; consequently, when his wife died (Callie was only two at the time), the four Porter children had to be reared by a grandmother. Callie's formal education was scanty and left her with a transient ambition to be an actress, and in her long life that followed she did indeed work for brief periods as an actress, both on the stage and in the movies. For the most part she supported herself as a journalist, freelance writer, scriptwriter for films, and, as her fame as a writer of fiction began to grow, lecturer and visiting professor at colleges and universities.

Her private life was unsettled. She traveled extensively, married four times, and engaged in numerous liaisons. Most of her stories contain at least some things that she re-created from data in her own life. At various periods she lived in Mexico and in Europe, notably in Berlin, and both locales are reflected in the stories. The sojourns in Mexico lent substance to "Flowering Judas" and "Hacienda," her residence in Nazi Germany to "The Leaning Tower" in her third collection. Echoes of her unhappy marriages add authenticity to several of the Miranda stories, and recollections of her dirt-farmer beginnings are recorded in "Noon Wine." Early critics found in the Miranda sequence, especially in "Old Mortality," a reflection of Porter's supposed upbringing among the "white-pillared crowd," but although many of the details there are derived from actual experiences, their patrician context is wholly imaginary—a circumstance supportive of the now commonplace view that in fiction the reality that matters is the reality that achieves an independent existence there, regardless of its derivation or mode of generation.

Critical approval came early for Porter, but financial success eluded her until 1962, when she published *Ship of Fools*. Reviewers were of several minds about that long-anticipated work, some praising it inordinately, others recognizing that for all the excellence of individual parts, it failed to cohere as a single unified performance. In 1965, however, all her best work appeared in *The Collected Stories of Katherine Anne Porter*, and for that she received both the National Book Award and the Pulitzer Prize. *The Collected Essays and Occasional Writings of Katherine Anne Porter* came out two years later, and in 1977, *The Never-Ending Wrong*, a memoir of the Sacco-Vanzetti case, against which she had protested vigorously fifty years before.

Many feel that Porter's best performances are the earlier pieces: "Flow-ering Judas," "Noon Wine," "Old Mortality," "Pale Horse, Pale Rider," and several of the shorter Miranda stories. In any case, taken together these con-tain developments of most of her recurring themes and exhibit that near per-fection of form that justifies the comparison of her work with that of the half dozen or so international masters of short fiction. "Flowering Judas," the ear-liest of her successes, is the story of a young woman, Laura, of Catholic back-ground and training, who, having come to Mexico City as a teacher, finds herself actively involved in the revolutionary cause. Inhibitions produced by Laura's background and training, however, keep her from giving herself freely either to the revolutionaries she presumes to serve or to the young men who try to woo her, or even to the Indian children whom she teaches for a part of each day. Without the capacity to love she languishes unaware of her spiritual poverty until through negligence she fails to prevent the death of an impris-oned revolutionary and suddenly is terrified at the recognition of her isolation and emptiness.

"Noon Wine" is the much longer story of a South Texas dairy farmer, Mr. Thompson, who hires an itinerant Swede to "help out" and keeps him on for nine years, profiting handsomely meanwhile by the Swede's many capabilities and his willingness to work for very little. When one day a stranger, Mr. Hatch, arrives to claim the Swede as a fugitive from a North Dakota asylum, Thomp-son resists, and the Swede, thinking his employer is being threatened, inter-venes. In the altercation that follows, Thompson inadvertently kills Hatch, and the Swede, hysterical and too terrified to be subdued without force, is taken to the local jail, where he soon dies of his injuries and shock. Thompson is exonerated at the trial but, branded as a murderer and unable to convince anyone that he is really not, finally commits suicide. In both of these stories about characters moved to despair by a recognition of their inability to relate to other human beings, Porter uses James's device of the central intelligence to present psychological studies of extraordinary complexity, and in "Noon Wine" she also makes it work to produce an action of intensity and power seldom achieved in short fiction.

"Old Mortality," however, the most elaborate of the Miranda stories, is Porter's masterpiece, a presentation in three stages of a young girl's passage from adolescence to early maturity. Paralleling that passage and linking its three stages is the girl's changing image of an Aunt Amy who had been beau-tiful, much loved, and unhappy and who had died young. The first section presents the family-approved version of the Amy story as Miranda and her sister Maria delight in reconstructing and embroidering it. The second brings them into contact with Amy's romantic lover, Gabriel, now dissipated and aging unattractively and living precariously on what remains of his squandered means. The third presents the mature Miranda as she is returning home after a failed marriage of her own to attend Uncle Gabriel's funeral. On the train she encounters a perennially disenchanted spinster, Cousin Eva, Amy's contemporary, who gives a revised version of the Amy story that may be closer to the truth than Miranda likes to think. As previously noted, the wealth of detail in all three parts caused early critics to assume that Porter was drawing upon her own experiences in life among the "white-pillared crowd," but the story seemed all the more remarkable when it became known that Porter had spun virtually all of it out of a fertile imagination. Even more remarkable was the technique displayed there: the skillfully manipulated shift from a roving narrator in Part I of the story to the use of Miranda as central intelligence in Part III; the ironic use of parallel details and characters between the first two parts and the recurrence of the story of Amy in contrasting versions throughout; the deft alternation between events recalled and incidents fully and credibly rendered—all these leading with cumulative force to a final powerful irony when the author presents Miranda's concluding "At least I can know the truth about what happens to me," and then adds, breaking the illusion in anticipation of the reader's judgment, "making a promise to herself, in her hopefulness, her ignorance."

The acceptance of death is an important theme in both "Noon Wine" and "Old Mortality." In the third story in Porter's 1939 collection, "Pale Horse, Pale Rider," Miranda in time of war falls in love with a young officer awaiting orders for shipment overseas, contracts influenza and slips into delirium, but waking learns that her lover, who has been infected by her, has in fact died. Miranda's bitter coming to terms with the finality of death is only chronologically the end of the Miranda series. *The Leaning Tower and Other Stories* (1944) contained several more, one of which, "The Grave," is considered by many to be the finest of all the short stories. *The Leaning Tower* as a whole, however, failed to match the sustained quality of Porter's first two collections, and readers began to look forward to the novel on which, Porter intimated repeatedly, she was at work.

Ship of Fools came out at last in 1962, sold well immediately, and soon was made into an equally successful moving picture. The ship in the novel is a German vessel, the *Vera*, which sails from Veracruz, Mexico, to Bremerhaven in 1931 with a complement of passengers and crew that includes Germans, Mexicans, Americans, Spanish workmen, a group of Spanish dancers, Cuban medical students, a family of Swiss, a Swede, and a Jew. Porter devotes the first part of her novel to an introduction of these characters and their interrelationships. In the second part she sets them all on their separate actions, which come to a conclusion in part 3 after the captain's gala, a fiesta that the Spanish dancers turn into a wild orgy. The novel has no plot in the usual sense. The network of episodes presents characters who do not develop but reveal themselves in their exchanges to be a speculum of humanity, good, evil and indifferent; and the movement of the whole is little more than the mechanical progress of the voyage itself. Porter has been quoted to the effect that the thesis of the novel is "the responsibility people must share for evil," but, as more than one critic has noted, that thesis never emerges with clarity. What is clear is the jewel-like precision with which Porter here, as in her previous work, presents the motley assemblage of people on the voyage. For most of her readers, of which she now had many, and a fair number of critics, that much was enough.

For any who may have felt that Porter's last book, *The Never-Ending Wrong*, provided an odd and perhaps inappropriate conclusion to a distinguished career, Porter's biographer, Joan Givner, had a ready answer. Many commentators had noted Porter's striking presentations of villainy in her best stories, Braggioni in "Flowering Judas," Mr. Hatch in "Noon Wine," and Herr Rieber in *Ship of Fools,* but Givner argued that these characters were not the focus of her attention any more than were the governor, judge, and jury in her account of the Sacco-Vanzetti affair. Throughout her career Porter was concerned with the passive villainy of "innocent people" who by their detachment permit and even encourage aggressive villainy to continue. This theme, brought home in *The Never-Ending Wrong*, serves both as a principle for seeing Porter's work as a unified whole and as a thematic bond linking Porter not so much to other southern writers as to Henry James, Joseph Conrad, and Ford Madox Ford, in whose company by virtue of her talent and commitment to craft she unquestionably belongs.

4
Two Major Novelists

Looking back it is easy to see that 1928, the year that Vanderbilt's poets published *Fugitive: An Anthology of Verse*, was a banner year for southern letters. Another such year came in 1930, the year of *I'll Take My Stand: The South and Agrarian Tradition*. Arguably more important than either of these was 1929, which saw the publication of William Faulkner's *The Sound and the Fury* and Thomas Wolfe's *Look Homeward, Angel*. At the time and for some years thereafter, most readers and reviewers would have placed Wolfe's novel well ahead of all these. At any rate, there it remained for at least two decades.

Thomas Wolfe (1900-1938)

Wolfe was born in Asheville, North Carolina, in 1900, the youngest son of an ambitious mother who helped support her large family by running a boardinghouse and a somewhat less ambitious tombstone-cutter father, much given to quoting poetry. There he received a better-than-average schooling, largely as the result of the persistence of his mother. When the time came, he was able to proceed to the University of North Carolina at Chapel Hill, presumably to prepare for the study of law. Four years later journalism, at least in his parents' mind, had replaced law on his agenda, but by then Wolfe was obsessed with the idea of writing plays. Accordingly, on graduation he persuaded his parents to let him go to Harvard, presumably to prepare for a career in journalism. Two years later, however, having brushed that plan aside, he received an M.A. in English and then stayed on for an extra year to study playwriting with George Pierce Baker.

The principal result of his new project was a series of disappointments, and when plays he had produced with gratifying success in Cambridge failed to hold the interest of even one New York producer, he was forced to settle for a position as instructor at New York University, a post he held intermittently for the next six years. During this period he made four trips to Europe, entered into a liaison with an older woman, Mrs. Aline Bernstein, who tried unsuccessfully to help him find a producer for his plays, and finally in 1926 decided, almost capriciously, to try his hand at a novel. At first he had no more success in selling fiction than he had had in selling plays, but eventually his manuscript, in a large packing crate, reached Maxwell Perkins at Scribner's, and Perkins showed him how to extricate from it the novel that he had all but buried in an unwieldy mass of extraneous material. The liberated book was published in October 1929 to considerable national critical acclaim. In Wolfe's native Asheville, however, where the citizens felt that he had exposed them to ridicule before the world, the reaction was anger, indignation, and pain from all except the members of his immediate family, who stood by him.

Perkins had foreseen that something of the sort might happen, but Wolfe was distressed. His idea of writing was to set down his experience, all of it, in a style that, like Walt Whitman's before him, would present a wealth of concrete detail in a seemingly inexhaustible flood of dithyrambic prose. In innocence he had tried to write truthfully about Asheville and its citizens, about his family, and above all about himself; and he never dreamed that truth could be offensive. When Perkins urged that he tone down some parts of the story, Wolfe objected on the grounds that to do so would be falsification; Perkins, who knew genius when he saw it, usually let him have his way. Fortunately he also insisted, with more success, on numerous excisions. In the end Wolfe's story of Eugene Gant's growing up stood clear, in writing that was all his own; but Wolfe scrupulously saved the discarded parts to use in future novels.

The plot of *Look Homeward, Angel,* if plot is the right word, is simply the first twenty years of Wolfe's life, which he tells as the story of Eugene Gant. The subtitle, *The Story of a Buried Life,* points to the action of the whole, which he saw as the desperate attempt of one maturing young man to meet the challenge of his human predicament by separating the presumably imperishable substance of his own identity from the morass of day-to-day ephemeral accident in which it seemed to be entrapped. In the end in a colloquy with his dead brother, Eugene comes to realize that he himself, transitory like everything else in creation, is the only world he can ever know. In retrospect, for us as for Eugene, the story of his life now becomes little more than a series of episodes, all leading up to that moment of recognition: his (or Wolfe's) first moments of awareness as an infant, his sojourn at the St. Louis World's Fair and the death of his brother Grover there, experiences in the school at Asheville and in his mother's boardinghouse, experiences at the university, an early love affair, a trip to Norfolk at the beginning of World War I, the death of his brother Ben. Scattered among all these at irregular intervals are prose poems unlike anything else in American literature outside

Leaves of Grass, and such passages in the eyes of readers and sympathetic critics at the time greatly enhanced the novel and confirmed its distinctively poetic character.

The prose poems became even more numerous in Wolfe's second novel, *Of Time and the River*, published in 1935. This book is considerably longer than *Look Homeward, Angel* and, according to at least one critic, more revelatory of Wolfe's method of writing and more characteristic of his style. A continuation of the story of Eugene Gant, it begins on the day after Eugene's encounter with his brother Ben and covers material corresponding to Wolfe's years at Harvard, his teaching at New York University, and his first trip to Europe. Memorable portions of the second novel present the death of Eugene's father, caricatures of the would-be playwrights in Baker's class at Harvard, his aimless wandering through England and France, his friendship and disillusionment with a young man whom he meets in Paris, and his subsequent return to America. This time the unifying action of the novel is Eugene's quest for a figure to replace the father he never really had and his discovery at the end that his real quest all along has been for an America he never understood until he went abroad.

The process of shaping *Of Time and the River* for publication was even more painful for Wolfe than the shaping of *Look Homeward, Angel* had been. This time the mass of manuscript was larger, and Perkins had to insist on even more extensive cutting, meanwhile requiring Wolfe to write additional material to bring the whole together in a continuous narrative. Wolfe described the process in a series of lectures that he gave at the University of Colorado in 1935 and published, first serially in the *Saturday Review* and then as a book, *The Story of a Novel*, in 1936. In these, however, his fecundity and enthusiasm began to offend many readers who had responded positively to the more restrained manifestations (restraint having been provided largely by Perkins) in the two novels. In a passage from one of the lectures, Wolfe described himself as spewing forth material like masses of lava from a volcano; in another he likened himself to a "huge, black cloud" pregnant with electrical discharges and rain and emptying itself in a "torrential and ungovernable flood." Reviewers were not tolerant of such effusions, and one of the most influential, Bernard De Voto, made an unfortunate reference to "the assembly-line at Scribners." Consequently Wolfe, already irritated with Perkins on other scores, began to look for a new publisher. Late in 1937 he moved into a three-room suite in the Hotel Chelsea in New York, signed a contract with Harpers, and began filling the place with manuscripts. His new editor at Harpers was to be a congenial southerner named Edward C. Aswell.

Wolfe worked all winter in the Hotel Chelsea; then after a short trip to

Baltimore, he made preparations to go to Purdue University for a lecture. Before leaving, he sorted out his packing crates of manuscript and left them for Aswell to familiarize himself with, but once in Indiana he impetuously joined two reporters for a tour of the western parks, which ended in a bout with pneumonia in a Seattle hospital in July. When he failed to recover as expected, his sister had him moved to Johns Hopkins Hospital in Baltimore. There he died in September of a tubercular infection of the brain caused when the pneumonia reactivated an old lesion in the right lung. Aswell, now with the Wolfe manuscripts on his hands and an obligation to Harpers, set to work to produce three more books, *The Web and the Rock* (1939), *You Can't Go Home Again* (1940), and *The Hills Beyond* (1941), the last of which consisted of a short novel and ten stories.

Aswell has subsequently received criticism from Wolfe scholars, who when the manuscripts became available discovered that in addition to putting Wolfe's material together and writing a few transitional paragraphs, he had revised, changed, and sometimes written whole portions, all without fully acknowledging his part in the published work. Most agree that the third and fourth novels are inferior to the first two, in which, Perkins insisted, not a word was printed that was not Wolfe's. Some have argued that Aswell's reconstructions do irreparable damage to Wolfe's reputation. Recognized for what they are, however, they probably do less damage than was at first feared. The hero in the two new novels is a character named George Webber, but both Webber and Gant are in the main projections of Wolfe himself, and many of the episodes in all four novels were taken directly from his life. Gant or Webber, the story is still that of one man's lifelong quest for identity in a world in which everything, including identities, is constantly in flux.

The leaner style of the last two books, Aswell insisted, was due to Wolfe's maturation as a writer; he had begun to create characters instead of merely recalling them, and he had learned to revise and rewrite and to curb his rhapsodizing. Perhaps so, but one wonders what Wolfe would have said of the books that Harper published posthumously in his name and whether his disapproval, if any, would have been as vehement as that of some of the literary historians who have elected to speak on his behalf. In any case, when Wolfe died at age thirty-nine, he had achieved a greater measure of literary capital than any other writer of his time, not excepting Faulkner, and like Faulkner he had done it alone. Moreover, his posthumous reputation would probably be the same if his last two books had never seen the light of day. Wolfe's career lasted less than twelve years, and during that time he matured in many ways, but he matured most as a man, one who never ceased to regard the phenomenal talent granted to him as his greatest responsibility and who at the end had also begun to escape his preoccupation with self and let art have its way.

WILLIAM FAULKNER (1897–1962)

Different as they were in most ways that mattered, Thomas Wolfe and William Faulkner were alike in one respect: both were loners in the literary world that fell to their lot. Both eschewed the company of other writers throughout most of their careers. They participated in no movements, literary or otherwise, and made few attempts to establish, much less cultivate, contacts with other literary figures of the time. But whereas Wolfe had the good luck to achieve fame and popularity at the outset of his career, a fact that tended to render him suspect among some of his contemporaries in the literary establishment, Faulkner, who had completed the bulk of his major work by the time of Wolfe's death in 1939, was only lightly regarded by the American public during that period. By 1945 only one of his books, the notorious *Sanctuary*, remained in print, and he had already begun to slip into semiobscurity as a minor master of what was commonly called Southern Gothic.

He was born on September 25, 1897, as William Cuthbert Falkner (the "u" in his name would come later) in the northern Mississippi town of New Albany, but by the time he was five his family had settled in the university town of Oxford nearby, which remained his home for the rest of his life. His first thirty years were a period of self-education, experimentation, and uneven maturation. During the first twenty he enjoyed a fairly normal childhood, indulging in the usual boyish games and pastimes, attending the local school (from which he never graduated), and engaging in an abortive romance with a local belle, Estelle Oldham, whose family regarded him as unpromising and unworthy. Nevertheless, for a time, still hopeful, he tried working in his grandfather's bank but soon abandoned that to pursue a career as a poet, a vocational choice that his father and most of the rest of the community dismissed as a frivolity. In June 1918, after Estelle had capitulated to her parents' wishes and married a suitor of their choice, he enlisted for a course of pilot training with the Canadian RAF, a pursuit that came abruptly to an end with the November armistice. Thereafter Faulkner began a restless period of reorientation that would end some years later with his decision to become a novelist.

For a time he remained in Oxford, unemployed but writing poetry, reading under the tutelage of a young lawyer, Phil Stone, who regarded him as his protégé, and to his father's profound irritation generally playing the bohemian. At one point he tried attending classes at the University of Mississippi but gave that up to work briefly as a clerk in a New York bookstore. Home again, he served as scoutmaster of the local troop, managed (with reprehensible indifference) the university post office, and formed a close friendship with Ben Wasson, an admiring young law student, who soon thereafter would become his agent and editor. He also managed to place a poem with the *Double Dealer* in New Orleans, his first to be published, and completed a book of poems, *The Marble Faun*, which came out shortly before Christmas in 1924. Earlier that year he had taken a train to New Orleans, where he met Sherwood Anderson, whose work he admired, along with Roark Bradford, Lyle Saxon, and others of the *Double Dealer* group. Returning there in 1925, he took up residence, wrote sketches for the *Double Dealer* and the *Times-Picayune*, and with Anderson's encouragement produced his first novel, *Soldiers' Pay*, which was published that same year by Boni and Liveright, and began another. The second half of 1926 he spent in Europe, for the most part in Paris, with a New Orleans friend and neighbor, the artist William Spratling. In April 1927 Boni and Liveright brought out his second novel, *Mosquitoes*. By that time, however, Faulkner was no longer able to support himself abroad, and he returned to Oxford to begin work on a third novel, which he planned to call *Flags in the Dust*.

Both *Soldiers' Pay* and *Mosquitoes* were respectable performances and moderately successful. The first, which centered on a wounded veteran who had returned home to Georgia to die, contained fractured images of Faulkner's own personality and constituted his contribution to the currently fashionable novel of postwar disillusionment. *Mosquitoes*, based upon an outing that he had taken with Anderson and others on Lake Pontchartrain, contained recognizable unflattering portraits of his *Double Dealer* friends, but neither novel gave any clear indication of the kind of work the mature Faulkner would produce. *Flags in the Dust* was quite another matter.

It had begun apparently in response to Anderson's suggestion that he ought to be writing something about the Mississippi he knew, and following that suggestion he had set to work on two stories, one about a clan of rednecks, the Snopeses, who had emerged from the backwoods to infiltrate and eventually dominate a town that he called Jefferson, and the other about an established family they challenged there, one reminiscent in many ways of the Falkners, whom he called the Sartorises. Within weeks he recognized that the possibilities in the first of these could not be dealt with adequately in a short story or even a novella, and that the second, which permitted development of the store of interrelated details and incidents from family history that filled his memory, was of more compelling interest to him. Accordingly he set the story of the Snopeses aside and concentrated on an account of the Sartorises.

Getting it all down in a coherent narrative, however, presented problems of control that he was not yet prepared to deal with and for which he had encountered no precedent in his reading, except perhaps in the Frenchman Balzac's sprawling chronicle. What came out in the end was not one story but at least half a dozen, all vigorously demanding attention and obscuring with their misdirections the clear story he was trying to tell. It should have been no surprise when Boni and Liveright declined to publish, but Faulkner, immensely pleased with what he had done, was devastated and tried without much success to put a semblance of order into the narrative tangle that filled his manuscript. The luck that saved him at that point came in the person of his friend Ben Wasson, now with a literary agency in New York, who agreed to help find another publisher and after some months did find one, Harcourt, Brace, who consented to publish provided Wasson would serve as editor. Thus what was to have been *Flags in the Dust* appeared in print as *Sartoris* in January 1929.

Meanwhile, he had forged ahead with a novel about another of Jefferson's patrician families, this time one that permitted a much simpler story line. He presented the story in four versions, the third and fourth of which were relatively straightforward narratives and presented no difficulties. Full comprehension of the novel, however, required comprehension of the first two, one of which was quite literally a tale told by an idiot, the second a Joycean stream-of-consciousness meditation by a young man on the point of committing suicide—devices that demanded more sophistication and patience than most readers at the time, including publishers' readers, could have been expected to provide. Harcourt, Brace rejected the work out of hand as unmarketable, but one of their readers, Harrison Smith, liked what he saw; and when Smith shortly thereafter joined with Jonathan Cape to form a new firm, he asked for the manuscript. Thus in the same month that Harcourt, Brace published *Sartoris*, January 1929, the house of Jonathan Cape and Harrison Smith accepted *The Sound and the Fury*, which they published the following October. Meanwhile, Estelle Oldham, now divorced, had come home to Oxford with her two children, and in June Faulkner impulsively married her. They honeymooned in the coastal town of Pascagoula, and Faulkner spent much of the time correcting proofs. He had written the novel, he said, mainly to satisfy a need to write as he wished to write without undue concern for what publishers or the public might think, and his writing merited priority.

These events of 1929 constituted a turning point for Faulkner, privately as well as professionally. His marriage would turn out to be a disappointment for both of them, and he would spend much of his life thereafter seeking, with only transitory successes, the companionship that Estelle through no fault of her own did not provide. The reception of the two new novels was equally disappointing, but in producing these he had discovered his medium as a writer. *Sartoris*, or rather the baggy monster from which it grew, proved to be the seedbed for most of what he was to write, including *The Sound and the Fury*. Most of the work on which his claim to fame would rest would deal with the inhabitants of that same northern Mississippi town he called Jefferson and the surrounding Yoknapatawpha countryside, a fictional world he had modeled after his hometown of Oxford in Lafayette County. More important, in *The Sound and the Fury* he discovered and unleashed the genius for innovative construction that would result in the three masterpieces of the 1930s: *As I Lay Dying* (1930), *Light in August* (1932), and *Absalom, Absalom!* (1936).

The central figure in the novel that Ben Wasson extricated from the tangle of *Flags in the Dust* was Bayard Sartoris, a young man, restless like Faulkner himself, who returned home from war in 1919 angry at the world and bent on self-destruction. In the end he did indeed destroy himself, but in the process he accidentally caused the death of his grandfather and left his bride, whom he had mainly neglected, to bear his child. Ostensibly Bayard's recklessness—manifested in such escapades as riding a half-wild stallion and driving his high-powered car furiously about the countryside—stemmed from grief for a twin who, in the tradition of male Sartorises before him, had died needlessly yet gloriously in war. The novel suggests that a deeper cause was his imagined inability, either in war or in peace, to conform to the family tradition as he understood it; but it also demonstrates how in the end Bayard, by persisting in his arrogance and rebellious behavior, ironically proved himself a true Sartoris.

For women the dilemma created by those parts of the lingering tradition that governed them was quite different, as Faulkner showed in the latently rebellious Narcissa Benbow, the character he created as Bayard's wife. In *The Sound and the Fury* he focused attention on Candace Compson, who by her escape from the restrictions of Jefferson and family infuriated her first brother, Jason, left a second, Quentin, with unresolved stirrings that eventually drove him to suicide, and hopelessly devastated a third, the idiot whom they called Benjy. To each of the brothers in *The Sound and the Fury* Faulkner gave a section of narrative, letting each reveal both himself and the personality of his absent sister and in addition the moribund tradition with its antiquated prescriptions of behavior appropriate to men and women that still governed at least three of them, Benjy being an innocent and therefore exempt. In a final section, in which Faulkner served as omniscient narrator, the story at last comes clear and by means of Dilsey, the family's black cook, who serves as the section's central intelligence, presents those virtues of compassion and understanding that in her person stand between the family and total disintegration in its last days. Most readers found the book difficult; but a number of critics praised it, and Faulkner, pleased and excited by even a modicum of success, set to work on another experiment, this one the account of an indigent farm family, the Bundrens, who set out on a bizarre journey with the body of a dead mother to satisfy her wish to be buried with relatives in Jefferson.

As I Lay Dying (1930) is a story of country people, similar to the Snopeses but without their rapacity. In it fifteen voices—seven of them Bundrens, including the dead Addie—alternately present the story, which in its ramifications proved almost as difficult for readers to grasp as *The Sound and the Fury*. This book also sold poorly; and Faulkner, having bought Rowan Oaks, the house that thereafter was to be his home, was in need of funds. To add to his income he had been forced to write *As I Lay Dying* while working night shifts at the university's power plant, and he had also begun trying to sell some of his accumulated short pieces to magazines. When this combination of strategies failed to provide enough, he wrote a "shocker"—to make money, he said—which, after some revisions to meet initial misgivings on the part of Harrison Smith, appeared in 1931 as *Sanctuary*. Both critics and readers were oblivious to the book's intrinsic merits, but it contained a gallery of dubious characters, several murders, and a rape, and it sold better than *The Sound and the Fury* and *As I Lay Dying* combined. It also made Faulkner temporarily famous—or notorious—as a writer of salacious fiction. Oxford was shocked, but New York began to pay attention, as did France and Britain. Still, the money was not enough; and the death of a child, born prematurely, and Estelle's declining health added to the difficulties.

In September 1931 Faulkner published his first collection of stories, *These Thirteen*. A second, *Dr. Martino and Other Stories*, would follow in 1934. In part the cache of short stories had resulted from his continuing need for additional funds, but only in part. It was also a reflection of his abiding compulsion to be writing something, however trivial, an activity that now for him was not merely an occupation but a way of life. Most of the stories had already appeared in magazines with a national circulation—*Saturday Evening Post*, *Harper's*, *Atlantic Monthly*, *American Mercury*, *Sewanee Review*, and *Forum*. Some were memorable in their own right: "Red Leaves," "A Rose for Emily," "That Evening Sun," and "Barn Burning." One, "Wash," became a crucial episode in *Absalom, Absalom!* (1936); another became the central episode in *Go Down, Moses* (1942), which was in fact an amalgamation of short stories. The same was true of his second novel about the Sartorises, *The Unvanquished* (1938).

During much of 1931, however, Faulkner worked on *Light in August*, which he finished the following February and soon after accepted the first of three offers he was to receive (1932, 1935, and 1945) to work as a scriptwriter in Hollywood. The plot of *Light in August* was the most complicated he had devised up to that point. In simple terms, it consisted of two plots. One was the story of a country girl, Lena Grove, on foot and pregnant, searching patiently for the man who had seduced her. In the course of her wandering she reaches Jefferson and finds companionship in the person of Byron Bunch, a planing-mill worker there. The other was the story of Joe Christmas, a social outcast of uncertain parentage and race, who becomes the lover and eventually the murderer of a spinster who years before had come South with her abolitionist father to educate the former slaves. Lena and Joe are among Faulkner's most memorable creations: Lena, the supreme embodiment of innocence and charity, and Joe, evil in his dispossession, forever lost in a world that has no category for him. The link between the two plots is the almost equally memorable Gail Hightower, onetime Presbyterian minister, now a recluse reveling in dreams of Civil War heroism. When Christmas is being sought for the spinster's murder, Bunch tries in vain to persuade Hightower to provide an alibi for the man, but he does succeed in getting him to deliver Lena's child. By this one act, Hightower manages to regain something of his lost self-respect. Joe Christmas, doomed in any case, is lynched by a fanatical racist, Percy Grimm and Lena, Byron, and the child continue their wandering as a family. More than any of the previous novels, *Light in August* transcends the southern setting that gives it substance and becomes a symbol of the universal human situation, redeemable only by the human capacity for compassion and endurance.

In May 1932 Faulkner, still in need of funds, left Oxford and Estelle temporarily to begin his first session as a scriptwriter in Hollywood. He soon found the work there tedious in the extreme, though his regular salary from MGM and the prospect of money for the movie rights to *Sanctuary* did help to compensate for the disappointing sales of *Light in August*, which came out the following October. By December he was back in Oxford, where he remained, still on salary and working halfheartedly on scripts; but the children's illnesses and Estelle's pregnancy compounded his frustration at not having some real project of his own in view. In desperation he put together a collection of old poems, published as *A Green Bough* in April 1933, and began to take flying lessons. Finally in May, when an impatient MGM released its absentee writer, he felt so relieved that he bought the plane, an indulgence that was to bring him far more grief than pleasure.

Then temporarily things seemed to improve. In June his daughter Jill was born, and he started working again in earnest, writing stories, reviewing his material on the Snopeses, and toying with a project about an adventurous planter whose ambitions brought him to disaster. Early in 1934 he flew to New Orleans to attend the dedication of an airport there, an episode that resulted in a potboiler about barnstormers, *Pylon*, which was eventually published in March 1935. In April his second collection of short pieces appeared, *Dr. Martino and Other Stories*. The year 1935, however, brought Faulkner to yet another crisis when his youngest brother, Dean, to whom he had sold his plane, crashed to his death during a barnstorming excursion. Faulkner for a time was inconsolable, but he finally found comfort in resuming work on the novel that he called *Absalom, Absalom!* and later declared to be his best. Many have since agreed, but reviewers in 1936 were bewildered by a strategy that involved the reminiscences and speculations of several narrators and a series of constructions and reconstructions and found the book unnecessarily confusing. In their struggle to clarify the story line they failed to grasp the significance of what Faulkner had done with it.

Absalom, Absalom! was the story of a young Harvard undergraduate, Quentin Compson of *The Sound and the Fury*, who was intrigued by the mystery surrounding a long-dead planter in Yoknapatawpha County, Thomas Sutpen, in whose legendary career he dimly perceived a possible clue to his own identity as a southerner. Initially, all Quentin had to go on was the bare outline of the legend: how Sutpen arrived in Jefferson some years before the Civil War with a retinue of wild blacks, acquired land (no one quite knew how) that came to be known as Sutpen's Hundred, built a mansion, married a local girl, sired a daughter and a son, and dreamed of a dynasty.

Yet following the war, which spared his land and mansion, Sutpen's hopes had collapsed when the wife died and the son murdered his sister's fiancé and promptly vanished. Thereafter he let the land go untended, the mansion fall into disrepair, and himself grow fat, but he stubbornly kept alive his dream of dynasty and vainly sought a female partner to enable him to begin again. To that end he seduced the granddaughter of one Wash Jones, a poor white living in Sutpen's abandoned fishing camp, but rejected her when the child she bore was a daughter. Jones, enraged, dispatched both granddaughter and child and then killed Sutpen with a scythe. To supplement this story Quentin adds details, many of them suspect, provided by Sutpen's sister-in-law, Miss Rosa Colfield, his own father's testimony, and his father's recollection of what his father had told him. He also has information gathered when he accompanied Miss Rosa on a mysterious trip out to the still standing mansion, and the report of what happened shortly thereafter when Miss Rosa sent out an ambulance to bring back the wasted figure of Sutpen's long vanished son and heir.

Faulkner presents his story partly as Quentin's report and partly as a continuing exchange between Quentin and his Canadian roommate, Shreve

McCarron, who has asked to know something about the South. Together they reconstruct Sutpen's tragedy, which involves murder, a series of racial interminglings, and the threat of incest; and the result—part fact, part inference, and part guesswork—embodies contributions by both but is an account that neither can reject. For Shreve acceptance is easy. Fascinated, he takes it to be symbolic of a violent social evolution that in the end may be beneficial, but sensing that Quentin is disturbed, he asks a final question: "Why do you hate the South?" The novel concludes with Quentin's confused and agonized reply: "'I dont hate it,' he said. *I dont hate it* he thought, panting in the cold air, the iron New England dark; *I dont. I dont! I dont hate it! I dont hate it!*"

Perceptive critics have agreed that the significance of the novel is implicit in Quentin's breathless response. In a single work Faulkner had presented more of the essential truth about the self-proclaimed aristocracy of the deep South than anyone before him: its genesis in an amoral wilderness and its human roots in a tide of adventurers who, unprepared by their cultural heritage for the situation they found themselves in, necessarily abandoned that heritage to ensure not only the advancement they sought but their very survival and who thereafter, having achieved both, with the same ruthlessness sought to reconstruct that heritage in the alien soil. Men like Sutpen in their failure exposed the reality that Faulkner's luckier adventurers—the Sartorises, Compsons, McCaslins, and their descendants—had been at pains to deny. Faulkner, perhaps without fully comprehending what he had produced, had with one stroke rebutted not only the romantic image promulgated by Thomas Nelson Page and his kind but the subtler image of the Agrarian apologists—their view of the South as an inchoate nation of yeoman farmers, destined to confirm the Jeffersonian dream if allowed to develop without interruption. Reviewers, however, in the North and the South alike, saw it as mainly another sensational offering by a southern author given to sensationalism and to presenting what should have been a straightforward tale in a barrage of unnecessarily obtuse stylistics.

In the years immediately following, Faulkner would publish four more novels: *The Unvanquished* (1938), dealing with Bayard Sartoris's antecedents during the Civil War; *The Wild Palms* (1939), an unsuccessful attempt to fuse two dissimilar stories by the mechanical device of relating them in alternate chapters; *The Hamlet* (1940), the first and best part of what was to become a Snopes trilogy; and *Go Down, Moses* (1942), a brilliant but sprawling examination of most of his themes, pieced together mainly out of earlier stories but focused on a minor masterpiece, "The Bear," which symbolized all America's confrontation with the great wilderness it neither respected nor understood. At this point in his career a lesser writer might easily have succumbed to the temptation to put aside novel-making and present in essays or lectures the wealth of insights his writing had engendered, but Faulkner would remain an artist to the end. By 1945, however, he had had few encouragements to continue. His public, such as he could claim, regarded him as a colorful but minor eccentric on the literary scene, and practically all of his work was out of print. Few saw that in probing the roots of the southern experience he had provided a definition of the South that would enable a new generation of writers to avoid the path of stultifying romanticism and exploitations of local color and begin to create a literature fully representative of the region's diversity and complexity. All that was needed was a credible public recognition of his achievement that might prompt a speedy revaluation.

5

Southern Playwrights

Literary historians have often noted that America had no indigenous theater until after World War I. Of course, theatrical houses did a flourishing business in all the major cultural centers—New York, Boston, Chicago, New Orleans, and San Francisco—and there were similar establishments in the secondary cities of the South as well as the North. Towns of more modest size usually had at least one multipurpose "opera house" to accommodate shows by local talent and other special events such as traveling musicians, lecturers, and evangelists as well as the occasional traveling troupe of actors. Buildings themselves, however, do not give sustaining life to the theater, which in nineteenth-century America and to an only slightly less degree in England during the same period was, to put it charitably, stagnant and produced scarcely enough actors, directors, and managers to establish and maintain a professional tradition—and no playwrights at all of distinction.

Encouraging signs of genuine life in the American theater began to appear early in the twentieth century, however, when the activity of the Little Theatre movement in England and Ireland extended its influence across the Atlantic and prompted aspiring Americans, including a number of southerners, to consider writing plays as well as fiction and poetry. At first, few of the southerners were alert to the techniques of writing for the stage. To develop that kind of awareness they needed the practical experience that was available mainly to those with access to legitimate theater, and the only legitimate theater available to the average southerner was miles away in New York.

One southerner who recognized early what he needed and was clever, or lucky, enough to make the necessary adjustments to achieve it was the novelist Stark Young (1881–1963), who after acquiring an M.A. degree at Columbia in 1902 and directing student productions at universities in Mississippi and Texas had ventured in 1921 to try his hand at freelance writing in New York. There his native talent surfaced, and he quickly established himself as a drama critic with both *Theatre Arts Magazine* and the *New Republic*. Within four years he also managed to write two plays for off-Broadway production, neither of which was more than moderately successful except with other critics. Yet as a dramatic critic and writer of novels, including the masterly *So Red the Rose* (1934), Young achieved a degree of prominence on the New York literary scene; and in the late thirties and forties he produced translations of Chekhov's plays—among them *The Sea Gull*, *The Cherry Orchard*, and *Three Sisters*—that were highly successful, both commercially and artistically, on Broadway.

North Carolina's Thomas Wolfe (1900–38), born two decades later, found a temporary substitute for Broadway in Frederick Koch's Carolina Playmakers at the university in Chapel Hill and from there went north in 1920 to enroll in George Pierce Baker's newly established drama workshop at Harvard. In 1924 Wolfe actually made it to New York with a play in hand, but he failed to find a producer and settled for teaching at New York University and writing novels. Andrew Lytle followed a similar path and studied with Baker at the Yale Drama School, but although he pursued the theater long enough to win a small part in a Broadway production, he wrote no plays, found existence in New York intolerable, and returned to Tennessee. Other southerners who dreamed intermittently of writing for the stage included William Faulkner, Robert Penn Warren, and Peter Taylor, but Faulkner wrote instead, and always unhappily, for Hollywood, Warren's plays were successful only as closet drama, and Taylor, although he succeeded in emulating Chekhov in prose fiction, lacked Chekhov's inspired knack for theatrical writing. A fair number of southern writers—among them DuBose Heyward, Erskine Caldwell, Faulkner, Warren, Margaret Mitchell, and Carson McCullers—have either collaborated with others to make their novels suitable for stage or screen or permitted others to adapt them.

The only southerner to achieve real success in New York and then settle in the South to write plays there has been Paul Green (1894–1981), and Green accomplished that feat only by creating both a special kind of play and a new kind of theater. Like Wolfe he began his career with the Carolina Playmakers and wrote a number of short folk plays, five of which the Playmakers performed. Then after an interlude of several years, during which he studied philosophy at Cornell and returned to teach philosophy at Chapel Hill, he made his assault on Broadway, taking with him a well-developed folk play, *In Abraham's Bosom: The Biography of a Negro*. To the astonishment of doubters, the play was produced successfully in 1926, was highly praised by reviewers, and was awarded a Pulitzer Prize the following year. Two more successes, *The Field God* (1927) and *The House of Connelly* (1928), the second of which was the initial production of the newly established Group Theatre, put him temporarily in a position second only to Eugene O'Neill in the eyes of New York's critics.

These three plays made Green a prime candidate for a Guggenheim Fellowship (1928–29), which enabled him to go to Berlin. There he met and exchanged ideas with Alexis Gronowsky and Bertolt Brecht and began to develop, partly from their precept and example, his own idea of "symphonic drama," one that would consist of a fusion of many elements, word and music, acrobatics and dance, farce and fantasy. It would also, he thought, provide him an opportunity to project some of his own deep convictions, not all of them theatrical: a strong egalitarianism, a concern for blacks, a respect for authenticity, and a belief that coherence in drama requires a sensitive and intelligent manipulation of scenes, characters, and separate actions—like motifs in music—to reveal a unifying rhythm underneath. Nevertheless, of the four plays Green wrote in this form only one achieved any measure of success. This was *Johnny Johnson*, which anticipated the device Faulkner was to use in *A Fable*, that of a guileless innocent who manages for a time to bring World War I to a halt. Green wrote it in the summer of 1936 in Chapel Hill in collaboration with Kurt Weill, then newly arrived in the United States and eager to work with an American, and the Group Theatre produced it the following November—also subsidized it, because for nine weeks they took half pay to keep the play running.

Discouraged with all things connected with Broadway, Green returned to North Carolina, where luckily local, state, and national authorities were planning to establish an outdoor theater near Manteo on Roanoke Island to celebrate the 350th anniversary of Raleigh's ill-fated colony. Almost immediately he began work on a play, *The Lost Colony*, which was ready for rehearsal in the spring of 1937 and opened on July 4. This new, somewhat modified version of the symphonic drama was not only successful that year; with the exception of four years during World War II, it has played to enthusiastic audiences every summer since, and it set the pattern for a kind of theater that has continued to flourish during summer months at historical sites throughout the South.

Historians have noted that one of Green's achievements in this play, though one that was probably unintentional, was to embody the function and aims of "people's theater" as the founders of the short-lived Federal Theater Project of 1935–39 understood them. This production was a dramatization of an action that presumably took place on the spot were the play was being given, and it presented values and ideals that all the members of the American audience, unsophisticated and sophisticated alike, could grasp. The settings, costumes, music, and hints of archaic speech all bespoke authenticity and thus added credibility to the values that emerged as the play progressed. The vehicle for these values was the hero, a simple English tenant farmer who discovers in his New World surroundings the initiative and talents that would have been suppressed to extinction in the stratified society from which he came. In the end, self-realized and free, he leads the settlers to an unknown destiny inland rather than accept enslavement by Spaniards who have threatened them in Raleigh's absence.

The success of *The Lost Colony* led to requests for more of the same. Accordingly for Fayetteville, North Carolina, Green wrote *The Highland Call*, a dramatization of the problems encountered by a community of Scottish Loyalists during the Revolution. Then for the Federal Theatre he provided one on Thomas Jefferson, *The Common Glory*, which Williamsburg, Virginia, seized upon when Congress terminated the theater in 1939. Requests for still others continued, but Green paused long enough at this point to produce, with the author's blessing and assistance, a dramatization of Richard Wright's *Native Son*, which under the direction of Orson Welles added still another Broadway success to his laurels. After 1941, however, he returned to his symphonic people's theater and wrote fourteen more outdoor historical plays for production by localities widely scattered across the country.

A number of these late plays were still in production more than a decade after Green's death in 1981. Fittingly, the University of North Carolina had named a theater for him in 1978, but the theater that more appropriately memorializes Paul Green continues transitorially season after season in a dozen or more amphitheaters where his plays and those of his imitators continue to delight and perhaps edify summer audiences. Green was meticulous in his craftsmanship. He published most of his plays, several of them more than once, and he revised each time he published, hoping to bring them to a degree of perfection that would justify preservation. Even so, few critics have granted him more than minor status. There is nothing profound in his work and, in the final analysis, nothing very original. Yet as a southerner who achieved with apparent ease the transition to Broadway, flourished there, and then returned to the South to create a unique kind of regional theater that continues after his death, Green deserves more than passing notice in the literary history of the area.

Lillian Hellman (1905–84), whose dramatic successes were largely confined to the Broadway theater, is another special case. Some might even decline to consider her a southerner. She was born in New Orleans and spent her earliest years there, but financial difficulties soon dictated that the family move to New York and, to make matters more awkward, live there with her mother's people during the winter months, returning to New Orleans during the summer to spend the rest of each year with her father's. Thus, although she maintained southern roots, she attended high school and college in New York and then with easy access to the worlds of publishing and theater found work as a reader in a publishing house, meanwhile writing reviews for the *Herald-Tribune* and reading scripts for a prominent New York producer. The South was never again her home. Married early, she removed to California in 1930, where she read scenarios for MGM, then divorced (amicably) and made new friends, among them Dashiell Hammett, who became her permanent companion and mentor. It was with Hammett's encouragement that she wrote her first play, *The Children's Hour*, produced in 1934 and afterward revised as a film.

The next twelve years were a happy period for Hellman. In them she produced all the dramatic work for which she is best known: five more plays, only one of which was a failure, and the script for a successful movie about Russia during the German invasion, *The North Star*, admired at the time but destined to be a source of embarrassment to her during the early postwar years. Looking back, one can admire the skillful construction of her plays but note that they are melodramatic and dated. Good and evil are simplistically differentiated and presented as absolutes, reflecting popular attitudes of the time, and the predilections of the author, rather than a compulsion to explore the subject at hand.

For example, in the most popular play of the lot, *The Little Foxes* (1939), set in small-town Alabama of 1900, she depicts with broad strokes the callosity and greed activated among members of a supposedly respectable family, the Hubbards, when northern entrepreneurs move in to set up a cotton mill. The Hubbards are undoubtedly representative of the South's many little foxes who without regard to anything except their own self-interest leaped at opportunities to collaborate with outsiders in the despoliation of their vineyard. Foremost among these characters in the play is Regina, married to local banker Horace Giddens, who is dying of a heart ailment but painfully aware of the exploitation of blacks and poor whites that must accompany the proposed industrialization. As the action proceeds Regina sees that her brothers have no compunction about leaving her out of their plans to participate in the new firm and seeks help from her husband. When he refuses, she withholds his life-sustaining medicine and lets him die. As the play ends, life among the Hubbards goes on, each family member trying to outmaneuver the others, but diabolical Regina, equal to her brothers in ruthlessness and their superior in resourcefulness, seems certain to survive and likely to triumph.

Some critics have compared Hellman's work here and in the other plays of this period to that of Ibsen, but the resemblance is probably superficial at best. Both used the tight construction of the well-made play, and both exhibited the inclination to focus attention on a problem; Hellman's characters, however, tend toward the two-dimensional. Her dialogue lacks the cumulative intensity that makes the exchanges in Ibsen exciting, and she falls short of Ibsen's mastery of irony and symbolic detail. Her plays are best seen as well-crafted devices for exploiting popular attitudes. The most memorable character in them, Regina, follows in the wake of approval that greeted Margaret Mitchell's portrayal of a Scarlett O'Hara ruthless in her assertiveness and determination to survive. With the impressive Tallulah Bankhead, herself an Alabamian, playing Regina, Hellman created a piece of memorable theater that added to the unflattering picture of the South still running on Broadway at the time in the adaptation of Caldwell's *Tobacco Road*. Her attempt several years later to present a dramatic explanation of how the Hubbards came to be as they were, *Another Part of the Forest* (1946), lacked the focus and guaranteed appeal of the first play and did less well.

Hellman wrote two plays depicting the Nazi menace. The first, *Watch on the Rhine* (1941), though less popular than *The Little Foxes*, had a more complex plot and a greater variety of characterizations, and it deservedly won the Drama Critics Circle Award. Her second, *The Searching Wind* (1944), dealt with America's failure in the prewar years to recognize the threat to its existence and, coming as it did after an aroused nation had already turned the tide of war, was received with great enthusiasm. Neither of these plays, however, has survived the memory of the events that gave them immediacy, and their patent patriotism and antifascist sentiments did little to protect Hellman from the near disaster that befell both her and her companion Hammett during the Communist-baiting that followed World War II.

In addition to writing the script for the manifestly pro-Russian *The North Star* (1943), considered a patriotic gesture at the time, Hellman on a trip to Europe in the late thirties had visited the Soviet Union, which she admired, and Spain, where like most of the literary community she was openly supportive of the Loyalists. Then in 1944 at the request of the U.S. government she had gone on a cultural mission to Moscow. By 1948, however, the political climate in the United States had changed, and Hellman discovered that she was on a Hollywood blacklist. By 1951 Hammett had also fallen under suspicion and, after refusing to testify before the McCarthy committee, was sentenced to six months in prison. Hellman herself declined to testify before the House Un-American Activities Committee but managed to avoid imprisonment. Other disappointments added to her woes during this period. Two of her plays, an adaptation of Edmund Robles's *Montserrat* (1949) and *The Autumn Garden* (1951), did poorly, and for a while she found herself in serious financial difficulties. At about the same time Dashiell Hammett's health began the slow decline that ended in his death in 1961.

Nevertheless, as the fifties advanced things seemed to improve for her.

The Autumn Garden had represented a shift from Ibsen in the direction of Chekhov, and in 1955 she brought out an edition of several of Chekhov's letters. Her adaptation of Anouilh's *The Lark* was a success on Broadway, and *Toys in the Attic* (1960) had a long run and brought her a second Drama Critics Circle Award.

Hellman was to write one final play, *My Mother, My Father, and Me* (1963), which promptly failed, but for the next two decades she enjoyed her celebrity—traveling extensively, lecturing, teaching at universities, and receiving honors. Her principal works during this period were four books of memoirs, the first of which, *An Unfinished Woman* (1969), won a National Book Award. The second, *Pentimento* (1973), was a collection of portraits of relatives, friends (some famous), and her black maid. The third, *Scoundrel Time* (1976), dealt with her political difficulties in the fifties, and the last, which seems to have been partly fictitious, *Maybe* (1980), was an account of a mysterious friend who had touched her life at various points. Scattered in these four volumes are passages that constitute Hellman's most significant contribution to literature about life in the South. Four of the plays are also valuable in that regard: the two dealing with the rapacious Hubbards and *The Autumn Garden* and *Toys in the Attic*, set respectively in a boardinghouse on the Gulf Coast and in New Orleans. Nevertheless, Hellman, for all her southern roots, wrote primarily as an outsider. She came on the literary scene with her extraordinary talents at a time when things southern happened to be fashionable, and by accident of birth she was able to write about them with authority but without seeming to be involved—as in fact she was not. Her South was one that tended to confirm the expectations of audiences in New York, Chicago, and San Francisco but offered little that might make a contribution to their understanding of the real South or to the self-knowledge of audiences in Atlanta, Memphis, and New Orleans.

The third important southern playwright of the twentieth century was Tennessee (born Thomas Lanier) Williams (1911–83), who did not have a play on Broadway until his thirty-fourth year. Yet Williams, unlike his predecessor Paul Green, continued as a part of the Broadway scene for all his productive life; and unlike his contemporary Lillian Hellman, he remained committedly southern, wrote about the South in most of his plays, and reflected authentic, if eccentric, aspects and dimensions of the southern experience. Moreover, unlike both of the foregoing he achieved the status of a major dramatist in American literature and (to the irritation of some southerners) was recognized as such during his own lifetime. Among the many honors that came his way were four New York Drama Critics Circle Awards, two Pulitzer Prizes, and the Gold Medal for Drama from the American Academy of Arts and Letters and the National Institute of Arts and Letters. When he died in 1983, he left a large portion of his considerable estate to the University of the South (which his grandfather had attended, though he himself had not) as a fund for young writers.

A fair amount of what Williams wrote reflected the circumstances of his own life, particularly those of his preadult years. He was born in Columbus, Mississippi, in the northeastern part of the state, but spent his first six years or so in his Episcopal grandfather's rectory at Clarksdale, in the Delta. His father, a large, boisterous fellow much like the character Big Daddy in his notable *Cat on a Hot Tin Roof*, was a traveling salesman for the International Shoe Company. When he received a promotion to an executive position, he moved his family with him to St. Louis, generally thought of as a hospitable place for southerners. Young Williams and his sister Rose, however, were never happy there; they missed their grandfather and the happy days in Clarksdale, and Rose began a long period of decline that eventually ended in madness. There were periods of respite, of course; and one of these came when Williams went on a summer tour of Europe conducted by his grandfather. There in Cologne Cathedral he had some sort of mystical experience, or so he thought, which anticipated by several years his joining the Catholic Church. College, in addition to an opportunity to escape, brought more difficulties, and after Williams had spent a troublesome year at the University of Missouri, his practical-minded father put him to work for more than two years in a shoe factory. Later he would subtract those years from his age, declaring them totally lost. Finally, after a stint at Washington University in St. Louis, he tried the University of Iowa, from which he graduated in 1938 at the age of twenty-seven. During these college years he experimented widely with literary forms, published poems and stories, and began to write plays. He also experimented with sex and discovered his own orientation to be homosexual. Thus prepared, he began his career as playwright.

In 1940 Williams won a Group Theatre prize for four one-act plays, which collectively he called *American Blues*. This accomplishment won him no fame, but it brought into the picture an agent, Audrey Wood, who opened doors for him, among them one that led to the production of his first full-length play in that same year, *Battle of Angels*, by the Boston Theatre Guild. That production, which pitted the sensitive poetic figure against the crass materialism and brutality of the modern South, was a failure; but Williams, ever defensive of his plays, did at least two revised versions before turning it into a film, *The Fugitive Kind*. Thereupon, determined to do something "safe," he wrote *The Glass Menagerie*, focusing upon a young girl reminiscent of his sister Rose and recapitulating with pathos, humor, and compassion the sense of estrangement during the years in St. Louis. The play opened successfully in Chicago in 1944 and moved in 1945 to even greater success in New York, where it won the Drama Critics Circle Award. From that point on until the midsixties, Williams's name remained one to reckon with in any serious consideration of contemporary American drama.

The next fifteen years were Williams's best. He cared for his sister Rose until an institution became the only solution for her, but this domestic sadness was compensated for by the happy liaison he established with Frank Merlo, who was his companion for more than a decade. Williams settled down, bought a home in Key West, and assumed responsibility for his aging grandfather, the person in his life who previously had been the nearest thing to a stabilizing influence. These were also the years in which he kept alive his early dream of becoming a general man of letters. He published a novel, *The Roman Spring of Mrs. Stone* (1951), which critics thought more amusing than praiseworthy, and his movie script, controversial at the time, for *Baby Doll* (1956). He continued to write stories, three volumes of which were published during the sixties, after his fame as playwright was secure. It was the plays of this period, however, some eleven of them, that are memorable. Not all were successes comparable to *The Glass Menagerie*, but three were, and these have become a part of the standard repertory of the American theater.

The first was *A Streetcar Named Desire* (1947), a play in which as in his first success he dramatized the contrast between the crass materialism and tunnel vision of America generally and of the South in particular with the South's dream of a world of grace and charm that had faded and all but vanished during the years following the Civil War. The setting for the play is a slum section of New Orleans, ironically called Elysian Fields. In it lives an insensitive and rootless Stanley Kowalski with his wife Stella Dubois, member of once proud planter aristocracy but more or less resigned to her present depressing circumstances. Into this ménage comes Stella's sister Blanche, fragile, unstable, still maintaining for herself the illusion that the antique glory has not faded, and, as is inevitable, in time she falls victim to Kowalski, who in a combination of resentment and animal lust brutally rapes the woman and precipitates her descent into insanity. In the end it is Stella who maintains illusions, choosing to believe that Blanche's tale of the rape is the fantasy of madness. Many argue that Williams never surpassed his work displayed here: the characters are completely credible, the dialogue that ties them together reveals the essential isolation that dooms them, and the emotional impact of the conflict that develops continues to overwhelm audiences year after year. This play won both the Drama Critics Circle Award and the Pulitzer Prize.

The other two plays that mark Williams's mastery of the theater are *Cat on a Hot Tin Roof* (1955), which also won both prizes, and *Night of the Iguana* (1961), which won the Critics Circle Award. The first of these has the same powerful dramatic impact as *Streetcar,* but the overwhelming character in it is an aging (actually dying) and domineering but loving southern father called Big Daddy, reminiscent to those in the know of Williams's father. It is hardly an accident that the intimidated young man who serves as his foil in the play is a latent homosexual. *Night of the Iguana* takes place in a decrepit "Bohemian hotel" in an out-of-the-way Puerto Barrio on the Pacific Coast, but the central figure here is a defrocked Episcopal priest, Shannon, leading a group of Texas Baptist ladies on a near disastrous tour of Mexico. One is tempted to see much of the rebellious Williams in the priest and much of his grandfather in the aging poet he encounters, who dies in the course of the play. One is hard put, however, to find a parallel for the remarkable Hannah Jelkes, spinster granddaughter to the aging poet, who by precept and example shows Shannon what calm acceptance of life means and why acceptance is infinitely preferable to the rebelliousness he seems to find necessary. All four of these plays by means of television or cinema effectively made the transition to film, and all seem destined to remain indefinitely in the active repertory of the legitimate stage.

The other plays that Williams wrote before 1961 were less successful but no less characteristic of the man himself. Some of these were *Summer and Smoke* (1948), *Suddenly Last Summer* (1958), *Sweet Bird of Youth* (1959), and *Period of Adjustment* (1960). He experimented with comedy, as in *Rose Tattoo* (1951), and tried dispensing with verisimilitude, as in *Camino Real* (1953). His penchant for innovation continued undiminished, and often it tried the patience of producers, who believed, rightly or wrongly, that Williams's real talent lay in his genius for exploring and presenting realistically the deleterious effects of modern materialism and prejudice upon persons, like himself, of unconventional sensibilities. By his own testimony, much of what he wrote may be thought of as self-therapy, but the best of it dramatizes a search for love that is universal—love conceived of as acceptance, the kind proffered to Shannon and other characters in *Night of the Iguana* by the selfless Hannah Jelkes.

In 1960 Frank Merlo died, and the resulting confusion for Williams is reflected in the unsuccessful plays that he wrote during his last years. In desperation he turned to drugs, tried Catholicism for a while, and spent time in a mental institution. His fame continued by means of repeated revivals of his best work (in some of which he himself appeared), occasional productions of new experimental plays, lecturing at universities, and the appearance of a collected edition of his dramatic work, published by New Directions in five volumes (1971–76). In 1975 he published his memoirs and in 1978 a volume of prose pieces, *Where I Live: Selected Essays*. He died in New York in 1983.

From time to time, the South has produced a drama critic capable of holding his own in the theatrical world of New York. In the years between the two world wars, that critic was Stark Young (1881–1963), already noted as a novelist and a participant in Vanderbilt's Agrarian movement, but Young during his active years was best known for his reviews, collections of which were published, and for his translations of the plays of Chekhov. As previously noted, his own efforts at writing plays were only moderately successful. In the years immediately before and after World War II, however, Louisville-born John Mason Brown (1900–69) in the view of many was New York's premier reviewer of plays, turning out material of high literary quality, sometimes witty but invariably urbane, perceptive, and unbiased. Brown wrote successively for *Theatre Arts Monthly Magazine* (1926–28), the *New York Evening Post* (1929–40), the *New York World-Telegram* (1941–42), and after the war, until 1955, the *Saturday Review of Literature*. The most inclusive collection of his work is *Dramatis Personae: A Retrospective Show* (1963), which contains a complete reprint of his earlier *The Modern Theatre in Revolt* (1930).

Part, but only part, of Brown's success was due to the quality of the material he had to write about. His active years in New York were a time of good, occasionally great, plays and superior acting, directors, and stagecraft. He had the luck to be an observer when Arthur Miller, Lillian Hellman, and Tennessee Williams were doing their best work, Clifford Odets and the Group Theatre were flourishing, and the modern American musical was coming into being. As the fifties drew to a close, however, it became evident that Broadway's inner light had grown dim, and people with theatrical talents were beginning to look elsewhere for opportunities that a decade before they would have sought in Manhattan. To meet the clear need for alternatives, vigorous regional theaters of various kinds began springing up in other urban centers across the nation: Atlanta, Dallas, Los Angeles, Seattle, Baltimore, and Charleston. The most successful of these has been the Actors Theatre of Louisville, which since 1975 under the imaginative leadership of its producing director, Jon Jory, has sponsored a highly successful playwriting contest with handsome prizes for the winners and in general has provided aspiring young dramatists with opportunities to have their work performed by professionals in a professional setting.

A number of southern novelists—among them Harry Crews, Wendell Berry, and Roy Blount Jr.—have taken advantage of this new chance to deploy their talent, but by far the most prominent young southerner to rise to the Actors Theatre's challenge has been Marsha Norman (b. 1944), herself a

Louisvillian, whose first play, *Getting Out* (1977), won the American Theatre Critics Association award for best play in that year. Five years later she had received supportive grants from the National Endowment for the Arts and from the Rockefeller Foundation, had seen five more plays reach production, and with the last of these, *'night, Mother* (1983), had made it to Broadway, still the lucrative goal for all playwrights, and won the Pulitzer Prize. Unfortunately, Norman's pattern of advancement underscores a fact that applies to all the regional theaters: they are essentially regional extensions of Broadway, which in spite of limitations continues to serve as America's premier center for theater, a role that since World War II it has shared only with Hollywood. Nevertheless, for southerners the regionals have opened a door to theater that previously was lacking. What further use, if any, they will make of it remains to be seen.

As always, however, a southern writer occasionally makes his or her way directly into the mainstream of American theater. A conspicuous example in recent years is Romulus Linney (b. 1930), by birth a Philadelphian but of southern stock, who spent most of his formative years in North Carolina and Tennessee and later lectured at Chapel Hill and served for a time as director of fine arts at North Carolina State University in Raleigh. Like Norman, Linney has written for the Actors Theatre, but before that he made a modest name for himself as a novelist and then turned successfully to theater. Several of his thirteen long plays and twenty-two short ones have had professional productions, on Broadway and at the Kennedy Center in Washington, and some of his best work has southern settings, notably the comedies *Holy Ghosts* (1974) and *Just Folks* (commissioned by the Kennedy Center; 1976) and *Appalachia Sounding* (1976), a chronicle play written for the nation's bicentennial. The authenticity of these "southern" plays derives in part from summers Linney spent in Boone, North Carolina, which also gave him the material for his first novel, *Heathen Valley* (1962).

An even more recent example of a successful southern invasion of American theater has been that of Robert Schenkkan (b. 1953), born in Chapel Hill, North Carolina, and educated at the University of Texas (B.A., 1975) and Cornell (M.F.A., 1977). Schenkkan wrote a number of producible plays before he turned out one that brought him a measure of fame, or notoriety. His two-part work *The Kentucky Cycle*, covering two hundred years of life in eastern Kentucky, was first produced in Seattle in 1991. From there it quickly made its way to New York, where it failed on Broadway and produced cries of outrage from knowledgeable Appalachians but won a Pulitzer Prize.

An older southerner whose original work during the postwar years has been characterized by authenticity as well as skill is Texas-born Horton Foote

(b. 1916), who served an apprenticeship as an actor for ten years (1932–42) before he discovered his talent for writing. Foote thus began as a playwright just as television, live in those days, was starting to offer genuine opportunities, and he was able to develop his skills by writing plays for all the principal networks, NBC, CBS, and ABC, and also the BBC. Some of his best early work went into the productions of Playhouse 90 and Kraft Playhouse. A number of Foote's shorter plays are based upon his own early life in Wharton, Texas, which he has renamed Harrison, and in 1959 he was able to publish a collection of eight of these, entitled simply *Harrison, Texas*. Meanwhile, he had begun to make his way back into the theater—his *The Chase* was produced on Broadway in 1952—and into the ranks of the novelists—*The Chase* as a novel was published in 1956. In 1962 he became a celebrity of sorts when his screenplay for Harper Lee's *To Kill a Mockingbird* won an Academy Award. By that time, however, live television was beginning to disappear, and during the seventies he went into semiretirement, emerging only at the insistence of his friend Robert Duvall, for whom he wrote a totally original screenplay, *Tender Mercies* (1983). That, too, won an Academy Award. Then for another friend, Geraldine Page, he adapted a television play for the stage, *The Trip to Bountiful*, which also became a successful film (1983), the last one to have Page as a star. Since that time Foote has received numerous awards and honorary degrees and returned to limited activity, writing plays mainly for regional theaters.

In sum, it is fair to say that to date the South's principal contributions to theater have been made by those few who by lucky circumstances were able to come to terms with the New York establishment and its more recent extensions in cinema and television. Successful drama requires a vital medium in which aspiring dramatics can work, learn, and develop whatever special contributions they are capable of. The South has never had the means—or perhaps the need—to develop such a medium of its own. The "people's theater" of Paul Green, though it has had a few imitators, began and ended with Green himself. Its surviving remnants have become for the most part diversions for summer tourists rather than models of a medium in which serious artists may explore the human condition in their region.

In fact, as many have observed, during the latter half of this century the whole American theater, perhaps for economic reasons, has become increasingly a place for entertaining performances, and serious drama has tended to move toward film, where wider distribution may provide an adequate return for the costs of production. Southern authors have proved quite as ready as any others to take advantage of this uncertain medium and enjoy some of the financial benefits of letting their novels and stories be adapted by professional scriptwriters and producers for presentation on the screen. So far, however, writers for film and television have been in the main little more than competent journeymen, and serious writers who have from time to time joined their number—Faulkner, Hellman, Williams—have usually found the experience limiting if not stultifying.

PART TWO

A Renaissance in Full Swing

6

The Beginning
of Recognition

By the end of the 1930s the South had produced an impressive number of writers of fiction, poetry, and criticism who collectively within less than a decade would prompt outside observers to begin speaking of a "Southern Renaissance." In 1952 Randall Stewart in his foreword to a new anthology of southern literature would note the already widespread use of that term, but fully aware that rebirth at best imperfectly characterized what had happened and was continuing to happen in the region, he compared the situation to that of Elizabethan England and, borrowing a phrase from Samuel Johnson, declared that the South inexplicably and without much warning had become "a nest of singing birds." Actually, at that point the American South had been singing, loudly, for the better part of a generation, yet as recently as the outbreak of war in Europe in 1939, few had been inclined to pay attention. Even so, as war was all but absorbing the attention of the public, books of special significance to an understanding of the South's situation did manage to get published and read by a national audience.

Two of these books have survived to mark the wartime transition between a South still nostalgic for a way of life that was never enjoyed by any but a small minority and one newly self-aware and alert to the contrasts and contradictions in its pluralistic culture. The first of these was written by William Alexander Percy, a fifth-generation member of a prominent Mississippi planter family and thus in the public's eye qualified by blood to serve as a representative of that Old South the sentimentalists continued to be nostalgic about. Percy's collection of reminiscences and reflections, written at various times and published in 1941 as *Lanterns on the Levee*, was more than a collection of essays; it constituted a fairly authentic bildungsroman of a southern intellectual at the time and showed as accurately as any book could have done where the more enlightened and responsible southerners were standing on political and social matters eighty years after the outbreak of their war with the North.

In Will Percy's eyes the finished book amounted to a celebration of the kind of life that would be the good life, not just for southerners but for all people in all places. A number of his twenty-seven chapters are profiles of people who helped him see what that life might be: his maternal grandparents, his black nurse, black playmates in childhood and black dependencies in later life, his teachers, unofficial as well as official. Several deal at length with significant passages in his active career; others are essays that treat generally of places, classes of people, and institutions. One is called simply "A Bit of a Diary," which is what it is. The two pieces that conclude the book are focused respectively on Percy's garden and the Greenville cemetery and serve as meditations on what these places signify to him about the meaning of his life.

Percy's vision of the good life is by no means the sentimental one of an Eden "befo' de war." The world that matters to him is the purely personal one that circumstances, including his own efforts and intelligence, have conspired to make possible in the here and now, and he finds that world in mortal jeopardy. "The World I know is crashing to bits," he writes in 1941—with an eye to more than the expanding war in Europe—and adds, perhaps here with an eye to the imminent end of his own existence, that he considers it "better to remember, to be sure of the good that was, rather than of the evil that is, to watch the spread and pattern of the game that is past rather than engage feebly in the present play." When he died in 1942, in his fifty-seventh year, many of his declarations of the good in his Mississippi life brought him posthumous censure by reviewers outside the region, the kindest of whom called him an example of the unreconstructed southern gentleman and the most unforgiving, a snob and a racist. On the basis of excerpted passages, Percy was probably vulnerable to such charges, but most would now agree that the book as a whole is redeemed by the spirit of broad humanity, tolerance, and charity that informs it.

Without question Percy conformed to the popular notion of a southern gentleman; whether or not he was unreconstructed is a matter of semantics. He had been born and reared in Greenville, which since 1850 his forebears had used as a base for managing their holdings in the adjacent countryside. Somewhere around the turn of the century his father, LeRoy Percy, astutely disposed of those holdings, then pretty much worn out, and put together some 3,300 acres to form a new place that he called Trail Lake, a genuine plantation with just under 150 black families living and working on it. Like any good father, he saw to it that his son should enjoy the educational advantages appropriate to one of his class and expectations: tutors as needed during the early years, an A.B. degree from the prestigious University of the South at Sewanee (1904), a year of travel abroad, and a law degree from Harvard (1908). Thereafter, off and on for twenty years, Will Percy dutifully and successfully practiced law in Greenville, but his heart was never in it. His secret ambition, never fully realized, was to be a man of letters, and between 1915 and 1930 he managed to publish four volumes of respectable low-keyed lyrics—in the nineteenth-century manner, one reviewer said—and gained, in the South at least, a modest standing as a poet. For a time (1925–30), he served as editor of the Yale Series of Younger Poets.

Increasingly, however, the limitations of small-town life made him ill at ease, and in 1916 he found himself so deeply moved by events in Europe that he left Greenville to work with the Hoover Commission for Relief in Belgium and after that served courageously with the Thirty-seventh Division in France, for which he was awarded the croix de guerre. Back in Greenville, however, restlessness continued and he was soon taking an active part in what turned out to be a successful fight against local intrusion by a revived Ku Klux Klan. In 1927 he headed a Red Cross unit responsible for the care and feeding of more than 100,000 homeless people, mostly blacks, during the great Mississippi flood. At one point in the course of that episode he found himself supervising a tent city seven miles long strung out along the levee, the only available dry land thereabouts, which is the significance of his reference to lanterns in the title of the book and suggests his abiding instinct for survival and his readiness to call it into action in a desperate time. At the death of his father in 1929, Percy assumed the management of Trail Lake and after several discouraging Great Depression years turned it into a profitable enterprise. He never married but in 1930, when his financial expectations were lowest, he took into his home the widow of his first cousin and her three small sons. At her death in 1932, he adopted the boys and proceeded to rear them as his own. One of these, the novelist Walker Percy, later wrote of his guardian, "He was the most extraordinary man I have ever known; . . . I owe him a debt which can never be repaid." Readers of Will Percy's autobiographical essays may begin to understand why.

Most of them are a witness to the man's capacity for being interested in almost everything that crossed his path: people of all kinds and stations, places (he was an inveterate traveler until family responsibilities required him to remain at home), history, the arts, farming, gardening, politics (if need required), and religion. He had firm opinions and expressed them when appropriate but apparently seldom pressed views when doing so might make others uncomfortable. By all accounts he was generous to a fault, with time, money, hospitality, and, insofar as was possible, his approval.

Percy did not live to see the adverse reaction that his book would produce in some quarters, but he probably anticipated it. In his view the social and economic dependency of the black, especially the rural black, was something to be corrected gradually and until corrected, endured with as much grace as possible. As regards the black's ultimate situation in the South—or, for that matter, in the nation at large—he was uncertain, but he made no apologies for doubting the fashionable liberal view that he and his black tenants had been created equal in all essential respects. He saw even greater innate differences among the white population, however, though pedigree had less to do with those differences than his critics imagined. What mattered in the makeup of black and white alike was the strength of character that manifested itself in the individual's willingness to accept and make humane use of the gifts and conditions of life allotted to him. For Percy, humane use involved recognizing, however dimly, the responsibility of fostering that universal brotherhood on which all civilization rests. He usually tolerated childlike selfishness when he encountered it in the black population because he considered that population more primitive than his own, but he was contemptuous of the same selfishness in whites, regardless of birth, though he sadly conceded that it was often their selfishness that put them on top of the social heap.

The part of *Lanterns on the Levee* that most disturbed liberal readers of the early 1940s, however, was Percy's unapologetic defense of sharecropping, which he said was a genuine partnership between planter and worker and "one of the best systems ever devised to give security and a chance for profit to the simple and unskilled." Sharecropping, he argued, involved the worker's responsibility to use the planter's property to produce goods in due season and the planter's responsibility to see that the worker lived comfortably in security and dignity: "If the white planter happens to be a crook, the sharecropper system in that plantation is bad for Negroes, as any other system would be. . . . But, strange as it may seem to the sainted East, we have quite a sprinkling of decent folk down our way. . . . Leveling down's the fashion now, but I remember the bright spires—they caught the light first and held it longest." Egalitarian liberals in the sainted East were not amused.

Thirty years after his death the Louisiana State University Press brought out a second edition of *Lanterns on the Levee* with an introduction by his now famous cousin, Walker Percy, who, reflecting on the changes of the past thirty years, acknowledged his own disagreements with his onetime guardian but referred to him as "a fixed point in a confusing world." "Even when I did not follow him," he said, "it was usually in *relation* to him, whether with him or against him, that I defined myself and my own direction." Many other southern authors who had their coming of age, chronological or literary, in the forties might have said much the same thing—if not specifically about Will Percy and his book, then about the hopeful attitudes he projected.

By 1940 most writers, including several who had taken their angry stand as Agrarians—Ransom, Tate, and Warren—were no longer concerned with perpetuating a cold war with the North and East. Even so, they were unwilling to accept the stereotypes by which liberals in all parts of the country had continued to characterize the South and define their relation to it. In their view, the "decent folk" of the region in post–Civil War years had in many respects made the best of a bad situation that was not of their creation, and the best solution in those years following reconstruction had been a temporary continuation of peonage in the form of sharecropping. The trouble with that solution was the inclination among too many southerners to cease to think of it as temporary—that and a dearth of selfless landowners like Will Percy. Fortunately, World War II brought a watershed in northern thinking about the South and the South's thinking about itself. Old stereotypes were threadbare, and the region was ready for reassessment from an existential point of view.

A step toward such a reassessment came in the second of the two landmark books of the forties—surprisingly, to some, from one of Vanderbilt's Fugitive-Agrarians, Robert Penn Warren, who, having begun as poet, and completed his degree at Vanderbilt, had taken another at Berkeley (M.A.) and in 1928, Rhodes scholarship in hand, was studying at Oxford when the urge to write fiction overtook him. Warren never recovered entirely from that seizure. In the decade and a half following, he would teach at several institutions, produce a memorable biography of John Brown, write two novels that were never published and two more that would gain him a modest reputation, with Cleanth Brooks create and edit the *Southern Review*, coauthor three revolutionary textbooks, publish three volumes of poetry, and in 1944 occupy the Poetry Chair at the Library of Congress. Yet none of all this quite prepared the public, or his former associates at Vanderbilt, for the book that he would contrive out of materials he had originally intended to use in a play and publish in 1946 as *All the King's Men*. Popularly, this work turned out to be far and away the triumph of Warren's career. It received the Pulitzer Prize in 1947 and was promptly made into a successful film. Subsequently, knowledgeable critics have pronounced the book a masterpiece.

Initially, much of the public's interest in *All the King's Men* was due to the widespread notion, understandable but erroneous, that it was based upon the career of Huey Long, who was assassinated in Baton Rouge during Warren's second year of teaching at the university there. Undoubtedly, Long was one of several factors that prompted Warren to develop a character, the governor of an unnamed southern state, whom he ultimately called Willie Stark. Nevertheless, except in the most general way the career of Willie Stark cannot be related to that of Huey Long. He remains a character in his own right, a responsible artist's credible three-dimensional fiction, one unrestricted by the particularities of any documentable history but, thanks to the author's ingenuity, revelatory of many. That ingenuity is nowhere more clearly manifested than in Warren's creation of Jack Burden, the narrator who presents the character of Stark and everything else in the novel. Burden is a native of Stark's state, a onetime graduate student of southern history turned newspaper reporter, who, having gone to work for Stark out of curiosity and almost for want of something better to do, suddenly finds himself increasingly preoccupied with a problem of meaning that has vexed interpreters of human events from time immemorial. His attempts to come to conclusions about the matter constitute the substance of the novel's central action, in the course of which he discovers unsuspected truths about himself, his family, and his heritage; in these discoveries, or disillusionments, lies the special significance of *All the King's Men* in the advance of southern letters.

The title of the book alludes obliquely to the context of Burden's disillusionment by calling to mind a Humpty Dumpty irreparably fractured by his great fall, thus prefiguring the fate of the idealistic redneck Willie Stark. Throughout most of the novel Warren presents in Stark a fascinating composite image of selfless reformer, dictator, and Machiavel whom the more sophisticated Burden, of better birth and inheritor of a lingering belief in social hierarchy and an overarching moral order, in his supposed detachment inclines to regard as an amusing special case. In the course of things, however, Burden discovers that Humpty Dumpty's tumble symbolizes a universal proclivity from which nothing is spared, neither king nor dictator, aristocrat, commoner, commonwealth, or principality. Two of his friends from childhood days at Burden's Landing, the reclusive young physician Adam Stanton and his sister Anne, son and daughter of a former governor widely remembered for his incorruptibility, demonstrate their vulnerability before his eyes. Anne Stanton, whom for a time he has wanted to marry (and eventually does), momentarily becomes Boss Stark's mistress; and the sensitive Adam, having reluctantly agreed to fill an important post under the boss's administration, is so chagrined when he learns of his sister's capitulation to a person of Boss Stark's character and station that he assassinates his would-be employer and is himself shot on the spot by one of the boss's henchmen.

These unfortunately are two of Burden's lesser disillusionments. Earlier, on the boss's orders, he has undertaken to examine the past of his most respected older friend, Judge Montague Irwin, at one time Governor Stanton's attorney general and presumably another model of patrician rectitude. To his dismay he uncovers documents that indicate both the judge's venality and Governor Stanton's complicity. Stanton, of course, is dead and beyond accounting, but Jack takes his evidence to Irwin, confident that the judge can and will clarify matters. Instead, the judge acknowledges his guilt and almost immediately thereafter commits suicide. Jack's disillusionment reaches its culmination that same afternoon when he receives a hysterical call from his mother, with whom he lately has had strained relations, telling him not only that Judge Irwin is dead but that Irwin was in fact his father.

With these revelations Burden is finally forced to acknowledge to himself that no one can be spared Humpty Dumpty's fate—Willie Stark, proud Judge Irwin and Governor Stanton, his mother, friends Adam and Anne Stanton, and himself—and since he and Anne, the two principal survivors in his immediate circle, are manifestly the products of corrupted seed, they will be committed hereafter to think of themselves as having been at least potentially tainted from the start. Jack, moreover, has reason to think that his corruption goes even farther back. In his graduate school days, he had begun a doctoral thesis on the journal of one of his own Civil War ancestors, Cass Mastern, and learned there how Mastern, although outwardly a model of breeding and ethical behavior, had unhesitatingly seduced the wife of his best friend, thus prompting the friend's suicide and inadvertently causing his erstwhile lover to sell an innocent slave, accidentally aware of her mistress's misstep, down the river. Mastern, to his credit, had tried unsuccessfully to find the unfortunate girl and make restitution, but failing in that, he had gone off to war and subsequently died in a military hospital, leaving his papers in lieu of a confession.

Burden's narration of the Mastern episode constitutes the better part of one chapter out of the book's ten, and critics insistent on thinking of the novel as a veiled criticism of the career of Huey Long have censured Warren for what they consider an intrusion in his narration. What that episode does, however, is to extend, strengthen, and, for attentive readers, make explicit the centrality of the novel's internal action, in which Burden moves from a prideful and cocksure cynicism at the beginning of the novel to a final sober awareness of his involvement with the rest of the human race in history's unremitting flux of events, wherein values are relative, moral order is a dream, and falling is the universal fate of mankind. Thus, in the final chapter the voice one hears is that of a soberer Burden who, having inherited Judge Irwin's home, returns to Anne Stanton at Burden's Landing and discovers from her how Willie's enemies managed to convey the news of her defection to Adam and so ignite his murderous rage. For a brief moment he contemplates a revenge of his own, but soon thinks better of that and instead simply confronts the manipulators, terrifying them with the realization that their machinations are known and, if he chooses, can be made public. He does not choose. At the end Burden and Anne, now married, leave the Landing, their fallen paradise, and like a modern Adam and Eve go out to face the convulsions of the modern world.

Successful as *All the King's Men* was, Warren's use of Burden as narrator left even some of its most ardent champions uneasy. Poe in several of his stories had employed with great effectiveness a similar device, that of a narrator writing from an achieved conclusion. In these short runs the device worked well enough, but in a novel it strained credibility, particularly a novel in which the narrator for the greater part of his account withholds from the reader the key bit of information that has climaxed his radical change from relative innocence and easy cynicism to the position of full awareness from which he has told his story. In spite of this defect, if it is that, Warren's novel, especially on a first reading, has an impact unmatched by previous works of southern fiction, and the author's deft sleight of hand at crucial points more than compensates for any technical lapses he may have committed. What is most important, however, is that for readers unencumbered by irrelevant preconceptions his account of the maturation of Jack Burden stands at the center of attention.

The effect of Burden's maturation is that he accepts and consents to live in a world which he cannot change. Traces of the old cynicism remain, but for the most part it has been transmuted into a kind of wise pessimism that is, or may be, the prelude to wise compassion. Warren makes this point by giving Burden a foil, who makes an appearance at midnovel when Jack seeks him out to see what, if anything, he knows about Judge Irwin's possible missteps in the past. This character, formerly the judge's "Jonathan," as Jack once refers to him although routinely he callously calls him the Scholarly Attorney, is the man he has always considered his father. Now long divorced from Jack's mother and prematurely aged, he lives a reclusive existence in what resembles a section of New Orleans and tells Jack nothing except that he has forsworn forever the "foolishness and foulness" of the world he has abandoned.

Such a retreat is not an option for Jack Burden, who for all his cynicism never loses sight of the goodness mingled with the evil that taints most people— Anne and Adam Stanton certainly, his mother, the judge, and even Willie Stark. He sees, too, that the human mix's dram of evil is an inextricable part of the nature of things. Nothing escapes its taint—not his and Willie's state, whatever its name, nor the South as whole, with its presumed hierarchy of persons and its substratum of moral order. All are and always have been parts of the world, which to all appearances is the continuing "convulsion" that naturalists see. Accordingly with Anne as companion he will go "out of history into history"—that is, out of the illusory world fallen from a Paradise that never was into the world as it is, declaring it neither foolish nor foul.

After *All the King's Men* poets and novelists would find it difficult to write convincingly of the South as envisioned by most of her latter-day apologists, even the more sophisticated ones among Warren's mentors and colleagues at Vanderbilt. These had readily acknowledged a fallen South, but each in his way had clung to the romantic notion that the region in its inception as a protostate had been the perpetuation of an orderly society begun in Europe perhaps as far back as the Middle Ages. Faulkner had anticipated Warren's realistic stance, most notably and brilliantly in *Absalom, Absalom!*, but in 1946 Faulkner's novels were still for the most part out of print and his reputation was only on the threshold of recovery. Warren's candid portrayal of the South, so rich in authentic detail that contemporary readers could hardly avoid taking it for veiled history, opened the door for implied critiques in poetry and fiction that at the time were the prerequisite, still unacknowledged, for a healthy continuation of the so-called Southern Renaissance. His prize-winning work eased the way for a public reception of Faulkner's last two Snopes novels and after these for the unsettling novels of Walker Percy and Cormac McCarthy. More important, perhaps, it was the prelude to major work of his own: at least two of the later novels, *World Enough and Time* and *Band of Angels;* the remarkable verse drama, *Brother to Dragons;* and a body of poetry that would dominate the field in the second half of the century and more than justify the nation's conferring upon him the title of poet laureate.

If *All the King's Men* had not been enough to turn that nation's eyes southward, the declaration the year before by a major New York critic that in William Faulkner, whose work even much of the South had tended to regard as an eccentric embarrassment, America had at last produced another author of stature comparable to that of Hawthorne, Melville, and James just might have turned the trick on its own. Faulkner himself, hoping and half believing that this statement might be true, had taken wry satisfaction from the fact that European critics were of a similar mind, but at home his books simply did not sell, and peddling stories to magazines scarcely brought in enough to pay the current bills, much less rescue him from debt. Consequently, after the publication of *Go Down, Moses* in May 1942, he signed a long-term contract with Warner Brothers at three hundred dollars per week (later raised to four hundred dollars) and returned to Hollywood. There he lived intermittently for the next three years, working more or less diligently at scripts and daily generating more frustration. Happily the year 1945 proved to be a turning point, both for him and for the southern writer generally.

The first sign of a change, undetectable at the time, came when, still under contract to Warners, he was approached by the director Henry Hathaway and the producer William Bacher with the suggestion that he produce a synopsis for a movie script about a second coming and crucifixion of Christ during the First World War. The synopsis would become the property of Hathaway and Bacher, but Faulkner would retain the right to develop it into a novel if he chose and also share in the profits from any movie that might ensue. Without pausing to consider the complications that might arise from his contract with Warners, Faulkner plunged into the proposed project with enthusiasm and for the next decade worked, often with an agony and frustration that he could not have anticipated, on what he thought might in the end become his magnum opus.

A more recognizable harbinger of a new order, this time one that would include all southern writers, came with the publication of an article on Faulkner in the *New York Times Book Review* by Malcolm Cowley, a critic whom Faulkner respected. In retrospect Cowley's praise may seem modest, but his voice was one that the literary establishment listened to, and it served to prepare readers for a second move toward the rehabilitation of Faulkner's reputation, Cowley's publication of *The Portable Faulkner* in 1946. Faulkner had enthusiastically given his approval to this project, participating in the selection of things to be included and providing a map of Yoknapatawpha County and a lively summary of the action of *The Sound and the Fury* to serve as a preface to the Dilsey section, which he thought one of his best. The finished book went a long way toward the restoration of his faltering self-esteem and also prompted reviews that did almost as much as the book itself to establish his reputation: an appreciative one by Caroline Gordon in the *New York Times Book Review* and major articles by Robert Penn Warren in the *New Republic* and Jean-Paul Sartre in the *Atlantic*.

Important as these developments were for Faulkner, they were even more so for southern literature as a whole. One supposes that even without them some sort of national awakening to what had taken place in the South since 1920 would eventually have come about, but it probably would have proceeded at a much slower pace. Luckily Faulkner's work was all that Cowley and the others declared it to be; otherwise their ardent championing might actually have delayed recognition of the new southern writing. As it was, recognition of Faulkner's superior status was long overdue. Within less than two decades he had produced five major novels—*The Sound and the Fury, Light in August, Absalom, Absalom!, The Hamlet,* and *Go Down, Moses*—all of which readers now discovered to be far more accessible and infinitely more challenging than they had appeared at the time of publication, and that discovery led almost inevitably to reconsideration of the work of Faulkner's contemporaries—first in the Deep South, then in the coastal South, and finally in the border states. Thus the long-neglected awakening of the South had at last been complemented by an awakening of the Northeast, with its superior opportunities for publishing and marketing and a veritable army of readers willing and able to pay for books.

For Faulkner, however, the euphoria of 1945 soon dissipated. Free at last to work on *A Fable*, he found to his dismay that the anticipated great novel simply would not come; for several years, while his new public waited for another masterpiece, he repeatedly put it aside to work on other things. In 1948 he published *Intruder in the Dust*, a modest but thoroughly competent novel featuring the arrogant Lucas Beauchamp of *Go Down, Moses*, falsely accused of killing a white man. Sophisticated reviewers were disappointed, but readers in general liked it and bought more copies than they had of any of Faulkner's previous books. Moreover, his share of Random House's sale of the movie rights put a temporary end to financial difficulties, and when MGM brought a crew to Oxford to shoot the film there, he cooperated enthusiastically, making suggestions and scouting out suitable locations for individual scenes. Gavin Stevens, Jefferson's liberal-minded bachelor lawyer, also from *Go Down, Moses*, was another prominent character in the novel, and Faulkner promptly put together a group of previously published stories about Stevens, wrote a new story to serve as centerpiece, and published the whole as *Knight's Gambit* in 1949.

In 1950 Random House brought out his *Collected Stories* and the following year, *Requiem for a Nun*, a hybrid, originally planned as a play but finished as a novel, which continued the story of *Sanctuary*'s Temple Drake. From that point on Faulkner was a prophet with honor, both at home and abroad. His best work was behind him, but in the slightly more than a decade remaining he would publish four more novels: the long-delayed *A Fable* in 1954, *The Town* in 1957, *The Mansion* in 1959, and *The Reivers* in 1962, only a month before his death at Oxford on July 6 of that year. The judgment of the critics would continue to be mixed, but regardless of what any critic wrote or said, the fame and fortune he had long coveted were his.

From 1948 until his death in 1962, recognitions and honors in a variety of guises continued to accrue: election to the American Academy of Arts and Letters (1948), the academy's Howells Medal for Fiction (1950), two National Book Awards (1951 and 1954), and two Pulitzer Prizes (1951 and 1963). In November 1950 the supreme international recognition came with the announcement that he had won the Nobel Prize for Literature, the fourth American citizen to achieve that distinction, and in 1951 he received France's award of the Legion of Honor. On four occasions the U.S. State Department invited him to represent the nation abroad—first in Brazil (1954), then in Japan (1955), in Greece (1957), and in Venezuela (1961)—and each time he dutifully accepted. In 1955 he experienced a brief interval of notoriety after firing off a series of letters on segregation to the *Memphis Commercial Appeal*, followed by articles on integration in *Life*, *Harper's*, and *Ebony*, but none of this activity prevented his receiving visiting appointments at the University of Virginia and invitations to visit West Point and the White House, the last of which he declined. At the time of his death Faulkner was unquestionably the ranking man of letters in the United States.

Of the four novels that he published during the last decade of his life, *The Reivers* (1962) was the least significant, though it was good enough to have guaranteed a lesser writer a place in literary history and fully worthy of the Pulitzer Prize it was accorded posthumously. Years before he had toyed with the idea of writing such a book but put the project aside to cobble together a larger mass of related material that resulted in his near masterpiece *Go Down, Moses*. In *The Reivers* a sixty-seven-year-old Lucius Priest relates in complicated and often amusing detail an escapade in which as an eleven-year-old he borrowed his grandfather's new automobile and with the help of two of his grandfather's employees—the part-Chickasaw giant Boon Hogganbeck of *Go Down, Moses* and a black coachman—drove it from Jefferson to Memphis. There Boon and the coachman inveigled the boy into an elaborate scheme to swap the automobile for a stolen racehorse, whereby they hoped both to recover the vehicle and reap a handsome profit. In the course of their picaresque adventure both Boon and Lucius take giant steps toward maturity—Boon by falling seriously in love with a reformed prostitute, whom he eventually marries, and Lucius with the help of the worldly-wise grandfather, who has tracked him down, by learning that he must take responsibility for his own actions in a society in which good and evil are relative matters and human imperfectibility is the norm. Critics, with some warrant, were quick to compare *The Reivers* with Mark Twain's *Huckleberry Finn*, a belated compliment to an author whose real accomplishment in that area twenty years before had received scant attention.

By contrast his more ambitious *A Fable* of 1954, which received both a National Book Award and a Pulitzer, was a failure but one that was probably inevitable. At the core of the plot was the unsuccessful attempt by an obscure French corporal in the First World War to promote a battlefield mutiny designed to end a senseless conflict. A comparison with the action of Jesus of Nazareth was already a part of the plan, but in dealing with it Faulkner elected to go the route of formal allegory, providing the corporal and his action with a multitude of details suggestive of the Christ story, among them twelve male followers (or disciples) including a traitorous Judas and a reluctant Simon Peter, a temptation episode, a magdalen, two friendly sisters reminiscent of Mary and Martha, a crown of thorns, a death between thieves, and an empty tomb. The burden of it all, in the minds of those who had urged the project upon him and initially in Faulkner's mind as well, was to have been that mankind, now embarked on a second world war, must somehow be prevented from repeating the disaster of the first. Had the work thus remained at the level of a cautionary fable, it probably would have missed greatness but might have avoided the epithet of failure.

During the process of composition, however, Faulkner for reasons of his own ventured to add to his objective a critical exploration of some of the fundamental aspects of a Christianity that constituted the avowed substructure of Western civilization, among them its tribal notion of an authoritarian God, its insistence on the irreducible duality of good and evil, and its heavy reliance upon the genius of a Paul of Tarsus to serve as its coordinator, apologist, and advocate. Biographical evidence leaves no doubt that Faulkner thought of what he had done as a major accomplishment, perhaps the most important one of his career; but even uncritical admirers have found it difficult to adjust their sights to a work that is in itself stylistically inconsistent and in most aspects irreconcilable with the rest of the Faulkner canon. One suspects that Faulkner himself may have found it disconcerting that as he explored the implications of its context, a work which had begun as a simple moral fable on a subject about which he felt deeply grew into something that all the narrative devices at his command could not present convincingly within the scope of a single work of fiction. Even so, *A Fable*, failure though it may be, is probably the most ambitious attempt at a comprehensive religious novel yet produced in America and one that in time may come to be regarded as a historically important critique of the complex of myths that for more than a thousand years served as a vehicle for Christian belief and enabled it to generate and support a major civilization.

The other two novels that Faulkner published during the last decade of his life—*The Town* (1957) and *The Mansion* (1959)—are the last in a series of stories and novels that chronicle the rise and proliferation of the Snopes family in Yoknapatawpha County. With *The Hamlet*, published in 1940, they constitute a trilogy of sorts in which we see the career of the archetypal Snopes, Flem, who after consolidating a base in the hamlet of Frenchman's Bend manages to penetrate the larger community of Jefferson, bringing with him a host of rapacious relatives. Thereafter, raising them and himself by varying degrees through the stages of power and superficial respectability, he manages to achieve a position of dominance in the demoralized town only to fall victim to the combined outrage of one of his own kind whom he has neglected to protect, the weasel-like Mink Snopes, and the un-Snopeslike daughter of the wife whom he has driven to adultery and suicide.

Neither of these two late novels reaches the level of technical brilliance that a younger Faulkner had managed to sustain throughout much of *The Hamlet*, but they are essential parts of the Yoknapatawpha story, which includes all the major novels, with the exception of *A Fable*, and most of the short stories. A just appreciation of Faulkner's achievement requires that all these pieces, minor as well as major, be read individually and as integral parts of the larger unit. By the time *The Town* and *The Mansion* appeared, Faulkner had a public prepared and eager to read him in this fashion. Of comparable importance, that same public was now prepared and eager to read the work of other southern authors—people such as Porter, Welty, and Warren as well as a host of younger writers with talents and techniques to which a decade earlier it might have given little more than passing notice.

7
Southern Regionalism
Comes of Age

Part of William Faulkner's popularity among northern and eastern readers after 1950 was due to a residual interest in southern literature as a species of exotica, which in turn was an outsider's response to the strong regional char acter of much of it. Regionalism was a significant aspect of Faulkner's best work, and it would continue to be an important aspect of the work of many, if not most, of the writers who would come to prominence in the years following World War II. As the critic R.B. Heilman wrote in 1953, a strong sense of the concrete was from the start a primary characteristic of the southern temper, and the better southern writers have usually manifested their regional affiliation either in direct presentations of their sensory world or by using that world as a platform for their presentations of worlds beyond its fringes, past or present.

For many readers, however, at least in the North and East, regionalism had usually meant local color—a succession of caricatures, potential stereotypes, who spoke in dialect, or convincing facsimiles thereof, and exhibited amusing folkways and attitudes. It was regionalism of this sort that had accounted in part for the ephemeral popularity of such writers as Joel Chandler Harris, Mary Noailles Murfree, and John Fox Jr. and initially for the popularity of Faulkner, Erskine Caldwell, and Zora Neale Hurston. It also served during the thirties and early forties to bring into temporary prominence a trio of writers from Appalachia who would continue to write and after the war confirm for themselves a permanent place in southern literary history.

The first of these to make a mark on the national consciousness was Jesse Stuart (1907–84), a native of W-Hollow in Greenup Country in eastern Kentucky. Intent on becoming a teacher and possibly a writer, Stuart made his way to tiny Lincoln Memorial University at Harrogate, Tennessee, where he earned a B.A. degree in 1924 and received the encouragement of Harry Harrison Kroll, who was himself trying to become a writer. Thereafter he returned to Greenup County, which remained his home, taught school for several years, and published (at his own expense) an undistinguished book of poetry. A year at Vanderbilt (1931–32) brought him in contact with Donald Davidson, who urged him to write about his own bailiwick, advice that resulted in the remarkable *Man with a Bull-tongue Plow* (1934), a collection of 703 rough but vigorous sonnets, largely autobiographical. Thereafter he published an equally remarkable collection of stories, *Head o' W-Hollow* (1936), an autobiography, *Beyond Dark Hills* (1938), and, after a year in Scotland on a Guggenheim, a novel, *Trees of Heaven* (1940). By this time reviewers were repeatedly calling Stuart a Kentucky Robert Burns and comparing his work to that of John Fox Jr., but few serious critics considered him anything more than an amusing but passing phenomenon. Residents of Greenup County, however, thought otherwise, and many there took offense at Stuart's accurate but undiscriminating portrayal of their ways, attitudes, and speech. Stuart, who found no cause for embarrassment in any aspect of his culture save perhaps its poverty, which he considered pardonable, and its ignorance, which he regretted but found amusing, expressed bewilderment and dismay at the hostility of his neighbors but continued to live in W-Hollow, continued to accept fully in all its diversity the life he found there, and continued as before to put it all into his stories and poems.

During the forties two of his richest longer works made matters even worse. The first of these was *Taps for Private Tussie* (1943), a seriocomic novel about a shiftless and carefree family who came into possession of an insurance settlement of one of their number mistakenly reported dead and riotously plunged into the pursuit of a better life. In the course of the changes that ensue, various members manifest their fundamental natures, the family disintegrates, and the narrator, a young boy, discovers the not altogether pleasant truth about his identity. As in much of Stuart's work the vigor of the telling obscures its numerous flaws, at least on a first reading. Nevertheless, the novel sold more than two million copies and secured for its author a $2,500 Thomas Jefferson Southern Award for the best southern book of the year. It encouraged Stuart to push forward with a second volume of poetry, *Album of Destiny* (1944), which he, though not his critics, thought his best, and honed his talent for yet another effort at long fiction.

During part of 1944 and most of 1945, Stuart served as a lieutenant, junior grade, in the U.S. Naval Reserve. Assigned to the Naval Writing Division, he amused his colleagues with more tall tales from the hills, some of which found their way into a third novel, published in 1946 as *Foretaste of Glory*. The book is actually a collection of stories related to a single imaginary incident, a display of the aurora borealis in September 1941 and its effect on the eastern Kentucky town of Blakesburg. In the first chapter, which sets the pattern for the rest, Liam Winston, spatula in hand (he has been frying eggs), races into the street panting, "The goddamned world's a-comin' to a end," in hopes of finding and killing in such time as remains the brother with whom he has long been at enmity. In subsequent chapters other citizens of the town, high and low, generous and mean-spirited, make similar frantic preparations in anticipation of the doom they believe is upon them. Readers outside Appalachia found all this entertaining, perhaps recalling another instance shortly before the outbreak of war in 1917 in which the aurora had provoked similar reactions in small towns throughout the viewing area. Stuart's tale, however, was set specifically in 1941, and his people were suspiciously familiar. Hence, on coming home he found that hostility among the residents of Greenup had reached a new intensity, and for a time he seriously considered abandoning plans to spend the rest of his life in W-Hollow. Luckily the crisis passed, and he was able to write there for thirty-four more years (a stroke silenced him in 1980), producing a total of more than forty volumes and establishing himself nationally in the eyes of the reading public, if not in those of sophisticated critics, as the principal literary figure in southern Appalachia. Since Stuart's death in 1984 critics have been kinder, taking note of his narrative skill, his almost unerring eye for significant detail, and his native ability to respond generously and sympathetically to every aspect of the world that surrounded him. Fortunately, Stuart's best work, all written before 1950, has now been reprinted for the benefit of generations more receptive to the early manifestations of serious literary activity in the South.

A slightly younger contemporary of Jesse Stuart, and in some respects an even more gifted one, was the novelist and social historian Harriette Simpson Arnow (1908–86), who was born Harriette Simpson in Wayne County, Kentucky, on the fringe of Appalachia, and lived for a time in nearby Burnside. She attended college in Berea for two years, taught school in Pulaski County for two more, earned her degree from the University of Louisville, then worked at a variety of jobs in Cincinnati, where she began to write. For four years after her marriage to newspaper reporter Harold Arnow in 1939, she lived with her husband on a farm on the Big South Fork of the Cumberland River, but in 1944 Arnow returned to newspaper work on the *Detroit Times*, and Harriette accompanied him. After years of residence in Detroit the Arnows retired with their two children to Ann Arbor, where they were living at the time of her death in 1986.

Harriette Arnow's first novel, *Mountain Path*, appeared in 1936, her second, *Hunter's Horn*, in 1949. In *Mountain Path* she tells the story of a young woman from Lexington, Louisa Sheridan, who took a teaching position in a remote valley at a bend in the Cumberland River and there began to learn about the life of the mountain people—their ways, customs, traditions, and values—things Arnow herself knew from experience as well as from the extensive research she undertook in preparation for her serious writing. Louise's most valuable lessons, however, are not restricted to the folk wisdom of Appalachia, though Jesse Stuart was exhibiting them in full measure. These she learns from a young man, wanted by the law, with whom she falls in love. In the seven months before he is killed, he teaches her the joy that comes from living in the present, fully and intensely day by day, and inadvertently at the end the lot that befalls most mountain women, who while their men follow precarious courses outside the home must remain there and endure the passive burden of waiting.

In the thirteen years that intervened between her first, quite respectable effort and her second, Arnow reached maturity as a novelist. *Hunter's Horn* is the story of farmer Nunnelly Ballew, by avocation a fox hunter, who becomes obsessed with the prospect of killing a particularly elusive animal that has been killing his chickens and his lambs. In the two and a half years that his pursuit lasts, he neglects farm and family and sees his hounds and those of his neighbors repeatedly outwitted and his own best dog lured to his death. Ballew's friends urge him to go the route of expediency and use a gun on old King Devil, as he has come to call him, but the rules of the game forbid and Ballew plays by the rules. In the end he sells valuable livestock to buy two pedigreed pups that finally manage to track the creature down and make the kill only to reveal that the formidable King Devil was actually a vixen, now pregnant and temporarily slowed by the litter she is carrying. Soberly Ballew recognizes that he has sacrificed everything for a hollow victory: the happiness of his wife and children, the livestock on which he and they depended to keep them solvent in increasingly hard times, and, perhaps most important, the joy of the hunt that once made his tedious existence tolerable. In the madness of a fool's pursuit he has let life itself slip through his fingers.

Arnow's third novel, *The Dollmaker*, the one for which she is best known and her masterpiece, came in 1954. In it she addresses the situation of the displaced Appalachian who, discouraged by the alternatives of working land that can no longer support him and life in the coal camps, has seized the opportunity for profitable war work and moved family and possessions to northern manufacturing centers. Her representative mountain family is that of the Nevells, Clovis and Gertie and their five children, Clytie, Reuben, Enoch, Amos, and Cassie; their promised land is a government housing project in Detroit and a makeshift life in its heterogeneous community of factory workers. Arnow's central figure in the novel is rawboned Gertie Nevells, the mother, who recognizes that permanent adjustment to the new life will mean spiritual death and feels diminished but does not stand in the way when Reuben seeks to return to Kentucky. For comfort she turns to her one conspicuous talent, whittling, making dolls and other objects that she can turn into ready cash and working meanwhile on a large block of cherry wood that she hopes to turn into a bust of Jesus. The death of her most imaginative child, Cassie, in an accident, however, all but destroys Gertie, and she despairs of ever finding a suitable face for the Jesus she has hoped to discover in her piece of wood. In the end she surrenders this as well, allowing it to be cut into sections suitable for making marketable trinkets. Critics found *The Dollmaker*, like Arnow's two previous novels, almost unbearably bitter yet powerful and moving in its portrayal of the enduring human spirit. A younger novelist, Joyce Carol Oates, in an afterword appended to the 1971 paperback reprint suggested that in it Harriet Arnow had transcended the naturalistic tradition and pronounced it "one of those excellent American works that have yet to be properly assessed."

One might say much the same for Arnow's work as a whole. She published two more novels, both competent performances but hardly so distinguished as *Hunter's Horn* and *The Dollmaker*. In the last decades of her life the history of her region increasingly became a preoccupation, and two of the works that she published during those years were models of social history at its best, authoritative, well written, and, as one professional historian noted, charming. These appeared within three years of each other—*Seedtime on the Cumberland* (1960) and *Flowering of the Cumberland* (1963)—works that made explicit the strong base she had created for her own best fiction and set it forth in a form that readers could enjoy and future writers use.

A third Appalachian writer, James Still (1906-), has published less (as pages go) than either Stuart or Arnow and consequently has sometimes been overlooked or undervalued by critics surveying the postwar period. Strictly speaking, Still is neither Appalachian nor Kentuckian. He had his beginnings on a farm near Lafayette, Alabama, in the Piedmont section of the state; but he attended college at Lincoln Memorial University, where he knew Jesse Stuart and learned about books. Graduating in 1929, he went on to Vanderbilt for an M.A., which he earned in 1930, but made no special impression on the members of the Fugitive group who were still there, and he took no interest in their new Agrarian movement, already well under way. The following year, with teaching school in mind, he earned a B.A. in library science at the University of Illinois, but by 1931 the Depression was at its worst, and jobs were scarce. For two years he wandered about taking work wherever he could find it, until finally in 1933 a college friend asked him to come to the Hindman Settlement School on Troublesome Creek, not far from Hazard, Kentucky. He stayed there six years, the first three for no more than room, board, and laundry. Later he would say of that interval, "I joined the folk life of the scattered community, attending church meetings, funeralizings, corn pullings, hog butcherings, box suppers at the one-room school, sapping parties, and gingerbread elections." He also wrote, both poems and stories, placed many of them in national magazines, and in time began to feel the need for isolation. When that happened he moved nine miles back into the hills and took up residence in a century-old log cabin. "When I moved from Troublesome Creek to the backwoods of the county," he later confessed, "I had expected to stay only for a summer. I have remained forty years."

No one knows for sure how much Still wrote during those years, but he has proved a good critic of his own work and released only those things that he considered worth keeping. In 1937, while still at Hindman School, he published a remarkably good first volume of poems, *Hounds on the Mountain*, which Katherine Anne Porter later said should be read in connection with the book he retreated to the backwoods to write, the superbly crafted short novel *River of Earth* (1940). This was followed almost immediately by his third book, a collection of stories, *On Troublesome Creek* (1941). Thereafter Still settled down to tending his garden and his beehives, reading as shifting interest and whim dictated, writing poems and stories, and publishing them at the rate of something fewer than one a year—nothing in hard cover, however, until 1974, when G.P. Putnam brought out his first children's book, a slender volume entitled *Way Down Yonder on Troublesome Creek: Appalachian Riddles and Rusties*. A similar volume, *The Wolfpen Rusties: Appalachian Riddles and Gee-Haw Whimmy Diddles*, appeared in 1975, and in 1976, *Pattern of a Man and Other Stories*, a collection of his previously published short fiction. Another children's book, *Jack and the Wonder Beans*, this one an Appalachian version of the familiar "Jack and the Beanstalk," came out in 1977.

Since then Still has occupied himself mainly with gathering up pieces previously published only in magazines, revising some, adding a few new ones, and presenting them all in book form. The first of these collections was *Sporty Creek: A Novel about an Appalachian Boyhood*, actually short stories arranged as a novel (1977), followed by *Pattern of a Man and Other Stories* in that same year, then *The Run for the Elbertas*, short stories (1980), *River of Earth: The Poem and Other Poems*, privately printed (1982–83), and finally, in what is the closest he is likely to come to producing a complete collection of his poetry, *The Wolfpen Poems* (1986).

In 1991 Still let the University Press of Kentucky bring out *The Wolfpen Notebooks: A Record of Appalachian Life*, jottings of expressions, phrases, observations, and anecdotes collected over a period of more than forty years from the speech and conversations of the people who had long since accepted him as one of their own. In these notebooks one may discern the primary source of strength in Still's work and its potential for greatness. He has often been called "a writer's writer" by those who would stress his superiority as a regionalist, and it is true that among his greatest admirers have been some of the nation's most sophisticated literary craftsmen and critics. The notebooks made it clear, however, that in addition to a good regionalist's concern for authenticity and a southern raconteur's delight in story Still has always possessed a poet's passion for the living language at all levels. Whether writing in prose or verse his objective has remained the same: to make the reader see, hear, and respond to, without apparent benefit of intermediary, the scene set before him.

In his one genuine novel, *River of Earth* (1940), now acknowledged to be one of the masterworks of southern fiction, the voice throughout is that of a young boy, seven years old at the beginning, who recounts a two-and-a-half-year passage in the life of the Baldridge family as they make their hopeful transition from a meager existence farming the hillside land of eastern Kentucky to an illusory promise of a richer life in the transient coal camps. The action of the story is the boy's gradual awakening to the uncertainty of his identity and his recognition that the guiding dream of his life must be to work with animals. Escape from his world is neither an option nor a desideratum; like his invisible creator, he responds positively and impartially to all manifestations of the natural world that surrounds him, and his narrative frequently turns perception into poetry. "I'm aiming to cure all manner of beings, aside folks," he declares shortly before the end of his story, and we rejoice in his determination, but in the dispiriting gloom of the coal camp fulfillment of any such dream seems unlikely, and Still to his credit does not encourage us to imagine otherwise. The most his novel allows us is to acknowledge the inevitable movement of the universal "river of earth," a phrase that surfaces a third of the way through the story as the Baldridges listen to the mountain preacher's sermon on Psalm 114: "Where air we going on this mighty river of earth, a-borning, begetting, and a-dying—the living and the dead riding the waters? Where air it sweeping us?" The question, unanswerable, itself bespeaks the human condition, and Still, who in presenting the sensitive boy's re-creation of his world has done as much as poetry can do, leaves it at that.

Marjorie Kinnan Rawlings (1896–1953)

It has already been noted but probably will bear repeating that during the early 1940s members of the reading public outside the South were prone to dismiss writers such as Stuart, Arnow, and Still as mere regionalists, hardly masters of work that one would expect to turn to again and again. Even

Faulkner had been touted principally as the readable and sometimes salacious chronicler of a mythical county that most assumed to be an authentic
representation of semirural Mississippi. Jesse Stuart was the acknowledged
chronicler of Greenup Country, Kentucky, James Still of Knott County, and
Harriet Arnow of the hill counties of the upper Cumberland Valley. In 1940
the time had not yet arrived when readers generally would look beyond the
regional aspects of southern literature for evidence of those values they expected to find in works of merit from other parts of America and the world.

Even then, however, change was already in the air. In 1939 Marjorie
Kinnan Rawlings (1896–1953) had received both election to the National
Academy of Arts and Letters and a Pulitzer Prize for *The Yearling*, a novel set
in the Florida backwoods that she had published a year earlier. From the
southerner's point of view Rawlings's claim to authenticity was questionable.
Although a native of Washington, D.C., she had grown to maturity in Wisconsin, graduated from the university at Madison, and subsequently made her
home in upstate New York. The Florida scene had been only recently quite as
exotic to her as it was to most of her readers. Nevertheless, with a dedication
comparable to that of Still to his adopted Knott County, she had identified
herself with the region and written with genuine knowledge and sympathy
about its landscape and its people. In the eyes of the latter she had become an
outsider they could accept, but in the eyes of her northern readers she luckily
was still one of their own and so wore the mantle of objectivity. They had
taken that mantle for granted when they read with relish her short pieces in
Scribner's about Florida's "crackers," and these reports from the deepest South,
so to speak, had prepared them to accept not only *The Yearling* (1938) but the
three book-length publications of substance that followed: her collected stories in *When the Whippoorwill* in 1941, the engaging, partly autobiographical
Cross Creek in 1942, and *Cross Creek Cookery* later that same year.

The success of these works as items of compelling interest quite apart
from their regional coloring helped establish a new public receptivity for a
succession of women writers who were actually natives of the regions they
presumed to speak about but who also had considerably more than local color
to offer in their novels and short stories—first Carson McCullers (1917–67),
then Eudora Welty (b.1909), and finally Flannery O'Connor (1925–64). These
three merit detailed consideration in a separate chapter, but their indebtedness to Rawlings as precursor should be noted at this point and remembered.
In the same way, her success as a regionalist helped prepare the way for the
reconsideration of Faulkner's Mississippi stories that began later in the decade and led in turn to the reconsideration of those other regionalists of the
thirties whose work had received little more than passing notice. In itself

Rawlings's reception by the general public was not a major factor in the turn of literary events that occurred on the American scene as World War II was coming to an end, but it was an important sign of the coming change that would provide opportunities for a host of new southern writers, most of them at least initially regionalists in some degree, who would swell the chorus of "singing birds" and confirm the fact of a Southern Renaissance.

PETER TAYLOR (1917–94)

Foremost among these new writers was the youthful Peter Taylor (1917–94), who was not only a regionalist but to all appearances a protégé of Vanderbilt's leading Agrarian, John Ransom. For the second reason alone, critics of a decade earlier might have been inclined to deal harshly with him or at least regard his work with skeptical amusement. With the publication of *A Long Fourth and Other Stories* in 1948, however, most critics, even those who professed to find in it traces of Agrarian sentiment, acknowledged that an important new talent had emerged. From that point on, Taylor repeatedly proved himself able to go it on his own. During the following forty-five years he published seven more collections of his stories, three volumes of plays (mostly unperformed), and three novels. His first novel, *A Woman of Means* (1950), was praiseworthy but little noted, and it quickly went out of print. By the time his *Collected Stories* (1969) appeared, however, critics were regularly comparing Taylor's work in that form to the best of Chekhov and Joyce. Their praise grew even louder when *In the Miro District and Other Stories* appeared in 1977 and louder still for *The Old Forest and Other Stories* (1985), which received the PEN/Faulkner Award for Fiction in that year. His second novel, *A Summons to Memphis* (1986), was accorded the Pulitzer Prize for 1987. His third, *In the Tennessee Country*, developed from a short story, appeared in the year of his death, 1994.

Yet in spite of such accolades Peter Taylor, like James Still, remained largely a writer's writer, and laments about the general public's indifference to his superiority became standard clichés in reviews of his work. The principal reason for the neglect was that during most of his career Taylor deployed his energy in perfecting a form for which there was no longer a popular market. His novel of 1950 was quite short, scarcely more than a novelette, and most readers were not prepared to relish the subtle ironies that gave it distinction. For the next thirty-five years he published only short stories and occasionally short plays, and these, since there were no longer popular outlets for such things, mainly in little magazines—the *Sewanee Review, Kenyon Review, Encounter, Virginia Quarterly Review*—and finally in the *New Yorker*. In each of these publications his work was guaranteed an appreciative audience; but in all but the *New Yorker* both audience and pay were small. In the postwar world of television, Faulkner's option of last resort, submitting short fiction to popular publications like the *Saturday Evening Post*, had all but vanished.

The "region" that Peter Taylor grew up in and continued to write about throughout his career is different from other so-called regions in that it is roughly contemporary, urban rather than rural and, most important, geographically distributed in pockets scattered over two-thirds of one state and a small part of another. Even so it is quite as distinctive as any other region that southerners have celebrated, with a nexus of values, attitudes, habits, traditions, and customs all its own. This is the world of Middle and West Tennessee's established families, originally landed for the most part but since Reconstruction transplanted to the larger cities, where having flourished in finance, law, and politics, they have until recently been able legitimately to consider themselves shapers of the state's destiny. The principal loci for this small but still influential group are, of course, the markedly different communities of Nashville and Memphis, long rivals for power and prestige but united in their exclusiveness.

Smaller pockets of the same region flourish, or at least they did so in Taylor's youth, in St. Louis (where Taylor spent much of his adolescence) with its colony of expatriate southerners, here and there in the small towns from which many of the urban families originally came (the Taylors came from Trenton in West Tennessee, called Thornton in the stories), and seasonally in such watering places as Beersheba (pronounced Burshaba) and Monteagle (which Taylor refers to as Owl Mountain). By the time he was twenty-one, Taylor had lived in both Nashville and Memphis, and even when his characters wander abroad, as he himself did throughout his adult life—to Chattanooga, Washington, Manhattan, or Charlottesville—they carry the credentials of their region with them and look back to Memphis, or Nashville, or perhaps some small town like Thornton, as the point around which their lives ultimately revolve.

Part of Taylor's narrative skill is traceable to its roots in the southern tradition of storytelling, at which his mother, by his own account, was particularly adept. From the beginning he adopted many of the devices of the folk teller of tales, particularly as regards the flow and articulation of his narrative. At first (perhaps intimidated or impressed by academic mentors) he seemed to favor Henry James's device of the central intelligence, focusing on a single character and limiting himself to that character's impressions and evaluations. As his confidence increased he tried other devices but seems to have settled at last on the straightforward first-person narrative, a reminiscence delivered gratuitously by someone who has observed or been involved in the event related. His three novels make use of this device as do those stories that critics have called, almost unanimously, his masterpieces, among them the title stories from two of his most recent collections, "In the Miro District" and "The Old Forest." Invariably, however, the real substance in a Taylor story lies not in the event related but within the focus of narration, whether that focus is a detached intelligence or a first-person narrator. In employing the latter, he frequently creates the effect of a personal "remembrance of things past," in which the speaker unwittingly reveals more than he intends to tell—a personal attitude, bias, or conflict that complements or sometimes radically alters the superficial import of the story.

In his best works, such as the two long short stories just mentioned and *A Summons to Memphis*, he went even farther. These three in particular involve a conflict, or at least a series of contradictions, between the collective persona that middle-class Tennesseeans have created for themselves and realities they prefer not to confront. Usually, as in these stories, the contradictions are presented through the medium of a middle-aged narrator who, only partially understanding them, looks back to the years of his late adolescence or early maturity and makes a conscious attempt to come to terms with some person, event, or combination of events that has had a shaping effect on his adult identity. The contradictions become clear in the course of his narrative, and he puts his immediate concern to rest in proportion as he recognizes and accepts them for what they are.

In "In the Miro District," for example, the figure that haunts the narrator's memory is that of his long dead maternal grandfather, Major Manly, a Civil War veteran from rural West Tennessee, who for years successfully resisted the efforts of his daughter and son-in-law to move him to Nashville. Once there, they assumed in their ignorance and simplistic miscalculating, the old man would serve as companion and inspirational model to their adolescent son. The difficulty, which Major Manly understood better than they, was his reluctance to assume the image they confidently expected him to present to the boy and to Nashville at large, a city he had often referred to contemptuously as "the Miro District" (the name of the region when it was still Spanish territory) "because he said only an antique Spanish name could do justice to the grandeur which Nashvillians claimed for themselves." As the narration proceeds we see how Major Manly, whose past as a whole (which his family regards as largely irrelevant) has been far more interesting and "heroic" than his relatively trivial involvement in the Civil War, inevitably capitulated to their repeated pressure, his own advancing age, and his grandson's manifest need for some kind of stabilizing presence—how he put on black suit and

string tie, grew an appropriate white beard, generated a fund of Civil War
stories to tell, and in general assumed the role of captive antique that his
children, grandchild, and fashionable Nashvillians of the twentieth century
were prepared to understand. The narrator senses the tragedy in his grandfather's enforced self-betrayal but stops short of acknowledging his own involvement in it.

Much of the richness of this story is the result of Taylor's adroit use of the
seemingly aimless but subtly manipulated reminiscence, a notable device even
in his earliest work but here compounded as he shifts from straightforward
reminiscence to reminiscence within reminiscence and sometimes counter-
points one reminiscence against another. For example, to introduce Major
Manly's view of the past, Taylor has the narrator tell how in attempting to
ingratiate himself with the old man he asked him leading questions about his
encounters as a young lawyer with West Tennessee's outlaw night riders: how
he escaped from them with great difficulty and greater luck, how he hid in
the lake for a time and then wandered for days, fearful, hungry, and often out
of his head—matters which the old man, sensing that he is being humored,
talks about with reluctance. Yet in these recollections we see, perhaps better
than the narrator, a principal source of the major's character and of his contempt for the romanticized version of a glorious war that Tennesseeans have
traded for the hard truths of their past.

As the story proceeds, the narrator also recalls fishing trips with his father to Reelfoot Lake, where during long evenings he listened as the men,
Grandfather Manly among them, drank and recounted stories about the place.
Especially gripping were the old man's recollection of tales about the New
Madrid earthquake in 1811, how it brought chaos again to that part of the
world, turned the river out of its course, and left behind a region of lake and
swamps. These were the tales, he now recognizes, nightmares from a childhood only a generation removed from the frontier, that long before had meta-
morphosed into those hallucinations that bedeviled his grandfather as he
wandered out of his head about the countryside after escaping from the night
riders. In the retelling the narrator catches glimpses, if only briefly, of a heritage far richer than that provided by the old man's command performances,
stories of Forrest's raids and accounts of battles, most of which he never saw,
all fashionably sanitized. For the contemporary Nashvillians in the story, this
rehabilitated version of their past seems to be heritage enough, but for Taylor's
reader it stands as a painful emblem of one honest man's defeat and, presumably in Taylor's view, as an example of the pottage still preferred by many
southerners to an unappreciated and all but forgotten birthright.

The narrator in *A Summons to Memphis* is less concerned with the distant past and more immediately involved in the narrated action. As the story begins, Phillip Carver, forty-nine years old, a bachelor recently separated from his longtime live-in companion, Holly Kaplan, has received a call from his two spinster sisters in Memphis, both older than he, frantically sounding an alarm at the threatened remarriage of their eighty-one-year-old father. Phillip, for twenty years now an editor in a New York publishing house and a devotee of rare books, no longer professes ties either to Nashville, where his family spent its earlier years, or to the less fashionable Memphis, to which his domineering father later moved them without much thought for their happiness or well-being. Nevertheless, even before he boards the plane for Tennessee, he finds himself involved in a skein of reminiscence that provides an unfolding context for the incidents he is proceeding to relate. The incidents themselves are considerably less startling than the change they precipitate in Phillip's attitude toward his father. Soon after arriving he discovers that the years have had a softening effect on the stressful relationships within the Carver family. His father is no longer the intransigent parent he once seemed to be and behaves with commendable restraint when they manage to frustrate his hopes of remarrying. The sisters, themselves a bit wiser as well as older, make plans to sacrifice some of their independence and return to the family home, and Phillip, after two decades of alienation, rediscovers a friendship with his father that after his return to New York he maintains by frequent telephone conversations until the elder Carver dies the following year.

A Summons to Memphis, unlike "In the Miro District," contains no striking evocations of the past and no semitragic figure, but true to the regional tradition from which all of Taylor's work springs and of which his second novel is in one sense a culmination, it presents a context, an evocation of place, that is as credible, authentic, and interesting as the ostensible action and is, in fact, the conveyor of the real action that takes place within the psyche of Phillip Carver. From it one gains, however, an insight into the way Nashville and Memphis participate in a common subculture and yet within that subculture stand in opposition to one another. In this phenomenon one can find interesting parallels in other southern states: in Kentucky's Lexington and Louisville, Georgia's Atlanta and Savannah, South Carolina's Charleston and Columbia, and Alabama's Montgomery and Birmingham. Taylor happily has never attempted to present the nuances of dialect that set his community of southerners apart from other groups in the region, at least until the end of World War II—"genteel city speech as it is spoken in the great heartland," he calls it in one of his later stories. He has, however, captured neatly the distinctive attitudes, both those that unite the sexes and those that differentiate between them, and the shared sense of decorum that determines procedures in such basic social activities as marrying, burying the dead, and the human interchanges of daily life.

Among the older members of Taylor's community, there is also the subliminal awareness of their pioneer experience, which among Tennesseeans involves such things as the Donaldsons' push down the Tennessee River, the advance of the Watauga men toward the Holston, and the expulsion of the Cherokees to make way for an undiluted Anglo-Saxon civilization. In "In the Miro District" the conflict between that deeper awareness and impulse to glorify a more recent South provides the condition for the action that takes place within the troubled mind of the narrator and the irony that characterizes his inability to see where he has failed. In the novel the conflict and irony lie in the conflict between the whole concatenation of class mores, which the narrator sees as hopelessly passé, and the liberated order that he thinks he has found in his Manhattan refuge. Such things "mean nothing to us nowadays," says Phillip Carver confidently of himself and Holly Kaplan, his Jewish mistress from Cleveland, at the conclusion, but Holly probably knows better. They remain a part of Phillip Carver, at least, even after twenty years in the subculture of Manhattan, where he is always to some extent an alien and where he achieves partial independence from the tyranny of his heritage only by a singular act of remembering and accepting.

Taylor's focus of narration, sometimes equated with Taylor himself, is usually characterized as that of the urbane, well-educated southerner who views his region and its peculiarities with impeccable sobriety and detachment as well as authority, but this view is hardly the whole truth. If it is a straightforward narrator who brings us the story, his appearance of detachment is frequently belied by our awareness, progressively developed by Taylor's control, that the narrator's authority is deficient in some way: either he does not fully understand the events he is relating or else he understands and for one reason or another resists acknowledging that he does. The same is true if the focus is on a central intelligence or if, as in some instances, the focus wanders. Some of Taylor's better stories come to us by way of a narrator who seeks to hide, from us and from himself, the significance of what he is relating, usually the manifestation of an implicit challenge to some widely received attitude, custom, or taboo: a relative or neighbor who has abandoned without reasonable justification the mores or even the company of the society that has sustained him, a child who willfully ignores his filial responsibility, a servant who ignores the demeanor befitting his or her station, a guilt-obsessed country cousin who chops off her hand. When the challenge is shockingly violent, as in the last case, Taylor's stories fall into the category created by some northern critics, Southern Gothic, where they keep company with stories of the supernatural that occupy about half the space in his final collection, *The Oracle at Stoneleigh Court* (1993). Such stories, however, have appeared sporadically in the work of other southern authors—Faulkner, Welty, Lytle, to name only a few—and have been an occasional staple of modern fiction ever since Defoe published his convincing *Apparition of One Mrs. Veal* (1706). Suffice it to say that Taylor's work is full of surprises, and many of the generalizations about it do not bear scrutiny. Within the range of his subject matter and the form of the short story, he has experimented, usually successfully, with more techniques, themes, and devices than any other southern writer, and the comparisons with Chekhov and Joyce that appear in reviews and later critical studies are not entirely misplaced.

Andrew Lytle (1902–95)

It fell to Andrew Lytle, Peter Taylor's older contemporary and longtime friend, to complete the metamorphosis of regional writing. Lytle first made a significant mark on the body of southern literature with his essay "The Hind Tit," by far the liveliest, and some would add the most authoritative, of the contributions to the manifesto of the Vanderbilt Agrarians, *I'll Take My Stand* (1930). After that he had a remarkable career as an editor, teacher, and critic but above all as a writer, in which role he did as much as any other, with the exception of Faulkner, to demonstrate that southern regional writing can be made to sustain art of a high order. By comparison with Faulkner's prodigious output, Lytle's was modest: a biography, three novels, a novella, a family chronicle, four first-rate short stories, and a fair number of essays and reviews. Nothing that he wrote, however, lacks quality. More than almost any other of his contemporaries he deserves to be called a writer's writer.

Of those Vanderbilt Agrarians whose literary accomplishment can be termed major, Lytle was the most consistently Agrarian in sympathy and literary practice. He was also the only one who repeatedly put his agrarianism to the test and thus understandably the only one whose agrarianism matured into something more practical than a reactionary program and more substantial than a nostalgic retrospective. For more than a decade after *I'll Take My Stand*, he spent most of his time managing his father's cotton farm in north central Alabama—Cornsilk, they called it. Then after the TVA had flooded most of the place, he sold the remaining portion and off and on for five years (1943–48) attempted, futilely as it turned out, to rehabilitate a "throwed-away" farm in Sumner Country, Tennessee. During these years, he continued his writing, acquired a family, and to supplement his income took brief vacations from both farming and writing to teach, first at Southwestern University in

Memphis, then at the University of the South (where he also served as managing editor of the *Sewanee Review*), at the University of Iowa, and from 1948 to 1961 at the University of Florida. Finally, from 1961 until his retirement in 1973, he served as professor of English at the University of the South and once more as editor of the *Sewanee Review*, this time for thirteen of its better years. Thereafter except for a brief period of farming in Kentucky, he lived in Monteagle, Tennessee, in the large log house that his father bought as a summer home in 1907. He died in 1995.

Lytle's "region," like Peter Taylor's, is a widely distributed one, in his case over much of the lower South. Although town-born in Murfreesboro, Tennessee, he belonged to that race of upland farmers that has always constituted most of the rural population of Kentucky, Tennessee, Georgia, Alabama, and Mississippi. These are of Anglo-Saxon or Scotch-Irish extraction for the most part, Protestant, and owners of sizable but not large tracts of land. In the early days they had a few slaves to help with the work; in later times they replaced these with white or black tenants. Some grow cotton, others tobacco; some raise animals. Most of them at least keep animals for food and companionship, grow corn to feed them, and plant other crops to meet their own needs and tastes. Their abiding aim is to live comfortably and well on what they have, care for it as a trust, and in good time pass it along intact to heirs who will do the same. Until recently they did not anticipate revolutionary change.

This was the kind of life that Lytle knew in his youth, not only in the time spent at Cornsilk but in the routines he regularly observed in the lives of relatives and neighbors on their small self-sufficient farms of his native Rutherford County, and it was such a life that he presented in rich detail in his essay "The Hind Tit" as a tangible symbol of what he and his fellow Agrarians were working to preserve. It was a life in which human beings lived in harmony with the natural world that sustained them. One may characterize it as a complex network of symbiotic relationships among human beings of both sexes, animals, wild as well as domesticated, crops, forest, field and stream, all mutually supporting one another in a world in which the unpredictable variations of sun, rain, frost, and wind are to be accepted as normal and rejoiced in.

This is the world inherited by Pleasant McIver in Lytle's first novel, *The Long Night* (1936), but during protracted intervals of revenge-taking and participating in war McIver so neglects to relish his inheritance that the capacity for relishing all but dies in him. Nevertheless, Lytle sets that world before the reader in glowing particularity and expects him to see, hear, and taste for himself the things that leave McIver unmoved. His authority for this presentation, if proof of that were needed, would be amply demonstrated in his *A Wake for the Living: A Family Chronicle* (1975), an account of lives lived and lives remembered that is virtually unique in contemporary letters. Suffice it to say that in Lytle's story of the Nelson and Lytle families from colonial days down to 1942 the way of the upland South stands clear with a genuineness that is unmatched in southern writing except perhaps in Lytle's own "The Hind Tit," published forty-five years before.

Robert Penn Warren in an afterword to the 1973 paperback edition of *The Long Night* took appreciative note of the vast amount of authentic data that Lytle with his "elephantine memory" had amassed about "the world of the plantation and the deeper backcountry," its language, its objects, and its practices. Warren might have added that in the process Lytle had "carried to the heart," almost as if preparing himself for an existence of backwoods self-sufficiency, a reservoir of details about the traditional methods of farming, gardening, animal care, carpentry, cooking, and housekeeping, much of which he had already put to practical use. Lytle's strategy here in his first novel and elsewhere for reporting backcountry practices and skills, especially those predictably foreign to modern readers, was to present them integrated dramatically with the rest of the plot, letting readers experience for themselves the way to chase a swarm of bees, the steps to take in jugging the flesh of pigeons for preservation, or the proper method of preparing a body for burial. For less esoteric matters, he simply made references to the business at hand in appropriate idiom and without apology left the rest to be interpreted by whatever vestigial remnants of backcountry knowledge his readers might possess. The result is a body of regional writing characterized by unusual dignity as well as richness, beginning with "The Hind Tit" (1930) and Lytle's early biography, *Bedford Forrest and His Critter Company*, and including three of the four stories he published, "Mr. MacGregor" (1935), "Jericho, Jericho, Jericho" (1936), and " The Mahogany Frame" (1945); *The Long Night*, of course; *The Velvet Horn* (1957), his final novel; and that masterpiece of history, autobiography, and reminiscence, *Wake for the Living*.

In addition to these Lytle wrote two major works about the Spanish conquest, *At the Moon's Inn* (1941) and *Alchemy* (1942); one other southern novel, *A Name for Evil* (1947); and some forty political and critical essays that have been reprinted in such collections as *The Hero with the Private Parts* (1966), *Southerners and Europeans. Essays in a Time of Disorder* (1988), and *From Eden to Babylon: The Social and Political Essays of Andrew Nelson Lytle* (1990). With the exception of the political essays and one or two of the critical pieces, these works show few of the overt marks of the regional author, but they all are related thematically in one way or another to that regionally oriented part of the literary production for which Lytle is best known.

For example, *At the Moon's Inn*, his novel about De Soto, emphasizes an insight that even in the thirties had set Lytle apart, at least by a few degrees, from his fellow Agrarians at Vanderbilt. Like them he always stood firmly against the encroachment of northern industrialism with its threat of social homogenization, but the reasons for his stance were somewhat different. As a moralist as well as student of history Lytle understood better than they— better even than the historian Owsley—that the Yankee industrialism they deplored was only incidentally the enemy. Behind industrialism he descried a tendency common to Europeans and their American counterparts to think of themselves as superior beings and the world as something they were free to exploit for their own comfort and gain, and while he readily acknowledged the prevalence of what he could only regard as depravity and cruelty in some of the primitive cultures, Native American as well as African, he deplored even more the arrogance and greed that had prompted Europeans to take advantage of them. He saw arrogance and greed as the primary motives behind the Spanish assault on the new world, and he described both at length: in the novella *Alchemy*, as manifested by Pizarro in the conquest of Peru; and, in the novel, by De Soto in his ruthless trek through the southeastern quadrant of North America. The climax of the latter comes as De Soto's outraged priest threatens him with excommunication unless he promises immediately to leave the Indian town of Mauvilla, which he has just despoiled. De Soto's refusal there is the beginning of the end both for him and for the ancient agrarian culture of the Indians of the southeast, and De Soto died soon thereafter. The final blow to the way of the Indians, as Lytle was painfully aware, had come at the hands of the northern Europeans, who followed the Spaniards into that region.

Fortunately, for the land at least, most of those European latecomers were seeking the same thing as the Indian. Following a countertendency in their culture, they were inclined to behave responsibly toward the land they took from the Indians and like them become husbandmen rather than exploiters. Not that no exploiters remained among them. Lytle's third novel, *A Name for Evil*, deals with the tragedy of one of these, Henry Brent, who took possession of a decayed ancestral farm and sought to rehabilitate it, mainly as a means of projecting his own ego; his fourth, *The Velvet Horn*, presents another in Pete Legrand, who, like the Yankee and his Spanish predecessor, thought of land primarily as something to be manipulated for profit. Legrand, however, stands at the periphery of an action that brings into simultaneous focus a wide range of characters, themes, and conflicting points of view, all essential to the comprehensive picture of the South that Lytle would have us see.

Two years after *The Velvet Horn* appeared, he published a remarkable essay, "The Working Novelist and the Mythmaking Process," in which he told what he had set out to do in the novel and described in some detail the process by which forces beyond his control had taken over and made it something more than he intended. "I thought I wanted to do a piece of fiction on a society that was long dead," Lytle wrote in his first paragraph. Instead he ended up writing a fictional projection of the universal process by which societies—and, indeed, all forms of life, corporate and individual—undergo perpetual change, renew themselves season by season, and ultimately pass away. The society that he had symbolized in the closely knit family of *The Velvet Horn* is the same one he had evoked so brilliantly in "The Hind Tit" and would write of again with moving nostalgia in *Wake for the Living*. It is also the society that he and his fellow Agrarians had once dreamed of recovering from the tattered remnants of a vanished South.

Ostensibly, of course, *The Velvet Horn*, which Lytle valued above everything else he wrote, is the story of a young man, Lucius Cree, and his coming of age. The key to that understanding which is usually the final achievement of the protagonist of such a novel rests undisclosed with his mother and two others in the story. One of these is the adulterous Legrand, whom Lucius thinks is his real father, and the other an eccentric uncle and mentor, who in the final moments takes a bullet intended for Lucius and so dies without telling. What Lucius does not know—and, Lytle would have us believe, never needs to know—is that he is actually the child of a union between his mother and her favorite brother, an incestuous relationship that symbolizes for Lytle the incest of spirit inevitable in the "complex interrelationships of blood and kin" which at once constituted the culture of the South and threatened its continuation. Thus when Lucius, unwilling to perpetuate what he mistakenly thinks is a continuing pattern of adultery in the family, decides to marry the sturdy poor white whom he has seduced and give their offspring a legitimate name, he avoids the penalty of death that Lytle sees as the unavoidable consequence of incest of whatever degree (it symbolizes mankind's forbidden attempt to return to Eden) and participates instead in an act that makes possible the reconstitution and continuation of the family. One may wish that Lytle had seen fit to develop this theme in a full interpretation of southern society as he understood it, but the novel is sufficient to make his point.

In any case, *The Velvet Horn* marks the maturation both of Lytle's art as a writer of fiction and of the agrarianism that in its various stages affected almost everything he did. It liberated him to write *A Wake for the Living* (1975), which begins, "Now that I have come to live in the sense of eternity, I can tell my girls who they are." That sense of eternity had for him two sources, which in the end are the same. The first consists of those subliminal impulses—

symbolized by mythmakers from time immemorial and formulated in various ways by the depth psychologists he happened to be reading at the time—that keep us consistently human throughout the cultural flux in which our race moves and has its being. The second and most important is the Christian religion, which Lytle professed openly without apology throughout his career. During their early days at Vanderbilt he and his friend Tate shared the view that the most serious obstacle to the establishment of a vital culture in the pre–Civil War South had been the absence of an adequate religion. At that point Lytle was beginning to feel uneasy about the evangelical Methodism he had been reared in, but as a student of history he considered it impossible to follow the Tates in their advance toward authoritarian Catholicism. In time he found an acceptable form of worship in the orderly yet more relaxed discipline of the Episcopal Church, which in early adulthood became his own expression of the faith. Even so, it was Christianity, not a particular version of it, that mattered to Andrew Lytle—Christianity with the eternal verities of faith, hope, and charity at its core—and in his view it was the last of these virtues that must sustain both the institution of family through all its natural vicissitudes and a southern agrarian society that was nothing more than a confederation of such families. Where charity prevails, man's dominion over the land and its creatures needs no apology; man takes his place within, not above, the universal scheme of things, and Lytle's dream of agrarianism is thereby realized.

8
Women Extend Fiction's Range

In retrospect it is easy to see that by the beginning of the 1940s women writers had assumed a position of dominance in the realm of southern fiction. To be sure, no woman had achieved the stature that at the time was being popularly accorded to Thomas Wolfe or that we now almost unanimously recognize in William Faulkner, but with these exceptions, one of them destined soon to disappear and the other not yet realized, fiction in the South was already well on its way to becoming largely a woman's province. By 1940 for most readers the work of James Branch Cabell had slipped out of memory, that of Pulitzer Prize winner T.S. Stribling had lost most of its luster, and Erskine Caldwell's popular Gothic notorieties, as they were frequently termed in the North, were considered by most southerners to be little better than caricature. Critics and reviewers in both the North and South would probably have ranked Ellen Glasgow along with Faulkner if not above him, although Glasgow was not to receive the national recognition of a Pulitzer Prize until 1942, and by the time Faulkner achieved that honor, with *A Fable* in 1955, three other southern women had preceded him: Julia Peterkin for *Scarlet Sister Mary* in 1929, Margaret Mitchell for *Gone With the Wind* in 1937, and Marjorie Kinnan Rawlings for *The Yearling* in 1939. In the estimation of academic critics the supreme practitioner in the field was Katherine Anne Porter, although Porter had yet to write a proper novel, and not far behind her was the theoretically oriented Caroline Gordon, novelist and lecturer, who within the decade would collaborate with her husband, Allen Tate, on influential formulations of the art of fiction.

By 1941 two younger authors had emerged to claim positions of distinction among women writers on the literary scene. The first of these in point of time was Carson McCullers (1917–67). McCullers was born Lula Carson Smith in Columbus, Georgia, the place that she repeatedly drew upon for material throughout her career but in which after 1937 she disdained to live. Altogether she wrote five novels or novellas, two plays, some twenty short stories, and a number of creditable pieces of nonfiction and poems. Her permanent fame, however, may very well rest upon two popular novels that she published in the early forties.

The unifying theme of McCullers's life was loneliness, for which her domineering mother was at least partly responsible. Quick to recognize her daughter's genius, Mrs. Smith, from the first encouraged her to set herself apart from her peers, indulged her adolescent whims and idiosyncrasies, and later promoted a marriage that proved to be a longtime disaster. Until her own death in 1955 she zealously maintained a crippling role in her daughter's life as confidante and counselor, but from that point on McCullers's health, never strong, deteriorated steadily and with it her writing.

A better marriage might have helped. Throughout her life she reached out desperately for the human relationships she had never quite learned how to make, but her marriage to the emotionally unstable James Reeves McCullers Jr., in 1937, though seemingly happy enough for one year, ended in divorce in 1941. Thereafter, having abandoned Georgia for New York, she sought comfort in a variety of infatuations—for women as well as men, although it is doubtful whether any of these were consummated. For a time during the early forties she was intermittently a member of a Brooklyn Heights ménage that included W.H. Auden, David Diamond, Gypsy Rose Lee, and Benjamin Britten, but this arrangement ended with a remarriage to her husband in 1945 that unfortunately was merely the prelude to a series of painful separations and reconciliations, followed by his suicide, in Paris, in 1953.

The two novels that most readers remember are the ones that draw heavily upon the author's early days in Columbus. In both she presented the portrait of an intelligent and highly sensitive young girl, like herself desperate to establish a human relationship and fearful of being permanently trapped in the isolation of her painful midpassage between an androgynous adolescence and early womanhood. The first of these, *The Heart Is a Lonely Hunter* (1940), is her best. In it the protagonist, Mick Kelly, poor but passionately in love with music (which was also McCullers's first love), dreams of one day buying a piano of her own. Meanwhile she continually seeks someone to whom she can communicate her passion and finally focuses her attention upon John Singer, ironically a local deaf-mute, who comprehends neither music nor the girl's need of his friendship and who kills himself when his own bulwark against loneliness, an amiable but mentally retarded young Greek, suddenly dies. Mick makes other futile attempts to connect with people and comes only reluctantly to a recognition that her isolation is a common condition, shared by many.

Frankie Addams, the central figure in McCullers's second popular success, *The Member of the Wedding* (1946), has the friends that Mick lacks, but these are an equally lonely six-year-old cousin, John Henry, and the black cook Berenice, whose years have made her wise and resigned to the loneliness that Frankie in her inexperience tries to camouflage by extravagant gestures and devices. When Frankie's older brother marries, she at first fantasizes about accompanying bride and groom on their honeymoon and then actually tries to join them. Afterward she makes an abortive attempt to run away. In the course of it all, however, she slowly grows up and at the end finds a friend her own age with whom to advance into maturity. The success of *The Member of the Wedding* brought McCullers a welcome but temporary euphoria, in the flush of which, and also with some encouragement from Tennessee Williams, she rewrote her novel as a play. In this form under the direction of Harold Clurman it was equally successful on Broadway (1950) and won several awards, among them the coveted New York Drama Critics Circle Award as best play of the year.

The fate of McCullers's other works, however, was less happy. Her second novel, *Reflections In a Golden Eye* (1941), written hurriedly in the months following her first, presents a gallery of characters whose loneliness has turned them into freaks, and who in their vain attempts to relate to one another destroy either the object of their attentions or themselves. Her fourth, *The Ballad of the Sad Café* (1951), a novella, is better focused, but it too deals with the theme of loneliness and unrequited love. The central figures here are Miss Amelia Evans, a recluse in the house in which she once ran a popular café, a hunchback called Cousin Lymon, largely responsible for her success and to whom Miss Amelia is strangely attached, and Amelia's former husband, Marvin Macy, who returns from the penitentiary to disrupt her life, kill the spirit of the café, and lure the hunchback away forever. For these two works McCullers gained a certain amount of critical attention and a reputation for "Southern Gothic," which was reinforced by her second play, a failure, *The Square Root of Wonderful* (1957/58), and by her last novel, *Clock without Hands* (1961), also unsuccessful.

Since her death in 1967, critics have become less severe, acknowledging that the inadequacies of McCullers's last works are in part attributable to the wretched health and personal loneliness that made her final years miserable. Most have dispensed with the term "Gothic" in reference to her less successful writing and begun to appreciate the psychological and social realism that in varying degrees characterize all her work. In her best moments she presented convincing pictures of life in south Georgia and during the war years produced studies of adolescence that are as authoritative as they are compelling. It may be said that her development as a writer faltered with her disintegration as a person; she was on safer ground writing about herself, and her work had the strength that confidence alone gives. Unfortunately, in spite of her gifts, which were many and remarkable, she remained the self-centered adolescent to the end.

The second southern woman to emerge as a major figure during the fifties was Eudora Welty (b. 1909), who, by contrast with McCullers, at a crucial point in her career unhesitatingly contributed ten of her best years to the care of a terminally ill mother and thus in addition to literary achievements of the first order has presented us with the example of an author who had the fortitude and character to put aside ambition, break stride at a crucial point in her development, and thereby perhaps risk her chances of fulfillment as a writer. The body of that achievement consists of four volumes of stories (one of these a series of related stories that many have treated as a novel), five novels, a book of children's stories, a remarkable collection of photographs (the product of a hobby passionately pursued), a collection of essays on writers and writing, and a book of autobiographical reminiscence. For her literary work she has received many honors, among them four O. Henry first prizes, the Gold Medal for the Novel from the National Institute of Arts and Letters, and in 1973 a Pulitzer Prize for fiction. Since 1960 she has taught or lectured at a number of colleges and universities in the United States and in England, has received several honorary degrees, and in 1971 was elected to membership in the American Academy of Arts and Letters.

All but a small part of Welty's fiction has for its setting some portion of Mississippi—either the Jackson area, where she was born and has continued to live for most of her life, the Delta region, the hill country, or Mississippi's near relation, New Orleans. Given her powers of perception a lesser writer might have produced superb local color out of the material she found ready to hand, but like Faulkner she made that color, in words she used in an essay in 1956, "an instrument, not an end in itself," a medium by means of which she could explore the manifold aspects of the human comedy. In this respect the body of her work has been judged worthy to stand beside that of her more prolific contemporary in Oxford to the north and well above that of the rest of her peers.

Welty seems to have made her formal decision to become a writer during two years as an English major at the University of Wisconsin, from which she graduated in 1929. On the advice of her insurance executive father, however, she prepared for a more marketable career by studying advertising at Columbia for a year but abandoned that project at his death in 1931, at which point she returned to Jackson. For the next five years she worked at various jobs in and around town, writing stories on the side, and collecting rejection slips. Better luck began in 1936, when a little magazine accepted "Death of a Traveling Salesman," and within a year she had managed to catch the attention of Brooks and Warren at the *Southern Review* and through them the attention and encouragement of Katherine Anne Porter and Ford Madox Ford. In 1940 she secured the services of Diarmuid Russell, son of the poet A.E., as agent. From that point on she was a writer by profession and nothing more.

The following decade was one of Welty's most productive. Three of her best collections of short fiction came out during those years—*A Curtain of Green* (1941), *The Wide Net* (1943), and *The Golden Apples* (1949)—and three novels, *The Robber Bridegroom* (1942), *Delta Wedding* (1946), first serialized in the *Atlantic Monthly*, and *The Ponder Heart* (1949). She also received her first Guggenheim Fellowship (1942–43) during that period and worked for a year in New York composing astonishingly expert battlefield reports for the *New York Times Book Review* under the pseudonym Michael Ravenna. Thereafter except for three trips abroad, one of them during a renewal of her Guggenheim (1949–50), and travels in the States to lecture, teach, or receive honors, she has remained in Mississippi writing. One volume of short stories, *The Bride of the Innisfallen*, containing some of her best work, appeared in 1955. During her mother's long illness in the later 1950s she published little.

Understandably the sixties for Welty were also relatively lean, but after that the pace of her publication accelerated. In 1964 she did bring out her book for children, *The Shoe Bird*, and from time to time she published essays on writers she especially admired—Jane Austen, Katherine Anne Porter, and Henry Green—as well as essays on writing, among them the remarkable "Must the Novelist Crusade?" (1965) with its tribute to Faulkner. In 1970, however, Random House published her long labor of love, *Losing Battles*, a novel set in the Mississippi hill country, which many critics consider her best work, and in 1972 the same publisher brought out her prize-winning *The Optimist's Daughter*, a shorter work enriched by details taken from her own life and that of her mother. In between, it published the photographs she had taken during her apprentice days, *One Time, One Place: Mississippi in the Depression: A Snapshot Album* (1971), and in 1978 a collection of her best nonfiction pieces, some written as far back as the midforties: *The Eye of the Story: Selected Essays and Reviews*. In 1980 Harcourt Brace Jovanovich, the house that had published all but the first of her books of short fiction, brought out *The Collected Stories*. Then in 1984 to the delight of critics and general readers alike the Harvard University Press published a Welty public performance in the engaging reminiscence, *One Writer's Beginnings*, part of which she had delivered as a lecture there. In that same year the University Press of Mississippi ensured the permanent currency of her personal wit, wisdom, and charm by bringing out a valuable collection of the interviews she had given over the preceding forty years, *Conversations with Eudora Welty*.

The remarkable range, in style, subject matter, and theme, of Welty's first book, *A Curtain of Green* (1941), would have justified giving it the subtitle "Experiments in Fiction." Equally remarkable for a first book was the number of her experiments there, if that is what they were, that succeeded as pieces of respectable professional quality. What was extraordinary, however, was that in subsequent volumes, novels as well as collections of short stories, Welty's "respectable quality" in the various modes she had developed quickly gave way to "high quality"; and by the end of the decade she had established herself as both a major talent among southern writers and one of the most versatile.

From the beginning Welty has been one of those rarer artists on whom, to use Henry James's criterion, nothing is lost. The basic ingredient in most of her work, as in Faulkner's, is the representation of the world she knows best, rendered faithfully, without condescension, and usually with compasssion. Her characters include Mississippians of all classes and age groups, principally white. Early in her career, critics reproached her for failing to deal adequately with blacks, but the relatively few blacks who do appear, from Powerhouse and Phoenix Jackson in her first collection to the blacks in her *New Yorker* story of 1966, "The Demonstrators," are treated with dignity and understanding. Welty hears as well as she sees, and some consider her greatest strength to be the ability to represent accurately and convincingly the wide variety of dialects and levels of speech in the state. At any rate, this capability has had a lot to do with her success in creating credible portrayals of such contrasting aspects of Mississippi life as those of the Delta plantation (*Delta Wedding*), the hill country (*Losing Battles*), and the small town (*Golden Apples*). Even if these alone represented the full extent of her talents, Welty would still stand as one of the foremost local-color writers in American literature.

Like Mark Twain, however, she has other talents and resources in abundance, and her first novel, *The Robber Bridegroom* (1942), provided readers with an anticipatory glimpse of several of those. Unfortunately, to many of them that work appeared to be little more than a fantastic and only partially successful montage of familiar fairy stories, Hellenic myth, and southern tales of folk heroes and villains, but with it Welty began her public probing beneath the unambiguous surface layer of such materials to demonstrate what she called the essential doubleness of things, in a world to be understood and appreciated only by means of the techniques and vision of poetry. Welty's second novel, *Delta Wedding* (1946), was totally different from her first. Here she displayed her ability to develop and control a complex narrative involving a large cast of characters, most of whom were identifiable with the life she herself was leading. The focus was upon family, or in a larger sense community, and in her hands what might have passed as a diverting story of rural life in Mississippi's Delta became an exploration of the love that is essential if human beings are to live in communion with one another.

The Golden Apples, which came out three years later (1949), is ostensibly a collection of short stories, but all of these deal with members of three or four families as they flourished in the small town of Morgana, Mississippi, during the years following World War I, and all the principal characters are wanderers at heart, most of them young people, destined eventually to leave their base and go in quest of impossible and vaguely realized dreams. The source of their restlessness is symbolized by the shadowy figure of Jove-like King MacLain, an itinerant tea and spice salesman, who has seduced many of the town's wives and thus physically and spiritually fathered children who will never know their true parent but in growing up must discover experientially their common patrimony in his irrepressible wanderlust. In Welty's telling, this patrimony is symbolized both by figures from Greek myth that her characters call to mind and by stanzas from Yeats's "Song of Wandering Aengus" that keep recurring in the head of one of them, teenage Carrie Morrison, herself not a wanderer. Fittingly the collection takes its title from that poem. Chief among the younger wanderers is one of Welty's most memorable characters, Virgie Rainey, who inherits both her father's wanderlust and his capacity for dreams and under the tutelage of an expatriated German piano teacher, also a wanderer, confirms and enlarges that double endowment. In the final story wandering Virgie returns to Morgana for her mother's funeral, a typical small-town affair that Welty with a combination of humor and sympathy renders in rich, authentic detail, and there has a remarkable final encounter with her now senile biological father, who recognizes with angry frustration that she has in effect replaced him. Afterward Virgie wanders in the rain to a nearby village where all the MacLains are buried, sits on the stile in front of the ancient courthouse, and in the falling raindrops hears the sounds of heroes past, present and to come and recognizes her kinship with the rest of perennially wandering humanity.

Welty's *The Ponder Heart* (1954), a short novel, which had appeared the previous year in the *New Yorker*, was her one attempt at pure comedy after the manner of "Why I Live at the P.O.," the most popular story in her *A Curtain of Green*. In it a benevolent Edna Earle Ponder, manager of the Beulah Hotel in Clay, Mississippi, prepares a casual visitor, unavoidably detained there for the afternoon, for a supper encounter with her mildly retarded

Uncle Daniel, a permanent resident at the hotel. Throughout the garrulous Miss Ponder's long narrative we come to appreciate Uncle Daniel's greatness of heart, his joyful habit of irresponsibly giving away everything he owns, and his equally joyful but ill-fated marriage to the poor white Bonnie Dee Peacock, who dies of fright during a thunderstorm. Charged with murder by Bonnie Dee's grasping parents, Daniel convinces the court of his innocence and promptly gives away the remainder of his inheritance to all present, including the astonished Peacocks. At the end of the story we find him still happily making gestures of giving even though he no longer has anything to give, as Edna Earle urges her visitor to go along with the pretense and accept Daniel's routine offering with thanks. The popular success of *The Ponder Heart* as a novel prompted playwrights Jerome Chodorov and Joseph Fields to write a dramatic version of the piece, which played on Broadway in 1956 with equal success.

In 1969 Welty published, again in the *New Yorker*, a second short novel, *The Optimist's Daughter*, in many respects a subtle and more ambitious variation on the theme of *The Ponder Heart*. This time the forbearing guardian of the irresponsible elder is Laurel McKelva, lately returned from Chicago to comfort her father during what turns out to be his last illness. Like Daniel Ponder, Judge McKelva late in life has optimistically married beneath him to a much younger woman, this one an unwashed Texan named Wanda Fay. For the funeral (reminiscent of the one the Peacocks arranged for the unfortunate Bonnie Dee) Wanda Fay, much to the embarrassment of Laurel and the judge's older friends, brings in a host of relatives and then returns home with them for a family visit. Laura remains briefly in the house preparing it for Wanda Fay's return. At first contemptuous of her vulgar mother-in-law, she recalls as she goes about the house that her own mother (like Eudora Welty's) had come to Mississippi from her native West Virginia to make a life in what was for her alien territory and then gone on to live out her days with divided and sometimes contradictory emotional attachments. In the end Laura returns to Chicago reduced in pride and more respectful of her father's charitable optimism. For this work Welty belatedly received a Pulitzer Prize in 1973.

Eudora Welty's latest novel, *Losing Battles* (1970), shares a relationship with *Delta Wedding* of 1946 that is similar to the one between the two intervening shorter novels. Like *Delta Wedding* it is a family novel, this time, however, set in Banner, Mississippi, a small community in the hilly northeastern part of the state. Like the characters in *Delta Wedding* the people in Banner are blood relatives for the most part, mainly Beechams and Renfros, poorer than their Delta counterparts but equally proud and equally inclined to clannishness. The subject explored and ultimately vindicated in this novel, as in its predecessor, is one that persists as a theme in much of Welty's work: the communion in love between and among human beings that she sees as essential equally to marriage, family, and community. The manifestation of such communion here is the annual gathering of the Beecham-Renfro clan to celebrate the birthday of their family matriarch, Granny Vaughn (actually her ninetieth, although she persists in declaring it her hundredth). This time two other events coincide: first, the death of Miss Julia Mortimer, local schoolmistress long retired, who has taught most of the Renfros and the Beechams and attempted with only partial success to inculcate in her students the virtue of independence and make them aware of a world beyond, and in her view superior to, Banner, Mississippi; and second, the return of young Jack Renfro from the state penitentiary at Parchman in the expectation of a happy reunion with his wife, Gloria. Gloria Renfro, however, an outsider reared as an orphan, is the protégé of Miss Mortimer and her successor at the school, and she privately resists exchanging her independence for allegiance to a family, Jack Renfro's or anyone else's. The resulting "battle," which duplicates the struggle most of the characters in the novel are undertaking in one way or another, is a battle to be lost if genuine love is to triumph over selfishness, confirm the marriage, ensure the continuity of family, and triumph in defeat, as it does in Welty's hands, convincingly and without sentimentality.

Part of Welty's success is due to a masterful method of presentation, in which she balances on one hand the business of narration between an omniscient interlocutor with humor and an eye for hard detail and on the other a rendering of virtually all the activity by means of extended conversations. The greater part of her success, however, must be attributed to the understanding and wisdom of a major author, evident in retrospect even at the beginning of her career, now fully revealed at the peak of her maturity. Here, as in virtually everything that Eudora Welty has done, her writing has on it the identifiable marks of Mississippi—the geography, which she has observed at first hand, the language, which she has reproduced almost infallibly, and the people. Such marks, however, even in the early works, become less noticeable as one reads and rereads. The local coloring in her work, authentic though it is, soon ceases to call attention to itself, and her progressive revelation of the universal human condition stands clear in a series of arresting actions and a wealth of particulars. What distinguishes Welty from the best of those writers who were her contemporaries in the early years—Ellen Glasgow, Elizabeth Madox Roberts, and Katherine Anne Porter—is her attainment of something that can only be characterized as ripeness. In this aspect of her achievement she stands with her only equal in the literature of the South, William Faulkner, and like him with America's best—Hawthorne, Melville, and Mark Twain.

In the early fifties, however, Eudora Welty was by no means an isolated phenomenon. Several other women of her generation were also beginning to attract attention with fiction of genuine technical sophistication and interest, among them North Carolina's Frances Gray Patton (b. 1906), Kentucky-born Elizabeth Hardwick (b. 1916), and West Virginia's relatively prolific Mary Lee Settle (b. 1918). Patton's reputation, then as now, rests principally upon her humorous and beautifully crafted short stories, which have since appeared in three collections, *The Finer Things of Life* (1951), *A Piece of Luck* (1955), and *Twenty-Eight Stories* (1969). Patton also developed one of her stories into a novel, *Good Morning, Miss Dove* (1954), which became a best-seller and later the basis for a successful film. The multitalented Elizabeth Hardwick has spent most of her mature life in New York, but several of her short stories have a southern setting, as do two of her novels, especially *The Ghostly Lover* (1945), which is a psychological study of a perceptive young woman's attempt to come to terms with her Kentucky family and upbringing. Hardwick's genuine talent for fiction, however, has tended to be overshadowed by her contributions as an essayist to such periodicals as *Harper's*, *Partisan Review*, and the *New Yorker* and by her skill as an advisory editor of the *New York Review of Books*.

Mary Lee Settle has made a career out of writing about her native West Virginia and perhaps for that reason until recently has attracted less critical attention than those writers whose provenance and subject are, to some minds, more distinctively southern. In 1978, however, her novel *Blood Tie* (1977), set in Turkey, won a National Book Award, and since then five of her West Virginia novels, collectively called the Beulah quintet, have belatedly brought her some of the notice she deserves. The titles are worth remembering: *O Beulah Land* (1956), *Know Nothing* (1960), *Prisons* (1973), *The Scapegoat* (1980), and finally *The Killing Ground* (1982), which is actually a reworking of an earlier work published in 1964. From these novels we get the story of the Lacey, Catlett, and McCarkle families, who began their ties with one another in Cromwellian England but subsequently migrated to America, establishing fresh roots in the part of Appalachia that was to become West Virginia and there continued their interrelated lives through the divisiveness of the Civil War and the progressively hard and troubled times that followed. Earlier critics praised Settle's "instinct for panorama," which in addition to her considerable novelistic skills she clearly possesses, but she has also produced a valid symbol of the making of at least parts of modern America, particularly those sections of rural New England and the agrarian South that have maintained a cultural coherence and preserved their unique identity.

By the time this trio of writers had established positions on the literary scene, however, even younger women were beginning to compete successfully with them for public attention. First among the newcomers was Elizabeth Spencer (b. 1921), who was destined in the course of a public career to earn a respected place in Mississippi's literary pantheon. Spencer's background was Carroll County in the state's Bluff Hills section, where her family had lived for almost a century; her education was Jackson's Belhaven College and the Vanderbilt Graduate School, where she studied under Donald Davidson and received his strong encouragement to continue writing. Since then she has produced nine novels, several essays, and a number of short stories for which she has received five O. Henry prizes and an Award of Merit Medal from the American Academy of Arts and Letters. The short stories, most of them, have been collected in four volumes: *Ship Island and Other Stories* (1968), *Marilee* (1981), *The Stories of Elizabeth Spencer* (1981), and *Jack of Diamonds* (1988). During the course of her career Spencer has lived and written in a number of places—Mississippi, of course, Italy, Montreal, and most recently North Carolina—and impressions of all these locales have served as material for her work.

As might be expected her first novels—*Fire in the Morning* (1948), *This Crooked Way* (1952), and *The Voice at the Back Door* (1956)—draw heavily upon the scenes and people she knew in the hill country where she grew up. The first of these, a novel reminiscent of Faulkner's work but in no pejorative sense imitative of it, deals with the attempt of a young Mississippian to reconcile his sense of ethical behavior and justice with the complex and sometimes contradictory heritage of values that undergirds his life and the life of the community in which he lives. The second, somewhat less suggestive of Faulkner, depicts the progressive humbling of another young man destructively obsessed with the notion that he has a divine mandate to pursue material wealth. *The Voice at the Back Door*, as its title suggests, confronts a similar problem as manifested in Mississippi's struggle with its race relations and suggests—too optimistically, according to some—a resolution in charity and good will. The praise elicited by these three early novels called attention to qualities that would characterize all of Spencer's subsequent work: superior plotting, convincing characterization, and a graceful and accessible prose style. These alone would justify the epithet "master storyteller" accorded her by a recent critic, but they hardly take into account the subtle craftsmanship and depth of feeling that have increased with each new work.

Both qualities are exhibited in her short novel of 1960, *The Light in the*

Piazza, the moving story of an American woman in Italy who confronts an emotional and moral crisis when a young Italian falls in love with her beautiful but retarded daughter and seeks to marry her. This, probably the most successful of all her works, appeared first in an issue of the *New Yorker* and was later made into a film. Critics found Spencer's other two novels of the 1960s, *Knights and Dragons* (1965) and *No Place for an Angel* (1967), less arresting but came to attention once more in their reviews of *The Snare* (1972), which recounts the attempt by a respectable young woman from New Orleans's Garden District to find a meaning for her life in the chaotic entertainment world of a decadent French Quarter. They were enthusiastic about *The Night Travellers* (1991), a mature work of fiction, set in two of Spencer's adopted locales, North Carolina and Canada, which tells the love story of two intelligent young people caught in the turmoils of those years.

Two other even younger southern women managed temporarily to catch the attention of both critics and readers at midcentury: Alabama's Harper Lee (b. 1926) and New Orleans author Shirley Ann Grau (b. 1929). Harper Lee's claim to fame rests upon her first and only novel, *To Kill a Mockingbird* (1960), in which she incorporated reminiscences of her early years in depression-ridden Monroeville. The novel's widespread popular success at the time (it received numerous awards, including a Pulitzer) was due in part to its principal subject, race relations, and to Lee's sympathetic portrayal (presumably based upon her father) of a young lawyer in the Deep South courageous enough to defend a black man falsely accused of rape. Equally commendable, and well ahead of its time, was her perceptive portrayal in a related plot of the retarded Boo Radley, white but nevertheless a victim of local prejudice and ignorance. From a critic's perspective, however, the remarkable thing about *To Kill a Mockingbird* was the display of confidence and skill, rare in a first work, that gave the book sufficient strength to transcend the timeliness that made it popular. A movie version by Horton Foote appeared in 1962.

Shirley Ann Grau also received a Pulitzer Prize (in 1965), at approximately the same age as Harper Lee had, but Grau received the award for her third novel, *The Keepers of the House* (1964), at which time she had been enjoying literary fame for almost a decade. Critics were unstinting in their praise of her first book, *The Black Prince and Other Stories* (1955) and compared it with the work of such established authors as McCullers and Welty and also with that of another youthful author, Flannery O'Connor, whose *Wise Blood* had appeared three years before to more mixed reviews. The virtues they found in that early collection were those that would continue to characterize Grau's work at its best: a concern for craftsmanship, especially in the shorter forms, a lush prose style, a perceptive treatment of rural characters and blacks, an interest in the forms that evil assumes in human behavior, and, as with Eudora Welty, an inclination to suggest a mythic dimension in the actions presented.

The three novels that followed *The Black Prince* were her most successful. *The Hard Blue Sky* (1958) deals with a colony of Cajun fishermen and the effect on their normally monotonous lives when a luxury sloop drops anchor there in advance of a hurricane and its one-man crew elopes with one of their women, whose character Grau delineates at some length. *The House on Coliseum Street* (1961) concentrates on the character of another young woman, this time a neurotic one in New Orleans, who is all but destroyed in her ill-advised strategies for coming to terms with the people whose lives are unavoidably intertwined with her own. By most estimates, however, Grau's best work is her prize-winning *The Keepers of the House* (1964). In it she undertakes, in a manner reminiscent of Faulkner's *Absalom, Absalom!*, to trace the consequences of an interracial marriage through several generations of a single family. The narrator of the story is the racially mixed granddaughter of that marriage, and her steadfast concern when the community discovers and denounces the "miscegenation" is to affirm the dignity of the house she represents and preserve its integrity. Since 1964 Grau has produced two new collections of stories—*The Wind Shifting West* (1973) and *Nine Women* (1986)—and two more novels—*The Condor Passes* (1971) and *Evidence of Love* (1977). These are all respectable achievements and in no way detract from Grau's stature, but her early novels and stories and the ambitious *Keepers of the House* remain her best work.

In the opinion of many critics, however, the one young writer of the fifties who seemed most likely to establish a permanent niche for herself in American literature was Flannery O'Connor, who was born in Savannah, Georgia, in 1925 and died, a victim of lupus, at Milledgeville in 1964. In her brief career as a writer, O'Connor produced two novels, *Wise Blood* (1952) and *The Violent Bear It Away* (1960), two volumes of short stories, *A Good Man Is Hard to Find* (1955) and *Everything That Rises Must Converge* (1965), a number of occasional pieces and reviews, and scores of letters. The essays were collected, edited, and published posthumously as *Mystery and Manners* (1969) by her lifelong friends Sally and Robert Fitzgerald. A selection of the letters edited by Sally Fitzgerald came out ten years later as *The Habit of Being* (1979). A volume of *Complete Stories* appeared in 1971, making available several unpublished stories and early versions of the two novels. In 1983 the University of Georgia Press brought out *The Presence of Grace*, a collection of short reviews that she wrote for two Catholic diocesan newspapers in Georgia.

O'Connor's family was Catholic on both sides; and she attended paro-
chial schools during her early years in Savannah. When her father fell fatally
ill, however, with the same lupus that would eventually end her own life, she
moved with the family to her mother's home in Milledgeville, completed her
secondary work in the local high school, and attended Georgia State College
for Women there. In the latter she distinguished herself for her wit as a car-
toonist on the school paper and for her writing as the editor of the literary
magazine, and so, supported by the guarantee of a fellowship, on graduation
was able to enter the Writers' Workshop at the University of Iowa. There she
earned her M.A. degree, began writing in earnest, and met established professionals who in addition to providing stimulation and camaraderie helped
her to find her way in the world of grants and publishers. Thereafter with the
help of a year at Yaddo, five months of writing in New York, and another year
or so boarding with her friends the Fitzgeralds, who had bought a comfortable place in the Connecticut countryside, she was well on her way to becoming the writer she aspired to be. She was just finishing the first draft of her
novel *Wise Blood* when the symptoms appeared that sent her back to Georgia
to confront the disease that was to be the condition of her life for the thirteen
years she had left.

Wise Blood came out in 1952, when O'Connor was just twenty-seven
years old. The germ of the novel had been published as a short story in the
Sewanee Review some months earlier, but otherwise nothing quite like it had
ever appeared in American literature, and critics scarcely knew what to make
of it. Some dismissed the work out of hand as a belated example of Southern
Gothic. Others declared it a satire on popular evangelical religion in the South.
Still others called it black humor at its bleakest. What saved *Wise Blood*, and
with it O'Connor's budding career, was the powerful vitality of the work that
for most readers quickly manifested itself and thereafter would not be denied
even though some of those reading as religionists protested the implications
of her narrative and others as lovers of form descried flaws in its structure and
technique.

The theme of the novel was the human race's perennial thirst for truth,
which for O'Connor was Christ, God incarnate, and fallen mankind's only
hope for redemption. More than once she would declare that her primary
objective in writing was to proclaim that truth, her talent being merely a divine gift to further that end. Actually no one ever studied technique more
assiduously than Flannery O'Connor, and no one worked harder at her craft
than she or was more receptive to advice and direction from the acknowledged masters who from time to time advised her (among them Caroline and
Allen Tate). Truth as she understood it, however, came first, and the truth she

believed in was that embodied in the Catholic Church, to which she gave complete assent and obedience. Fortunately for her literary pretensions, public acknowledgments of religious faith during the conservative fifties had ceased to be anathema. With T.S. Eliot's announcement of his conversion in 1928, a change in attitude among the literati had begun to be noticeable, and by the end of World War II the company of publicly professing Christians included such figures as W.H. Auden, Evelyn Waugh, Allen Tate, and Katherine Anne Porter. By 1950 C.S. Lewis and Thomas Merton had achieved the status of popular apologists with many followers, especially among the young. Thus, almost as soon as *Wise Blood* came out, Flannery O'Connor began to assume willy-nilly the status of a cult figure.

She later described her hero in the novel, a recently discharged veteran from East Tennessee, Hazel Motes, who like O'Connor herself felt a compulsion to proclaim truth, as "a Christian *malgré lui*." Motes, however, was shrewd enough to recognize that the versions of Christianity's ancient paradoxes and moral code that had come to him by way of his semiliterate elders and preachers were hopelessly flawed with inconsistencies and improbabilities; consequently he set out to prove the irrelevance of both and to proclaim a religion without Christ. His trouble, according to the novel, was that a longing for the Christ he had never known lurked in his subconscious and would not let him rest. Thus, blind to the truth he passionately desired, he stumbled into one sin after another until eventually, in desperation trying to find the light that the world could not provide, he literally blinded himself, never realizing that by virtue of his quest he had himself become the light he was seeking. O'Connor in a headnote to a later edition attributed Motes's salvation, or "integrity" as she called it, to his inability "to get rid of the ragged figure who moves from tree to tree in the back of his mind," but she acknowledged that this bizarre figure represented a mystery which a comic novel like hers could only be expected to deepen.

The term "comic," although perhaps not in the sense she used it here, points to the aspect of caricature that characterizes all her writing and caused it to be read by some as a Catholic author's satire on the fundamentalist religion of the South's Bible Belt. It came as a shock to some readers of the title story in O'Connor's first collection, "A Good Man Is Hard to Find," that she regarded the grandmother there as the heroine. Most had thought of the grandmother mainly as a stereotype, an ignorant and foolish old woman, who in her senility causes the family to stumble into the path of an escaped criminal called The Misfit and by recognizing him as such prompts him to kill them all. Almost none had been able to read sympathetically O'Connor's representation of the old woman's frantic attempts—even as The Misfit's cohorts are leading her family away to be shot—to appeal to the man's better nature and persuade him to turn to Jesus. Nevertheless, O'Connor insisted that for all the woman's general lack of comprehension she has a moment of real insight when, having seen the deaths of the others and now facing her own, she murmurs, "Why, you're one of my babies. You're one of my own children!" and moves to touch her murderer-to-be on the shoulder. At this point he shoots her three times in the chest. There is nothing grotesque here, O'Connor later declared, simply the literal depiction of an action of grace and the inevitable satanic reaction to it.

She said essentially the same thing about the transformation that takes place with Mr. Head, the central character of "The Artificial Nigger," her favorite among all the stories. Mr. Head is a north Georgia primitive, inordinately proud but unaware of his limitations. Consequently, when he takes his young grandson, Nelson, to see Atlanta and black people for the first time (he himself has been there only three times), he fails in his roles both as parent and as guide—first, abandoning the boy when he innocently stumbles into difficulty; then, having boasted grandly of wisdom and superior knowledge, managing to get them lost in the maze of Atlanta's streets. For a time the two are estranged, with Nelson angry and hurt in his disillusionment and Mr. Head humiliated, but they come together at last in common astonishment before the plaster figure of a black boy sitting on a garden wall. "They could both feel it dissolving their differences," writes O'Connor, "like an action of mercy." Consequently when Nelson's eyes plead for an explanation, Mr. Head hears himself saying, "They ain't got enough real ones here. They got to have an artificial one." Where his words have come from, Mr. Head does not know, but the boy is reassured by his grandfather's ability to come up with an appropriate answer, and Mr. Head himself recovers a measure of his credibility. In this fashion, O'Connor would have us believe, divine grace has miraculously restored the harmony between the two and taught Mr. Head his perpetual need for a forgiveness that is abundant and always available even to prideful old men.

In her view it was also miraculous grace that brought about the resolution in *Wise Blood*, and it is manifestly grace that guides the erring younger Tarwater to a fulfillment of his destiny in her second novel, *The Violent Bear It Away* (1960). O'Connor set great store by this work, and more than one critic has since declared it to be her masterpiece. At any rate, by the time it appeared her readers, at least some of them, had learned, as she had hoped they might, to look behind the comic, cartoonlike surface of her narratives for the action that she had meant them to take seriously. Here the action was the way of God's grace with fallen mankind in a world all but dominated by the devil, and she demonstrated that way with another story of a prophet, Francis Marion Tarwater, who was blind to the nature of the hound that was pursuing him. Tarwater, an orphan aged fourteen, has lived most of his life at Powderhead, a "gaunt two-story shack" in the middle of a corn patch. There his great-uncle, a self-proclaimed prophet and recluse much given to violence, has provided him with Christian instruction and named him his successor. The elder Tarwater has also provided his nephew with specific instructions for his own burial (ten feet deep with a cross above) and directed him, as a first assignment in his career as prophet, to baptize a mentally retarded cousin then living in the city with his agnostic schoolteacher father. Tarwater does not resist taking the role of prophet, but he considers his great-uncle a madman and an unreliable teacher and plans to begin his own career with a more appropriate project than baptizing an idiot. Consequently, he disregards the burial instructions and sets out for the city, determined to disregard the assignment as well. In his rebelliousness he is abetted by a mysterious stranger (presumably the devil) who appears from time to time with advice and suggestions to support his defection. Accordingly, when circumstances that Tarwater does not understand dictate that willy-nilly he encounter the child, whom he has tried desperately to avoid, he proceeds to drown him—in the process, however, inadvertently saying the words of baptism. At this point, still failing to recognize the persistent action of grace in his life, he heads back to Powderhead to begin again, once more encounters the devil, this time in the guise of a homosexual seducer, and at last recognizes his enemy. Now more furiously the prophet than his great-uncle ever was, he sets fire to the thicket where the seduction took place, receives a vision of Christ feeding the five thousand, and prepares to return to the somnolent city, this time as the violent agent of God's mercy.

The Violent Bear It Away was the last work to appear during O'Connor's brief lifetime. The best of her stories had appeared in the collection she published in 1955; but there were others, including some that she had written during her last years, and these too she prepared for publication. They came out in 1965 with the title *Everything That Rises Must Converge*, which she had borrowed from Teilhard de Chardin, the priest-anthropologist whose work she greatly admired. These stories are not so arresting as the ones she had published earlier, but they were good enough to justify reprinting six years later in *The Complete Stories*, which won a National Book Award. All the work of her productive fifteen years taken together was certainly sufficient to earn O'Connor a place of distinction in America's literary annals, although the exact degree of that distinction is still difficult to predict. As an example of sustained wit and craftsmanship her work undoubtedly will continue to stand on its own. The religious bias of it, however, which contributed in large part to the extraordinary vogue it enjoyed among academic critics during the late sixties and early seventies, has become less attractive as the climate of literary criticism and study has shifted, and the audience that produced the flood of books and articles about O'Connor's work even while she was still alive has for the most part found other authors to explicate. This change will be all to the good if an interval of inattention can be followed by a return to her novels and stories and a revaluation of them without reference to what she intended them to do and the heroic effort required of her to produce them.

9

The New Black Writers

Before World War II American readers tended to regard black writing with the same amused detachment they accorded works of local color that happened to be sufficiently removed from their own experience and thus unlikely to cause them private embarrassment. Even when the black author had avoided the stereotypical, readers were likely to read stereotypes into the work before them, and these stereotypes frequently tended to be indistinguishable from those served up by white authors imagining they were writing in a black mode. After the war this situation began to change. Part of the shift was attributable to public pressure from the black community, most of whom were unwilling to tolerate indefinitely the manifest inequities in their lot when they had just completed a war presumably to end similar inequities elsewhere. Part, however, was certainly due to a mounting anger expressed in the work of an unusually talented black author whose personal circumstances had so aggravated the pain caused by the circumstances he shared with American blacks generally that his rage demanded extraordinary expression.

Much of what Mississippi-born Richard Wright (1908–60) put into his short stories and novels had a basis in the dark data of his own life. His mother was a country schoolteacher, who contrary to her parents' wishes had married a millworker, Nathan Wright, who by some accounts was illiterate. Wright, however, was eager for better things, for himself at least, and moved his family, now consisting of a wife and two sons, to Memphis, where shortly thereafter he abandoned them. The mother, unable to provide adequately for herself and two small boys (Richard was only five at the time), was forced to place them temporarily in an orphanage. After a year she found a promising haven for all three with her sister and brother-in-law in the small Arkansas river town of Elaine, but that situation came abruptly to an end when the brother-in-law was lynched and sisters and children were forced to take refuge in nearby Helena. To make matters even worse, in less than a year the mother suffered a series of crippling strokes from which she never fully recovered. Richard and his brother went to Jackson, Mississippi, there to live for six years with maternal grandparents in a household that was supportive but rigidly Seventh-Day Adventist.

In 1925, having graduated with honors from the ninth grade (all the formal education he was ever to have), Wright moved to Memphis, found a place for his brother and ailing mother, worked at odd jobs, and began to read widely and voraciously. Then in 1927, in high expectations of finding the good life in a more genial North, he moved to Chicago, where in spite of repeated disappointments and mounting frustration he remained for ten years, again working at series of jobs and this time writing as well as reading. Within a year he had fared well enough to bring his mother and brother to Chicago. In 1933 he took an unanticipated but for him fortunate step when he joined the Communist Party, began associating with young intellectuals in the John Reed Club, and started expressing his pent-up feelings in poems, essays, and reviews, a number of which were published in such periodicals as *New Masses*, *Partisan Review*, and *Left Front*. During this period he also worked with the Federal Negro Theater in Chicago and with the Federal Writers' Project and wrote two novels and a number of short stories, but with the exception of one story, "Big Boy Leaves Home," none of his Chicago writing saw print, at least immediately.

In 1937 Wright moved to New York, where again his manuscripts at first were rejected, but he found work there on the magazine *New Challenge* and became Harlem editor for the *Daily Worker*. In December of that year a first prize in a contest at *Story* led to publication early in 1938 of the short story "Fire and Cloud" and indirectly to the publication of *Uncle Tom's Children: Four Novellas* (1938). Thereafter he had little trouble getting things into print. In 1940 Harper, which had published *Uncle Tom's Children*, was willing to try his *Native Son*, which to his delight was selected by the Book of the Month Club, became an instant success, and almost overnight established Wright as the country's leading black author. To capitalize on this signal success, Harper also brought out an expanded version of *Uncle Tom's Children*, and when in 1941 a stage version of *Native Son*, written by Wright in collaboration with Paul Green, was given a successful Broadway production by Orson Welles and John Houseman, Harper published that too. In the same year Viking published Wright's first book of nonfiction (written in collaboration with Edwin Rosskam), *Twelve Million Black Voices: A Folk History of the Negro in the United States*.

With one possible reservation *Native Son* may be called Wright's major work. In it one repeatedly hears echoes of the author's experience and reflections of his personal anguish. Its central character, Bigger Thomas, a southern black relocated in Chicago's ghetto, finds himself trapped in the dilemma imposed upon him by white society. Forced by an environment of that society's making to assume the image of a monstrous animal, he desperately dreams of full humanity but ironically begins to achieve it only in violence that brings about his own destruction and that of two white women. Bigger Thomas hardly possesses the epic stature one enthusiastic commentator has attributed to him, but he does stand as the supreme symbol of America's angry black man, coming at a time when complacent whites, in the South and elsewhere, were congratulating themselves on their efforts to improve the black man's lot.

Wright had married in 1939 and soon thereafter, buoyed by the success of *Native Son*, traveled to Mexico on a Guggenheim Fellowship, where the marriage fell apart. A second marriage in 1941 proved happier, and Wright continued his work. Some of the stories he produced during this period appeared later in *Eight Men* (1961); but the principal result was *Black Boy: A Record of Childhood and Youth* (1945), a fictionalized autobiography that some critics have felt is superior to *Native Son*. Arguably the writing, reminiscent of Dreiser's circumstantiality, is better; but the sharper focus of the novel is missing as is the iconic significance of Wright's Bigger Thomas. Nevertheless, *Black Boy* remains the best account of what it meant to grow up black in a Mississippi scarcely half a century removed from slavery and the Civil War. Wright seems to have left out little if anything: the black child's hunger, fear, and loneliness, his vulnerability to the contempt of whites and the harsh discipline imposed by his black elders, presumably to prepare him for life in a world where blacks were expected to know their place, his repeated exploitation by black and white alike, his perpetual humiliation. There is also the intelligent young black's seemingly unquenchable hope that somewhere else, perhaps in a Chicago of his dreams, there existed a place where the South that was bred in his flesh and bones and was not to be repudiated might blossom into a life that could be lived with dignity.

Chicago obviously had not been that place nor had New York. In 1947 Wright, having visited Paris the preceding year, moved to France, where after renouncing his connections with the Communist Party he settled permanently. During the remaining thirteen years of his life, he made trips to the Gold Coast (Ghana), Indonesia, and Spain, which resulted in a series of travel narratives, and lectured in Germany and Scandinavia. He also published two more novels, *The Outsider* (1953) and *The Long Dream* (1958), neither of which added to his stature as a literary figure. After his death of a heart attack in 1960, two works appeared, *Eight Men* (1961), a collection of stories that did add to that stature, and *Lawd Today* (1963), an apprentice novel written during his Chicago days.

Wright did not remain in America long enough to participate in the civil rights movement or directly profit from the renewed interest in black literature that accompanied it, but he was a key figure in both. More than any other writer before him he opened the eyes of American—including southern—readers, deplored the long-standing disparagement of black people, affirmed their essential dignity, and marked a path of exit for southern black writers who within two decades would produce writing equal in sophistication to anything being produced by their white contemporaries. Even so, on the broader stage he seems destined to be remembered principally as a powerful writer of protest who came at a critical juncture in the course of American letters. His successor, less powerful only because he did not come first, was Ralph Ellison (1914–94).

Ellison was born in Oklahoma City on the fringe of the South proper and grew up there. He was, as he said of himself, "by geographical origin a South-westerner," and added, "in a state which [possessed] no indigenous tradition of chattel slavery." Thus the segregation Ellison knew, though real enough, lacked the intensity of that segregation which Wright had described with corresponding intensity and bitterness in *Black Boy*. He was also luckier in other ways. His father, a man of educated taste who named his son Ralph Waldo, died when the boy was only three, but his mother saw to it that the child developed his parents' passion for reading and, more important at the time, acquired an appreciation for theater and music. She exposed him to classical music, supported his interest in jazz, bought him a secondhand cornet, and encouraged him to learn to play. Thus music dominated Ellison's ambitions during the early years, so that in 1933, with two years' savings in hand and a small scholarship, he was able to ride the rails to Alabama and enroll in Tuskegee Institute with dreams of becoming a great composer.

Ellison never returned to Oklahoma. At Tuskegee he discovered a gallery of new and exotic writers: Pound, Hemingway, Fitzgerald, Freud, Marx, Sherwood Anderson, Gertrude Stein, and especially T.S. Eliot, whose *The Waste Land* so intrigued him that in short order he decided to make writing rather than music his career. A pressing need for funds, however, dictated that temporarily he seek work, so in 1936 he made an exploratory foray into New York but within a year was forced to abandon that and return south as far as Dayton, Ohio, where his mother, now seriously ill, had moved in the interval. When his mother died the following year, he returned to New York and through Langston Hughes, with whom he had formed a friendship, met Richard Wright. These two introduced him to the remaining members of the Harlem Renaissance and broadened his horizon to include Conrad, Dostoyevsky, and Malraux, especially the last of these. In addition Wright set him to work doing reviews and trying his hand at fiction. During the next five years Ellison published short stories, worked for the WPA and the Federal

Writers' Project, and served briefly as editor of *Negro Quarterly* before joining the merchant marine as a cook in 1943.

The merchant marine served Ellison well. There quite literally he broadened his horizons and was able in infrequent moments of leisure to begin
writing a war novel. Both his service, however, and that first attempt at a novel
were interrupted in 1945 by a period of sick leave, during which he put war
out of his mind and began work on a very different kind of writing project. By
1952, having already published two sections of it, he was able to publish the
whole as *Invisible Man*, which almost immediately became a popular and
critical success and in 1953 won both the National Book Award and the National Newspaper Publishers Russwurm Award. Overnight Ralph Ellison had
unwittingly replaced Richard Wright in the public's eye as America's premier
black writer of fiction, a position he held throughout much of his long life.
Ironically, neither man ever again published a major work of fiction.

Invisible Man has often invited comparison with *Native Son*, principally,
one may suppose, because both reflect in realistic detail circumstances that
their respective authors encountered while growing up black in a segregated
South. Wright's Bigger Thomas, however, like Wright himself, has grown up
in Mississippi, where the shadow of slavery has persisted, and the traumas
forced upon him in youth have rendered him permanently angry at being
denied the dignity that he instinctively knows is rightfully his. Sadly the adulthood that Bigger's author allows him is too brief to permit more than a gesture toward control of the resentment that has dominated his life. By contrast, the nameless hero of *Invisible Man*, although repeatedly advised by
whites and blacks alike that his place in society is somewhat lower than that of
his Anglo-Saxon counterparts, has grown up with parents who encouraged
him to taste the bounty of a European culture that he is intelligent enough to
appreciate—done so, moreover, in a society that seemingly has no great interest in denying him access to it. In addition, from the fierce words of a dying
grandfather he has derived the insight that his life as a black must be one in
perpetual conflict with both white arrogance and black complaisance. Briefly,
the substantive difference between the heroes of the two novels is that Wright's
engages the enemy with outright hostility, Ellison's with dogged but passive
resistance. For Bigger Thomas the consequence of his engagement is destruction; for Ellison's nameless hero, protracted invisibility in a context of
willful white misunderstanding and misguided black activism.

Formally, the difference between the two novels is even greater. Wright,
not only in *Native Son* but consistently in all his narratives including *Black
Boy*, made use of a naturalistic style reminiscent of those American authors
he most admired, Theodore Dreiser, Sherwood Anderson, and Sinclair Lewis.

Ellison used the same mode in *Invisible Man* but only in the beginning. Thereafter he shifted to a picaresque formula and in a succession of symbolic incidents, replete with folkloric materials, dream sequences, and passages of stream of consciousness, presented a black bildungsroman in which the central figure advances from an innocent anonymity to an awareness both of his identity and his invisibility and the realization that many others less aware than he, white as well as black, share his ambiguous situation. Wright's *Native Son* had both predecessors and successors, but Ellison's novel stands alone, though as a serious examination of the predicament of blacks in America it anticipated the writing he himself would do throughout the rest of his life.

Soon after *Invisible Man* appeared, rumor began to hint at a second novel, but although Ellison published several more pieces of fiction, collectively referred to as the Hickman stories, nothing resembling a novel came out during his lifetime. Since his death, however, John F. Callahan, his literary executor, has worked at putting together both published and unpublished material to produce something that may suggest the kind of novel Ellison had in mind. During the more than forty years remaining to him after 1952, he lectured, held university posts, and continued to write—essays, reviews, formal addresses, and conference talks—in which he explored at length many of the aspects of the black situation that he had dealt with novelistically in *Invisible Man*. He published some of these in collections, *Shadow and Act* (1964) and *Going to the Territory* (1986), and gave his executor permission to reprint both collections after his death, along with twenty-two additional uncollected items. These appeared with a preface by Saul Bellow as *The Collected Essays of Ralph Ellison* in 1995 and constitute, if one chooses to read them so, an extended commentary on the themes of the novel. In any case, they provide fascinating glimpses into the mind of an intelligent black man coming to terms with his situation in an era of stressful transition.

The writer who has dealt most authoritatively with that transition, in published novels and stories about twentieth-century blacks in the Deep South, is Louisiana's Ernest F. Gaines (b. 1933). Gaines has come by his authority naturally. He was born on a plantation near Baton Rouge and, as was still the custom there, began work in the fields by the time he was nine years old. Because his parents soon separated, he was raised by an aunt, Augusteen Jefferson, a sterling example of courage and fortitude, who unable to walk nevertheless carried out her household duties alone and by crawling on the floor; her indomitable spirit is preserved in several of Gaines's older characters, notably Miss Jane Pittman. At fifteen he moved with his mother to Vallejo, California, where a good school and a supportive stepfather helped to point him in the direction of great books. Many of the best authors, he found, had dealt extensively with peasant life, and these became his favorites: Chekhov, Tolstoy, Turgenev, and of course Faulkner.

Within a year he was writing his own stories, and after attending high school and junior college and serving briefly in the army, he entered San Francisco State College, earned a B.A., and in 1958 received a Wallace Stegner Creative Writing Fellowship for study at Stanford, where Wendell Berry and Ken Kesey were classmates. Since then Gaines has maintained a home in San Francisco, where he has done the bulk of his writing: a collection of stories, *Bloodline* (1968), and six published novels, all set in the fictional parish of St. Raphael, similar to the parish in which he was born. He regularly returns to Louisiana, however, which he calls his "spiritual home" but adds that it is not the place he prefers to live. Since 1981 he has held the post of tenured professor of creative writing at the University of Southwestern Louisiana in Lafayette, where he spends three or four months out of every year.

From the beginning, the body of Gaines's fiction has been unified both by geography and by a comprehensive understanding of his part of the South. The range of his work, like Faulkner's, covers a span of time from the Civil War to the present, a period in which Louisiana witnessed the decline of the old plantation economy, the rise of the Cajun class to a position of control, and the progressive displacement of black labor by machinery with a corresponding challenge to the integrity of black communities throughout the region. His first novel, *Catherine Carmier* (1964), set in the time of the Freedom Riders, was a reworking, largely done at Stanford, of a youthful attempt at fiction. Told in the third person, a mode that he seems to find uncongenial, it presents the troubled and inconclusive relationship between Jackson Bradley, a young plantation black, like Gaines educated in California, and Catherine Carmier, a Creole black, deeply attached to her father, Raoul, a proud man who resists the Cajun encroachment that threatens in time to deny both groups of blacks their place on the land and in the social structure. Jackson, contrary to the hopes and expectations of the aunt who has reared him, sees that he can never live happily in Louisiana, but he is deeply attached to Catherine, who cannot break away. In the end both are victims of caste and history, with almost no prospect of ever finding a means of making a life together. This novel received a Joseph Henry Jackson Literary Prize but otherwise attracted little notice.

With his second, *Of Love and Dust* (1967), Gaines began to receive the respectful attention that critics and readers alike have since accorded him. Here he dropped back to the forties, at a time when the Cajun poor whites had made only a few disruptive forays into the older and faltering social structure, and tells the story of Marcus Payne, a rebellious "bad nigger" who has killed another black in a tavern brawl and having been "bonded out" to a plantation for his term of five years continues to rebel and eventually brings about his own death. The principal narrator throughout is Jim Kelly, a black foreman, who serves under the Cajun overseer, Sidney Bonbon, and has the responsibility for seeing that Marcus works and stays out of trouble. In the course of the narrative Marcus continues his rebellion, which includes seducing Bonbon's wife and attempting to elope with her. In so doing he brings about his own death at the hands of the outraged Cajun wielding a scythe. The real action of the novel, however, consists of transformations that take place within the two principals: Marcus, who changes from the stereotypical angry man to a believable human being poised on the threshold of full awareness with the courage if not the means to escape from the animal existence to which his race has doomed him; and Jim Kelly, who at first despises his charge but comes to recognize that Marcus's rebellion is symptomatic of a crisis that is shortly to confront all black people. Almost as remarkable as the skill with which Gaines presents these developments is the care he has taken to render the context in which they take place: the life of rural blacks in the quarters of a Louisiana plantation, the caste system that persists within their community, and the uneasy tension between an old landed class of whites and the increasingly rapacious Cajuns. Suffice it to say, this novel and those of Gaines to follow possess a coherence and a vitality unsurpassed by those of any other black writer in America.

The year after *Of Love and Dust* Gaines's publisher, Dial Press, brought out *Bloodline* (1968), a collection of five previously published stories, in which he had explored at length the aspects of black manhood and continued his depiction of change in the Deep South. He expanded the range of that depiction in his third and most popular novel, *The Autobiography of Miss Jane Pittman* (1971), with a central character based in part upon the aunt who had reared him. Miss Jane is the principal observer, and her remarkable longevity enables her to present the story of black people in Louisiana over the course of a century from the Civil War to the civil rights movement of the 1960s, the women providing a spiritual continuum for their community while the more aggressive men initiate its advances, frequently at the cost of their own lives. This work, publicized by a remarkably effective television version, prepared a wide public for the three novels to follow.

In My Father's House (1978), published seven years after *Miss Jane Pittman*, saw a return to and mastery of the detached observer that Gaines had used as narrator in his first novel. It also presented an honest but less encouraging view of the immediate prospects for black society in the South. The main character there is a minister in a small Louisiana town who has put

behind him a youth of drinking, gambling, and whoring and become a respected community leader, only to be confronted by the inescapable presence of his past life in the person of an illegitimate son, whom he has abandoned. Try as he will, he is unable to suppress what he was or what he has
done and fails utterly to come to terms with the young man, who is not convinced that a slave heritage can sufficiently account for his father's irresponsible behavior. The novel ends on an even more desperate note, with the son
a suicide and the father disconsolate.

On the surface it would appear that Gaines's two more recent novels deal
with equally depressing subject matter, but actually they are astute celebra-
tions of reservoirs of strength. In the first, *A Gathering of Old Men* (1983),
the reservoir has lain unsuspected and untapped in a group of old men who,
in order to protect a young black whom they believe guilty of murdering a
Cajun, suddenly overcome their lifelong slavish subservience and stand together, heroically taking on themselves the responsibility for the deed. The
story, told from different points of view, is itself a gathering and cumulatively
suggests the coming to awareness of a whole black community. The other
novel, *A Lesson Before Dying,* published a decade later (1993), is even better
and more powerful, but it addresses the same capacity for strength latent in a
black population subdued by generations of servitude.

The ostensible focus of attention here is again upon a young black man
accused of murder, this time a murder he witnessed but took no part in. At
the trial his public defender had represented him as subhuman and incapable
of plotting a crime, but the all-white jury nevertheless convicted him, and the
judge's sentence was death by electrocution. The narrator, Grant Wiggins, a
college-educated black schoolteacher, reluctantly accedes to the request of
the condemned man's godmother that he visit her godson (whose name ironically is Jefferson) in jail and prepare him to die with dignity. In the narrative
that follows Gaines presents the painful process by which Jefferson discovers
his manliness, but more important he portrays a profound transformation in
Wiggins, who in his exchanges with a local minister bent on saving Jefferson's
soul, with others in the community, and with Jefferson himself begins to comprehend the depths of his own ignorance about the nature of humanity and
the loneliness that death compels all human beings equally to confront. With
this latest novel Gaines has confirmed his place among the best contemporary southern writers. Although he has yet to receive a Pulitzer or a National
Book Award, he has been the recipient of honorary degrees, a Guggenheim
Fellowship, a National Endowment for the Arts grant, and a prestigious Mac-
Arthur grant. Among southern black writers he is probably the one for whom
the art of fiction has the most meaning.

PART THREE

*Postwar Development
and Diversification*

10

The South
after World War II

Even before the end of World War II, the South was no longer the Sahara that Mencken back in the twenties had declared it to be. Even so the literary capital of America was still New York, and many of the South's authors were tempted to set up shop either there or at some hospitable location in the North or East. Accordingly, some of its best writers left the region to spend all or part of their careers elsewhere, among them Allen Tate and Caroline Gordon, Robert Penn Warren, John Crowe Ransom (though for different reasons), Katherine Anne Porter, Carson McCullers, and after the war William Styron, Ralph Ellison, Randall Jarrell, Ernest Gaines, and A.R. Ammons.

A typical example was James Agee (1909–55), who except for occasional visits to the South and one protracted stay there at midcareer, spent all but the first sixteen years of his life elsewhere—first in New England attending Phillips Exeter Academy and Harvard, and then mainly in New York, where he served as staff writer for two of the Luce publications, *Fortune* and *Time*. He had been born in Knoxville, Tennessee, and lived there until 1919, when three years after his father's accidental death he moved with his mother to Sewanee, Tennessee, and enrolled in St. Andrew's, an Episcopal school for boys. These two events, the death of his father and his stay at St. Andrew's, resulted in his two principal works of fiction, both autobiographical, *The Morning Watch* (1951) and his more ambitious *A Death in the Family*. The latter was published posthumously in 1957 and awarded a Pulitzer Prize that same year. Earlier, during his tenure at *Fortune*, which for the most part Agee found uncongenial, he had published a collection of poems, *Permit Me Voyage* (1934). In that book he tentatively explored the roots of a melancholia that had plagued him for most of his life and was still plaguing him when in 1936 his editors at *Fortune* sent him to Alabama to do a piece with the photographer Walker Evans on the sharecroppers there.

Once back in the South he began to see more clearly the nature of his uneasiness: so torn was he between feelings of belonging and alienation that he found it impossible to turn out a coherent story on sharecroppers or anything else. Consequently, he began to produce brilliant segments that ultimately, after much torment and struggles with the editors at *Fortune*, he combined with Evans's pictures to make the book that Houghton Mifflin finally published in 1941, *Let Us Now Praise Famous Men*. This work, both as a testament to the dignity of the all-but-forgotten pariahs of South Alabama and as an account of one displaced southerner's desperate but honest attempt to come to terms with his heritage and humanity generally, is a minor masterpiece. Agee originally thought of it as the first installment in a three-part work, but he never completed parts two and three. What remained was the very personal prelude to the two novels he would finish more than a decade later. It was the success of the second of these, *A Death in the Family*, that precipitated the public's "discovery" of Agee two years after his own death and made him briefly a cult figure. Within another decade most of his writings, including his movie reviews for *Time* and five film scripts, were collected and published, and in 1971 Houghton Mifflin brought out a collection of Agee's letters to Father Flye, his priest and mentor at St. Andrews.

Another and very different example of the southern expatriate was Truman Capote (1923–84), whose career in fiction differs from Agee's in almost every conceivable way save one: it too constitutes a postwar shift away from self-conscious Jamesian formalism as prescribed (though not always practiced) by Tate, Gordon, Brooks, and Warren. With the ingenuity of youth, Capote and Agee and others like them in the South were discovering the legitimacy of more mansions in the house of fiction than some of their elders had been willing to acknowledge, and to many of these writers straightforward autobiographical narrative seemed more attractive and far easier to produce than the rigorously dispassionate presentations of action demanded by Tate and Gordon and their mentor Ford Madox Ford.

At least part of the new sense of freedom that now began to permeate the writing community may be attributed to a normal youthful self-centeredness and aversion to discipline, but whatever the cause its appearance signaled the advent of a vogue of confessional literature that was shortly to sweep the country as a whole. With it the line between fiction and reportage would become indistinct, and writers would shortly pass freely between the two territories. An anticipatory example was Capote's largely autobiographical first novel, *Other Voices, Other Rooms*, which created a mild sensation when it appeared in 1948.

Capote was born in New Orleans to parents who divorced when he was four years old. For the next six years he lived with relatives in Alabama and then at age eleven moved north with his mother. There he received an education in private schools and at seventeen began a brief stint with the *New Yorker*, during which he rose from mailing clerk to feature writer and established himself in the role of journalist. After that he returned to New Orleans, but finding New York more to his liking, chose to live either there or abroad for the rest of his life. At first he undertook to turn his Alabama experiences into fiction and wrote those popular books that in the public eye made him forever a southern author; in addition to *Other Voices, Other Rooms*, these include *A Tree of Night and Other Stories* (1949), *The Grass Harp* (1951), and *A Christmas Memory* (1956/1966). To these one should add the central character in *Breakfast at Tiffany's* (1958), which as a whole reflects details from his adult life. Meanwhile he put together a collection of travel sketches that he had written for the *New Yorker* and published as *The Muses Are Heard* (1956) and still later other essays written during his career as a practicing journalist, including memorable pieces on Marlon Brando and Marilyn Monroe in *The Dogs Bark* (1973) and *Music for Chameleons* (1980). Capote appears as himself in a number of these, as he does also in what is perhaps his best-known work, *In Cold Blood*, a superior piece of "fictionalized" journalism dealing with the murderers of a Kansas family in 1959. According to friends and associates, however, Truman Capote's most interesting creation was his own public persona as an eccentric artist about town, party goer, party giver, and perennial gossip—a figure that appears also in some of his writing, though not his most enduring.

Had Agee and Capote, both ambitious men with conspicuous literary talents in addition to their journalistic inclinations and capabilities, remained in the South, they might have found the postwar situation limiting. To be sure, the *Virginia Quarterly Review* had been going since 1925, and the *Kenyon Review*, established in Ohio in 1939 under the editorship of John Crowe Ransom, seemed more likely than most to give a southern writer the benefit of the doubt. Moreover, the best hope of publication in the region, the *Southern Review*, begun in 1935, had ceased publication in 1942, apparently with no hope of renewal; and the long somnolent *Sewanee Review*, although recently brought to new life by Allen Tate during his brief tenure as editor (1944–45), had scarcely begun to make its impact on any but a small coterie of writers. All the other prestigious periodicals were still in the Northeast as were the established publishing houses.

Nevertheless, for those aspiring writers who could afford to wait, hints of change were in the air. By 1947 the *Georgia Review* had made its appearance, to be followed by the *Mississippi Quarterly* in 1948. Then with the growth of higher education in the South during the fifties, established university presses at such places as North Carolina and Louisiana State began to expand. Several new presses were created at that time, as well as a number of new literary journals, among them *Southern Studies* (1961), *Southern Quarterly* (1962),

Southern Literary Journal (1968), and *South Carolina Quarterly* (1969). In addition, the *Southern Review*, considerably expanded and under able new editorship, resumed publication in 1965. These developments, though they were not decisive in transforming the literary climate, were enough to change it from bleak to only partly cloudy.

Of equal importance in the long run were the newly emergent university courses in southern literature, at first mainly in southern institutions but increasingly after 1960 in colleges and universities across the nation and even abroad. Once established, these played a crucial missionary role in the establishment of a public awareness of the unique character of southern literature as a distinct entity that was interesting aesthetically, at least in its more recent developments, with cultural roots significantly different from those that had nourished the literature of the rest of the nation. In 1952 Vanderbilt's Richmond Croom Beatty in collaboration with two of his former students, Floyd C. Watkins and T.D. Young, and with Randall Stewart as advisory editor, had brought out an anthology, *The Literature of the South*, that for several decades (it was revised in 1968) provided a reliable model for those college courses in which much of the popular interest in southern literature would be generated. In addition, the production of supportive works in literary history and criticism in the field was already under way at major universities all across the South. Foremost in this enterprise were such prominent scholars as Jay Hubbell at Duke (already recognized as a pioneer in the field), Richard Beale Davis at Tennessee, C. Hugh Holman and Louis Rubin at Chapel Hill, and Lewis P. Simpson at Louisiana State; and these were by no means alone. By 1968 the rapidly increasing number of workers and students in the field made it feasible to create a Society for the Study of Southern Literature, which within two decades would grow to several hundred members and support valuable bibliographic and reference works.

As the interest in southern literature grew, so for better or worse did the number of aspiring writers. During the late 1930s a few of these had headed uninvited to Baton Rouge, perhaps hoping to benefit there from simple proximity to the brilliant new *Southern Review*, but that opportunity, if it was one, evaporated in 1942. Here and there in southern schools one might find a gifted teacher with a love for writing and a special knack for guiding the young—for example, William Blackburn at Duke or Donald Davidson at Vanderbilt, who was allowed to offer a graduate fellowship in writing once a year—but such people seldom received much recognition for that part of their efforts. Even as late as the 1950s aspiring poets and writers of fiction in southern schools were usually told to consider the graduate writing classes at the University of Iowa.

There were sad precedents for such neglect. Major universities before the war, especially in the South, had not been especially kind to practicing writers. Vanderbilt, for example, had been embarrassed by its Fugitives and made only token objections in 1937 when John Ransom received an opportunity to go north to Kenyon College at a decent salary and establish a literary magazine there that by rights should have been Vanderbilt's. Louisiana State did little better by Brooks and Warren and after the demise of their *Southern Review* made little effort to keep Warren on its campus when he received an offer from Minnesota in 1942 or Brooks when he received one from Yale in 1947. In 1948, however, the University of Florida with the hiring of novelist Andrew Lytle became one of the first of the larger southern universities to follow the lead of the University of Iowa in including writing among its professional disciplines. Thereafter—slowly during the fifties but with quickened pace during the sixties—academia, for better or for worse, became the acknowledged training ground for most, though not all, of the South's new generation of writers. After 1960, with the rapid expansion of graduate work, degree programs in writing became common, varying widely in quality as the school offering them was able to attract writers of some note to its faculty.

With these developments, change and diversification became the order of things, and by 1960 some were preparing to announce a new era in southern letters. Certainly by that time the Vanderbilt version of the New Criticism had all but ceased to be new, and many of the values promulgated by John Ransom, Tate and Gordon, and Brooks and Warren were no longer being taken for granted either by teachers or by their students, many of whom were openly intrigued by the livelier and less orthodox pronouncements of poet novelist-critics such as Randall Jarrell and James Dickey. Moreover, defensive theorizing about the nature of the South, clearly under attack ever since the publication of W.J. Cash's remarkable but iconoclastic *The Mind of the South* (1941), had begun to give way both to the careful scholarship of men like C. Vann Woodward and Lewis Simpson and to the gifted journalism of Mississippians like Hodding Carter (1907–72) and Willie Morris and Arkansas's Shirley Abbott. Henceforth young southern males in the new era would find it easier to respond to Morris's bittersweet autobiography, *North toward Home* (1967), than to the nostalgic essays of Andrew Lytle and John Donald Wade in *I'll Take My Stand*, and southerners of both sexes and all stations would be able to rejoice at the revelations of themselves in Shirley Abbott's brilliant *Womenfolks: Growing Up Down South* (1983), the account—some have said inspired account—of her youth compiled of her own memories and those transmitted by her elders.

To the names of these writers one should add, if space permitted, a host of others who complemented the picture of diversity that increasingly would characterize southern belles lettres in the second half of the century. Several of these, however, demand at least brief notice at this point. Prominent at one end of the spectrum is Robert Drake (b. 1930), native of Ripley, Tennessee, graduate of Vanderbilt and professor at the University of Tennessee, who has produced widely praised collections of engaging and manifestly autobiographical stories about small-town life in an imaginary Woodville, among them *Amazing Grace* (1965) and *Survivors and Others* (1987). Writers in a similar vein who like Drake have concentrated on a single imaginary locale are James Wilcox (b. 1949) with his novels about Tula Springs, Louisiana, and T.R. Pearson (b. 1956), whose fictitious town is Neely, North Carolina; North Carolina's Clyde Edgerton (b. 1944) has written comic novels about the region that evoke comparisons with both Thurber and Mark Twain. Each of these in his distinctive way adds to the picture of southern small-town life that constitutes the basis of some of Peter Taylor's best work and most of Eudora Welty's. Varying the pattern significantly, Randall Kenan (b. 1963), in two important collections, *A Visitation of Spirits* (1989) and *Let the Dead Bury Their Dead* (1992), has concentrated on the community of Tims Creek, North Carolina, and enriched his presentations of local color with a store of information drawn from black folklore and history.

Balancing these portrayals with some from an authentically feminine perspective, we have on the one hand two regionalists, Josephine Humphries (b. 1945), who has written of South Carolina, and Kaye Gibbons (b. 1960), of North Carolina; on the other Annie Dillard (1945), who during the time of her marriage to the professor-poet R.H.W. Dillard, lived at Hollins College, Virginia, and wrote there a series of perceptive and often moving essays about the nonhuman life she had observed in and along the small stream running past her house. These pieces, published in 1974 as *Pilgrim at Tinker Creek*, have made available an aspect of the southern world that far too many, including southerners themselves, take for granted, brought Dillard universal praise, and in 1975 won her the Pulitzer Prize. Another distinctively innovative writer, West Virginia's Jayne Anne Phillips (b. 1952), in her novels and short stories, most notably the recent highly praised *Shelter* (1992), has pressed beyond depictions of the local scene to deal with the intricacies of family life and the agonies attendant on loss of innocence. Similarly, Richard Ford (b. 1944)—like Eudora Welty a native of Jackson, Mississippi, but with a very different perspective—has bypassed local color to deal with more universal themes, depicting in his best-known novel, *The Sportswriter* (1986), a sense of futility identifiable with postmodernism. And Percival Everett (b. 1956), Georgia-born but with even less regional affinity, who in *Suder* (1983) began with a young man's bizarrely comic quest for freedom, has since moved on to deal with traumas confronting a returned Vietnam veteran and the crisis of a physician driven to despair by the specter of contemporary moral disintegration.

In the postwar years several purveyors of journalistic fiction (the "New Journalism") have followed in the wake of Truman Capote's success. The most talented of these has been Virginia's Tom Wolfe (b. 1930), who began as a reporter but soon discovered an idiosyncratic style that he deployed in a series of essays, part satire and part social criticism, which he has since collected in a succession of volumes beginning with *The Kandy-Kolored Tangerine-Flake Streamline Baby* (1965). In 1980 Wolfe received the American Book Award and the National Book Critics Circle Award for his account of the astronauts in *The Right Stuff* (1979) and then in 1987 moved ahead to a satirical novel, *Bonfire of the Vanities*, both of which have been made into popular films. Another journalistic writer of fiction, Winston Groom (b. 1943), has followed a less varied course. Groom has produced novelistic accounts of events in both the war in Vietnam and the Civil War and dealt with the first of these in at least one novel, but his *Forrest Gump* (1986) has overshadowed everything else he has written and become both a best-seller and a prize-winning film (1994).

One contemporary southerner, James Lee Burke (b. 1936), has been successful in the field of detective fiction, evoking in a series of novels about an ex–New Orleans police officer a vivid sense of life in that city and the surrounding bayou country, and at least two academics have successfully melded literary activity with their professional interests. The first of these is the Renaissance scholar Richard Marius (b. 1933), who in addition to solid biographies of Martin Luther and Sir Thomas More has produced a series of novels centered in a fictitious Bourbonville, Tennessee. The other, at the far end of the spectrum of postwar southern diversity, is the brilliant and curiously erudite South Carolinian Guy Davenport (b. 1927), essayist, translator, and all-around man of letters, who has spent most of his professional years teaching at the University of Kentucky. Davenport's work includes, among other things, four collections of his collagelike short stories—*Tatlin! Six Stories* (1974), *Da Vinci's Bicycle: Ten Stories* (1979), *Eclogues: Eight Stories* (1981), and *Apples and Pears and Other Stories* (1984)—and a collection of forty critical and personal essays, *The Geography of the Imagination* (1981). Predictably his subjects in the last of these are mostly literary figures (Whitman, Pound, Melville, Louis Zukofsky, Jonathan Williams, and so on), but he also includes pieces on Louis Agassiz, Charles Ives, the Soviet painter Tchelitchew, the philosopher Ludwig Wittgenstein, Lexington photographer Eugene Meatyard, and the *American Heritage Dictionary of the English Language*.

Poets of this new postwar—some would characterize it as postmodern—era, no longer intimidated by the brilliance of the Fugitives' achievements, have been unwilling to follow slavishly the lead of Ransom, Tate, and the early Warren; and a few whom some critics have ventured to accord a place of permanence in the southern canon—Randall Jarrell, A.R. Ammons, and, for a time at least, James Dickey—have elected to make little overt use of the southern context that produced them. Most, however, including the three just mentioned, have sooner or later manifested their southernness, some by casual allusions and others by occasionally exploring their own early experiences in poems of some length. Nevertheless, all the postwar southern poets are in one way or another beneficiaries of their distinguished predecessors in the twenties and thirties whose pioneering work made it possible for genuine poets at midcentury to claim a habitat, however modest, in the postwar world. What they have not and probably could not have inherited from the older poets is that bone-deep perception of the defining facts and events of an older South that previous generations were able to take for granted. One is reminded that the younger writers, novelists and short-story writers as well as poets—with the possible exception of Jarrell, who spent his formative years in southern California—have all been children of the New South, for whom southern history and southern myth were alike nostalgic curiosities or at best matters of mainly academic interest.

Most of the new poets as a matter of simple survival have found it expedient to accept the relative security of the new posts offered by academia. After teaching several times a week in such havens, the luckier ones among them have often found themselves free to spend the rest of their time writing or, on occasion, traveling about the country reading poems to other poets and their students. This arrangement has not always been good for the health of southern letters, but where poets like Jarrell and Dickey are concerned it sometimes has had the effect of encouraging the production of interesting or even better-than-average poetry by young aspirants with unrealized talent. For a few writers poetry has become an anchor for indulgence in other activities, artistic but nonliterary.

For example, the energetic and multitalented Jonathan Williams (1929–) of the Black Mountain group, in addition to writing poems the most memorable of which preserve the rhythms and nuances of Appalachian dialects in verse that owes more to his mentor Charles Olsen than to any of the older southern poets, became with his brilliantly managed Jargon Press the publisher of some of America's best avant-garde poetry. Another multitalented writer, Kentucky's James Baker Hall (1935–), gifted novelist and short-story writer as well as poet, has achieved distinction as a photographer and in addition to producing shows of his work has taught photography as well as poetry at both the University of Connecticut and the Massachusetts Institute of Technology. Randall Jarrell and his younger Greensboro colleague Fred Chappell (1936–) both turned early to music as an alternative to the poetry and fiction they wrote, and although neither ever aspired to compose or become a performer, both acquired a knowledge of composition and music history not found in many professionals. By contrast Sylvia Wilkinson (1940), Jarrell's pupil at Greensboro, took undergraduate degrees in painting as well as writing and since graduation has produced respectable specimens of both, meanwhile indulging to the full her passionate interest in sports car racing.

So far it is too early to say which, if any, of these newer writers has the genius or the staying power equal to those who made the Southern Renaissance a reality. Nevertheless, several of the older figures—for example, Eudora Welty, Andrew Lytle, and Robert Penn Warren—continued to produce significant work through the seventies and eighties and kept the spirit of the older renaissance alive. Welty, as has been noted, received a Pulitzer Prize in 1973 and other national and international honors well into the nineties. Lytle remained editor of the *Sewanee Review* until 1973 and published *Wake for the Living*, one of his best works, in 1975. Warren, who had received a Pulitzer for his third novel in 1947, another for poetry in 1958, and the distinction of being America's first poet laureate in 1986, would continue to be a major figure on the literary scene until his death in 1989. Three other writers of affinity with these but younger would make strikingly original contributions to the dimensions of southern letters: Shelby Foote, with his monumental history of the Civil War, Walker Percy, author of southern novels mirroring a broader America's spiritual crisis, and Wendell Berry, who in poetry and prose would give a revived agrarianism new meaning and become its national and international prophet. These and a host of other writers, none of whom could remember the renaissance's beginning—William Styron, Ernest Gaines, Reynolds Price, Anne Tyler, Fred Chappell, Cormac McCarthy, Barbara Kingsolver, and Bobbie Ann Mason—would continue to give substance to the argument that the southern literary scene, whatever historians might choose to call it, in an era seemingly dominated by sociological and political imperatives retained much of its old coherence and vitality.

11
Postwar Poetry

As the number of graduate programs in writing increased nationwide after World War II, so did the number of writers with academic credentials in either fiction or poetry. A few found positions in established writing programs, but most simply entered English departments, taught the usual courses in composition and literature, and hoped that courses in creative writing, as it was commonly called, would materialize. The initial result was a modest increase in the audience for poetry, not because of any sudden demand for poetry among the general readership but because of the number of students newly trained to read the kinds of poetry their professors were writing and willing to attend readings and take part in creating journals (usually short-lived) to publish their work. In short, after World War II poetry in America, in the North as well as the South, became and for the most part has remained an academic phenomenon, produced, read, judged, and supported by academic audiences.

A few southerners elected to move out of the region. As already noted, A.R. Ammons (b. 1926), one of the most distinguished, after trying various other careers ultimately accepted a position as poet at Cornell (1964) and has remained there ever since. Another poet, Donald Justice (b. 1925), whose early work bespeaks an admiration for disciplined craftsmanship and delicate irony reminiscent of John Crowe Ransom, followed the customary postwar path through academia. A native of Florida, he earned his bachelor's degree from the University of Miami (1945) and his master's from the University of North Carolina (1947), then studied at Stanford, where he responded positively to the formalism of Yvor Winters, and at Iowa, where he studied under John Berryman, Karl Shapiro, and Robert Lowell and in 1954 earned a Ph.D. Since then Justice has taught at various schools, mainly in the North and West but most recently at the University of Iowa, where since 1971 he has remained. His later work, as beautifully crafted as ever, calls to mind the sparely elegant verse of Wallace Stevens, and principally for that craftsmanship his *Selected Poems* received a Pulitzer Prize in 1980.

In general, however, postwar southern poets have chosen to remain more or less in the region. Occasionally one has circumvented the pattern and managed to develop a career outside academia—for example, Eleanor Ross Taylor, wife of fiction writer Peter Taylor, and Texas-born Vassar Miller (b. 1924), especially noteworthy for the religious aspect of much of her work. Most, however, have settled in colleges and universities in the South: Dabney Stuart at Washington and Lee, R.H.W. Dillard and W.J. Smith at Hollins, Heather Ross Miller at Pfeiffer, Fred Chappell at the University of North Carolina at Greensboro, James Applewhite at Duke, Wyatt Prunty at Sewanee, and James B. Hall at the University of Kentucky. Several have also identified themselves wholly or in part with Appalachia, which after the war quickly established an identity of its own: Western Kentucky University's Jim Wayne Miller, for example, Betty Sellars of Georgia's Young Harris College, and again Fred Chappell, whose verse transcends the regional but often reflects his early years in Canton, North Carolina.

Two black poets have achieved unusual prominence during this period. The first, Maya Angelou (b. 1928), although a native of St. Louis is usually associated with Arkansas, where she grew up in a bleak climate of rural segregation. Not surprisingly the first half of her life was a protracted struggle, and she survived it only after triumphing in a series of encounters that would have brought a weaker person to her knees. In time, however, after putting together a career of sorts as a performer, she became active in the early civil rights movement and attracted the attention of Martin Luther King, Jr., who appointed her northern coordinator for the Southern Christian Leadership Conference (1959–60). Since then she has not lacked either for leadership roles or for public recognition. Angelou's literary career has been primarily an exposition of her life in prose and verse. The first of her five books of autobiography, *I Know Why the Caged Bird Sings* (1970), was an immediate bestseller and remains an essential complement to her *Complete Collected Poems* (1994), which brings together five previous volumes of verse and concludes with the piece she read at the inauguration of President Bill Clinton in 1993.

As a poet, Angelou is popular for several of the reasons that Edgar A. Guest and James Whitcomb Riley became popular. Whatever she writes, though totally unlike their work in subject matter and tone, is simple, unpretentious, and completely accessible, and her poems, taken together, like her prose constitute an optimistic celebration of a life that has refused to be destroyed. The caged bird sings, she declares in one of her best poems, simply because that is the only freedom it has left. Like the bird, her great virtue— and her salvation—has been an ability to accept the conditions dealt her, however grim, with grace, good humor, and an unfailing resourcefulness. Now widely regarded as a role model for repressed womanhood everywhere, Angelou holds the respected position of Reynolds Professor at Wake Forest University in Winston-Salem, North Carolina.

The second black poet to achieve prominence, Louisiana's Yusef Komunyakaa (b. 1947), has done so mainly among critical readers and his fellow writers, who have found exciting his presentation of a southern black's concurrent explorations of the world he remembers from childhood and the largely inhospitable world into which he emerged as a young adult. The verbal underlay of his poems, signaled to the reader by repeated intrusions of black colloquialisms, is presumably that of the primitive who thinks in concrete images, but the images themselves and the mosaiclike patterns into which they fit are the work of a sophisticate, university trained, widely read, and conversant with musicians and painters. The result for some can be puzzling and for others irritating, but the reader who grants Komunyakaa his donnée may find in the body of his poetry an entry into the black experience that is like no other. Five volumes of his work have been published thus far, the last of which, *Neon Vernacular: New and Selected Poems* appeared in 1994 and received in that same year both the Kingsley Tafts Poetry Award and the Pulitzer Prize. In 1985 Komunyakaa was appointed professor at Indiana University in Bloomington.

Another poet with a very different background, Virginia's Henry Taylor (b. 1942), has also created a body of poetry out of his experience, the various contexts for which include his immediate and extended families, the farm where he grew up and worked until college gave him another vocation, the Quaker community that provided the ethical context for his formative years, his love of horses and horsemanship, his circle of friends at college (faculty and colleagues at the University of Virginia and Hollins College's graduate writing program), and his professional associations after graduation. Since leaving Hollins with an M.A. degree in 1966, he has published five volumes of poetry, a textbook, and a collaborative translation of Euripides's *Herakles*. His last volume of poetry, *The Flying Change: Poems* (1984), received the Witter Bynner Prize for poetry, an award from the American Academy and Institute of Arts and Letters (1984), and the Pulitzer Prize (1986). Taylor's work from the outset has exhibited a blend of unobtrusive craftsmanship (simple forms, some poems rhymed and others not) and colloquial speech. In his earliest volume, largely written at Hollins, he indulged in good-humored parodies of friends' work and that of established poets (James Dickey, Howard Nemerov, J.V. Cunningham, George Garrett, Robert Creeley, James Wright, and Robert Bly) and, as was his custom with allusions, naming names in every case. Later he confined his attention to more serious subjects but retained the same good humor and the directness that even then had become his hallmark. That directness, moreover, as some now recognize, is simply one aspect, along with his honesty and lack of pretension, of Taylor's Quaker commonsense acceptance of things as given combined with a semimystical conviction of their ineffable worth. It is also an aspect of his prosody, in which the elegance of precise statement all but obscures the unobtrusive metrical regularity and rhyme that signify a given order of things and their ultimate relatedness. Taylor holds a professorship at the American University in Washington, D.C.

Although most of the postwar poets have seemed content to be thought of simply as poets, a few have ventured into other literary fields, fiction or criticism or both, and at one time or another prompted observers to refer to them as men of letters. Three who have manifestly earned that epithet— Randall Jarrell, James Dickey, and Wendell Berry— will be given extended treatment elsewhere in this study, but two others merit at least a brief examination here. The first is North Carolina's Fred Chappell (b. 1936), whose offhand public manner for a time masked his remarkable productivity, most of it of high quality. The count, however, is now clear: six novels, a collection of stories, a volume of essays entitled (after a passage from Virgil) *Plow Naked* (1993), and ten books of poetry. The unique appeal of Chappell's poetry derives at least in part from a playful inventiveness freely indulged in, a rare eye for significant detail, a fecundity with words matched by few of his contempo raries (R.P. Warren may be one of these), and an ability to integrate the whole with a voice that at once is and is not the voice of Fred Chappell. (The persona he uses is that of "Old Fred" or sometimes "Ole Fred," the rustic from Appalachia, but a sophisticated Chappell, almost never visible in his public demeanor, remains firmly in control.)

Chappell's literary virtues are perhaps most strikingly exhibited in the four volumes of poetry that he published between 1975 and 1980—*River* (1975), *Bloodfire* (1978), *Wind Mountain* (1979), and *Earthsleep* (1980)—all published again as a tetralogy, actually a single long poem, called *Midquest* (1981). Many critics have since commented on the virtuosity he displays in this work: specifically, his ability to move effortlessly from one style to another, in one poem the music of the French symbolists, in another the percussiveness of Anglo-Saxon half lines, and in yet another the witty manipulation of the colloquial idiom after the manner of Auden. Sometimes by subtle allusiveness he manages to invoke two or more of these simultaneously, occasionally throwing in echoes of still other poets he has admired: Virgil, Lucretius, Dante, Milton, Dr. Johnson, or perhaps even Robert Graves.

One of Chappell's fellow poets, Dabney Stuart, in a generous explicatory appreciation (*Southern Review* 27 [1991]) has called attention to the quest that unifies all four parts of the poem, a spiritual one analogous to Dante's but set in solid earth and the context of the present century's expanded awareness, and, as another has noted, a quest that begins and ends in the bed of his devoted wife, Susan. Subsequent volumes of poetry, *Castle Tzingal* (1984), *Source* (1985), and *Spring Garden* (1995), which contains a number of new poems, have continued the same quest on the same terms and with similar skills and invite the conclusion, eminently supportable, that Chappell's work, fiction as well as poetry, will eventually be seen as pieces of one multitextured fabric. Among the many recognitions that have come his way are a T.S. Eliot Award for Creative Writing, a Bollingen Award in 1985, which he shared with John Ashbery, an Aiken-Taylor Award from the University of the South (1996), a prize from the Académie Française, and an Award in Literature from the National Institute of Arts and Letters.

The second southern poet with a substantial claim to the rank of man of letters is George Palmer Garrett (b. 1929), a native Floridian, who began his career with a volume of poetry in 1957 and then with seemingly inexhaustible energy proceeded to add all the other literary strings to his bow: the novel (eight of them), short stories (six volumes), plays (two), biography (James Jones), and an assortment of valuable literary reviews and essays in criticism. That first volume, *The Reverend Ghost: Poems,* was followed within four years by two more, *The Sleeping Gypsy and Other Poems* (1958) and *Abraham's Knife and Other Poems* (1961). Since then he has published several additional volumes, including *For a Bitter Season: New and Selected Poems* (1967). Garrett has been widely praised for wittily amalgamating a remarkable range of impressions—from early life, family legend, travels, experiences in military service, and even the classroom—with an equally wide range of classical myths, biblical stories, and assorted legends. He is also one of the few modern southern poets (Vassar Miller is another notable exception) to exhibit a specifically Christian cast in his work. If in recent years other activities have taken precedence in Garrett's literary production, the course of contemporary poetry remains one of his major concerns and has occupied an important place in his lectures and critical writing. Moreover, being as generous as he is gregarious, he has contributed much in less formal ways over the years to the support and encouragement of other, especially younger, writers.

Of the three postwar poets whose achievements have already clearly earned them the right to be called men of letters, Wendell Berry has tended to regard his poetry, perhaps mistakenly, as secondary to those other interests and activities that give him a special place in southern letters and make it expedient to consider his work as a whole in an extended treatment elsewhere in this survey. Randall Jarrell and James Dickey, however, for all their versatility remain noteworthy primarily as poets and should be looked at here. Finally, still another, A.R. Ammons, who has ranged less widely but nevertheless produced a body of poetry in quality second to none among the work of his contemporaries, is appropriately dealt with in the concluding portion of the present chapter.

RANDALL JARRELL (1914–65)

During the early years of Jarrell's career as a poet, many thought of him as a possible successor to the Vanderbilt Fugitives. To all appearances he had the qualifications for such a role. His birthplace was Nashville, where after an interlude in California with grandparents he had spent his adolescence, graduated from Nashville's prestigious Hume-Fogg High School, and then earned a bachelor's degree at Vanderbilt University. He had majored in psychology rather than literature at Vanderbilt, but as luck would have it, three of his English teachers had been prominent Fugitive-Agrarians, John Crowe Ransom, Robert Penn Warren, and Donald Davidson, who by their example as much as by their instruction prompted him to enroll in the graduate program for a master's degree in English. There he made plans to write a thesis under Ransom's direction on the poetry of W.H. Auden, but with Ransom's abrupt departure for Kenyon in 1937 he followed his mentor north. At Kenyon Jarrell taught for two years as an instructor, completed work on the master's thesis in absentia (on Housman, however, and under Davidson), and began seriously to write poems of his own, twenty of which he published in John Ciardi's *Five Young American Poets* (1940). Finally, when ready to publish his first independent volume, *Blood for a Stranger* (1942), he dedicated it to yet another of the Fugitives, Allen Tate, whom he had known mainly through his poetry.

From this point on, however, Jarrell seems to have taken pains to maintain a discreet distance, at least publicly, between himself and his Vanderbilt predecessors—and, for that matter, from the entire Nashville scene. One might argue that he did so out of an understandable wish to be distinctive in his own right, but he soon extended the distancing to include the entire South and whenever a southern setting was called for in a poem manifestly autobiographical—Texas, Washington, D.C., North Carolina, or wherever—simply denoted it as something incidental to his purposes and interest. In fact, the only American setting he wrote about with any warmth was Los Angeles, where he had spent the happiest months of his early youth. Other than that, the settings he preferred were all European and most of these Austrian or German. His interest in things German, especially German poetry and fairy tales, was also warm, almost passionate, and toward the end of his career he developed a similar interest in Russian life and literature. By contrast, he showed at most a casual interest in things Italian, and in things French scarcely any at all.

Nevertheless, except for a year after the war teaching at Sarah Lawrence College and serving as literary editor for the *Nation*, occasional visiting lectureships, and three trips abroad, Jarrell spent most of his adult life in the South. After his years at Kenyon he taught for a time at the University of Texas, where he married a colleague, Mackie Langham, and saw *Blood for a Stranger* through the press. During the war he served at airfields in Texas, Arizona, and Illinois, and although never in combat or even overseas, he wrote poems that established his reputation as a major poet of World War II. These appeared in two collections, *Little Friend, Little Friend* (1945) and *Losses* (1948), which presented with remarkable empathy a wide variety of characters, male and female, combatant and noncombatant, living and dead, all of whom had been touched in some way by events in the main theaters of the twentieth century's two major wars. Several of the poems showed extraordinary technical skill, especially the much anthologized "Death of the Ball Turret Gunner," perhaps the best known of all Jarrell's poems, and "Eighth Air Force," which he considered most representative of his own attitude toward war and used as lead poem in the war section of his *Selected Poems* (1955). In that poem he speaks as a poet and combat survivor who has come to the realization that he and all his comrades, collectively representative of the human race's last savior, man himself, have actually been mankind's murderers in the missions assigned to them. Accordingly, like Pilate, the speaker declines to judge, but unlike Pilate recognizes that he cannot evade responsibility—that in his case any washing of hands must be done in blood. Thus here, as in the rest of Jarrell's war poems, anger at the senselessness of war is transcended by compassion for the bewildered and suffering human beings trapped in it or victimized by it.

In 1947 both Jarrells accepted positions at the Woman's College of the University of North Carolina (later called the University of North Carolina at Greensboro), where except for a two-year stint as poetry consultant at the Library of Congress and a visiting professorship at Princeton (1951–52) he remained for the rest of his life. In 1952 Jarrell divorced Mackie and married Mary Von Schrader, and their home in the rural surroundings of nearby Guilford College became the setting for some of the happiest and most productive years of Jarrell's life.

To readers acquainted with some of the criticism Jarrell had written up to this time—brilliant but often devastating in its wit—sensitivity to the feelings of others was hardly the quality one might ascribe to the work of this most waspish of prose writers. Yet Jarrell had never forgotten the pain of alienation that growing up in the context of a dysfunctional family and a society suspicious of native genius had imposed upon him, and to his credit even as a witty young adult he usually reserved his stings for the pretentious and for those indifferent to human suffering. In maturity he expended most of his energy conferring the blessings of sympathy and understanding on the humble, the eccentric, and the innocent sufferer. A good example from *Losses* is "Burning the Letters," in which he assumes the persona of the wife of a pilot killed in the Pacific and relives with her the painful process by which she manages to accept his death and the meaning of death itself in human life. One of the poems in *Losses* that had nothing to do with war was an indication of things to come: "Lady Bates," a moving address in child's terms to a little black girl, named "Lady" by southern custom but dead before she "even had [her] hair straightened," in which he acknowledges without condescension the dignity of the limited life the child had led and the heaven she was capable of imagining to be in store for her.

Jarrell's fourth volume of poems, *The Seven League Crutches* (1951), contained some of his richest examples of this kind of empathetic portraiture, and he chose several to represent "Lives" in the first section of his *Selected Poems*. One that he especially liked to read to audiences was "A Girl in a Library," a sympathetic meditation on an adolescent student—student in name only—asleep in the corner of a library, oblivious now and forever to the wealth of past experience at her fingertips but destined to recapitulate, perhaps unknowingly, the essentials of that experience in the life that awaits her. Another is a monologue by the aging Marschallin in Richard Strauss's *Der Rosenkavalier* as she acknowledges but still resists accepting the painful cost of living. The most remarkable of the poems of this kind is "Seele im Raum," in which a former mental patient recalls the time of her illness when she imagined improbably that she owned an African antelope, an eland that lived with the family and partook of their meals at the table. Now recovered, she reflects that her fantastic illusion, even though it grew out of her wretchedness, at least generated the expressions of love from family and friends that made its momentary existence worth all the pain. These poems and others like them—for example, "The Woman at the Washington Zoo," from the collection published under that title in 1960, and the beautiful reminiscence in terza rima of his California youth in *The Lost World* (1965), his final collection—are unlike anything else in southern letters and, for that matter, anything else in the broader range of American literature. They are also representative of the kind of poem Jarrell did best and so probably are among the poems for which he will be best remembered.

From these pieces alone some might launch the argument that Jarrell's primary passion was not poetry but psychology. Undoubtedly, it was a passion during his college days when Vanderbilt's psychology department consisted of a single charismatic teacher, the German-trained Herbert Sanborn, whom he greatly admired. At any rate, thereafter his literary idol and role model was Sigmund Freud, with whom he shared a birthday (May 6), whose works in translation he virtually memorized, and in partial emulation of whom he wore a beard for much of his adult life. Hence it is hardly surprising that he should have written serious dream poems at various times during his career—for example, "90 North" and "The Skaters" from his first collection, "The House in the Wood" from his last, "The Night before the Night before Christmas" with its rare reminiscence of Nashville, and "Windows"—or that he should have turned familiar fairy stories, Hansel and Gretel, Cinderella, Sleeping Beauty, and Cinderella, into perceptive explorations of the dark wood of the human subconscious. Moreover, his skill at analysis, sometimes deployed gratuitously on the psyches of friends and acquaintances, provided the substance and strength of many of his poems, especially those in his last two collections, *The Woman at the Washington Zoo* (1960) and *The Lost World*, in which like Allen Tate before him he resorted to Dante's terza rima as the medium for a deceptively straightforward examination of formative episodes in his own youth. It may be worth noting that the project he most frequently talked about near the end of his life, one that he probably never actually undertook, was an essay in Freudian analysis and corrective interpretation of the poems of T.S. Eliot.

Throughout his life, however, Jarrell had written brilliant essays on a variety of other subjects. His earlier prose pieces, many of them reviews, were collected in *Poetry and the Age* (1953). A second collection containing both literary essays and social criticism, *A Sad Heart at the Supermarket*, came out in 1963, and two volumes of essays appeared after his death, *The Third Book of Criticism* (1969) and *Kipling, Auden & Co.: Essays and Reviews 1935–1964* (1980). When writing as a literary critic Jarrell steadfastly refused to theorize, preferring simply to record, often wittily, his observations about the author at hand, often adding a list of selections to which the reader should pay particular attention. Professional critics, most of them academics, tended to undervalue these pieces at the time of their writing, but Jarrell's lively sallies kept them afloat, and in time the accuracy of most of his judgments have proved their worth.

Jarrell also published fiction and translations. Strictly speaking, the latter, some in prose and some in verse, were mainly adaptations, but he tried his hand at a variety of texts, from Rilke (included mainly, with other translations, in *The Woman at the Washington Zoo*) to Chekhov and gave them all a distinctive new life in English. In 1964 he published two small volumes of children's stories, one from Grimm and the other from Bechstein. His encounter with Chekhov resulted in a version of *The Three Sisters*, performed off-Broadway but published only after his death (1969). The best of Jarrell's fiction, however, was totally his own. Early in the fifties he had announced to his friend Peter Taylor, who by then was an established writer of short stories, that he was putting together a novel. The result, to Taylor's astonishment and gratification, was *Pictures from an Institution* (1954), a brilliant comic novel set in a small southern women's college, rich with recognizable portraits of people Jarrell had known at Sarah Lawrence, Greensboro, and Vanderbilt, and constructed moreover with a precision that should have pleased even the strictest formalist. By any standard it was the best of those novels with an academic setting that were appearing at about the same time; and two years after Jarrell's death John Crowe Ransom, never given to exaggeration in his praise, declared that it just might turn out to be his masterpiece.

Ten years after the novel Jarrell again surprised his friends, this time with *The Gingerbread Rabbit* (1964), a story for young people with illustrations by Garth Williams, which he took a special pleasure in reading aloud whenever a group could be collected to sit at his feet. Meanwhile he had been working hard at another very different kind of story, one ostensibly for children but more appropriate for sophisticated adults, *The Bat Poet*, which came out later in that same year, this time with illustrations by Maurice Sendak. The idea for it had come from a small colony of bats that to Jarrell's great delight had chosen his front porch as their roosting place, and from that germ he developed a fable of the nature of poetry, at least poetry as he understood it, and the role of the poet in his world. Two more so-called children's stories followed, both with illustrations by Sendak. The first of these was *The Animal Family*, published shortly after his accidental death in 1965. It was an eccentric but skillful recasting of the myth of Adam, here presented simply as an unnamed hunter: how he came into the world and acquired an Eve (in Jarrell's version, a mermaid) as a helpmate, how together the two tried unsuccessfully to live on equal terms with the other animals in their world but eventually succeeded in creating a family when a man-child unaccountably arrived to fill the void in their lives. Somewhere during his last years he wrote one other story, *Fly by Night*, a fable in prose and verse about a boy who dreamed he could fly. This work was essentially a private poem recapitulating many of the deep-seated aspirations and fears that had made up the complex personality of Randall Jarrell. It did not appear until 1976, a decade after the author's death.

JAMES DICKEY (1923–97)

After Jarrell the next person to occupy a place of preeminence among southern poets was James Dickey, who in the year of Jarrell's death (1965) had published *Buckdancer's Choice*, his fourth volume, destined a year later to receive a National Book Award. The two men had a few things in common: a Vanderbilt connection, an interest in animals, substantial achievement in the writing of war poetry, and a talent for criticism and fiction as well as for poetry. In their approach to poetry, however, as in their personalities generally, they could hardly have been more unlike.

Dickey was born in 1923 in Buckhead, Georgia, a middle-class suburb of Atlanta, and grew up there. A passionate interest in athletics, especially football, determined his decision in 1942 to enroll at Clemson College in South Carolina, where (it being wartime) his prowess on the gridiron as a freshman was sufficient to warrant early promotion to the varsity. Clemson and football, however, soon gave way to war, and he left at the end of the first season to enlist in the Army Air Corps. Unlike Jarrell, who promptly "washed out," Dickey became a pilot and flew a number of combat missions in the Pacific, including one on the firebombing of Tokyo. Out of these experiences he later created the war poems that are scattered through all the volumes he published during the sixties and seventies.

After the war, he transferred from Clemson to Vanderbilt and there encountered a tradition that sparked his interest in literature. The only one of the Fugitive-Agrarians remaining on campus was Donald Davidson, but Dickey had the good fortune to study also under some of Vanderbilt's younger bright lights: the graduate instructor William Hunter, who gave him free rein in his writing; Vanderbilt's first astronomer, Carl Seyfert, who turned a childhood interest in the mysteries of the cosmos into a lifelong fascination; and Monroe K. Spears, who recognized Dickey's literary talent, read and criticized his early efforts, and convinced him that at least in poetry and fiction the "creative lie" may be a better avenue to truth than strictly matter-of-fact reportage. While at Vanderbilt he married Maxine Syerson, a B.A., and completed his M.A., in that order, and also saw his first publications (in the student literary magazine and in the *Sewanee Review*). With all these credentials he managed to secure an instructorship at Rice Institute, but his stay there was interrupted, first by a recall to service in Korea and then by the offer of a *Sewanee Review* fellowship, which enabled him to spend a year in Europe (mainly in Italy) writing poetry. A similar appointment at the University of Florida in 1956 ended abruptly when Dickey, having offended squeamish listeners at a public reading of his poems, resigned rather than apologize.

For the next few years he successfully pursued a career in advertising, first in New York and then in Atlanta. Nevertheless he continued to write poetry, which in the end won out, with the publication of *Into the Stone* in 1960. Then came *Drowning with Others* in 1962, a Guggenheim Fellowship in Italy in 1961–62, *Helmets* in 1964, *Buckdancer's Choice* in 1965, a National Book Award in 1966, numerous visiting appointments as poet in residence, two years as consultant in poetry at the Library of Congress (1966–68), and in 1967 his first general collection, *Poems 1957–1967*. During this productive period he also served as poetry reviewer for the *Sewanee Review* and published several volumes of essays, the most significant of which was the collection *Babel to Byzantium: Poets and Poetry Now* in 1968.

In Dickey's early reviewing, Jarrell was his acknowledged model, but lacking Jarrell's rapier-like wit he often came across as a hatchet man. Subsequently, with his more tactful observations in *Self-Interviews* (1970) and *Sorties* (1971), he began to fare better. Even here, however, he often ignored, or failed to recognize, the difference between the compelling intensity of his own daily living and that of others and required that poets give priority to their personal experiences, no matter how come by, and present them truthfully and with a vitality sufficient to move ordinary readers. Thus in varying degrees he expressed disapproval of contemporaries (Hecht, Wilbur, and Merrill) who he believed had allowed technical elegance to substitute for straightforward presentation of meaningful experience and dismissed with something like contempt those fashionable confessional poets (Sexton, Plath, and sometimes even Lowell) who in his opinion had merely affected poses of full disclosure or assumed postures of guilt (e.g., for the Holocaust) they had not earned the right to assume.

By 1969 Dickey, aged forty-six, was widely recognized as one of America's leading poets, and in that status he accepted a position as Professor of English at the University of South Carolina. In the view of many of his critics, he was now at the peak of his career. Most would agree that at this point he had established his individuality as a poet and unconsciously laid a groundwork for the different kind of poetry he would write in the two decades following. Some have referred to his work of this period and later as postmodern, a term that in his case is appropriate mainly in a chronological sense. Dickey is best understood as an American romantic, a semisolipsistic Whitman, who writes enthusiastically and without apology of his own experiences and impressions. In *Babel to Byzantium* he declared that his aim had always been "to find some way to incarnate my best moments" and impose them on his readers, "whoever they may be."

Thus it is not surprising that marks of identity abound in his poetry: details of his suburban upbringing and of his family life, references to his penchants for flying, hunting with a bow and arrow, and playing the guitar, as well as evidences of a growing preoccupation with blindness. Yet at no point have Dickey's best moments been limited to the documentable kind of data and

events that the more introspective confessional poets celebrate. His tempera-
ment is one that leads him to seek out new and sometimes bizarre experiences, particularly those involving risk. Where actual participation in such
experiences proves impracticable, he participates vicariously or empathically
by "way of exchange" with other persons, female as well as male, and even
with animals: for example, a Japanese soldier who has served as an execu-
tioner of American prisoners, a fiendish voyeur, a slave owner approaching a
defenseless black woman, a young girl, a deer, a dog, a snake, a shark. Preferably he spreads his mantle of self to encompass creatures that exhibit the
primitive responses and strategies that have enabled them to survive in their
indifferent or even hostile worlds, for as he is fond of saying, he himself is a
survivor—partly by virtue of great good luck, of course, but also by virtue of
his energy, ingenuity, and willingness to ignore the constrictions of custom
and face reality on its own terms.

All this and more can be seen in Dickey's first collection, *Poems 1957–
1967* (1967), in which his explorations of experience are spread out for inspection, many of them experiences by way of exchange and several of them
developed in ways seemingly designed to offend readers easily offended and
accustomed to expecting more restraint and attention to technique from a
southern poet. The first poem in the collection, lengthily but descriptively
titled "May Day Sermon to Women of Gilmer County, Georgia, by a Woman
Preacher Leaving the Baptist Church," presents a speaker who is abandoning
the restrictions imposed by Scripture and church in order to respond to the
higher mandate of her body. Urging her female listeners to do likewise, she
recommends the example of a country girl who has responded to the same
mandate by making love with an itinerant motorcyclist and thereafter, when
her father tried to whip her into submission and penitence, consummates her
liberation by killing the old man, setting all their farm animals free, and flee-
ing with her lover.

An even more remarkable example is the last poem in the collection,
"Falling," in which Dickey re-creates the thoughts, sensations, desperate strategies for survival, and ultimate resignation of a doomed airline stewardess
accidentally swept through an emergency door to her death on the Kansas
plain below. Both of these poems affirm his abiding faith in the human ability
to achieve at least spiritual deliverance from externally imposed restrictions
by violent and, if need be, self-destructive means. His most startling celebration of that same human capacity, however, in this case one by a creature only
semihuman, comes in a shorter poem, "The Sheep Child," which is half a
meditation on country boys' tales about monstrous creatures born of their
indiscriminate copulating and half a meditation by one unfortunate product

of it, a dead sheep child reputedly preserved in alcohol in an Atlanta museum, who triumphs in spite of his insensitive and irresponsible creators.

The same characteristics are manifest in Dickey's commercially successful first novel, *Deliverance*, published in 1970 and rewritten by him for an equally successful movie in 1972. The story in both versions is that of four Atlanta suburbanites—one an accomplished outdoorsman, the other three novices—who undertake to navigate white water in a North Georgia river. During the excursion they are forced to kill two malevolent mountain people who attack them and in the process lose one of their own number. Of the three survivors, Bobby, who has been sodomized by his attacker, simply tries to put the whole affair out of mind; Lewis, the real outdoorsman in the trio, seems to have learned little that he did not already know; but Ed, the narrator, is sadder and wiser, having ensured the survival of himself and his friends and in the process achieved his own deliverance from the protective illusions of a presumably sophisticated society.

Deliverance came under fire from one quarter in particular. By 1970 Dickey had been embroiled for three years in a noisy challenge to his preeminence largely inaugurated by a fellow poet and former friend, Robert Bly, and vigorously perpetuated by partisans of the New Left. Bly had charged, among other things, that *The Firebombing*, Dickey's lead poem in his award-winning *Buckdancer's Choice*, manifested the crass insensitivity that many believed had characterized America's intervention and participation in the war in Vietnam. On that score Dickey was probably guilty as charged, but few in America at the time were prepared to acknowledge that insensitivity had played any part in the bombing of Tokyo. Nevertheless, his critics had other excuses for their displeasure and made the most of them: Dickey's fondness for semiviolent activities (particularly athletics, archery, and blood sports), his celebration of acts of violence in his poetry, his blunt and outspoken criticism of other writers in the *Sewanee Review*, and above all his phenomenal popularity, which seemed to validate the things about him they found most offensive.

In addition, some of the more determined detractors, disregarding Dickey's strong support of Eugene McCarthy's bid for the presidency in 1968, noted that he was a southerner and automatically representative of a region notorious for its "redneck" behavior and attitudes. Thus the popular success of the manifestly violent *Deliverance* added fuel to a fire that was fanned still further by the novel's success as a movie with Dickey himself performing convincingly in the role of Sheriff Bullard. The controversy did little to deter Dickey, who continued to write and publish as before, but it helped to confirm a growing division among readers, even in the South, some admiring his work extravagantly and others professing to despise it. In 1976 his admirers won a victory of sorts when they persuaded the newly elected southern president Jimmy Carter to have Dickey read a poem, "The Strength of Fields," at an inaugural celebration.

Nevertheless, with the publication of *The Eye-Beaters, Blood Victory, Madness, Buckhead and Mercy,* Dickey's poetry had taken a different direction, or so he later declared. Up to this point, he had been writing anecdotal narratives; now, he said, he would turn to new subjects and new methods. The new methods, however, at least with respect to form, mainly involved abandoning what he called the "block format" (that is, lines of predictable length arranged more or less in stanzas) in favor of a freer arrangement of lines of irregular length, sometimes split to indicate units of stress, often with three beats to the line. A few of the poems in this mode can properly be classified as shaped verse, depending for their total effect on the appearance of the poem on the page, but most seem to have been shaped for dramatic effect, letting the spaces contribute as meaningfully as the words. The poem that Dickey later singled out as illustrative of his change in method was "Pine," a piece of some ninety-four lines in which by the use of associational imagery he suggested the speaker's identification with a stately tree. Several of the others are startling after Dickey's earlier manner: "Diabetes" and "The Cancer Match," in which he presents a speaker's accommodation to the threat of disease; "Mercy," the account of a more or less desperate assignation in a nurses' dormitory; "Madness," an account of a household pet's fatal encounter with rabies; and "Eye-Beaters," in which the speaker visits an orphanage where a group of blind children have to be restrained from beating their sightless eyes to produce an illusion of light. In most of these poems the persona appears to be a thinly disguised image of Dickey himself, explicitly so in the poem "Messages," addressed to his sons, and "Two Poems of Going Home," which celebrate a return to his native Buckhead.

Dickey's next two collections, properly so termed, *The Strength of Fields* (1979) and *The Eagle's Mile* (1990), created less stir among critics and readers than had the earlier, more spectacular volumes. The first of these has been commended for its subdued tone of acceptance, and the second for its abandonment of what had seemed to some an unnecessary straining of syntax to the point of unintelligibility. *Strength of Fields* contains both the poem he wrote for President Carter's inaugural celebration and his respectable but not altogether successful efforts at translation. In *The Eagle's Mile* a lyrical capability not evident in much of Dickey's earlier work manifested itself, nowhere more effectively than in the title poem, addressed with obvious admiration to the late semiblinded Justice William O. Douglas, whose physical prowess and courage had become legendary. Both collections indicate a deliberate movement toward resolution of tensions in the author and his poetry as well as in the speakers represented.

During this period Dickey published two other volumes of poetry, *Zodiac* (1976) and *Puella* (1982), both major contributions to his canon. The first of these was a translation (more properly an imitation, as Dickey himself noted) of a poem by the late Hendrik Marsman. In Dickey's version the voice of the drunken narrator seems to be that of the frustrated poet himself, at last in command of a suitable medium but desperate to relate it and himself in some meaningful way to the universe. Like other contemporary long poems with which admirers have compared it—Crane's *The Bridge*, Eliot's *Four Quartets*, and Tate's *Seasons of the Soul*— Dickey's poem represents an attempt to objectify a personal crisis that had been mounting over the years. Predictably, like his predecessors, he was only partially successful in this objective. Nevertheless, the poem moves in the direction of an acceptance of the human condition which continues in the volumes that follow.

Acceptance, however, implies a fullness of knowledge that thus far was lacking. Coincidentally in 1976, the year of the publication of *Zodiac*, Dickey's wife Maxine had died of cancer, and this painful loss may have forced recognition of a personal deficiency that had gone unnoticed. In any case, on marrying again the following year, he undertook the composition of a sequence in which he temporarily abandoned his male perspective and adopted that of his second wife, Deborah. This series of poems, in which he presents by means of an increasingly complex nexus of images her development from girlhood to womanhood, is among his most difficult and is accessible principally to the minuscule audience willing and able to participate in the rigors of creative reading. Yet these poems are a necessary complement to the progression of Dickey's previous poetry and essential to an understanding of his work as a whole.

Puella was published in 1982, but Dickey had already begun to think of his poetic output as a work of coherence. In 1981 he reissued two of his earliest volumes as *The Early Motion: Drowning with Others and Helmets*. Two years later he published a second collection, *The Central Motion: Poems, 1968–1979*, and in 1992, just short of his seventieth birthday, a third, entitled *The Whole Motion: Collected Poems, 1945–1992*. In addition to poetry and essays, Dickey in these years went on to publish two more novels, both reflective of his own wartime experiences. The title of the first, *Alnilam* (1987), refers to the central star in the belt of Orion. It is the story of the renewal of one Frank Cahill who, having fallen victim to diabetes and blindness, hears of the death of his son Joel whom he has never known or even seen and goes in search of a clearer vision of the dead young man as the star that may possibly give meaning to his life. The second, *To the White Sea* (1993), is at least ostensibly another survival story: the account of a flyer shot down over Tokyo who survives the subsequent firebombing and pursues a murderous course northward toward the island of Hokkaido and a surprise ending. Neither novel has met with the success of Dickey's *Deliverance* or added appreciably to his stature as a writer of fiction. For most readers he remains the writer of a unique body of poetry—inventive, vigorous, sometimes violent, occasionally offensive, and always interesting.

A.R. AMMONS (B. 1926)

Archie Randolph Ammons is vastly different from his two slightly older contemporaries in that his preparation for poetry seems to have been prompted by no particular mentor or tradition but resulted as the unanticipated by-product of an attempt by a hardheaded pragmatist to understand the world around him and assess his own relation to it. In other words, Ammons, coming relatively late to poetry, began at a point that both Jarrell and Dickey reached much later in their careers. Apparently the production of poems of competitive character and quality was no significant part of Ammons's initial aim. Thus his first volume, *Ommateum* (1955), privately printed and put together for mainly private reasons, attracted little attention. Nearly ten years elapsed before he was ready to declare himself a poet and publish another, *Expressions of Sea Level* (1964)—this time, however, with a respected university press. In the same year, Ammons, aged thirty-eight, joined the faculty of Cornell University as an instructor; since then he has written and published steadily, maintaining thereby a development as thinker and writer that seems likely to continue indefinitely.

During the almost forty years that have elapsed since the publication of *Ommateum*, Ammons has produced some twenty-two volumes of new poetry and collections of poetry and gathered an impressive array of awards. For his *Collected Poems: 1957–1971* (1972) he received his first National Book Award for Poetry (1973). The following year for *Sphere: The Form of a Motion* (1974) he received the 1973–74 Bollingen Prize in Poetry. In 1981 for *A Coast of Trees* (1981) he won the National Book Critics Circle Award for Poetry, and for *Garbage* (1993), a second National Book Award. Ammons's most recent volume, *Brink Road: Poems* (1996), is a collection of more than 150 new and previously uncollected poems, all written since 1973, that testifies to the wide range and continuing excellence of his work. Important recognitions that have come his way, in addition to the awards for individual volumes already mentioned, include a Guggenheim Fellowship, a Levinson Prize, a Lannan Foundation Award, a MacArthur Prize Fellow award, a Robert Frost Medal from the Poetry Society of America, an award from the National Institute of Arts and Letters, and honorary degrees from Wake Forest University and the University of North Carolina at Chapel Hill.

The experiences that molded Ammons's unique sensibility began in his birthplace, Columbus County, North Carolina, an essentially rural part of the state near enough to the ocean to allow him to partake routinely of its sand, sounds, and salt sea breezes. After high school he worked briefly in a shipyard, spent two years in the U.S. Navy, and attended Wake Forest College (then still at Wake Forest, North Carolina), from which he graduated in 1949 with a B.S. in science. For the next fifteen years he did a variety of things, serving briefly as the principal of an elementary school at Hatteras on the Outer Banks, attending the University of California at Berkeley for a year, and working as an executive in a New Jersey firm that manufactured biological glassware. Somewhere in these early stages of his career he achieved the maturity as a poet that is exhibited in *Expressions of Sea Level*. In any case, once established at Cornell, he managed in less than a decade both to rise to the rank of Goldwin Smith Professor of Humanities and to establish himself as one of America's leading poets. More recently he has begun to establish himself in a parallel career as a painter.

Ammons's poems come in a variety of shapes and sizes: epigrams and small haiku-like pieces, book-length poems, long verse essays, and medium-sized meditative lyrics, frequently on some aspect of nature visually perceived. These according to several critics place him in a "practical-visionary succession" of poets that includes Emerson, Wallace Stevens, and William Carlos Williams. The classification serves well enough, provided one emphasizes the word "succession." Ammons resembles his predecessors in various ways but derives from none of them. He also resembles Walt Whitman (another practical visionary, at least in a collateral line) in that he usually writes from a personal point of view, although without Whitman's garrulity and exaggerated ego. With Ammons, singing of self is not assertiveness but simple honesty. In his scheme of things the poems that he presents for inspection have all been developed by a mysterious process of accretion in the "sound stream" (his own term) of a unique consciousness (he would consider all consciousness unique); since he is the only one who can possibly be speaking in them, in his more recent works he has avoided making suggestions to the contrary.

Early in his practice he abandoned the use of personae (no more "I am Ezra," as in early poems) and took to writing in a personal idiom that increasingly he has made even more recognizable by expressions, terms, and specific data from the various areas of his experience: rural east Carolina, the shipyard, and the navy, as well as his successive immersions in scientific study, life in New Jersey, and the provincial climate of American academia. Nevertheless, whether drawing images from the sea or New Jersey or the closed world of the university, he has remained the born southerner, tempering his images of alien settings and climates with images from a reservoir filled during his Carolina youth and salting the whole with southern colloquialisms and circumlocutions. Understandably some of his longer works—specifically *Tape for the Turn of the Year* (1965) and *Garbage* (1994)—have been labeled diaries in verse, but Ammons has always been a diarist of sorts, each poem, long or short, reflecting a transaction between himself and some other aspect of reality.

As a practical thinker Ammons also resembles certain of his predecessors but again derives directly from none of them. For example, the classical philosopher he most obviously resembles is Heraclitus, an echo of whose familiar "You cannot step twice into the same river" the careful reader will detect in the concluding lines of one of his best-known poems, "Corsons Inlet." Thus prompted, the same reader may go on to find similar parallels throughout the poems between Heraclitus's ever-flowing universe indifferent to human concerns and the world of Ammons's poetry. A modern philosopher whom he frequently calls to mind is Alfred North Whitehead, whose presentation of nature as a weblike process of infinite complexity in which the entities we perceive are continually being born, maturing, and perishing bears at least a superficial resemblance to the universe we infer from Heraclitus's fragments. Whitehead, however, does not fit comfortably into the context of twentieth-century existentialism, which is the real matrix of Ammons's thought. There, for all his scientific training as an undergraduate, he shares with Heidegger, Sartre, and Camus the view of an irrational universe and a humankind liberated, sometimes in fear and trembling, from its long Platonic dream. In poem after poem he presents the world as a place where Being is no philosopher's abstraction but the materiality we see and hear and touch, and that materiality, mysterious and magnificent in its indeterminacy, has been his tutor. From it he has learned to accept each ephemeral event or thing—stone, spider's web, goldfinch, or holly tree—as being "totally its apparent self," requiring no philosophy or metaphysical apologetic to justify its existence. More important, he has learned therefrom to avoid the futility of assuming that all things must be part of some larger scheme and to acknowledge that each entity—man, beast, bird, insect, or stone—has equal dignity and the freedom to exist as it will. In his philosophy, if one may call it that, there are no walls, no boundaries, no finality of vision, and the honest observer settles more or less contentedly for a stance of humility and patience before the spectacle of eternal becoming.

Ironically, maintaining a stance of humility and patience before the inevitable almost automatically made Ammons a rebel at the time of his setting forth. In his view a poem is a free entity like everything else but at the same time a transitory process reflective of the activity of an inquiring mind in its continuing attempt to grasp momentary completions in the flux of existence. That viewpoint put him at variance with the exponents of a prevailing formalism who tended to see the ideal poem as an end in itself, an artifact sub specie aeternitatis, something to be valued as an organic entity rescued from time and mortality. Ammons's initial bow to formalism consisted of roughly symmetrical stanzas in some of his shorter lyrics, but even in these what appear to be formal elements turn out for the most part to be anomalies, like the superficial resemblances one sometimes encounters between plants and animals of the different species. In 1963–64 he tried abandoning customary conventions altogether and wrote a long verse diary covering some thirty-five days on a roll of adding-machine tape, letting the width of the paper be the formal limit for the length of the lines. The result was *Tape for the Turn of the Year*, a caricature of formalism, unfair perhaps but a remarkable demonstration of what poetry at its best is to him: the unpretentious, straightforward rendering in language of an active mind's continuing attempt to bring the ever-changing aspect of reality into focus.

One enthusiastic admirer has credited Ammons here and elsewhere with repudiating the ironic strategies that characterized the work of those established poets who at war's end would continue for a time to dominate the literary scene. If so, he was probably unaware of it. A nonconformist by nature, Ammons has always done what came naturally to him. At any rate, he has never repudiated irony itself, as a number of his passing observations about pretentious poets (unnamed) and about critics who fancy their kind of activity as superior should make clear. As a poet he stands at the opposite end of the spectrum from John Ransom, but he resembles Ransom in his preoccupation with ontology, in his fundamental seriousness, and in his honesty. The main business of a poet, Ammons has said, is "to put things together and touch a source that feels like life." At least half a dozen of his best pieces do that as well as any written in America during this century, among them "Gravelly Run," "Still," "Corsons Inlet," "The Arc Inside and Out," and "Easter Morning." When poems such as these appear, the South can take pride but hardly claim exclusive rights.

12
Mainstream Fiction

During the midfifties, as the dislocations of wartime were disappearing, south-ern writers quickly resumed their modest place in the book lists of commer-cial publishers, practically all of which were centered in New York. The an-cient argument that northern publishers were sectionally discriminatory, if it had ever had much validity, now had virtually none at all. At first, authors who displayed a regional orientation fared best, particularly those who were able to cater to a national taste for fiction with a romantic appeal. A good example of an older author who consistently turned out commercially profitable work, and one whose popularity survived World War II, is Frances Parkinson Keyes (1885–1970), who from 1919 until the time of her death published more than fifty volumes of fiction, biography, and travel, the most memorable of which dealt with New Orleans, where she lived for many years. A less prolific example is Margaret Mitchell (1900–49), whose lone novel, *Gone With the Wind* (1936), became an international best-seller, received a Pulitzer Prize in 1937, and as a 1939 film destined for perennial popularity garnered ten Academy Awards.

Another and better writer than either of these, although less prolific than Keyes and less popular than Mitchell, was Marjorie Kinnan Rawlings (1896–1953), discussed in a previous chapter, who celebrated a small segment of wilderness Florida in her works, notably *Cross Creek* (1942) and before that *The Yearling* (1938), for which she too received a Pulitzer Prize. Then there was Rawlings's contemporary, Lillian Smith (1897–1966), temporarily famous, or notorious, for her first novel, *Strange Fruit* (1944), with its sympathetic treatment of a love affair between a white man and a black woman. Popular but, perhaps as a consequence of deliberate discretion, hardly notorious was Georgia's Frank Yerby (b. 1916), black author of authentically historical ro-mantic novels about the Old South, who moved to Spain and continued year after year to turn out popular successes, mainly with white characters in them. Three of Yerby's works have deservedly received critical praise: *The Foxes of Harrow* (1946), *The Vixens* (1947), and *Pride's Castle* (1948). Earlier he had written of racial matters in his native Georgia, but once established in Europe he seldom dealt with race or depicted black characters. An exception is *Speak Now* (1969), one of his best, which has its setting in contemporary Paris.

The popularity in the marketplace of all these authors continued well into the postwar years, but as one would expect with the decline of popular taste for regional color and costume narratives, younger writers with a fondness for contemporary interests and settings have since tended to replace them. One novel that achieved immediate success was Harper Lee's lone attempt in the form, *To Kill a Mockingbird* (1960), the story of a young lawyer's brilliant but unsuccessful defense of a black man in a small Alabama town. Lee's novel won numerous awards including a Pulitzer Prize in 1961. In 1962 a screen version by Horton Foote received an Academy Award, as did Gregory Peck, who portrayed the young lawyer. A new writer whose productivity has continued and whose esteem among critics has lately matched her public popularity is Anne Tyler (b. 1935), pupil of Reynolds Price, the successor to William Blackburn at Duke. Tyler is actually a native of Minnesota, but she grew up in North Carolina and has spent the years of her married life in Baltimore. Her short stories (still uncollected) and eleven novels reflect a familiarity with both of these places. Baltimore, however, is the setting for the two novels that marked Tyler's emergence as a writer of stature, *Dinner at the Homesick Restaurant* (1982) and *The Accidental Tourist* (1985). Both of these exhibit the qualities that distinguish all her work and give it, at least potentially, a place in the canon of the South's better writing: honest and accurate presentation of scenes and people, a fine sense of form unobtrusively maintained, and a perception of the action or actions that can develop credibly from the characters she has chosen to portray. Frequently her characters are reclusive and ill at ease with the society that surrounds them, but Tyler, unlike some of her contemporaries, has chosen to focus on their unawakened compassion and innate ability to make accommodations. Consistently in her work she affirms the possibilities of rebirth and renewal.

Other competent writers—Gail Godwin (b. 1937), Alabama-born but reared in North Carolina, Georgia's Pat Conroy (b. 1945), and Arkansas's John Grisham (b. 1955), have found considerably less favor with literary critics than Tyler but have enjoyed greater commercial success. One reason is that all three of these have written principally to provide readers with some form of diversion, made no special demands upon their attention, chosen subject matter of current and general interest, and kept the plot lines clear and uncluttered. Nevertheless, although southerners by birth and upbringing, they have made no essential use of their heritage—unless their penchant for storytelling be considered a part of that. In most of their works the South, when it appears, is simply an incidental aspect of the whole. Both Godwin and Conroy in such best-sellers as Godwin's *Glass People* (1972), *The Finishing School* (1985), and *Father Melancholy's Daughter* (1991) and Conroy's

The Great Santini (1976) and *Prince of Tides* (1986) have proved especially adept at presenting the intricacies of family relationships. John Grisham, by profession a lawyer, in six novels has shown himself to be the current master of the tale of suspense. All his works have sold well, among them *The Firm* (1991), *The Pelican Brief* (1992), and *The Rainmaker* (1995). Both he and Conroy have seen their novels made into successful films.

George Garrett (b. 1929), Florida-born novelist and all-round man of letters, after making moderately successful fiction out of his experiences in the South and elsewhere, achieved his most notable commercial successes with a series of historical novels about Elizabethan England. Garrett's first published work of fiction, *King of the Mountain* (1957), contained memorable short pieces made out of his experiences in the occupation forces serving in Yugoslavia and Austria during the time of the Korean War. By that time he had also published his first two volumes of poetry, earned an M.A. at Princeton, and accepted a teaching position at Wesleyan University in Connecticut. During his Wesleyan years, partially spent abroad on an award from the American Academy and a *Sewanee Review* fellowship, Garrett published his first novel, *The Finished Man* (1959), about Florida politics, and set to work on a second collection of stories, *In the Briar Patch*, which he published in 1961. More important, he also wrote (on the kitchen table, he later said) his war novel, *Which Ones Are the Enemy?*, published in 1961 but not fully recognized as an achievement of consequence until Southern Methodist University combined it with several short pieces, some previously published and some unpublished, and brought out the whole as *The Old Army Game*, with an introduction by George Core, in 1994.

In 1965 he published his technically most ambitious novel to date, *Do, Lord, Remember Me*, the story of an itinerant evangelist and faith healer, Red Smalley, who made his climactic last stand in the small southern town of High Pines. Six narrators participate in the telling—Smalley himself, the three members of his entourage, a local shopkeeper, and a nymphomaniac who has joined them seeking a cure. These characters narrate by turns the mildly sensational goings-on, usually with straightforward narrative but sometimes interspersed with stream-of-consciousness passages. The climax comes as Smalley in a protracted monologue lays bare the complex and conflicting impulses that are driving him to destruction. Critics were impressed by Garrett's performance but not enthusiastic, and he turned once more to short fiction and poetry. In 1971, however, he startled even some of his southern colleagues by publishing *Death of a Fox*, a novel, again with multiple points of view, on the last two days of Sir Walter Ralegh.

Perhaps buoyed in part by the critical and popular success of this enterprise, he produced two more Elizabethan novels, *The Succession: A Novel of Elizabeth and James* (1985) and *Entered from the Sun* (1991). Meanwhile he continued to write witty criticism of a high order and shorter pieces about the South. His latest novel, *The King of Babylon Shall Not Come Against You* (1996), marks a return to the southern setting and methods of his earlier work. Both in variety and in quantity Garrett's productivity in fiction has been remarkable to say the least: twenty-five books, eight of them novels. Many recognitions have come his way, including in addition to those already mentioned a PEN/Malamud Award and Guggenheim, Ford, and National Education Association fellowships. He has lectured and taught widely and most recently held the Henry Hoyns Chair of Creative Writing at the University of Virginia. In addition, for the past thirty years Garrett, more than any other single writer, has been a lively and salutary presence on the southern literary scene.

Garrett's slightly younger contemporary and friend, North Carolina's Fred Chappell (b. 1936), already noted as being especially distinguished for poetry, began as a writer of fiction and has continued with a series of novels and stories that some consider his finest achievement. The novels began appearing first: *It Is Time, Lord* (1963), *The Inkling* (1965), *Dagon* (1968), and *The Gaudy Place* (1973), at which point critics began to take serious notice. In 1980 a number of the stories, some reflective of his North Carolina upbringing and others, imaginative reconstructions (among them Ben Franklin and Franz Josef Haydn), were published as *Moments of Light*. A second volume of stories, *More Shapes Than One*, came out a little more than ten years later (1990).

Chappell's most accessible work and perhaps his best, *I Am One of You, Forever*, some of it previously published as short pieces, came out in 1985 to general acclaim, followed by a sixth novel, *Brighten the Corner Where You Are* (1989). In 1987 St. Martin's Press published *The Fred Chappell Reader*, an anthology consisting of some of his best poetry, the novel *Dagon* reprinted in full, selections from four other novels, and a selection of his short stories. Most of Chappell's fiction is reminiscent of his own life in some way, frequently in a combination of ways: his early years in rural western North Carolina; his youthful fascinations with science fiction, the modern existential novelists, and the macabre; his uneasy adolescence, which brought him into contact with the small-town street life of which he gives a brilliant account in *The Gaudy Place*; and his accommodation with the academic world. Critics and readers alike, however, have responded most enthusiastically to his presentations of Appalachia, comparing these to the work of Faulkner, Eudora Welty, and Mark Twain.

Of course, much of the fiction that appeared at the outset of what has come to be called the postmodern era was not by new authors, certainly not by authors who could be fitted into that classification. Throughout the period two established novelists continued to hold places of prominence. From 1950 to 1977 Robert Penn Warren wrote seven more novels, all of them competent work and at least three strong enough to be remembered along with his *All the King's Men*. And Eudora Welty, having begun to receive a measure of popular attention with her short novel *The Ponder Heart* in 1954 and even more with the dramatic adaptation that ran on Broadway in 1956, brought out her most finished collection of stories, *The Bride of the Innisfallen*, in 1955 and then after a long interval her most ambitious novel, *Losing Battles*, in 1970. For *The Optimist's Daughter* two years later she received a Pulitzer Prize.

A third major figure, Flannery O'Connor, in the brief span of life allotted to her (she died in 1964 aged thirty-nine) published only two novels and two collections of stories, yet throughout the sixties and seventies it was O'Connor who dominated the literary scene both regionally and nationally, and apparently she has assumed a permanent place there as a major southern author. As literary artists, however, these three stayed recognizably within the Flaubertian tradition as it had been continued by Henry James and Ford Madox Ford and popularized in America by the textbooks of Brooks and Warren and Caroline Gordon and Allen Tate. Other writers in the same tradition who emerged during this period are themselves now recognized as literary artists: John Barth, Elizabeth Spencer and Elizabeth Hardwick, both noted previously, and William Styron and Reynolds Price, both protégés of Duke University's William Blackburn. Still others, Shelby Foote, Walker Percy, and Wendell Berry, who have published major fiction during this period but have distinguished themselves in unique ways are dealt with at length in other sections of this survey.

A number of writers with talents that vary in kind as well as degree—men and women, white and black, and hailing from all parts of the South—have achieved momentary prominence but still lack general recognition. Some of these have written both short fiction and novels and a few, as has been noted, poetry and short fiction as well. One writer who had begun to publish poetry and short fiction shortly before World War II was Hubert Creekmore (1907–66), a native of Water Valley, Mississippi. Creekmore studied at the universities of Mississippi and Colorado, Yale, and Columbia (M.A., 1940) before interrupting his stride to serve three years in the navy. In 1946 he came into national prominence with the publication of his first novel, *The Fingers of Night*, set in the Mississippi hill country, and achieved distinction with a third, *The Chain in the Heart* (1953), which deals with three generations of a black family. For a time thereafter Creekmore turned to scholarly editing and translating but was resuming his writing at the time of his death. A somewhat younger writer, who actually developed his craft while serving in the navy, was William Goyen (1915–83), born at Trinity, Texas, and educated at Rice University. Although Goyen published three novels during his career, the short story was the form best suited to his talents. His repeated use of bizarre characters and situations prompted early critics to resurrect for him the term Southern Gothic, but it soon became clear that Goyen was also adept at presenting the life of east Texas and exploring intricate family relationships there. Much of his best work appears in *The Collected Stories of William Goyen* published in 1975.

Another writer whose work has received, at least occasionally, the epithet Southern Gothic is Atlanta's Calder Willingham (b. 1922). By any measure Willingham has proved one of the most prolific of the new writers of fiction, with nine novels and numerous short stories to his credit. One of his more ambitious longer works, *Eternal Fire* (1963), combines an array of Gothic devices with broad humor, but Willingham's most memorable work to date is still his first novel, *End as a Man* (1947), a satiric treatment of life in a southern military academy. He has since been successful as a writer of screenplays: *One-Eyed Jacks* (1961), *The Graduate* (1967), and *Little Big Man* (1970). Possessor of a wider range of talents although somewhat less prolific, Guy Owen (1925–81) turned his North Carolina tidewater country into a fictional Cape Fear County and made it the setting for a remarkable series of poems and novels, the most popular of which was the rollicking account of the adventures of one Mordecai Jones, *The Ballad of the Flim-Flam Man* (1965), almost immediately made into a successful movie. Owen's last novel, *Journey for Joedel* (1960), consisted of a penetrating portrait of a young boy from one of North Carolina's Lumbee Indian communities and gave promise, unfortunately cut off by Owen's untimely death, of even more powerful things to come.

Two other promising writers cut off by death even earlier in their careers were John Kennedy Toole (1937–69) and Breece D'J Pancake (1952–79). Toole had published virtually nothing at the time of his death, and his Pulitzer Prize–winning novel, *A Confederacy of Dunces* (1980), a simultaneously funny and sad satire on modern times set in New Orleans, saw the light of day only as a consequence of his mother's persistence and the support of the novelist Walker Percy. Pancake, a West Virginian, was a student in the University of Virginia's writing program and already publishing short stories of professional quality, mainly in the *Atlantic*, when he took his own life.

Two more locally prominent writers were at one time or another students of Vanderbilt's Donald Davidson. Walter Sullivan (b. 1924), now professor at

Vanderbilt, has written three creditable novels, notably *Sojourn of a Stranger* (1957), *The Long, Long Love* (1959), and most recently *A Time to Dance* (1995), by any measure his best to date, which makes one regret the long interval when no novel was forthcoming. Sullivan has also written a remarkable book of reminiscence, *Allen Tate: A Recollection* (1988), and three books of criticism that have established him as one of the more conservative Christian interpreters of southern letters. His friend and onetime fellow student, Madison Jones (b. 1925), since 1956 at Alabama's Auburn University, is the respected author of some seven novels, among them *The Innocent* (1957) and *A Cry of Absence* (1971), and occasional critical essays, notably on R.P. Warren and on Andrew Lytle, under whom he also studied.

Several other producers of substantial work and perpetuators of the southern tradition of storytelling deserve mention in any review of postwar writers of fiction: David Madden (b. 1933), a Knoxvillian, onetime assistant editor of the *Kenyon Review*, and author of seven novels and a collection of short stories, now settled at Louisiana State University; Andre Dubus (b. 1936), a Louisianian, once writer-in-residence at the University of Alabama, now a resident of Massachusetts, author of one novel and a collection of essays but primarily known for several collections of distinguished stories; Barry Hannah (b. 1942), professor at the University of Mississippi, winner of the Faulkner Prize for his first novel, *Geronimo Rex* (1972), and author of several more novels and collections of stories; Madison Smartt Bell (b. 1957), a Tennessean successfully transplanted in the Northeast, which is the setting for much of his work, versatile author of novels and short stories; and Mary Ann Taylor-Hall (b. 1938), a Floridian transplanted in Kentucky, wife of author James Baker Hall, and author herself of several well-crafted stories and a remarkable first novel, *Come and Go, Molly Snow* (1995).

Two native Kentuckians, both former holders of Wallace Stegner Fellowships at Stanford, Ed McClanahan (b. 1932) and Gurney Norman (b. 1937), have produced work that sets them apart from most of their contemporaries as regionalists reminiscent of those that flourished at the turn of the century. Ed McClanahan, who willy-nilly revived the tradition of the Old Southwest humor that nourished Mark Twain and later the Kentucky humorist Irvin S. Cobb, has demonstrated his unique talents in a remarkable collection of sketches, *Famous People I Have Known* (1985). These talents are best displayed in the painstakingly crafted *The Natural Man* (1983), an often hilarious but frequently perceptive account of the growing up of one Harry Estep of a mythical Needmore in a mythical Burdock Country, Kentucky. To amplify that setting he has developed three shorter pieces, which have now appeared in the collection *A Congress of Wonders* (1996).

Gurney Norman is the author of an equally remarkable bildungsroman called *Divine Right's Trip: A Folktale* (1972). Divine Right Davenport (his real name is David Ray) is a young man from eastern Kentucky who goes to California and participates wholeheartedly in the life there before returning to Kentucky to marry and make a life on the family's blighted coal-mining land. Even before it was published in hardcover, the book had appeared in an earlier version in *The Last Whole Earth Catalog* (1971) and in that form acquired a vogue as a novel of the counterculture. Now a quarter of a century later it remains, along with Harriette Arnow's *The Dollmaker*, one of the best witnesses to the deep-rooted cultural identity of a southern Appalachia that has remained essentially intact and in place even as overcrowding at midcentury temporarily propelled it outward. Norman's claim to lasting distinction, however, rests with his *Kinfolks* (1977), a collection of ten engaging stories, most of them previously published, about an East Kentuckian named Wilgus Collier and his family. These stories, whether or not by intention, constitute a novel and help to establish Norman as the only visible successor to Kentucky's James Still.

Since World War II, women writers in greater numbers have also emerged to take their places in the scheme of things. One woman of an older generation was already in place but largely unnoticed: Mildred Haun (1911–66), an East Tennesseean who had found her way to Vanderbilt in 1931 and flowered as a writer under the direction of John Crowe Ransom and Donald Davidson. In 1940 with the support of Vanderbilt's newly established writing fellowship, she put together a remarkably promising collection of tales that was published a year later as *The Hawk's Done Gone* (1941). Because of family illnesses and other reasons best known to herself, Haun published little else before her death in 1966, and it remained to Herschel Gower, formerly a student at Vanderbilt and now a faculty member there, to bring out a complete *The Hawk's Done Gone and Other Stories* (1968). Another but quite different feminine voice from Appalachia is that of Wilma Dykeman (b. 1920), a genuine student of the region and a vigorous activist for civil rights. In addition to producing numerous articles and essays, Dykeman has embodied her insights in two novels, *The Tall Woman* (1962) and *The Far Family* (1966), both of which trace the lives of members of a single mountain family, the McQueens.

Still another Appalachian writer of fiction, younger than either of these and more prolific, is Lee Smith (b. 1944), a native of Grundy in the mountains of far western Virginia. Smith, like Haun, sees herself as a storyteller, spinning tales out of her experience and a fertile imagination that is limited only by a compulsion to be true to the materials. One of her most remarkable achievements in this mode is her first novel, *The Last Day the Dogbushes Bloomed* (1968), written while she was still a student at Hollins, and in this and the works immediately succeeding it she has produced a series of portraits for contemporary Appalachia somewhat analogous to those Eudora Welty produced for Mississippi. With *Oral History* (1983), however, Smith's fifth novel and with respect to narrative her most ambitious, she took a new tack. As a framing device for the book she has a contemporary college student from a nearby community college set out to record the stories and experiences of mountain relatives for a class project. Stretched a bit, this device allows Smith to drop back to the late nineteenth and early part of the twentieth centuries and let the voices of the dead as well as those of the living tell their stories. In a later work, *The Devil's Dream* (1992), she has again spanned past and present to put together the story of several generations of a mountain family, this time one involved in the performance of country music, which some of them regard as "the devil's work." In her latest, however, *Saving Grace* (1995), Smith achieves the status of a mature artist. Here she allows a mountain woman, Florida Grace Shepherd, to tell her own story, from its beginnings in poverty and abject naivete as the child of an itinerant snake-handling evangelist to something approaching a mature woman's capacity for love, understanding, compassion, forgiveness, and the awareness of which humanity is capable. Honesty, talent, an ear for speech, and a keen eye for detail have made Lee Smith Appalachia's best chronicler, and in her more recent work she has become in the best sense its preeminent apologist.

A talented contemporary of Smith's and onetime pupil of Randall Jarrell, North Carolina's Durham-born Sylvia Wilkinson (b. 1940), has used a wider lens in her stories and novels to include both rural eastern Carolina and the mountains. Among other things (she paints as well as writes), Wilkinson has produced the biography of a racing car champion, *The Stainless Steel Carrot: An Auto Racing Odyssey* (1973), but in her five novels she has focused on the female psyche. In the three earliest, all set in eastern North Carolina, she depicts the partial success of unsophisticated country women struggling to achieve fulfillment without adequate models to guide them. *Shadow of the Mountain* (1977) tells the story of an educated social worker who partly through ignorance comes to disaster in trying to help the people of Appalachia. The more hopeful *Bone of My Bones* (1982) deals with a young woman who in spite of traumatic obstacles manages to come to terms with herself and her community.

Meanwhile, an older North Carolina writer, also a onetime student at Woman's College, Doris Betts (b. 1932), with little fanfare had been making explorations over a considerably wider range of human responses, including both black-white relationships and the broader challenges faced by southern womanhood. Her first attempts were mainly in short stories that for a long time failed to receive the recognition they deserved. In 1954 she published her first collection of these, *The Gentle Insurrection*, and at the same time enrolled briefly at the University of North Carolina in Chapel Hill to complete the undergraduate degree she had begun at Woman's College. From this point on her career assumed a clear direction; and by 1966, although she still had not completed her degree, she was allowed to assume the duties of a part-time teacher at the university. She also continued to publish: two more volumes of short fiction, *The Astronomer and Other Stories* (1965) and *Beasts of the Southern Wild and Other Stories* (1973); and four novels, *Tall Houses in Winter* (1957), *The Scarlet Thread* (1964), *The River to Pickle Beach* (1972), and *Heading West* (1981). In 1980 the university made Betts its Alumni Distinguished Professor of English. In subsequent works she has given extended treatment to themes announced in her shorter works, but in *Heading West* she has developed at length and with understanding one that puts her in the company of postwar feminists, that of the southern female trapped in a restrictive and stultifying culture.

Two Mississippi writers have taken places of distinction on the postwar scene. The first of these to make a stir was Mississippi-born Josephine Ayres Haxton (b. 1921), who writes under the name Ellen Douglas. Douglas has spent most of her adult life in the cultivated surroundings of Greenville, home of William Alexander and Walker Percy. Her first novel, *A Family's Affairs* (1962), brought her the Houghton Mifflin Fellowship, after which she published a volume of short fiction, *Black Cloud, White Cloud* (1964), and two more novels, *Apostles of Light* (1973) and *The Rock Cried Out* (1979). Douglas has been widely praised for breaking new ground with perceptive treatments of black-white relationships, especially in her short fiction and in *The Rock Cried Out*. Less well-known but equally talented and more inclined to experiment is Ellen Gilchrist (b. 1935), a native of Vicksburg, who received her education at Millsaps in nearby Jackson and at the University of Arkansas. Gilchrist has published one book of poems, *The Land Surveyor's Daughter* (1979), but her masterful explorations of the female psyche and its effect on human relations when allowed to run free are best displayed in her fiction: two collections of stories, *In the Land of Dreamy Dreams* (1981) and *Victory over Japan* (1984), which won the American Book Award, and two novels, *The Annunciation* (1983) and *The Anna Papers* (1988).

One of the most remarkable figures to emerge during the postwar years has been the black writer Alice Walker (b. 1944), born in Eatonton, Georgia, and educated at Spelman College and Sarah Lawrence. Since her own college days Walker has lectured widely, taught at Jackson State and Tougaloo in Mississippi, Wellesley, the University of Massachusetts, and Brandeis, and served as distinguished writer in Afro-American studies at Berkeley (1982), but she is best known as a writer of short stories (two collections of them) and an epistolary novel, *The Color Purple* (1982), which won both the Pulitzer Prize for 1983 and the National Book Award. Walker already had two novels to her credit: *The Third Life of George Copeland* (1970), which depicts the persistence of slavery's brutalizing effects upon the generations following emancipation, and *Meridian* (1976), an account of how one black woman found her own identity and enabled others to find theirs in the civil rights movement in Mississippi and Georgia during the sixties. Both of these earlier novels emphasize Walker's point that black people, vigilant black people, may find fulfillment in a South where they have roots in a land that is rightfully theirs. *The Color Purple*, however, is more ambitious than either of its predecessors. In its somewhat sprawling plot one encounters, often painfully, experiences shared by many black females in the South, including a compulsion felt by some and given forceful literary expression earlier by Margaret Walker and Alex Haley to understand those experiences in the light of a redemptive African heritage.

Another black writer, Gayl Jones (b. 1949), born in Lexington, Kentucky, and educated at the University of Connecticut, has produced works in authentic black speech that have offended some readers but elicited admiration from serious critics, including responsible members of the black community. Both in her two novels, *Corregidora* (1975) and *Eva's Man* (1976), and in her more recent collection of stories, *White Rat* (1983), she has presented with an honesty that cannot be dismissed as mere sensationalism the continuation of slavery's brutalization as the tragic heritage of a contemporary black community, male as well as female, still not emancipated either socially or economically. Her one volume of criticism, *Liberating Voices: Oral Tradition in African American Literature* (1991), is a landmark in the field. Although she has sometimes been accused of reclusiveness, Jones has recently taught at the University of Michigan.

Two other Kentuckians who have come into prominence within the last two decades are the slightly younger Barbara Kingsolver (b. 1955) and Bobbie Ann Mason (b. 1940). Kingsolver was born in Annapolis, Maryland, and since 1977 has lived in Tucson, Arizona; but she grew up in Kentucky and in noteworthy novels and short fiction has made effective use of the impressions and experiences of her formative years there. Her first novel, *The Bean Trees* (1988), is the story of a young Kentucky woman, Taylor Greer, who like herself settles in Tucson. Greer, however, is deeply moved by Arizona's dispossessed, adopts a motley family of the elderly, orphaned, and abandoned, and eventually espouses the cause of that state's illegal aliens. Kingsolver's more recent work includes both fiction and nonfiction, especially a much acclaimed sequel to *The Bean Trees*, *Pigs in Heaven* (1993).

The work that rescued her from some early false starts in writing, Kingsolver has told one interviewer, was Bobbie Ann Mason's newly published first collection of stories in 1982. At that point Mason, then nearly forty years old, had attended the University of Kentucky, spent several years writing for movie magazines, earned a doctorate at the University of Connecticut, married, published a scholarly study of the girl sleuth in children's detective stories, and taught for a time at Mansfield State College in Pennsylvania. In 1980, she managed to place her short story "Shiloh" in the *New Yorker*, and its republication two years later in *Shiloh and Other Stories* brought her nominations for both the National Book Award and the American Book Award. Other awards and grants, including a Guggenheim Fellowship, followed in 1983 and 1984.

Since then she has written a second collection of stories, *Love Life* (1989), and three novels, *In Country* (1985), subsequently made into a movie, *Spence + Lila* (1988), and *Feather Crowns* (1993). In all these works Mason's principal setting is western Kentucky, and increasingly in all of them she displays a remarkable eye for detail and an ability to deploy a significant selection of it to reveal action and character. Plot is never absent from these stories, but frequently the plot is internal and from the reader's point of view submerged like bedrock in a stream. In the novels, however, particularly *In Country* and *Feather Crowns*, Mason's rock and stream are equally visible.

Feather Crowns, her best to date and a major work by any measure, contains authentic data and locutions to gratify the most discriminating folklorist, but its focus throughout is on Christie Wheeler of fictional Hopewell, Kentucky, who on February 26, 1900, gives birth to live quintuplets. Predictably the children die, and Christie and her husband are prevailed upon to undergo a lengthy and exhausting tour of Tennessee, Mississippi, Alabama, and Georgia, exhibiting the preserved bodies in the interest of education and science. In the long section devoted to that enterprise, Mason manages to render life in America's mid-South at the turn of the century as richly and convincingly as she had previously rendered that of middle-and lower-class whites in a contemporary western Kentucky. More important, however, here and in the sections that follow she presents Christie's gradual escape from her limited awareness to something like a good-humored acceptance of the world as given. Happily, this is the same acceptance that seems to characterize the attitude of Mason herself as reflected in her works as a whole.

13
The New Major Writers

As has been noted, the newer southern writers of fiction after World War II moved in a variety of directions—almost as if, having glimpsed the form's multitude of possibilities and gained from their predecessors a sense of the discipline required to use it effectively, they were eager to experiment. The first of them to achieve any real preeminence was William Styron (b. 1925), for a time widely regarded, especially abroad, as Faulkner's legitimate heir. Styron, having been born and reared in Newport News, Virginia, was legitimately southern. He had attended several of the better schools in the area: Christchurch Episcopal (where, however, he did poorly), Davidson College, and finally Duke, where he profited greatly by the presence of William Blackburn, a master tutor who provided the essential intelligent guidance that he would later give other gifted Duke writers, among them Mac Hyman, Reynolds Price, Anne Tyler, and Fred Chappell. For a time during World War II, Styron served as an officer in the Marine Corps before completing his undergraduate work at Duke. After graduation in 1947 he spent a brief unsatisfactory period with McGraw-Hill in New York and then enrolled at New York's New School for Social Research. There he encountered the critic and editor Hiram Haydn and with Haydn's encouragement made his formal decision to become a novelist.

His first novel, *Lie Down in Darkness* (1951), was a success with reviewers (it received the Prix de Rome) and general readers alike but it clearly showed a susceptibility to the influence of other writers that, consciously cultivated, would characterize much of his best work. In this first novel the principal influences were R.P. Warren (especially the narrative technique in Warren's recently successful *All the King's Men*) and the early masterpieces of William Faulkner, notably *The Sound and the Fury* and superficially *As I Lay Dying*. In *Lie Down in Darkness*, however, the corpse to be brought home for burial is that of a suicide, a twenty-year-old girl of good family, Peyton Loftis, who like Faulkner's Quentin Compson has been driven to insanity by an inability to reconcile a crucial conflict in her southern heritage.

Peyton Loftis's estranged parents, who accompany the body home, are Styron's representatives of that conflict: the relaxed civility of her cavalier-like father contrasting sharply—and for his marriage, fatally—with his wife's in-grained Calvinism. Peyton, torn between love for both parents and unable to please either, has chosen death rather than a life of intolerable tension; and for some reviewers the resemblance here to Faulkner's portrayal of a similar situation in *The Sound and the Fury* tended to obscure the virtuosity of the new author's performance. But Styron's virtuosity stood clear in his second novel, *The Long March* (1953), a relatively short work that was compared with Melville's *Billy Budd* and accorded by some the status of a Greek trag-edy. Undoubtedly the conflict in this work, between the arbitrary exercise of authority by a marine colonel and the sane and compassionate humanity of a young reserve officer under him, does partake of the universal, but in retro-spect it also underscores still another characteristic of Styron's work as a whole—his conscious attempt to avoid the label of southern writer, or at least that of the southern regionalist.

Thus on leaving Duke, Styron moved north and never again maintained a residence in the South. In 1953 he married and after a period of wandering about Italy settled permanently in Connecticut, where he brought a third novel to completion, this time one with an Italian setting, *Set This House on Fire* (1960). Here the central figure is a southern expatriate painter, Cass Kinsolving, who falls under the domination of a rich bourgeois American, Mason Flagg. In the end he extricates himself by murdering the American and with the help of an understanding Italian policeman who rules the death a suicide is able to avoid punishment and reconstitute a life in his native South Carolina. The story of a southerner returned, one might say, but again the text is replete with echoes, this time to Fitzgerald's work rather than that of War-ren and Faulkner. Although most American reviewers disliked the book, in France an excellent translation helped place Styron, at least in Gallic eyes, among the first rank of American writers. During the next five years or so, he confirmed their opinion by writing—in the manner of Gide and Sartre—a series of polished essays on issues of current interest and publishing them in prominent journals, *Esquire*, *Harper's*, and the *New York Review of Books*. Eventually these journalistic pieces were to be combined with others that he wrote subsequently and published in a single volume, *This Quiet Dust* (1982).

Issues that Styron examined in these nonfiction pieces led in time to two of his finest novels. The first of these appeared, after many advance notices (mainly by Styron himself), in 1967 as *The Confessions of Nat Turner* and almost immediately precipitated a nationwide controversy. The 1960s were years of unusual tension in American race relations, and cries of "Black Power" were being heard in all quarters and at all levels. In disregard of the sensitive situation—almost in defiance of it—Styron, a white man of southern origin, ventured to tell in the person of the black Nat Turner an "authentic" version of the slave rebellion that had erupted in Virginia in 1831. For several reasons that attempt was an open invitation to trouble, which promptly developed. Criticism of the book divided along racial lines. White critics wrote highly favorable reviews in the *New Yorker* and the *New Republic*, while blacks responded in public denunciations and a collection of angry essays, *William Styron's Nat Turner: Ten Black Writers Respond* (1968). Nevertheless, in the end the judgments were in Styron's favor, and his "meditation on history," as he called it, received both a Pulitzer Prize in 1968 and a Howells Medal in 1970.

From that point on, Styron's rate of productivity began to slacken appreciably. As was his custom, he complained of being a slow worker; but for a time he pressed steadily ahead with a novel called *The Way of the Warrior*, and he also wrote a play, *In the Clap Shack*, which was published in 1973. Then he discovered a topic that compelled him to put lesser projects aside. The result, *Sophie's Choice* (1979), was a new meditation on history, this one concentrating on the Holocaust and pairing that twentieth-century event with the establishment of Negro slavery in America as glaring examples of the disasters produced by the ills of Western society. For the focus of narration he used an aspiring young southern writer named Stingo, recently moved north from Virginia, as Styron himself had done after graduating from Duke, and at the center he placed the story of a young Polish gentile and her Jewish lover, Nathan, whom Stingo encounters in his Brooklyn rooming house. These two, older and presumably wiser, preside over the maturation of the inexperienced Stingo, who learns more than he anticipates from the hidden tragedy that eventually destroys both of his self-appointed mentors. The woman, it turns out, is living with the unbearable memory of being shipped to Auschwitz and forced there by a sadistic commandant to choose which of her two children he will allow to live. In the end both she and Nathan commit suicide, victims of the willful inhumanity they have witnessed and in Sophie's case unwillingly participated in.

Sophie's Choice did well commercially, but reviewers were lukewarm initially. Polish readers chafed at inaccuracies, and Jewish groups were uneasy with Styron's subordination of their cardinal example of anti-Semitism to a broader and more abstract instance of human inhumanity. Still there was no general outcry over the book such as had confronted him with the publication of *The Confessions of Nat Turner*, and his essays, *This Quiet Dust*, which came out in 1982, met with widespread praise. For a less sensitive writer the outlook might have seemed promising. Unknown to his friends, however, and to himself, Styron was on the brink of a severe depression from which with treatment he would eventually recover, but only at the expense of several of his potentially most productive years. His account of that dark period, published first in *Vanity Fair* in 1989 and then in book form in 1990 as *Darkness Visible: A Memoir of Madness*, stands as an example of his nonfiction at its best and an unwitting tribute to the man's strength of character. Styron has continued to live and write in the northeast, but he returns to the South occasionally— notably to Sewanee in October 1993, where he received an honorary doctorate from the University of the South.

John Barth (b. 1930), five years Styron's junior, came to writing almost by accident and with his first two novels failed to receive much more than passing notice from readers and reviewers. A native of Cambridge, Maryland, he first attended the Juilliard School in New York for a short time, hoping to become a jazz musician, then returned south to Johns Hopkins to accept a scholarship in journalism that had come in response to an application he had all but forgotten. Working in the Classics Library there, he discovered short fiction, in particular *The Arabian Nights*, and literally devoured all the specimens of the form he could lay his hands on. Consequently, after graduation in 1951, he stayed on at Johns Hopkins to earn an M.A. in creative writing (1952). Then, lacking funds to support leisure or writing, he embarked upon a career of teaching—first at Pennsylvania State (1954–65), then the State University of New York at Buffalo (1965–73), and finally back at Johns Hopkins, where ironically as a professor in creative writing he conducted the seminar for which he had written an unpublishable novel as his thesis more than twenty years before.

Barth's first publishable novel demonstrated most of the salient characteristics of his work as a whole: a love for the short narrative or tale, a barely suppressed taste for the bizarre, and a persistent conviction that all the reality one perceives is a projection of the inventiveness of the perceiver. In fact, portrayal of the desire to achieve reality by means of creative activity is perhaps the most striking constant in Barth's work; in his presentations the fuel for that desire—the "archetypal fire," as he called it—is a rich imagination and the medium in which achievement takes place, living language. Barth is well endowed with all these attributes, and thus all his novels involve, in varying degrees, the reflexivity of the knowledgeable seeker after reality. The hero creates the novel he participates in, sometimes moving back and forth between his starting point and the mirror he has created—indeed, sometimes creating multiple mirrors and mirrors within mirrors to accommodate his narrative foci. Usually he succeeds in this technical legerdemain, but always in proportion as he maintains flexibility in the imaginative projections that he uses as metaphors, avoids letting them harden into dead referents, and keeps the movement of his action at the center of his reader's attention.

Barth's first two novels, *The Floating Opera* (1955) and *The End of the Road* (1958), gave enough intimations of all three of these characteristics to excite a small group of readers but hardly enough to generate sales. Both were commercial failures, as was his third, *The Sot-Weed Factor* (1960), the first of three meganovels and one that for the most part had the accessibility and style (though not the tight form) reminiscent of a novel by Fielding, a writer he greatly admired. The material for the novel was historical, at its base an eighteenth-century satirical poem of the same name by Ebenezer Cooke, whom Barth imagines to be the narrator in the poem. The story involves a young man's adventures in the raw and lawless New Eden of colonial Maryland, and Barth went to considerable lengths to authenticate the details he used. Even so, *The Sot-Weed Factor* has very little of the feel of primitive Maryland in it, and the substance satirized there, as in all his work, is the timeless and universal constituents of the human condition. In 1965 the publisher reissued the book as an inexpensive paperback, and college students, increasingly restive and wearied of fantasies by Tolkien and C.S. Lewis, claimed it for their own and so prepared themselves to receive the even more impressive *Giles Goat-Boy*, which came out in 1966.

Many consider *Giles Goat-Boy* to be Barth's best work. It is certainly one of his most complex. Ostensibly, the story is that of George Giles, who, having been reared as a goat and educated as a man, concludes early in life that he is destined to serve as Grand Tutor or Messiah to the world. The narrative is anything but simple and straightforward. Using the device of a recently discovered manuscript, a device sanctioned by Hawthorne and Henry James among others, Barth presents the book as an eccentric document, presumably transmitted to him by the son of the author, entitled *The Revised New Syllabus of George Giles Our Grand Tutor*. What we have before us, we are told, is Giles's computerized compilation of such things as his taped lecture notes and recorded conferences with "protégés," amplified and cemented together by commentary, and edited initially by the younger Giles (and then, of course, by Barth himself). In addition we have as front matter the conflicting reports of editors who reviewed the manuscript for publication and an essay by Barth as transmitter. This modest but bogus apparatus for the manuscript proper provides occasion for satire on the contemporary procedures and practices of publishers and the zealous industry of those textual bibliographers who pin their hopes for truth on the possibility of establishing an authoritative text. In the text itself we have what amounts to a bizarre bildungsroman of George Giles and in the course of that text a stylistic virtuoso's display of the range of narrative devices as well as discussions, digressions, wild and often bawdy comedy, elaborate puns, parallels, and parodies dealing with a wide variety of topics fundamental to Western civilization; all these components, if not already ambiguous and inconclusive, are rendered so by the multiple perspectives established in the frame. The result is a performance that delighted Barth's newly found student audience, invited critics' comparisons with Joyce, gave academic scholars numerous opportunities for busy work, and pleased the general public sufficiently to become a best-seller and a commercial success.

Still at Buffalo, Barth now turned back to his early love, short fiction, discovered the work of Borges, launched an investigation into the potentialities of oral narrative, and produced a collection of short pieces, *Lost in the Funhouse* (1968), which brought him a nomination for the National Book Award, though not the award itself. He also began another major project, *LETTERS*, which, however, gave him trouble and did not appear until 1979. Undaunted he took a finished part of that work and combined it with two more narrative pieces that he published as *Chimera* in 1972, and for this effort he won the National Book Award that had eluded him four years before. In 1973 he accepted the invitation to return to Johns Hopkins University in Baltimore, there to become the Alumni Centennial Professor of English and Creative Writing. At Hopkins his productivity continued without letup: *LETTERS: A Novel* (1979), *Sabbatical: A Romance* (1982), and a volume of collected essays, *The Friday Book: Essays and Other Nonfiction* (1984). His life had now come full circle, with fame, fortune, and academic prestige assured.

Barth's admirers in academia have disagreed about which of his works to declare the preeminent masterpiece. *Giles Goat-Boy* has had numerous advocates, *LETTERS* (for its encyclopedic dimensions) somewhat fewer, and *The Tidewater Tales* (1987) at least one. *Tidewater Tales*, however, may well be the most representative of the lot. First of all, it is a neat exercise in Barthian reflexivity: a novel about a writer and his writing, Peter Sagamore, who like Barth himself is completing a collection of stories to be called *Tidewater Tales*. Sagamore goes sailing on the Chesapeake with his pregnant wife, a specialist in folklore and oral history and a poet, who challenges her husband to tell his tales as they proceed. They then take turns serving as narrators for the novel, but the husband's part predominates. The stories he tells constitute both his projected book, the title page for which appears at the end, and Barth's book, which the reader holds in his hand. Other doubles and mirror images abound, including the twins that the wife gives birth to at the end. These are all typical characteristics of Barth's work, but they are not what holds most readers' attention. The compelling and perhaps most enduring aspects, served in full measure here, are those described by his fellow writer George Garrett as "lots of good food, good fun, good sex. . . . Solidly realized and completely credible central characters, people with lives and histories, living in a world as full of wonder and great danger (and suspense) as our own." It is these aspects that are most likely to ensure the endurance of Barth's novels, works by a southerner that without conspicuous reference to place speak to the general human condition. There is nothing distinctively southern about them—a point, of course, about which Barth seems to have concerned himself not at all.

Barth's more recent works, if anything, have enhanced his reputation for technical virtuosity, prompting use of the terms "brilliant" and "lapidary" and comparisons of his style with that of Nabokov. In 1991 he brought out what some might call another picaresque novel, *The Last Voyage of Somebody the Sailor*. This work is in part a playful exercise in emulation of *The Arabian Nights* that had fired his imagination in the library at Hopkins forty years before, a superbly told succession of incidents, anecdotes, and embedded narratives. As in all his previous works, here he also drew upon autobiographical material, transmuted beyond easy recognition but marking the work as idiosyncratically Barthian. This aspect was even more conspicuous in the work that followed, *Once Upon a Time* (1994), which Barth described as "a memoir bottled in a novel." Here again in a work with multiple references to family and friends and a Chesapeake setting he had an opportunity to write something distinctively southern but instead chose to transmute any localizing data rather than develop and explore it. Thus Barth has remained, like Edgar Allan Poe and James B. Cabell, for all his brilliance a southern writer at several removes from the scenes he designates and the activities he presumes to describe.

Another academic southern writer, only slightly younger than Barth, has chosen to explore a narrower range with equal intensity but in considerably greater depth. Reynolds Price (b. 1933), by contrast with William Styron, his predecessor in William Blackburn's informal succession of writers, elected to stay not only in the South but at Duke itself and pursue there a double career of teaching and writing. Price was born at Macon, North Carolina, a hamlet on the edge of North Carolina's Piedmont east and north of Raleigh. Nevertheless, as a child of loving but intermittently impecunious parents, he grew up in a succession of towns about the state and found at Duke for the first time a home that he could consider permanent. Thus except for three years at Merton College on a Rhodes Scholarship, he has remained there, unmarried and preferring to live alone in rustic surroundings outside the town. In the early eighties Price was stricken with a rare and devastating form of spinal cancer that, although now in remission, has left him permanently confined to a wheelchair. In cheerful defiance of the odds, he has continued to write and teach his classes—creative writing, Milton, and more recently the literature of the Bible. As James B. Duke Professor and author of some twenty-five books of fiction, verse, translation, and memoirs, he has achieved academic success and arrived at the status of a major writer, admired both for his work and for the sheer physical courage that made it all possible.

Unlike most writers, Price has never known absolute failure. Even those works in which unfriendly critics found real or imagined shortcomings have been reasonably successful by ordinary standards. Still, it is primarily as a writer of fiction that he is best known, and it is as a novelist that he seems most likely to be remembered. His first novel, *A Long and Happy Life* (1962), was warmly received by critics and the reading public alike. In addition to receiving the usual book publication, it had the distinction of being run by *Harper's* as an illustrated supplement, and the Faulkner Foundation gave it its award for the best first novel by an American author. It came out, perhaps unfortunately, just before the death of William Faulkner, at a time when critics everywhere were looking for someone, preferably a southerner, to "receive the mantle of the master." That game had begun much earlier, of course, when after the war it became evident that Faulkner's great work was behind him. As has already been noted, one of the first candidates for the role was William Styron, to Styron's discomfort and with a modest amount of detriment to his initial reputation. Price was luckier. His account of the Mustian family in *A Long and Happy Life* had all the earmarks of being the first work in a chronicle, as indeed after a fashion it was, but it did not invite comparison with any of Faulkner's less imitable triumphs such as his accounts of the bizarre trek of the Bundren family and of the suicidal meditations of Quentin Compson. Price's first book of short stories, *The Names and Faces of Heroes*, came out in the following year to widespread approval, and *A Generous Man*, delayed until 1966, was as anticipated a continuation of the first novel, although, as it turned out, the final one in a series of only two.

Actually, it was a series of three. The principal characters had already appeared in Price's first story, "A Chain of Love," which together with the two novels it anticipated was reissued as *Mustian: Two Novels & a Story* in 1984. In 1968 Price turned to a new subject, the study of a neurotic professor torn between contending claims of work and family, that he called *Love and Work*. This time some of the critics were less than kind, perhaps because in their eyes he was still wearing, albeit loosely, the mantle of Faulkner. That notion, however, had already begun to dissipate in the seventies when Price again turned to family chronicle for a major novel, *The Surface of Earth* (1975), followed six years later by the equally impressive *The Source of Light* (1981), the story of four generations of the Kendall-Mayfield families, concentrating on second-generation Hutch Mayfield's attempt to escape the tyranny of patterns established by his predecessors and shape a meaningful life on his own terms. By this time it had become clear that Price's principal source for material was his own life, his early years in Macon and other North Carolina towns, his experiences past and present in academia, and the tensions and stresses resolved there or simply confronted. The mantle he more justly might have been accused of assuming was that of Thomas Wolfe rather than Faulkner, but to Price's credit and the benefit of his still-developing talent he had avoided the temptation to romanticize. All his stories up to that point, like those that followed, had been objective and selfless presentations, even when manifestly autobiographical; all had been grounded in the perception of a capacity in the best people—female or male, rich or poor, black or white—for acknowledging the persistent human proclivity to err and accepting it in something like charity. This kind of hero gave Price's early work its distinctive appeal and is the kind he has continued to write about throughout his career, even as his narrative skills have sharpened and his stylistic range has increased.

Another aspect of Price's work, not noted at first, became apparent as his work proceeded: a persistent but undogmatic and unobtrusive form of Christianity that he seems to have inherited in part from his parents and in part from the simple pieties of the small communities in which he grew up. The first overt indication of this aspect, surprising even to some of his most sympathetic readers, was a series of translations, or adaptations from Scripture, that he published in three volumes during the seventies: *Presence and Absence: Versions from the Bible* (1974), *Oracles: Six Versions from the Bible* (1977), and the one that finally commanded serious critical attention, *A Palpable God: Thirty Stories Translated from the Bible with an Essay on the Origins and Life of Narrative* (1978). Both the versions in *A Palpable God* and the essay accompanying them have been widely praised, especially by critics who are themselves writers, and the Bible has been added to the formative influences on Price's life as well as his art.

By this time Price had established himself as a writer of extraordinary gifts. In addition to the novels and short stories for which he was best known, he had distinguished himself with several volumes of poetry, plays, memoirs, and essays and had established himself as a distinctively southern author, one with a mantle of his own making, which he continues to wear with ease. Unfortunately, this was the time when disease would threaten to end his career, but it was also the time when he stood on the threshold of his full majority as a writer. He met both challenges with a novel that many consider his masterpiece, *Kate Vaiden* (1986), the story of a woman in her midfifties who in fear and trembling undertakes to reestablish connections with the child, now man, she had abandoned forty years before. When at last she hears his voice on an answering machine and knows that he is alive and well, she decides to delay the final meeting until she can deliver a written account of her life and let him choose for himself whether or not he wants to acknowledge the relationship. The first-person narrative presented is presumably that account, told in authentic North Carolina idiom and with deftly concealed art, the self-portrait of a woman in the fully rendered context of her life that is scarcely matched by any other of its kind in American literature; for it Price received the National Book Critics Circle Award for fiction in that year.

In 1990 he published a slimmer but no less impressive novel, *The Tongues of Angels*, in which a middle-aged representational painter, Bridge Boatner, recounts for his son a homoerotic experience in a summer camp more than thirty years before that ended tragically for the beautiful young man to whom he was attached. The written account is in part Boatner's act of expiation, but it is also his moving acknowledgment that the young man's life has enabled him to achieve some level of fullness in his own. Since then, Price has published additional new fiction, a trilogy of plays, *New Music* (1990), and in 1993 *The Collected Stories*, which was a finalist for the Pulitzer Prize the following year. In 1994 he published a frank and crisply written story of the illness that all but rendered him helpless, *A Whole New Life: An Illness and a Healing*, an appropriate climactic work for a writer whose principal subject, sometimes obscured, has always been the mystery of health and healing. Here he demonstrates that the posture of acceptance, which has tempered his portrayal of the Piedmont South with a sweetness that few writers have approached without slipping into sentimentality, is in grain and a principal ingredient of Price's strength, both as an artist and as a man.

Not all the postwar southern novelists and short-story writers have worked from reverential or nostalgic or, as in the case of John Barth, even routinely noncommittal attitudes towards the region. Even before World War II a few authors—Erskine Caldwell, for example—established a precedent for displaying disparaging portraits of classes of people who were undeniably a part of the scene but who were innocent of tradition and had never participated in any part of the culture, folk or otherwise. Some more circumspect, like Faulkner, occasionally took what was regarded as a perverse delight in presenting examples of deviant behavior at various levels of society, but such departures from the norm were for the most part either deplored as aberrations or ignored by their contemporaries. Northern critics, however, sometimes delightedly treated these grotesqueries as typical and freely used the label Southern Gothic to refer to them.

Since the war, fewer readers in the North or the South have found such labeling meaningful. The postwar rehabilitation of Faulkner's reputation had brought about reconsiderations of *Sanctuary*, *As I Lay Dying*, and "A Rose for Emily," and a new generation of readers seemed prepared to receive, almost without demurral, the remarkable characters in the works of Carson McCullers and Flannery O'Connor. Yet these characters, for all their differences, appeared in stories and actions that stayed within the parameters of traditional fiction and so could be accepted as idiosyncrasies in an otherwise stable world. During the sixties, however, two writers appeared, Harry Crews (b. 1935) and Cormac McCarthy (b. 1933), both of whom, from the point of view of those who regarded themselves as representatives of the southern establishment, seemed bent on delivering a troublingly anarchic picture of southern life. Of the two, Crews at first appeared to be the one most likely to achieve a permanent place on the literary scene. In 1968 at the age of thirty-three he published his first novel, *The Gospel Singer*, which tells of the decline and fall of a cynical yet God-haunted purveyor of an illusory Gospel message that his naive followers dutifully maintain faith in, even as they destroy him, its patently faithless messenger. After that, he produced seven more novels in quick succession, almost one a year, in the course of which activity he explored in an unsystematic fashion the various options available to existential man, concluding pessimistically in the last novel with a portrayal of ultimate despair.

No southern writer, early or late, has had a more legitimate right to such a conclusion. Crews spent his earliest years in a part of the southern milieu from which few escape to write reports, and most of those who have attempted to describe it at a comfortable distance have reproduced at best surface details. His parents were South Georgia farm tenants, poor, uneducated, rootless, and prone to violence. Their tradition was an oral one, and their art, though they never called it that, was storytelling. Crews's father died when he was two years old, and his mother married again to a man equally rootless and violent and also given to drink. Quickly divorced, she drifted down to Jacksonville, Florida, where she worked in a cigar factory and where Harry contracted poliomyelitis, which kept him bedridden for a year. Nevertheless, Jacksonville also made it possible for him to attend primary and secondary school, after which, having no visible objective and no means, he joined the Marine Corps and served for four years. In 1956 with support from the G.I. Bill he entered the University of Florida in Gainesville.

While at the university he met Andrew Lytle, who understood tenant farmers, recognized Crews's genius and native talent for narrative, taught him the discipline of writing, and, although never able to lead him to the objective stance necessary for controlling his fiction, fired him with the urge to write professionally. Thus off and on for four years Harry Crews attended school, and wrote and rewrote, finally graduating in 1962. When his first novel was successful beyond expectations, he was asked to return to the University of Florida as a teacher.

In subject matter Crews's eight novels offer numerous parallels with details in his own life, and most commentators have surmised that the futile search for meaning they seem collectively to portray is at least in part his own. It can be argued, too, that Crews's failure to achieve a literary work of the first rank lies in his inability to escape a tyrannical awareness of a past he has alternately proclaimed and resented. For example, the first three novels portray satirically the religion he had known in youth and imply his bitter rejection of it in maturity. Thus having portrayed the failure of religion and its minister in *The Gospel Singer*, he proceeded to publish the even more dispiriting *Naked in Garden Hills* (1969) and *This Thing Don't Lead to Heaven* (1970), although two of his misfits in the second of these do seem to find a measure of solace in their affection for one another.

In one way or another all the characters in the next four novels are misfits, or freaks, as Crews preferred to call them. The locations of the settings are the contemporary Florida and Georgia that he knew, but the situations themselves are bizarre. In *Karate Is a Thing of the Spirit* (1971), he offers young lovers in a commune of karate aficionados; in *Car* (1972), a man raised in a junkyard who seeks to achieve a distinctive identity by eating an automobile; in *The Hawk Is Dying* (1973), a Georgia-born citizen of Gainesville who finds his only satisfaction in the medieval ritual of falconry; in *The Gypsy's Curse* (1974), a deaf-mute with withered legs who spends much of his time working out in a gymnasium with other male defectives. Here again love seems to offer hope for additional comfort; but when the deaf-mute's beloved becomes a disruptive influence in the all-male gymnasium, he feels constrained to kill her. In *A Feast of Snakes* (1976), the freak is a functionally illiterate high-school football star who marries and sires children but is unable to attend college or find an equivalent place to make use of his physical talents; consequently he turns to random violence, sex, and finally a series of murders. In the end members of an aroused mob pitch him into a snake pit.

Crews has provided some of the most useful commentary on his work in interviews over the years and in three works of nonfiction, which many feel contain his best writing: *A Childhood: The Biography of a Place* (1978), *Blood and Grits* (1979), and *Florida Frenzy* (1982). In all of his work, however, the autobiographical element is at least implicit, and the violence he depicts seems to be a projection of his own rather than the work of a creative imagination. Nevertheless, as an early and honest presentation of an aspect of southern life that was generally ignored but pervasive and persistent in spite of widespread improvements in educational and economic opportunities, it has a unique interest and value.

Cormac McCarthy, a writer often paired with Crews in notices of new writers in the late sixties and early seventies, has since then tended to attract an increasingly disproportionate amount of critical attention. McCarthy, a native of Rhode Island, came with his parents to Knoxville, Tennessee, at the age of four and with the exception of four years spent in the U.S. Air Force (1953–57) lived either there or nearby until he had established himself with four novels, all set in the East Tennessee area. Before going into the service McCarthy had made an abortive attempt at college, enrolling at the University of Tennessee for two semesters; afterward he returned and in 1961 completed his degree. Four years later he published *The Orchard Keeper* (1965), a novel displaying remarkable narrative skills but with such unconventional plotting and absence of authorial control that critics grown accustomed to formalism in southern fiction were at a loss how to deal with it. Nevertheless, it was in such denials of formal order as these that McCarthy revealed his basic assumptions and gave notice of things to come.

Actually, the plotting of *The Orchard Keeper* was unconventional principally in its lack of resolution. One reviewer suggested a number of ways in which another author might have developed the intrigue, but here McCarthy, as he has even more strikingly in the rest of his work, chose to portray characters at the unstructured base of society, people unaware, or barely aware, of the history and traditions of the rest of the South and thus unencumbered by its customs or moral conventions. For most of these people life is nothing more than the inconclusive succession of days that animals know, a sequence without comprehensive pattern or meaning; and their story, in a straightforward telling, can approach an undistorted reflection of the flux that involves everybody, an acknowledgment of which sometimes makes even the most hopeful human beings uneasy.

The central figure in the story is a young boy, John Wesley Rattner, who receives such positive direction as he gets during his growing up from two social misfits. The first of these is a bootlegger, Marion Sylder, who unknown to the boy has also been the unwitting murderer of his father. The second is the boy's mother, Mildred Rattner, who correctly suspects that her husband has met with foul play and sternly lays upon John Wesley the obligation of a revenge he actually has little interest in seeking. In addition there is a mountain hermit, Uncle Ather Ownby, who in a number of casual encounters contributes more to the boy's maturation than either of the others but who serves with them as a reminder of the mores of a simpler age when game abounded, government was minimal, and the Tennessee mountains were still frontier. In

the end, all of John Wesley's elders are shown to be stranded victims of changing times, and to avoid a similar entrapment John Wesley heads west.

In the two novels that followed *The Orchard Keeper*, McCarthy dipped
even further into southern society to bring out of the shadowy recesses of
East Tennessee life a presumably authentic conglomeration of people, predominantly white, who make Faulkner's Snopeses seem civilized. Many southern commentators expressed shock and resentment, and some were prompted
to consult their critical lexicons for such terms as indecent, naturalistic,
antipastoral, gnostic, and nihilistic. The first of the new novels, *Outer Dark*
(1968), presents the story of a simpleminded Culla Holme and his sister Rinthy
whose casual coupling produces a child. Culla gives the baby to an itinerant
tinker and tells his sister that it has died, but Rinthy, suspecting the truth,
begins a rambling search for her "chap" that ends many pages later after a
band of marauders has hanged the tinker, slit the child's throat, and left its
body to burn in the fire along with remnants of the tinker's equipment. There
she discovers the charred rib cage and other bones but makes nothing at all of
what she sees. A sympathetic reader may possibly find elements of the piti-
able here and elsewhere in *Outer Dark* but will be hard-pressed to find anything at all of the sort in *Child of God* (1974), which is the detailed story of
one Lester Ballard, voyeur and man of violence, whose excursions into necro-
philia exceed the gargantuan. McCarthy describes all these vividly and with a
directness that has caused most critics to doubt that he seriously expects readers
to see in Ballard anything but a parody, but in his refusal to suggest an escape
by way of gnostic dualism, McCarthy is probably a better Christian theolo-
gian than his critics. His early characterization of Ballard as "a child of God
much like yourself" indicates where he stands. Ballard may be an extreme
case, but he is inescapably one of us, bone of our bone, and, in McCarthy's
view, beloved of God as much as anyone else.

This premise is also true of the gallery of characters who drift in and out
of McCarthy's fourth East Tennessee novel, the one for which currently he is
best known, *Suttree* (1979). Such unity as this book possesses is provided by
the central character and focus of narration, Cornelius Suttree, an educated
refugee from the more acceptable levels of society, where he has been the
beneficiary of the upper-middle-class comforts of home and family. Suttree is
not, as some critics have imagined, a "dropout" from the planter aristocracy of
an older South. The Knoxville area, for all its affluence and occasional pretensions to the contrary, is still Appalachia in attitude and ways, and Suttree is
best seen as an East Tennessean who has repudiated all attempts by his
peers to deny their fundamental kinship with the inhabitants, transient or otherwise, of the disreputable McAnally district along Knoxville's waterfront. His

story, moreover, with its inconclusiveness (some have called it picaresque) makes it clear that the gestures toward resolution in the three works previously published were nothing more than that. Suttree's world, wherever he may find himself, is always that of people like the elder Rattner, the Holmeses, and Lester Ballard: an indeterminate process the meaning of which, if there is one, is known only to whatever God may preside over it. One cannot legitimately characterize it absolutely as nihilistic. Love has somehow found its way there, and in it some people do love their neighbor, express concern for their children, cherish a friend, or care for an animal. Such concern persists, even if it does not prevail, along with the violence and amorality that McCarthy seems to suggest constitute the common ground for southerners as they do for people everywhere.

For his fifth novel McCarthy moved himself (to El Paso) and his scene westward. Although most of the characters in *Blood Meridian* (1985) are from Tennessee, the impulse that moves them is not the one that caused others there to settle into an agrarian existence and develop an apologetics for a distinctively southern way of life but rather a continuation of that restless urge to exploit the frontier which in the first half of the nineteenth century was still a significant part of the average southerner's psyche. The central figure in *Blood Meridian* is an unnamed "kid," who shortly after the Mexican War goes west and falls in with a band of murderous scalp hunters headed by a historically identifiable cutthroat named John Glanton. The band's second in command, also historically identifiable, is a massive hairless figure named Holden, commonly referred to as Judge Holden—sophisticate, graceful dancer, molester of youth, philosophical apologist for their aimless enterprise, instructor to the kid, and ultimately his murderer. The novel conducts the reader through a succession of brawls, massacres, mass scalpings, encounters with despoiled mummies, severed heads, dead infants, and mutilated bodies, and ends in a dance hall with a protracted Walpurgisnacht of drunken drovers, hunters, soldiers, whores, and a captive bear, all orchestrated by a smiling and naked Holden, who, having just killed the kid presumably for his reluctance to participate in the reveling, declares the dance eternal and himself immortal.

As the eighties drew to a close, McCarthy's admirers, on the basis of these five novels, were comparing his work to the best of Melville and declaring him America's greatest writer and Faulkner's legitimate heir. Detractors, who were considerably more numerous, were deploring his gratuitous use of violence and flagrant indecencies, although for the most part even these critics were forced to acknowledge the subtleties of McCarthy's craftsmanship and the power of his prose. Few if any seemed to recognize the extent to which he had extended the range of southern fiction to explore at a childlike and amoral level of the region's society those impulses that its civilization had done its best to obscure or at least divert into acceptable channels. Admittedly McCarthy's own range up to this point was narrow, but the best fiction writers of the South—among them Mark Twain, Faulkner, Warren, and Lytle—had all recognized that range, understood it, and as their courage and larger vision required presented it to their readers.

McCarthy himself continued to maintain his indifference to the opinions of critics and commentators, especially those from academia. Having completed his apprenticeship, he announced a new "Border trilogy" of novels continuing his saga of the west. For the first five novels he had already received a number of important recognitions: a traveling fellowship from the American Academy of Arts and Letters, an Ingram-Merrill Foundation grant, a Guggenheim Fellowship, and awards from the Faulkner, Rockefeller, and MacArthur foundations. The first book of his new trilogy, however, *All the Pretty Horses* (1992), broke new ground. In it he broadened his scope to include a wider range of human specimens and their responses. The arresting rhetoric and the presentations of violence are still there, but these aspects now take their place in the body of the fiction and allow the questing of John Grady Cole, which is the action of the piece, to remain in focus.

The story is that of a young man's escape from his tangled associations in a South Texas milieu and his travels into uncharted Mexico to discover simultaneously a new world and a new self, and McCarthy presents the venture with an economy and directness that he had not maintained consistently in any of his previous works. For this work he deservedly received both the National Book Award and the National Book Critics Circle Award. Some might argue that here McCarthy, to a greater extent even than he had in *Blood Meridian*, abandoned the South, but that argument ignores the residue of the Spanish heritage in southern minds at least as far north as Tennessee and the persistence in people throughout the region of an urge to press south and westward. John Grady Cole in Texas remains very much the Tennesseean, and he takes the characteristics of a Tennesseean with him as he advances into the Mexican state of Coahuila. There, however, he discovers in the people, the animals, the air they breathe, and above all the changing landscape, which McCarthy renders with a precision and restraint sometimes lacking in his descriptions of East Tennessee, a mirror of something unexplored within himself and intimations of unexplored worlds beyond.

An even greater degree of precision and restraint and a focus on innocent characters amenable to enlightenment are salient characteristics of the second novel in McCarthy's trilogy, *The Crossing* (1994). In it two young boys,

Billy Parham, aged sixteen, and his brother Boyd, fourteen, confront reality as it impinges on their part of the world, the New Mexico of 1939. Boyd struggles to come to terms with all that he encounters there but does not survive the struggle. Billy, whose capacity for acceptance achieves the level of love, at least where his brother and the nonhuman creatures about him are concerned, lives to take things as they come, although not without tears—both the "inexplicable darkness" and the "godmade sun" that rises daily without distinction.

Superficially the picaresque plot of *The Crossing* resembles that of McCarthy's previous novels, but the spine that gives it character and distinction is Billy Parham's successive acts of instinctive charity—his futile attempt to return a pregnant she-wolf to the wild, his dogged and ultimately successful attempt to return the bones of his dead brother to New Mexico for burial, his care for an almost mortally wounded horse, and his efforts, reluctantly come to, to minister to a strange and horribly misshapen dog. Recently critics have become impatient with McCarthy's refusal to avail himself of some of the conventional compromises of the realistic novel, specifically his free use of Spanish dialogue, sometimes at crucial points in the narrative. This indulgence, however, if it may be called that, is consistent with the honesty that has characterized all of his work.

More legitimately vulnerable to criticism has been McCarthy's increasing tendency to use, or seem to use, a centrally placed character in the novel as a spokesperson for his view of such reality as can be known. Apart from this and other mildly questionable devices, however, the cumulative impression from seven novels is of a world inconsistent with any of the patterns of purpose, order, or value that we might be inclined to impose upon it. The sun and stars with regularity rise and set on all alike. Everything else is flux, indiscriminate, indifferent to animal pleasure or suffering. In such a world evil has no meaning; and good is that rare and unpredictable concern that one creature sometimes manifests toward another.

Good, however, is the subject of a closet drama that McCarthy published late in 1994, *The Stonemason: A Play in Five Acts*. The central character (and some would say spokesman for McCarthy) is Ben Telfair, a thirty-two-year-old former graduate student in psychology, now a stonemason, who has undertaken to salvage as much as possible from his disintegrating Louisville (Kentucky) family. Ostensibly Telfair's motivation is charity, but it is not without selfishness, and initially he lacks the fullness of wisdom that comes slowly though his association with his ancient grandfather. In asides to the audience Telfair explains that true stonemasonry embodies the secret of mankind's proper relationship with the universe: accepting and cooperating with the physical principles by which it has stood from time immemorial. In the end he learns the proper application of that insight from a vision of his now dead grandfather—that the better part of charity involves not large attempts to redeem and rectify but a selfless concern to rebuild where rebuilding is wanted and needed and a willingness to let people work out their own lives. Unavoidably some readers will see the views presented here as the abstractable substance of McCarthy's work as a whole and the stonemason's addresses as a thinly veiled apologetic for McCarthy's solid response to the well-made novel that has dominated southern fiction since the 1920s. It remains to be seen whether he is a special case or the first strong contender in the vanguard of a revolution.

14
Three Key Figures

Generalizing about any aspect of history is usually hazardous, one generation's mountain frequently becoming the next generation's foothill or vice versa. Yet looking back at the development of southern literature, the observer can distinguish a few eminences who seem likely to retain their character and position indefinitely. In the years between the two world wars, Thomas Wolfe and William Faulkner were eminences of this kind, as were three members of the Fugitive-Agrarian group at Vanderbilt—John Crowe Ransom, Allen Tate, and Robert Penn Warren. Eudora Welty and Flannery O'Connor are two whose reputation for work done before and since World War II also make them likely candidates for this category. Warren, however, perhaps deserves to be placed in a special category of one, for he more than any of these—perhaps more than any other figure in the century—embodied in his life and work the key elements that have made southern literature distinctive. For that reason it seems fitting to designate him as the supreme summary figure of the century and examine his career in that light as a final chapter in this book.

First, however, it will be necessary to consider three other figures, prominent in the last half of the century although less representative of the century as a whole, who have summed up with major achievements, not all of them strictly literary, separate significant developments that began early and reached something like fulfillment near the end. These figures deserve at least to be called key in any final accounting, and they will be so dealt with here. The first is Shelby Foote, who has recognized the significance of the Civil War as the defining event for almost everything we call southern and told the story of that conflict in an account worthy to stand with the other classic histories in American literature; the second, Walker Percy, who became a southern novelist almost by accident but used its techniques to examine the complex subliminal crisis that arose in the last quarter of the century to dominate both the South and the nation as a whole and so make them one in perplexity; and finally, Wendell Berry, younger than either of the other two, who by heritage, inclination, and genius emerged in the century's last quarter as the embodiment of the South's fundamental agrarianism and explored the meaning of that agrarianism in fiction, poetry, and discursive prose. These three figures, the subjects of the present chapter, stand tentatively as main markers on the map of the South's literature and its still growing self-awareness.

SHELBY FOOTE (B. 1916)

At the time of Faulkner's death in 1963, when eager historians were vying to be the first to identify the belatedly recognized master's successor, no one thought seriously of suggesting Shelby Foote. To be sure, some observers, alert to the potential for literary riches among newer writers in the South, had recognized him as a promising young novelist, one who within the space of a decade had written five respectable novels and edited a collection of stories about the Civil War. But no one thought of Foote as a candidate for greatness, and few took note that Random House, in hopes of meeting the upcoming Civil War Centennial with a literary flourish, had commissioned him to write a brief history for publication by 1961.

Foote had good natural credentials for such an assignment. He was a native of Greenville, Mississippi, where members of his family had settled in 1877, and at the time he himself had been living there for the past twenty-six years. At school he had formed a friendship with the novelist-to-be Walker Percy, the adopted son of the poet William Alexander Percy, and as a frequent participant in the civilized life of the Percy household, he had met and sometimes hobnobbed with the literary and political dignitaries, northern as well as southern, who visited there. In 1935–37 he attended the University of North Carolina but returned to Greenville to devote himself to writing. During World War II Foote served in both the army, from which he was dismissed for insubordination, and the Marine Corps. Immediately after the war he briefly tried working for a radio station and a local paper but quickly returned to the writing of a novel he had begun before the war. That novel, *Tournament*, was published in 1949, after which for the next eight years he worked at a steady pace, publishing three more novels, a volume of interrelated stories, *Jordan County: A Landscape in Narrative* (1954), and, as editor, a collection of short pieces by various authors that he called *The Night before Chancellorsville and Other Civil War Stories* (1957).

For the most part Foote had broken no new ground with his work. Like Faulkner he built at least three of his novels from characters and incidents in his own family history, centering on a mythical Bristol (Mississippi's Greenville) in Jordan (Washington) County. In all three the ancient claims of land and history on their modern inheritors provide the basic situation. *Tournament*'s plantation owner Hugh Bart, for example, loses the sense of identity with and responsibility for the land that sustained his predecessor and thereafter courts disaster as he begins to think of his holdings merely as a means of generating wealth. Another Jordan Countian, the lawyer Parker Nowell in *Follow Me Down*, Foote's second novel (1950), knows better and articulates the required corrective principle; but he does so impersonally in the course of his defense of one Luther Dade Eustis, who not only has come to think of the cotton he grows as a commercial product rather than a gift of the bountiful earth but also has succumbed to the region's religious fundamentalism and self-righteously has killed the prostitute he earlier had taken as a mistress. In *Love in a Dry Season* (1951), the decline of the twentieth-century characters is less spectacular, but these languish in a modern wasteland of materialism, jazz, and alcohol. Like the rest of Foote's failed characters, including those in his collection of stories, *Jordan County: A Landscape in Narrative*, all have denied the greater love that links them to the wellsprings of their being and as a consequence face what amounts to spiritual death.

The most successful of Foote's early novels, however, and the one that brought him to the attention of Random House, was *Shiloh* (1952). This remarkable account of two days of the bloodiest battle fought in the West was presented as a series of interrelated narratives by six participants, officers and foot soldiers, representative of both sides of the conflict. The result was an authoritative rendering of the battle sub specie aeternitatis but one that never averted the reader's gaze from the human actors who were performing, bleeding, and dying in it. It was an example of military narrative at its best but hardly the sort of thing that could have been extended, with values intact, to cover the whole of the Civil War in a brief one-volume account. Nevertheless, Foote accepted Random House's challenge, and Random House to its credit permitted him to continue at his own pace and on the scale he considered necessary. Other historians would produce valuable new one-volume accounts, although not in time for the centennial, among them the highly readable and authoritative *An American Iliad: The Story of the Civil War* (1991) by the historian Charles P. Roland. Foote would complete by 1958 only the 840-page first volume of *The Civil War: A Narrative*, a truly epic account that would require twenty years of uninterrupted labor to complete and run to a total of almost three thousand pages.

The work came out serially in three volumes, subtitled as "Fort Sumter to Perryville" (1958), "Fredericksburg to Meridian" (1963), and "Red River to Appomattox" (1974). Reception of the three volumes, individually and as a whole, was mixed. Reviewers in such publications as *Atlantic*, *New York Times Book Review*, *Newsweek*, *New Republic*, and the literary quarterlies were enthusiastic, although unfortunately their enthusiasm did not always translate into sales. Professional historians by contrast tended to be suspicious, preferring on the whole Bruce Catton's three-volume *Centennial History of the Civil War* (1961–65) or Allan Nevins's *The War for the Union* in four volumes (1959–71). Some chided Foote for failing to provide detailed documentation; Foote, however, had never pretended to be a professional historian in the contemporary sense. Rather, he was managing, perhaps without fully realizing it at first, to be an example of something rare in any age, the historian as artist.

His models were classical historians, Thucydides, Tacitus, and Gibbon; his American predecessors, Parkman, Prescott, Motley, and Henry Adams. The mere fact that he had begun his career as a novelist was not in itself significant. What mattered was the kind of novelist he had turned out to be in a decade of developing his form of the craft. Any artist worth his salt seeks to know his material by re-creating it, and novelists do their re-creating in words, but they differ vastly in what they seek to know and hence in the materials they elect to re-create. Most work with a motley collection of materials derived in part from experience, in part from patterns perceived in previous work or other disciplines, and in part from impulses, more or less recognized, from their own psyches. The resulting fiction is the rendition of new coherences, sometimes coherences unanticipated by the creator, and, if the artist is lucky, new adumbrations of truth, whatever truth may be. By contrast the historian normally re-creates only insofar as his use of language requires him to do so; his aim is to report, nothing more, and he is satisfied in proportion as he is able to marshal observed data so that the data may speak for themselves. The artist who elects to use the materials of the historian performs his unique function, first, in proportion as he faithfully respects the materials of the historian and, second, in the degree to which he is able to present a rendering of the events which will stand the scrutiny of impartial investigators and at the same time provide a surrogate of the original that is credible enough on its own to invite further exploration. In other words, the writer who makes an art of historical writing seeks to render in sensible form a re-creation of a significant part of his world, to know it and make it known.

In brief, Shelby Foote's *The Civil War: A Narrative*, although not the work of a professionally trained historian, nevertheless stands as a prime example of what all great histories must be, a dedicated attempt to comprehend a complex action, one that in this case is panoramic as well as linear. Like all the great historians of the past, Foote was self-taught in the techniques of his craft; and like them he knew, perhaps by instinct, how to detect the presence of a genuine action lurking beneath a mass of data and restore it to visible life. Unbiased professionals have acknowledged that as regards the significant parts of the conflict Foote's account is as complete as any that have been done and that the details, though not visibly anchored with documentation, are as accurate throughout as meticulous research could make them. Three aspects of the war are there, masterfully interwoven: the military, which Foote, perhaps again by instinct, understands better than most who have written about it; the political, with its principal arenas in Washington and Richmond; and the human, from the presidents and generals down to the foot soldiers and those who endured at their homes.

Given the same dedication and time, a similarly endowed professional might have achieved this result. What distinguishes Foote's performance is the comprehensive vision that sustained him through twenty years of single-minded labor and gives unfaltering coherence to his work from chapter to chapter, volume to volume. Surprisingly to many, especially those familiar with Foote's ardent southern sympathies in private life, the work is virtually without bias. As artist-historian he stands apart from and above the multifaceted drama unfolding before him and without predilection or preconceived thesis lets the events have their way. Davis, Lincoln, Lee, Grant, Jackson, Sherman, Forrest, McClellan, these and hundreds more all receive their due. Nothing is added to enliven either them or the events in which they participated. All are summoned from the mass of documents in which their memory has been preserved, and Foote lets them stand as they appear. "Many problems were encountered in the course of this study," he wrote in a bibliographical note at the end of volume 1, "but lack of color in the original materials was never one of them." The colors of war remain in *The Civil War: A Narrative*, dusted off by the author perhaps but without his artificial enhancement.

It would be gratifying to be able to say that Foote's work put an end to popular myths about the Civil War with their sentimental maunderings about the lost cause and tales of southern valor, but such easy glorifications, dubiously founded for the most part, remain invulnerable to criticism and survive as long as the perpetuators have need of them. Foote's three volumes as such were not destined to be popular; works comparable in magnitude to Gibbon's seldom are. Nevertheless, thanks to his engaging appearances on Ken Burns's PBS television documentary, Foote acquired an unexpected coterie of readers who were willing to buy the paperback edition (1986) that Random House had made available, whether they read it or not. In 1991 the same readership also bought, and probably read, the reissued *Shiloh: A Novel* and *September, September*, Foote's moderately successful 1977 novel involving a racial incident in the Memphis of 1957; and in 1993, a new edition of *The Night before Chancellorsville*, newly entitled *Chickamauga and Other Civil War Stories* to emphasize the war in the West.

With these works, new and revived, Shelby Foote belatedly and almost overnight became visible as a major figure in southern letters. In time the solidity of his achievement would be recognized: he had rendered for all readers willing to attend to it a literary facsimile of the complex series of events that initially had defined the South as a region and given a unique and relatively permanent coherence to an emergent culture that in its years of enforced pain and isolation would resist for more than a century the cultural homogenization of the rest of the nation and produce a distinctive literature in its own right. The war that had for present generations all but faded into the past and become an irrelevance was once more available to be felt, heard, seen, explored, and understood—perhaps for the first time.

WALKER PERCY (1916–90)

Shelby Foote's boyhood companion and lifelong friend, Walker Percy, came late to the profession of writing. By the time Percy at age forty-five was ready to publish his first novel (1961), Foote already had five novels to his credit as well as the first volume of *The Civil War: A Narrative*. When Percy died in 1990, however, he had not only closed the gap with six novels and three volumes of essays but had established himself as a major figure in southern letters.

Percy's slow and uncertain development as a writer during his formative years and early manhood may have been due in part to a succession of traumatic experiences that at once tested and augmented his inner strengths as a human being. The first of these events was his father's suicide when he was only thirteen and the consequent removal of the family from Birmingham, where Percy had been born in 1916, to the home of his maternal grandmother in Athens, Georgia. There he lived until the accidental death of his mother two and a half years later, at which point William Alexander Percy, a second cousin, affectionately called "Uncle Will," formally adopted Walker and his two younger brothers and brought them to live with him as his sons in the sophisticated ambience of the Percy home in Greenville, Mississippi.

Walker found the new arrangement congenial but not altogether comforting. Among the benefits he found there—in addition to care, comforts, and affection—were an exposure to the best southern mixture of liberal and conservative attitudes as embodied in Will Percy, an acquaintance with the world of artists, literature, and music, and above all a lifelong friendship with Shelby Foote. Nevertheless, he remained vaguely uneasy and uncertain about a meaningful direction for his life. In due time he went to Chapel Hill, where he earned a B.A. degree in chemistry and then mainly at his guardian's urging proceeded to Columbia, where he earned a degree in medicine in 1941. Percy did well enough in his studies at both places, but the years at Columbia brought his deep dissatisfactions and tensions nearer to the surface, and for three of his years there he underwent psychoanalysis although without gaining much relief.

Finally, during an internship at Bellevue in 1942 Percy contracted tuberculosis, which mandated rest and treatment at a sanitarium at Saranac Lake, New York. Two years later an attempt to resume his association with Columbia as a teacher of pathology precipitated a relapse and a second, briefer period of treatment, this time at the Gaylord Farm Sanatorium in Connecticut. During the first of these periods of retreat he read extensively in the existentialist philosophers, Kierkegaard, Heidegger, Sartre, and Camus; during the second, having abandoned all thoughts of medicine, he began to think of writing as a possible alternative career. Understandably, foremost among the models that caught his eye at this point were Mann's *Magic Mountain* and Dostoyevsky's *Notes from Underground*. Nevertheless, philosophy remained his primary interest. He carefully read Thomas Aquinas, then Thomism's current apologist, Jacques Maritain, and from the French existentialists he went on to read the Germans, especially Heidegger, and from there to Cassirer, Carnap, and finally Susanne Langer. His first published work was an essay on Langer's second major work, *Feeling and Form*. Throughout this period, however, Kierkegaard was his mentor; and when hoping to emulate Sartre and Camus he decided to turn philosophy into fiction, he produced a novel in which the influence of Kierkegaard was discernible throughout.

On first returning to Greenville, however, Percy had found himself at loose ends and an interval at Sewanee, where in years past he had spent happy parts of summers with Will Percy and where he still had friends, proved of little help. Desperate, he headed west and there in the desert air of New Mexico began to achieve the integration that thus far had eluded him. There, too, he made his firm decision to be a writer and began to develop in embryonic form the subject he would write about: man's spiritual alienation in a world dominated by empiricism and his need to seek and cling to some means of wholeness, if need be by violence.

Will Percy's death in 1942 had left his wards financially independent so that Walker in 1946 was free to begin a protracted apprenticeship. He was also free, he discovered, to marry Mary Bunt Townsend, to whom he had been attracted for some time, and with her in 1947 embark upon a commitment to Catholicism, which had been his guardian's faith and in which he hoped to find the path to complete integration he was seeking. It was at this point that with the enthusiasm of a convert he added other Catholic philosophers and thinkers to his reading. In 1950 the couple settled permanently in

Covington, Louisiana—a comfortable "nonplace," as Percy called it—across Lake Pontchartrain from New Orleans; and there as a prospective novelist he worked diligently, for a time with the guidance of Caroline Gordon (also a recent convert), on two apprentice novels, neither of which ever saw publication. At last Alfred Knopf, after requiring numerous changes and revisions and in almost total disregard of the lukewarm approval of all but one of his editors, agreed to publish Percy's third effort, provided he change the title from *Confessions of a Moviegoer* to simply *The Moviegoer*. Apparently Knopf expected very little to come of the book, but it appeared in 1961 and in 1962 to the surprise of many including Percy himself won the National Book Award for Fiction.

Throughout Percy's long and often discouraging period of apprenticeship, Shelby Foote had provided advice (not always heeded) and friendly encouragement. Principally he urged his friend to take with a grain of salt the formalist criticism of Caroline Gordon and her husband Allen Tate, and this part of Foote's advice Percy for better or worse heeded. Even so, the character of the achievements of the two could hardly have been more different, which had less to do with the subjects they wrote about, different as these were, than with the use they made of their respective skills. Foote in both his fiction and history had applied his talents to the recovery and rendition in literary form of a part of the factual past, which for him constituted the face of reality and embodied, in covert form if at all, any deeper realities that might inhere there. By contrast, Percy's way, or part of it, involved beginning with an intellectually perceived deeper reality, at which point he usually proceeded to explore his perception in an essay. Several of these essays—on such subjects as linguistics, semantics, and theology—he published in appropriate journals and in time collected in two volumes—*The Message in the Bottle* (1975) and *Lost in the Cosmos: The Last Self-Help Book* (1983)—the ones that he thought worth keeping. A volume of previously uncollected pieces on a wider variety of subjects, *Signposts in a Strange Land* (1991), was put together, edited, and published after his death. A number of the subjects that Percy dealt with in these collections, especially the first two, show parallels with subjects and themes of his six novels; and this connection, coupled with numerous parallels with details and events of his own life, adds strength to suggestions that much of Percy's fiction can be read as autobiography.

Within limits it can indeed be read so and probably should be. Given the romantic bent of his thinking, Percy turned naturally to the data of his own life for focal points in his novels and probed the depths of his own psyche for the subjects he felt a compulsion to explore, but the fictional surrogates that he created—Binx Bolling, Will Barrett, Lancelot Lamar, Dr. Tom More, to say nothing of the complementary characters that serve as their foils—have a life of their own and are at best uncertain clues to their author's private attitudes and views. All, however, share a condition that Percy felt to be the common lot of perceptive postmoderns everywhere: existence in a secular post-Cartesian world that offers at best illusory prospects of wholeness. Their options were either to accept passively their situation as aliens in that world or to seek a remedy that the world cannot provide.

Percy's first novel, *The Moviegoer* (1961), is at once the simplest and the most representative of the six that he published. It is the account of several crucial days in the life of Binx Bolling, a thirty-year-old New Orleans stockbroker whose sense of alienation has prompted him to take quarters in an unfashionable section of the city rather than live in the Garden District, where his Christian-Stoic Aunt Emily maintains a proper family establishment. When summoned by his aunt, however, Bolling still goes to receive corrective admonitions and gratuitous advice, much of it apparently like the guidance the maturing Percy had once received from his Uncle Will. Another, more revealing manifestation of his urge to withdraw from a world that sickens him is his habitual recourse to moving pictures for images of a stable and more palatable if trivial world, hence the title of the book. Yet Percy's Bolling is also a seeker, as indicated amusingly by his casual flirtations with the physically attractive but plebeian secretaries that he employs. The solution he eventually stumbles on derives from his innate capacity for love and self-sacrifice and in rapid sequence near the end manifests itself in a decision to comply with his aunt's earnest wish that he go to medical school, his concern for his dying half-brother whose Catholic piety he respects but does not share, his ready assumption of responsibility for his younger siblings, and his dedication in marriage to what may well be the lifelong rehabilitation of his aunt's stepdaughter, Kate Cutrer, whose sickness with the world has already brought her past Binx's point of malaise to the brink of suicide.

All of Percy's other novels in a variety of ingenious ways and with more verve address themes developed or adumbrated in his first. All of them work from the same basic assumption, which Percy maintained privately as well as publicly: that the Western world, having acquiesced long ago in the division of mind from body and both from soul, for the most part has now lost its ancient vision of wholeness. The rare few who still possess vestigial intimations of what a complete life might be have no alternative to an existence in despair but to become desperate seekers after something that is undefined and perhaps ineffable. All of Percy's principal characters are or have been such seekers, and for those in the know, most by one or more details call to mind Percy's own early malaise and the circumstances of his life.

For example, Williston Bibb Barrett, the central figure of his second novel, *The Last Gentleman* (1967), is a transplanted southerner recently aware of his predicament, adrift and desperate in New York. Like Percy his distress is complicated by the knowledge that his father on coming to a similar recognition of his situation committed suicide, but Will Barrett's response, again like Percy's, takes the form of a fruitless return to the South followed by a trek west to New Mexico. The bulk of the novel, however, presents Will Barrett's interaction with members of the Vaught family, who provide the immediate occasion for his journeying south and west and serve as foils for his faltering progress toward a recovery. The novel concludes, in a manner inversely reminiscent of the conclusion of Evelyn Waugh's *Brideshead Revisited*, with Barrett's seriocomic attempts to comply with the urgent wishes of a Catholic member of the family and get a dying Jamie Vaught baptized.

The plots of Percy's third and fourth novels both took new directions. *Love in the Ruins* (1971) has as its setting an America already descended into the chaos that Percy thought was probably inevitable. The principal figure is Dr. Tom More, a lapsed Catholic and sex-preoccupied psychiatrist, himself in treatment as an outpatient. The action of the novel is More's attempt by means of a device he calls the ontological lapsometer to take control of the minds of the populace and transform chaos into utopia; its happy denouement is his revelation of himself as a fool and his salvation of sorts under the sober ministrations of a sensible Presbyterian wife. There was nothing of the comic, however, in Percy's *Lancelot* (1977), into which he poured both his disgust with the world, exacerbated at the time by the progressively nauseating Watergate affair, and his latent misgivings about his own commitment to the Catholic faith. In it Launcelot Andrewes Lamar, imprisoned in a madman's cell, describes at length to a failed priest named Percival the context in which he feels justified in having destroyed by fire his unfaithful wife, the Louisiana mansion in which they lived, and a group of actors assembled there to make a film. At the end he is still imprisoned in his rage and developing a plan for a new order centered upon the Nietzschean superman; but the priest, who has seldom spoken throughout, indicates there is still more to be said.

Percy's last two novels strike more positive notes. *The Second Coming* (1980) returns to Will Barrett, this time retired to his native North Carolina, where as a disllusioned Episcopalian still hoping for some sign of an Apocalypse he surveys in vain all forms of religion in the Judaeo-Christian world. In the southern scene, presumably the most religious part of the United States, he finds only chaos. Hence he confronts in detail the circumstances of his father's suicide and contrives an elaborate plan for taking his own life.

Luckily when this attempt at a desperate resolution fails, he has at hand a guide in Allie Huger, a refugee from psychotherapy, who is hiding in an abandoned greenhouse. In her, whose neuroses are roughly complementary to his own, he finds the communion and perhaps the Second Coming that he seeks.

The Thanatos Syndrome (1987) reintroduces Dr. Tom More, now back in Louisiana but only recently released from serving a term in prison for trafficking in controlled substances. Percy's plot, similar to that of a popular suspense thriller, has More discovering and indignantly frustrating an attempt by local physicians and engineers to render the populace inoffensive and amenable by doctoring the water supply, but the plot's function is satire, the immediate object of which is the series of atrocities committed in the name of science during World War II by Nazi physicians and technologists. Ultimately, the object of Percy's scorn here is Western civilization's apparent compliance in science's usurpation of the role civilization once accorded the transcendent, real or imagined, in human life.

Even admirers agreed that this last novel, for all its readability, shows signs of hasty writing and the profound weariness that overtook Percy in the years immediately preceding his death in 1990. Nevertheless, in style, tone, and attitude it was of a piece with the other six and contributes, if only minimally, to the unique position that he established for himself in southern literature. It is too soon to say with confidence what Percy's eventual place will be. As the century draws to a close he seems to stand as one of its most interesting figures, but that may be due in part to his success in addressing its primary anxieties. By some standards he was not a great master of the craft of fiction, but for him that was a matter of choice. On approaching the role of novelist, he had allowed the demands of craft to weigh heavily and sought the advice of fiction's archformalist, Caroline Gordon. Thus *The Moviegoer* is at once the most cautious and the most carefully crafted of all his works. After the unexpected success of that novel, however, he felt free to give priority to concerns of greater personal urgency. In the face of what he conceived to be threats to the kind of society that meant most to him, he declined to put on conspicuous display manifest gifts for characterization, dialogue, and the evocation of place unsurpassed by those of any of his contemporaries. For him devotion to art as an end in itself was at best an evasion and at worst unpardonable idolatry. More prophet than poet, he aimed at presenting variable truths about his time, particularly as regards the materialism that had replaced a moribund spirituality and the consequent despair that had paralyzed some of society's best and driven others to suicide. In that much, at least, he was without peer.

WENDELL BERRY (B. 1934)

During the midsixties, when protests against the war in Vietnam were gathering momentum, people began to be aware of the eloquent and sometimes strident voice of Kentucky's Wendell Berry. With Berry, however, disaffection with the war was secondary to his indignation at the alarming practice of stripmining in the eastern part of his state, with its criminal disregard for land and people, and it was locally published strictures prompted by this indignation that brought him immediate attention and, unperceived at the time, signaled the broader and more constructive concerns his career was shortly to encompass. At the time few outside Berry's circle of friends and associates knew or cared that he had long entertained aspirations to be a writer, and none in the know could have predicted that he would succeed in this effort precisely in proportion as he subordinated his literary talents to nonliterary pursuits. To Berry, however, talents were gifts to be used rather than exhibited, and he was already prepared to deploy such talents as he had in promulgating a single conviction: that our human superiority—if it is that—carries with it a responsibility to respect and preserve the integrity of that part of the world in which by luck we find ourselves. In his view that responsibility takes precedence over everything else, including art, which as it approaches autonomy becomes precious and trivial.

Whatever Berry's views on such matters may have been at the outset, he began by following the customary path to success in the literary profession, which in his case involved an A.B. and an M.A. at the University of Kentucky, followed by two years on a Stegner Writing Fellowship at Stanford, another in Europe on a Guggenheim Fellowship, and finally the sought-after teaching post, at New York University. In addition, in 1964 Berry completed a southern variation on the pattern by returning to the University of Kentucky, where he taught for the next thirteen years, all the while maturing and achieving distinction as a writer.

In 1965, however, Berry had bought a small farm, Lanes Landing, at Port Royal in his native Henry County, intending, he said, to use it as a summer retreat. As things turned out, by that action he had unwittingly committed himself to the life of a working farmer, which meant that for the next twelve years he would work the land and also drive fifty miles to Lexington and back several times each week, over backcountry roads in all weathers, to fulfill his obligations at the university. In 1977, when this dual role became unduly burdensome, he resigned the teaching position to make his living farming, writing, and lecturing.

Since then, except for an interval of seven years (1987–94) in which he did a limited amount of teaching at the university, he has spent his time as a farmer-writer, emerging in that dual role as a prophet of national stature, widely respected if not always heeded. By the time he had completed his second stint at the university, Berry had added some eighty titles to the library catalogue. Many of these, of course, were second editions or reprintings, and a number of the volumes of poetry were elegant chapbooks, reflecting Berry's disposition to favor enterprises where pride in the work took precedence over profit. Even so, there were seven major works of fiction, ten collections of poetry, and a dozen gatherings of essays that by any measure could be considered major.

The first half-dozen titles in Berry's catalogue listing, all published within a space of less than a decade, had collectively set the categories and established an agenda for most of what he would write thereafter. The earliest item, *Nathan Coulter* (1960), a novel begun during his Stanford days, was the first in what was to become a series of five novels and three collections of short stories. All of these would deal with one or more members of several generations of related and associated families who lived in and about a fictitious Port William, and most would be reflective of places, people, and events in Berry's Port Royal. The next two works listed, both published in 1964, are poetry. The first, a single poem of eighty-one lines arranged in eleven uneven stanzas and titled simply *November twenty six, nineteen hundred sixty three*, had appeared in *Nation* shortly after the assassination of President John F. Kennedy and subsequently as a book with illustrations by the painter Ben Shahn. The other volume, *Broken Ground*, was Berry's first collection, and like the first novel it contained reflections of Berry's own experience, including some from Europe and New York as well as Kentucky. For 1967 the catalogue lists a second novel, *A Place on Earth*, and for 1968 an unassuming piece that may well turn out to be his most significant work up to that time: a personal essay entitled "The Rise," published in a limited edition by the University of Kentucky Library. This essay would appear again in two of Berry's collections, but standing alone in 1967 it provided a foretaste of the kind of work by which he would become known throughout the country and abroad.

Berry's ostensible purpose in writing "The Rise" was to recount a six-mile canoe trip down the Kentucky River, undertaken by himself and one other person (never named) on a cold, gray day in mid-December. What he has given us, however, is a perceptive native's meditation on the swollen river, as mile by mile the stream in full majesty of flood reveals the essentials of its nature: beautiful, swift and dangerous, willing to tolerate the traveler who respects its authority but unmistakably in control. Two voices alternate in the telling of the piece: the voice of the newly awakened poet, eager to make us see and hear, and that of the young protester alternately angry and sad at the failure of human beings to respect a natural world that ultimately sustains them. His specific targets are the vacationers from town who litter the riverbanks and the thoughtless sportsmen who later come to the wilderness for nothing more than the pleasure of killing, but he does not spare the country dwellers themselves, who sometimes fatally forget the power they are dealing with.

Midway through the essay he tells the story of "a man I knew in my boyhood" who on just such a day as this, having delayed his landing past sundown, capsized the boat he was using and drifted with the current until he grew numb and finally drowned. Farmers along the shore thought later they might have heard the poor fellow's cries in the dark but could not at the time imagine where the cries could be coming from or what they might mean. That man's folly came to a sad end, but another by luck presumably fared better when he tried to walk across the river with gallon jugs tied to his feet and found himself upside down in the water. Such protests and bits of local folklore mingle in the speaker's meditation with images of swirling water and submerged trees, brief sightings of cardinals that seem to blaze out in the grayness, and the cries of pileated woodpeckers, heard but not seen in the falling dark. All are parts of Berry's Henry County river world, which he deeply respects and loves and which he earnestly commends to our attention.

It is out of a similar but much broader recollection of Henry County in its manifold particulars, past and present—geography, winds and weather, flora, fauna, people, and their ways—that Berry has built his novels and stories and, with minor exceptions, his poems. His first novel, *Nathan Coulter* (1960), was written at least partly as a recollection, both of the place where he grew up and of his own growing up in it. *A Place on Earth* (1967), however, was written "on location" by an author who had come home to stay, and like its predecessor and the two novels that would follow, it represented the author's exploration of the implications of a position he had found himself in almost as soon as he decided to become a writer and make Henry County his subject.

The ground of that position was a conviction, in part inherited, that human beings have a natural obligation to respect the rest of the natural world and seek an accommodation with it. This conviction alone might have enabled Berry to become a naturalist of the first order, but as a child of rural Kentucky and the scion of several generations of Bible-believing farmers, he had taken to heart early in life God's mandate to Adam: to "fill the earth and subdue it; and have dominion over . . . every living thing that moves upon the earth." To him this obligation meant caring for whatever comes to one's hand— land and its produce, animals domesticated and wild, spouse, family, and neighbors. The terms Berry chose to express his obligation were "husbandry" and "marriage," and their substance provides the action for *A Place on Earth*, which is the story of one man, Mat Feltner, who when faced with an insurmountable crisis in his life finds in the therapy of work on his land and the acceptance of responsibility to care for the remaining members of his family a peace and a satisfaction with his lot that he has never known before.

By reflection and observation Feltner also comes to understand the significance of place, another key term in Berry's catalogue of values. The family farm in Port William with which he had made his primary marriage has ever since that transaction owned him at least as much as he owned it, but he grasps fully the nature of their interdependence only as he thinks back in his grief to the generations that have preceded him there and comes to realize that place has a dimension in time quite as important as its dimension in length and width. In electing to add his life to that context Mat Feltner without quite realizing it has indeed chosen something that in effect has already chosen him, and that choice combined with his own innate capacity for work and love makes possible the land's renewal and keeps Mat himself whole.

Berry's next two novels were more sharply focused than the previous ones, but both were marked by the same free use of omniscience to create a complex perspective, and both continued the exploration and presentation of principles that had emerged with clarity in *A Place on Earth*. The first, *The Memory of Old Jack* (1974), is ostensibly the reminiscence of ninety-two-year-old Jack Beechum, uncle to Mat Feltner, as on his dying day he stands on the porch of a small Port William hotel. Jack has long since retired there with his memories, which, when considered as a whole, serve as another example of Berry's deep-seated beliefs about the virtues of a life mainly spent in loving commitment to land, family, and community. The memories are not Jack's alone, however. As in the previous novel, what we see is partly the recollections of the central character and partly those of others who knew and were influenced by him. Thus the novel is a memory of old Jack in complementary senses, illustrating by its method of narration the principle that life as fostered by genuine agricultural communities like Port William is always to a significant degree communal.

The same point is made again in *Remembering* (1988), Berry's fourth novel, which also involves a reminiscence, this time one by a much younger man, Andy Catlett, Mat Feltner's grandson, who on maturing had left Port William, going first to college and then to work for an agricultural magazine. Experience, however, has brought disillusionment with the direction that American agriculture seemed to be taking, and he returns home, intending like his grandfather (and, one should add, also like Wendell Berry) to live out his days on the small farm and defend in place its practical and spiritual values. Ironically, there he encounters the enemy head-on in the guise of a modern mechanical corn picker, which destroys his right hand and ends, as he supposes at the time, any hopes of making a life as a farmer. All this we learn as Andy in his second attempt to leave the land finds himself lying sleepless in the "darkness visible" of a San Francisco hotel room. There in the course of his remembering he unfolds for himself an intricate web of precedents involving several generations of Port William's Feltners, Beechums, and Catletts—all enhanced and integrated by the unseen narrator of the story with threads of allusion and analogy, Miltonic, Dantean, and even Homeric—suggesting hopefully Andy Catlett Everyman's unwitting participation in the age-old patterns of departure and return, fall and redemption.

In his fifth novel, *A World Lost* (1996), Berry concentrates on a special case in the Port William community, Andy Catlett's irresponsible and fun-loving uncle, for whom Andy is named and whom for a time as a boy he admired even more than he now admires his father. Andrew's sudden and meaningless murder at the hands of a habitually angry neighbor, however, initiates in the ten-year-old Andy an inquiry that begins as childish questioning about the circumstances of the incident and continues into his early maturity without achieving complete resolution. Nevertheless, in after years he sees that his protracted inquiry was the means whereby he came to recognize the beauty of a life like his uncle's and to appreciate the wisdom of placing joy in people, family, and friends well ahead of rigorous devotion to duty and dedication to land. He now knows that his Uncle Andrew is and always was one of that company of immortals by whose light he himself has been able to discover in love the source of his being and his only true happiness.

No summary can do justice to this most satisfying of Berry's novels, one that marks his mastery of the craft and his complete transmutation of passionate private convictions into art. The novels, however, were never Berry's principal means of consolidating and circulating his views. To that end he has written essays, personal as well as polemic, on a variety of topics but mainly on the part that agriculture has played in the development of America's distinctive culture and the dangers he foresees in America's apparent willingness to redefine agriculture as an industry and reshape it in the image of manufacturing. By 1988, the year in which he published *Remembering*, Berry had written enough of these to fill ten volumes with a fair number of pieces left over. The first volume, called *The Long-Legged House*, came out in 1969, the year in which he turned thirty-five, and in addition to "The Rise" contained essays on both the disastrous effects of strip-mining in East Kentucky and the folly of America's war in Vietnam. *The Hidden Wound* (1970), written in 1968–69 but amplified with an important afterword in the second edition (1989), was and is Berry's word on racism—part analysis, part polemic, and part a moving memoir of two black people, Nick and Aunt Georgie, who unknowingly shaped his thinking on the subject. *The Unforeseen Wilderness* (1971), illustrated with photographs by his friend Eugene Meatyard, is a series of meditations prompted by a trip into Kentucky's Red River Gorge that functions as a protest against the plan (fortunately abandoned) to flood the place and provide water for the growing city of Lexington.

The next three collections indicate by their titles the principal subject matter in them: *A Continuous Harmony: Essays Cultural and Agricultural* (1972), *The Unsettling of America: Culture and Agriculture* (1977), and *The Gift of Good Land: Further Essays Cultural and Agricultural* (1981). Other topics turn up in these books—among them, American education, the poetry of William Carlos Williams (a strong influence on Berry's own work), and Homer's *Odyssey*—but the principal topic is the interdependence of culture and farming and the current rage for industrialism that threatens to destroy both America's land and its people. The second collection, *The Unsettling of America*, although prompted, Berry says, by the farm policies of Earl Butz, the secretary of agriculture during the Johnson Administration, can and should be read as a single, sustained essay. It presents most persuasively Berry's abiding conviction that until recently respect for the land, perpetuated by small farmers, has been a crucial part of culture in America, giving to farmers and nonfarmers alike a sense of community without which no nation can endure.

In 1981 Berry brought out a retrospective volume, *Recollected Essays, 1965–1980*, which contains eleven key essays, some slightly revised from five of his previous collections and one, "The Making of a Marginal Farm," that had been published the year before in the *Smithsonian*. In 1983, however, he published a new collection dealing almost exclusively with poetry, *Standing by Words*, in which he developed at length his belief that the dissociation of poetry, like that of agriculture, from other human concerns has been one of the disasters of our time. The theory of poetry implicit there is not one with which other critics are likely to agree, but it is one that wholly or in part has sustained such poets and artists as Wordsworth, Ruskin, Arnold, Tolstoy, Edwin Muir (another poet whom Berry admires), the sculptor Eric Gill, and William Carlos Williams. For students of Berry's own poetry, the whole book—especially the first chapter, which deals with modern poets, and the next to last, "Poetry and Place," which astonishingly ranges over the whole of English poetry—are mandatory reading. In 1987 two new essays appeared as *The Landscape of Harmony: Two Essays on Wildness and Community*, published in England, and both of these appeared again that same year in *Home Economics*, which contained twelve additional essays.

Since then Berry has published four more independent volumes of non-fiction. The year 1990 saw his *What Are People For?*, a collection of essays, reviews, and registers of opinion on a variety of subjects, notable people and books, poetry, Christianity in rural churches, feminism, and his refusal to use a word processor. In the same year the University of Kentucky published an expanded version of his Blazer Lectures, *Harlan Hubbard: Life and Work*, eight essays in tribute to a remarkable painter and writer and his equally re-markable wife, who in spite of the conventions imposed by time and place, lived a good life of work and self-sufficiency in a house they had built for themselves on the banks of the Ohio. *Sex, Economy, Freedom and Commu-nity* (1992) added eight more essays to the canon, including "The Problem of Tobacco" and "Christianity and the Survival of Creation," a lecture delivered at the Southern Baptist Theological Seminary in Louisville; and in 1995 *An-other Turn of the Crank* provided six more, described by the publisher as "six new essays on sustainability and stewardship," two of the key principles in all of Berry's thinking and writing from the first novel on.

Given the principles explored and presented in Berry's novels and essays, it was inevitable that readers should compare his work with that of Thoreau and the literary men among the Vanderbilt Agrarians. Obviously he has things in common with all of these, but in fairness he cannot be equated with any of them. Unlike Thoreau, Berry for all his love of nature is not a naturalist, and solitariness is not one of the virtues that he champions. Moreover, Berry, again unlike Thoreau, is a lover of farming and has been actively engaged in it for most of his life—something that cannot be said of the Vanderbilt group, not even of Lytle, who after reaching adulthood farmed only intermittently. Nei-ther has Berry been moved, as Ransom and Tate were, to preserve "the most substantial exhibit on this continent of a society of the European and historic order." For Berry such considerations of political science mean little. He is not even self-consciously southern. Where place is concerned, he says, his first loyalty is to Port Royal, after that to Henry County, then to Kentucky, and finally to the world.

Yet southern he is, in spite of having lived only a few miles south of the Ohio River; and like Donald Davidson and the other dedicated Agrarians, he stands in opposition to domination by technology and industrialism and to large-scale agriculture (agrobusiness, he prefers to call it), none of which he thinks of as exclusively or even distinctively northern. Nor apparently has it ever occurred to him to decry an alleged northern domination of the arts. For Berry the enemy abides wherever charity is absent. From the example of his family and others of the community that nourished him he acquired almost in infancy the habit of accepting as neighbor whatever creatures of the natural world were next to him—people, male and female, white and black, animals tame and wild, and land as given, regardless of its presumed utility—and, as already noted, a natural obligation to respect all these and care for them in the order of their nearness.

Critics have noted that Berry has portrayed his Port Royal mentors in all his fiction and especially in the short stories, now collected in three volumes, but too few have noticed the mastery of craft that manifested itself strikingly in the first collection, *The Wild Birds: Six Stories of the Port William Membership* (1986) and advanced progressively with the second and third, entitled respectively *Fidelity: Five Stories* (1992) and *Watch with Me and Six Other Stories of the Yet-Remembered Ptolemy Proudfoot and His Wife, Miss Minnie, Nee Quinch* (1994). These shorter pieces are somehow freer, almost as if in undertaking them he felt liberated from the constraint to make a point that haunted him in composing the longer works. In any case the short stories are clearly the work of a naturally talented writer and present for close inspection some of the lives that make up that extended community of souls past and present which he refers to as "the membership."

Some have compared Berry's achievement here to Faulkner's Yoknapatawpha, but the comprehensive term that he has chosen to apply to it indicates the difference between the two. The title of one of his stories, "Thicker than Liquor," about an incorrigible uncle who manages to be an embarrassment and burden to all concerned, emphasizes Berry's point. Most of the people in Port William are individualists, but they seem to have adapted to one another, tolerating eccentricities and differences that in Yoknapatawpha would almost certainly have made aliens of the possessors. The inhabitants of Berry's part of Kentucky (predominantly white, although traces of the slave days remain) are yeoman farmers and have been so since the early settlement. Over the years they all have become cousins by association, and frequently in fact as well. By custom they watch over one another and share one another's lives. When the rare feuds occur among them, they are considered family affairs and usually settled in-house. Directly or indirectly his experiences with this homogeneous group and the particular corner of the natural world that sustains them are the source and subject of all of Berry's fiction.

As already noted, the Port Royal membership and its nonhuman context also provide the subject matter for most of Berry's poetry, which he thinks of as a species of rhetoric, a strategy for the persuasive presentation of a message. His standard for poetry, announced after he was well into his career, is simply speech made memorable by measure; and his forebears in this pursuit are Emerson, Whitman, and the poet-prophets of the Old Testament. Thus it is not surprising that he especially admires Frost's use of direct colloquial statement and has expressed approval of William Carlos Williams's strategy of repudiating overt formality but subtly preserving the true essentials of form. Emulation of these styles, however, even had he been able to accomplish them to his own satisfaction, would scarcely have been enough to recommend him for consideration by conservative academic critics, who continued to declare irony and ambiguity the primary criteria for acceptable poetry, or by the new wave of iconoclasts, many of whom advocated dispensing with order altogether.

Berry's first collection, appropriately called *The Broken Ground*, was the immature work of a young man, but it gives a good indication of the variety of topics he would later write about and includes one long piece, "The Handing Down," in which in some 130 three- and two-line stanzas he reviews with perceptivity and commendable control the state of mind of a man grown old and wise in his community and aware of his approaching death. Since then he has produced nine more collections, eight of which consist almost entirely of new work. Their titles, in order of their publication, are as follows: *Openings* (1968), *Findings* (1969), *Farming: A Hand Book* (1970), *The Country of Marriage* (1973), *Clearing* (1977), *A Part* (1980), *The Wheel* (1982), *Collected Poems, 1957–1982* (1985), *Sabbaths* (1987), *Sabbaths 1987* (1991), and *Entries* (1994).

Berry's poetry began to come of age in *Farming: A Hand Book* (1970), the longest and richest of his collections up to this time. Some of the poems here simply versify the continuing irritation and anger of the polemical essayist ("The Morning's News," "The Farmer among the Tombs," "In This World," "March 22, 1968"), and occasionally one of them suffers from a deficiency in perception ("The Farmer and the Sea"). Many more, however, beautifully exemplify the motto Berry may have adopted from William Carlos Williams ("No ideas but in things"): "The New Roof," "On the Hill Late at Night," "Independence Day," and "The Grandmother." At least two poems, "The Birth (Near Port William)" and "Meditation in the Spring Rain," show a gift, unfortunately not indulged often enough, for narrative verse, and the second of these reveals a gift for transforming folk humor into poetry that is probably best exemplified in a later collection of anecdotal pieces which critics and even admirers often tend to ignore, *Sayings and Doings*, published by Gnomon Press in 1975. Then, too, there is the mad farmer, a Port William Dionysius who first makes his appearance in an uproarious poem presented "in homage" to his friend Ed McClanahan, at the time working on his own uproarious novel about a natural man. The same character appears in four other poems, in three of which the farmer acts as Berry's mouthpiece.

With *The Country of Marriage* (1973), his fifth collection, Berry brought his poetry into clear focus with what one at this point might call, pretentiously perhaps but accurately, his philosophy of farming. Henceforth, marriage would be a key term for all his commitments—to wife, family, animals wild and domestic, and land—in short, to the natural world in its endless variety. This book is the most representative of Berry's works and one of his best. Almost everything is in it: the poems in tribute to his wife, including the beautiful seven-stanza title poem; poems addressed to Allen Tate and William Butler Yeats; a recollection of Edwin Muir; poems to and about animals; meditations on a country funeral and on winter; more poems about the mad farmer, including "Manifesto: The Mad Farmer Liberation Front," surely the best of the lot; poems in free verse; and tentative experiments in formal prosody that would bear fruit in another collection, *Sabbaths*, to be published more than ten years later.

Sabbaths (1987) is different from anything else Berry has attempted and different from any other volume of poetry by a southern author. Together with its sequel, *Sabbaths 1987* (1991), it presents a series of fifty-three meditative poems in which he seeks to bring his passionate convictions about farming, family, nature's economy, and mankind's violations of it into line with religious convictions that remain from the Baptist pieties of his upbringing. The territory is the same as that for the earlier poetry. Details of the Lanes Landing farm and of the Port Royal community are recognizable, and there are addresses to members of his family (wife, daughter, and son), but the images of all these, especially those of creatures in the nonhuman world, are not rendered but declared, presented as occasions for rumination or without comment as metaphors for a comprehensive order that he accepts on faith. Together they speak to him of life, death, resurrection—recurrences that persist in spite of human perversity, manifestations of a greater Sabbath that asserts its existence in the quiet of a Sunday, when custom if nothing else requires both laborer and angry man to rest. Frequently the principle of order becomes explicit in these poems, as contrary to previous usage Berry turns away from free verse to rhyme and the simpler traditional verse forms; but even here the implicit order of normal syntax usually takes precedence. The most effective poem of the lot, couched in his usual free verse, comes at the conclusion of *Sabbaths 1987* when he goes to feed the animals on a cold Christmas morning, recalls "the Child bedded in straw," and senses the holiness that according to the best insight of his country faith has surrounded him always.

In 1994 Berry put together still another volume, *Entries*, which contains a number of poems that for unpretentious craftsmanship will surely stand among his best: "The Parting," "One of Us," "The Wild Rose," "The Venus of

Botticelli," "Spring," "The Widower," and "The Storm." There are more poems celebratory of his various "marriages": to his daughter, his wife, his mother, and his friend Hayden Carruth. One poem, "The Record," speaks of his conviction that active membership in a community is a person's best hope of participating in an extended life, and another, "The Mad Farmer, Flying the Flag of Rough Branch, Secedes from the Union," presents the essence of his many injunctions to a generation adrift from its moorings. These matters, however, are best and most movingly presented in a concluding section that consists of a sequence of poems about his father's last days and a dream poem in which he sees the old man abandon cane and broken stance to leap upon a frisking horse and sit upright.

Never at any point in his career has Berry written poems that conformed to prevailing fashion, yet even at his setting forth he found an audience of the select few who recognized his talent and the genuineness of his passion for wholeness (among them the poet Gary Snyder) and a much larger but less perceptive group of antiestablishment, protesting students, who appreciated his plainspokenness and thought they discerned in his return to farming a simple and easy way whereby they themselves might someday avoid the confusion and frightening contradictions of modern life. Unlike most writers, southern or otherwise, he has never, except perhaps at the beginning, made writing his goal, although writing has brought him numerous honors: a Guggenheim Award, a Rockefeller Award, several honorary degrees, an Emily Balch Prize for *Nathan Coulter* from the *Virginia Quarterly Review*, a Lannan Foundation Award for Nonfiction, and an Aiken-Taylor Award for Poetry from the University of the South.

All of Berry's activities have been the consequence of a set of passionate convictions that can be reduced to three simple principles: denial of self, love of one's neighbor, and an acceptance of the responsibility of stewardship over the "good gifts" of heaven and earth. In some hands a career spent in the exemplification of these principles might have degenerated quickly into tedious sentimentality, but Berry's sense of humor and above all his talent have resulted in a unique contribution to America's literature and the literature of the South. He is a southern agrarian who has proved his love of the soil by faithful tillage and a Kentucky Thoreau who has enhanced his love of nature by including the human race in it.

15
Robert Penn Warren

Of all the southern writers of the twentieth century—not excluding Faulkner, the one towering genius to emerge during the period—Robert Penn Warren (1905-89) has probably come closest to finding a point of equilibrium between honest portrayals of the various and sometimes contradictory faces of America's South and the integrity of their collective identity, tension between which had given the literature of this time and region a dynamic life unique in American letters. With one or two exceptions southern literature as we know it had begun shortly after the Civil War, and most authors in that period had taken pains in their fiction and verse to offer representations of life and manners acceptable to southern readers. In general they had excluded unflattering, or "tasteless," details (a practice that continued well into the twentieth century) and written with one eye on the objects being portrayed and another on a sentimental ideal order that served as a context. From that order, they suggested (or at least implied) that a nobler form of the present diminished state had fallen or been made to fall. For a time readers, at least in the South, accepted their suggestion at face value, approved the cautious selection of detail, and expressed loud disapproval whenever some upstart Caldwell or Faulkner instead gave them caricature or honest realism.

With World War I the tide of realism began to make advances even in the normally conservative South, and Vanderbilt's Fugitive-Agrarians, of whom Warren was a junior member, repudiated the romantic ideal of an Elysian antebellum South and replaced it with ingenious ideals of their own dreaming. Ransom and Tate maintained that the South had perpetuated on its foreign soil the semblance of a sophisticated European civil order which, being patrician and agrarian, had escaped corruption by puritanical Yankee merchants. Donald Davidson, ever the plebeian, formulated the image of a South that perpetuated the economic and moral austerity of those tall men of the frontier who had transmitted their virtues to the race of yeoman farmers that succeeded them.

Spirited discussions of both notions flourished in the ranks of the Agrarians, but to what extent, if any, Warren shared either of them is difficult to say. His essay for their Agrarian manifesto suggests that even as a young man his sympathies were already veering toward the way of newer American writers, second-generation inheritors of European naturalism and precursors of existentialism, who had put a high priority on realistic representation and committed themselves to no principle except that of letting facts speak for themselves. In any case the mature Warren to all appearances walked in the path of these people, good-humoredly maintaining his individuality, until at last the path became a highway filled with southern writers who remembered Ransom, Tate, and Davidson mainly as dedicated artists of a vanished era and the all-but-forgotten romanticists of post–Civil War days only as curiosities.

This is not to say that Warren was without a shaping ideal of his own. The difference between him and his onetime mentors was that his ideal was something patently unrealized, to be discovered and known, if at all, only by such exploratory tools as were at his disposal, principally that of writing poetry. This difference also existed between Warren and many of the twentieth-century southern writers who had responded to the stimulus of their realist predecessors earlier in the century. More recently, thanks to the influence of those predecessors, to which Warren added his own, the skills of the newer southern writers have come almost ready-made, but as the century has drawn to a close, neither the power of a shaping ideal nor the urgency of a need to find one has been sufficient to drive the creativity of emerging novelists and poets. The quest for a new image of the South that became necessary when the comfortable image of an idyllic past faded has gradually lost its power as year by year the region draws closer to full union with the rest of the nation and confronts the prospect of persisting only as a geographical designation.

Had Warren's career ended in 1950, the year in which he gave up his post of eight years at the University of Minnesota and moved to the Yale Drama School, he would still stand high among his southern peers—Ransom, Tate, Welty, Faulkner—but probably would come short of his current stature as one of the important figures in twentieth-century American literature. At that point his accomplishments consisted of three novels, one of which, *All the King's Men*, had received a Pulitzer Prize, a volume of short stories that included the memorable "Blackberry Winter," three distinguished volumes of poetry, and two major essays, "Pure and Impure Poetry" (1943) and "A Poem of Pure Imagination: An Experiment in Reading" (1946), both of which remain major contributions to the critical literature of the century. He had also been an active member of Vanderbilt's Fugitive and Agrarian groups, the co-editor of a series of revolutionary textbooks, and a cofounder of the *Southern Review*, at the time certainly the preeminent literary quarterly in America and according to some in the English-speaking world as well.

During the almost forty years that followed (1950–1989), Warren continued in his role as teacher-author, and although he published seven more novels, one of them a masterpiece and all of them interesting, the poet in him after 1950 took precedence over the writer of fiction, bringing him many additional awards and honors. Among these were two more Pulitzer Prizes, a Bollingen Award, and in 1986 designation as the country's first official poet laureate. In addition, during the same period this southern but border-state author, who in early maturity had seen more clearly than most that 1860–65 indeed marked the birth of the South, emerged as a perceptive and for the most part genial oracle to a nation still in the painful process of coming of age. Even so, throughout the second half of his life, as he had during the first, Warren remained manifestly southern in his choice of subject matter and in the scrupulous authenticity with which he presented it. That he also became a national author was due in part, but only in part, to his physical detachment from the region he wrote about. Genius, of course, had something to do with it, along with his capacity for industry, phenomenal from the beginning, and his congenital inability to relax from mental activity. Most important, however, was a key conviction, early arrived at but not held with complete confidence as long as he was surrounded by formalist friends and mentors at Vanderbilt: namely, that poetry and fiction are not ends in themselves but tools for exploring both the heterogeneous manifestations of human nature and the complex and mysterious nonhuman world that surrounds them. Poems and stories he saw as the products of a process of discovery, and ultimately he came to value both in proportion as they dealt honestly and faithfully with the subjects addressed and any subjects unexpectedly encountered along the way.

An existentialist, at least in part, long before he knew the term, Warren lived always in the transitory present, the Now, and derived most of his values from the ephemera of existence. In the early days this stance, of which he probably was not fully aware, set him apart from his Vanderbilt colleagues— particularly Ransom, who even in later years was sometimes disturbed by Warren's earthiness, and Davidson, who was so startled on reading "The Briar Patch," Warren's contribution to *I'll Take My Stand*, that he almost rejected it. Nevertheless, self-confidence in what was to be the young man's mature view was burgeoning by the time he wrote "Pure and Impure Poetry" in 1942, and it had reached full flower with *A Poem of Pure Imagination* in 1946. After that the first fully ripened creative work of Warren's maturity came with his second (and, as it turned out, final) major novel, *World Enough and Time*, published in 1950.

By comparison with the technically finished *All the King's Men* (1946), *World Enough and Time* was an impure novel, and critics were not sure what to make of it. Warren had chosen as his subject the once notorious but largely forgotten "Kentucky Tragedy," in which a callous young man had sought to remove the stain of seduction from a young woman by murdering her seducer. Instead of returning to his device of the single narrator who would bear in himself the focus of the action, Warren here used three voices—the hero's in his journal account, that of a scholarly redactor interpreting what the hero had written, and a third voice, presumably Warren's, controlling the performance but until near the end maintaining, more or less successfully, invisibility. The result was a sustained ambiguity taken for uncertainty by many of his readers, who were made even more uneasy by Warren's inversion of the ethical conventionalities: making the lady attractive but unlovable, the villain in many ways morally preferable to the young avenger, and the avenger himself too naive and unteachable to justify the convoluted course of his education. Many also missed the cautionary force of the title, which echoed Marvell's "To His Coy Mistress," and failed to see that like the poem Warren's novel recommended accepting the here and now instead of striving for a more satisfactory but unachievable ideal. It was, in short, a performance to be expected from an emerging major author ready to put on the mantle of Melville or Hawthorne but hardly one calculated to please an audience accustomed to being reassured.

During the fifties Warren published two more novels, both ambitious but neither equal to *World Enough and Time* in complexity or control. *Band of Angels* (1955) was the story of Amantha Starr, told throughout in her own words, who learns at her father's graveside that she is the daughter of a black slave and hence, being legally chattel, is subject to being disposed of with the rest of her father's assets. This unexpected blow to the woman's freedom, however, is secondary to damages that the news wreaks on her sense of identity, and the novel becomes the long account of her progress from self-pity ("Poor little Manty") to an acceptance of what she is and a recognition of the unique dignity that is rightfully hers. The ending of his next novel, *The Cave*, published four years later (1959), was somewhat less optimistic. This work constituted a digression for Warren in that, contrary to his practice elsewhere, he focused on no single protagonist but made his central character, Jasper Harrick (a noncharacter, as some have called him), fatally trapped and immobile in his Tennessee cave, the occasion for all the other characters to participate in a quest for identity that ultimately unites them and gives the novel its meaning. Suggestion for the story had come from the entrapment of Kentuckian Floyd Collins in Sand Cave more than thirty years before, an event that attracted worldwide attention and turned a remote spot in the middle of the state into the site for a bizarre carnival of hill-country neighbors, imported miners, the Red Cross, and the Kentucky National Guard. Warren's skillful use of that aspect of the situation adds much to the interest of *The Cave*, just as his re-creations of slave life had done in *Band of Angels*, yet neither of these novels captured the fancy of the public or the attention of critics to the same extent as his previous two successes.

The works that made the fifties a turning point in Warren's career were poems: a book-length dramatic piece, occasionally reminiscent of the Book of Job, called *Brother to Dragons: A Tale in Verse and Voices* (1953); and a fourth book of lyric poetry, *Promises: Poems, 1954–1956* (1957), for which he received the National Book Award, the Edna St. Vincent Millay Prize from the Poetry Society of America, and his second Pulitzer Prize. The first of these works, *Brother to Dragons*, presented the story of Thomas Jefferson's Kentucky nephews and their senseless murder of a black man on the eve of the New Madrid earthquake in 1811 and did so in the form of a colloquy, more oratorio than play, involving the disembodied principals of the affair, the spirit of Thomas Jefferson, and R.P.W., "the writer of this poem." In the course of the story the issue of human imperfection, addressed so forcefully in *All the King's Men* and *World Enough and Time*, is pushed to its desperate extremity, inexplicable evil, here ironically the fruit of the same lineage that had produced the most enlightened of America's founding fathers. On this pivotal point Warren's preoccupation with the puzzle of right action in individual human beings, evident since his biography *John Brown* (1929), became an inquiry into the perils attendant on national self-definition with a conclusion as ambiguous as the one he would come to at the end of his prose essay, *The Legacy of the Civil War: Meditation on the Centennial*, published in 1961. Thus in retrospect *Brother to Dragons*, revised and published again in 1979, can be thought of as the visible dividing line in Warren's career, the point at which as man of letters, neither wholly novelist nor wholly poet but both, he ceased to be exclusively a southern writer and began to confirm a position in the broad field of American literature.

This, contrary to early expectations, he would do mainly as a poet. *Promises: Poems, 1954–1956* (1957), Warren's first volume of lyric verse in more than ten years, differed sharply from all that had gone before. Of the formal structures, esoteric diction, and metaphysical complexities that had characterized his earlier poetry, significant echoes remained and would continue to be heard in later works although with diminishing frequency. The use of the second personal pronoun, partly as a device to involve the reader but, more important, to dramatize an internal debate, had been a distinctive feature of Warren's work ever since his employment of it in "Original Sin: A Short Story," and this feature also would continue, as would the disturbing concreteness of that early poem and the mixture of narrative and reflection that distinguishes another early and major achievement, "The Ballad of Billie Potts." Henceforth, however, his poetry would be freer in form and, primarily at least, a vehicle for personal concerns.

Ostensibly *Promises* is what the title suggests, a volume devoted to the new promises in his life, Rosanna Warren and her infant brother Gabriel, born in those years to him and his second wife, the fellow novelist and essayist Eleanor Clark. It contains two sequences of poems. The first and shorter one, "To a Little Girl, One Year Old, in a Ruined Fortress," is dedicated to Rosanna; the second, entitled "Promises," (in a somewhat different sense), to Gabriel. All the poems were written during a stay in Italy, but only those in the sequence to Rosanna reproduce the Italian scene, where, Warren later said in an interview, he acquired a new understanding of the roots of poetry and learned to follow a mood, a chance impression, even a whim, instead of taking an abstract idea or bit of story and making verse to embody it. In these poems, three of which have the structure of sonnets, the child Rosanna in her innocent capacity for enjoying the world as it is renews the promise that her father, saddened by experience, has all but despaired of seeing fulfilled. In the second much longer sequence, addressed to the infant Gabriel, Warren reviews starker images and impressions of his own early life, recalls the promises implicit in his relationships with his grandfather and parents, all now dead, and in these reminiscences delivers the sterner promises of things the child must encounter in his passage from infant sleep to final sleep. In a concluding lullaby he bids the child in his innocent rest to summon strength to know the world as it is and in the fullness of that knowledge come to see that time's deepest wounds are often the guise of its "irremediable joy."

The hard-bitten faith that lurks in the conclusion of this poem had appeared before in Warren's work and would prove to be a constant throughout the rest of it. After *Promises* he lived thirty-two more years and published twelve additional volumes of poetry, one every two or three years, all or most affirming in one way or another that God's love—he used the word for deity sparingly but always meaningfully—is for the world as it is, not for some ideal world from which the world we know has fallen. One of the twelve was a revision of *Brother to Dragons*, and two were long poems, *Audubon: A Vision* (1969) and *Chief Joseph of the Nez Perce, Who Called Themselves the Nimipu, "The Real People": A Poem* (1983). The remaining nine, however, are all best thought of as parts of a work in progress, the conclusion of which would be simply the ending of poetic activity with the publication of his last volume and death. These volumes vary in quality, but all were well received; and one of them, *Now and Then: Poems, 1976–1978* (1978), brought Warren his third Pulitzer

Prize. Three were recapitulations of work up to the point of their publication: *Selected Poems: New and Old, 1923–1966* (1966), which received the Bollingen Prize; *Selected Poems, 1923–1975* (1976); and the final volume *New and Selected Poems, 1923–1985* (1985), which contains as its first section what is in effect a new volume, *Altitudes and Extensions, 1980–1984.* In these publications, as the initial date in the titles indicates, Warren gave the reader a tentative overview of his life's achievement in poetry from his most recent pieces back to some that he had written shortly after joining the Vanderbilt Fugitives; and in each volume he made significant deletions, rearrangements, and revisions, indicating thereby his latest view of his work.

As has been noted, Warren's poetry undergoes a stylistic shift with *Promises: Poems, 1954–1956.* Even so, the entire corpus forms a coherent whole and is distinctively his from beginning to end. The diction remains much the same, ranging from the cerebral through the colloquial, occasionally to the scatological, and sometimes with a mixture of all three. Many of the poems are reminiscences of his Kentucky past, with data in abundance, scenes, people, encounters casual and otherwise with family members, friends, and neighbors, incidents seen directly or reported, all adding up to an impression of community with which the speaker (or Warren himself) still feels a strong affinity, even after years of separation. Repeatedly, especially in the later poems, with varying admixtures of affection, tension, and pain, he considers personal relationships with those elders who have meant most to him, notably his father. Whatever the subject, he presents it concretely and without condescension, as something worthy of respect and acceptance in its own right, and often in addition as a symbol to be explored.

Some have objected that Warren, once committed to poetry as his principal medium, wrote too much, but writing—all writing—for him was the equivalent of thinking, and from the beginning he wrote compulsively. The mark of his genius was that he knew that nothing worth seeing is ever finished, and he was good at recognizing when a piece of writing was at least tentatively worthy of being seen. Revision of work in a novel, once it had appeared in print, was scarcely practicable; the best way to achieve that was to write another. With poetry he could take advantage of both solutions, revising and writing anew, and frequently did. The wonder is that he wrote so many memorable poems and that these are distributed fairly evenly throughout his canon. Some that most critics have agreed with Warren's decision to preserve are the following, listed here in the order of composition: "Bearded Oaks," "Pondy Woods," "Original Sin: A Short Story," "The Ballad of Billie Potts," "To a Little Girl, One Year Old, in a Ruined Fortress," "Infant Boy at Midcentury," "School Lesson Based on Word of Tragic Death of Entire Gillum Family," "Mortmain," "Elijah on Mount Carmel," "Masts at Dawn," "Homage to Theodore Dreiser: Psychological Profile," "Old Nigger on One-Mule Cart Encountered Late at Night When Driving Home from Party in the Back Country," "Red-Tail Hawk and Pyre of Youth," "When Life Begins," "English Cocker: Old and Blind," "Rumor Verified," "Little Girl Wakes Early," "The Whole Question," "Old-Time Childhood in Kentucky," "Caribou," and "Three Darknesses," all of which appear in Warren's last general collection, *New and Selected Poems*, published four years before his death. These poems like all the others in that final volume are survivors of a rigorous selective process maintained for thirty years by a poet capable of extraordinary critical detachment even where his own work was concerned. Like all good poems their claim to quality begins in the timelessness of their relevance, yet all are poems that for reasons mainly personal the author chose to keep.

Of the two other poems (after *Brother to Dragons*) that Warren elected to publish separately during his career, *Audubon: A Vision* (1969) was most admired by critics, both as a poem (or rather a series of poems) of extraordinary skill and as a multifaceted symbol of the artist's relation to the world. It was short enough, only eighteen pages, to be included in his *Selected Poems* (1976) and *New and Selected Poems* (1983). It was also, like the other pieces in his collections, a deeply personal poem. In all but the final section the speaker, a Kentuckian, perhaps Warren himself, contemplates the figure of Audubon in a succession of meditative responses to his various aspects: ornithologist, naturalist, artist, charlatan, and genuine lover of the creatures that he nevertheless killed, presumably in order to know them better and so, as the speaker would have it, love them more completely. He prefaced the poem with a biographical sketch but in the work itself, as in *Brother to Dragons*, he freely modified factual data to fit his purposes. Thus the poem is best thought of as a series of "enactments," to use Warren's term, of selected moments in a documentable life that was itself an enigmatic enactment—a complex poem in flesh and blood—of a deeper and private life, the outward details of which must forever resist full explication, but a life that can nevertheless be known in the artifact that remains.

Warren's third long poem was a composition of a very different kind. Here the introspective quality of most of his later poetry is missing, and perhaps for that reason he chose not to include it in the *New and Selected Poems* of 1985, as he might easily have done. The subject of the poem is Chief Joseph of the Nez Perce, whose integration with both his tribe and his traditional segment of the natural world was heedlessly and tragically challenged by the advance of European civilization. Warren seems to have set considerable store by *Chief Joseph*, technically one of his most accomplished pieces.

Critics have noted obvious resemblances to *Brother to Dragons*: for example, the "freed-up blank verse" of *Chief Joseph* and Warren's use there of more than one voice in the narration. As in the earlier poem, the controlling voice is that of the poet, here clearly identifiable as Warren himself, but the voice that holds our attention is that of Chief Joseph, who speaks for almost half of the poem—at some length near the beginning as he presents the series of betrayals that preceded his ill-fated attempt to lead the Nez Perce to a refuge in the Canadian north, and again near the end as he recalls from his place of forced exile the long trek through what is now Yellowstone and north to the place of his defeat. These accounts constitute the heart of the poem, but the poet introduces it with a brief introduction and a quotation from the journals of Lewis and Clark (the first of several such links with documented sources), returns later to tell of the actual surrender of the Nez Perce and the indignities laid upon their despondent chief in after years, and concludes with an account of his own modern-day pilgrimage to the Bear Paw Mountains, where the Nez Perce's hope of temporary escape and ultimate return to their sacred lands ended forever.

Some have found Warren's language in *Chief Joseph* uncharacteristically restrained, but restraint there is appropriate given the dignified stature with which he obviously intended to accord the Indian leader, and readers who may consider such an intention strange in a southern poet with at best a tourist's acquaintance with the American West might keep in mind two ways in which this southern poet, at least, could have seen in the story of the Nez Perce analogies with the history of his own people. For one thing, the Nez Perce tribes' view of themselves as "real people" and their dedication to the dream of a unique destiny in a sacred land form an easily recognizable parallel with the unreconstructed southerner's view of his own confederation of like-minded tribes and those tribes' total readiness to resist an alien and unenlightened usurper. At any rate, such a view had once received vigorous support from Warren's unreconstructed friends in Nashville and achieved a classic restatement in Donald Davidson's memorable "Lee in the Mountains." Moreover, although Warren was mindful, as was Davidson, of the admirable resistance to dispossession made by the handful of Cherokees who had successfully sequestered themselves in the fastness of the Smokies, he also recognized that the Custers, Sheridans, and Shermans who later sought the dispossession, if not extermination, of America's remaining Indians were merely continuing a practice begun by the land-greedy southerners who years before had applauded Jackson of Tennessee in his ruthless dispossession of the Seminole, Creek, Choctaw, Cherokee, and Chickasaw. Even as an associate of Vanderbilt's Agrarians, Warren had been prepared to acknowledge that in racial pride and readiness to suppress minorities in their midst, white Americans in the North and South had been brothers from the beginning. In his view, the differences among Americans were largely due to economics and perhaps the southerner's unique sense of place.

Throughout those years of intense poetic activity, Warren also moved in a variety of new directions, writing essays on the racial question, on the Civil War, and on figures of American literature whom in his earlier years he had ignored. Typically his books on racism in America, *Segregation: The Inner Conflict in the South* (1956) and *Who Speaks for the Negro* (1965), were among the most judicious of their kind produced during those troubled times, and he alternately pleased and displeased partisans on both sides of the question. Like other writers, northern and southern, during the early sixties he observed the centennial with a major essay, *The Legacy of the Civil War: Meditations on the Centennial* (1961), discovering there still another example of the perennial pattern, similar to the examples he had developed in his best fiction, that of growth from innocence through a traumatic rite of passage and on beyond toward a seemingly unattainable fullness of self-knowledge. Years later he would retrace his steps in a penetrating *Jefferson Davis Gets His Citizenship Back* (1980), questioning in conclusion whether the discredited leader, if by some miracle still living, would have been pleased to accept it.

Meanwhile Warren undertook a review of American literature, especially those authors whose poetic output had been keyed to current events and who subsequently had been dismissed by his contemporaries as being mainly of historical interest. Whitman, of course, was in no danger of being neglected, but he plunged into a serious study of Melville's often discredited poetry, about which he had written approvingly years before (1946), and of the Quaker-Abolitionist Whittier's and published selections of their best work with introductory essays that initiated a rehabilitation of both. Then in 1971, to the astonishment of friends and admirers, he published *Homage to Theodore Dreiser on the Centennial of His Birth* and so welcomed into the circle of respectability a writer whose work many of the better critics, including himself, had previously found leaden and plodding. Finally, in 1973 with R.W.B. Lewis and Cleanth Brooks, now his colleagues at Yale, he published a two-volume anthology of American literature that represented, both for him and for his more academically minded colleagues, countless hours of assembling, selecting, and glossing the major documents. Two memorable essays were by-products of that enterprise, one on Mark Twain (1972) and another on Nathaniel Hawthorne (1973), both published in the *Sewanee Review*; and with these and all the rest of his late critical activity Warren transcended any doctrinaire limitations of the criticism that had been carelessly attributed to him over the years, making his advocacy of a catholic view of the function of literature clear to all who chose to pay attention.

Incredible as it may seem, during this period Warren also regularly taught classes, lectured widely, and wrote four more novels, all valuable additions to the canon but all of which initially proved disappointing to some admirers who continued to hope for another *All the King's Men* or even another *World Enough and Time*. The first of the four, *Wilderness: A Tale of the Civil War* (1961), was relatively short, uncomplicated, and in spite of the title little concerned with the South or details of the Civil War. It was the story of an immigrant clubfooted Jew, Adam Rosenzweig, who had come to the new world from his native Bavaria hopeful of finding in America's war confirmation of his belief in justice and mankind's right to freedom. What he discovered in his own behavior and that of two new companions, like him dispossessed but for other reasons and without his ideals, was a disturbing truth that transcended simplistic idealism and brought him to a willingness to deal pragmatically with the inequities of a life that defied perfection.

The protagonists of the remaining novels, mature and desperate in varying degrees of intensity, are all characters whose experience with life has shown them little of its meaning. For example, the writer Brad Tolliver in *Flood: A Romance of Our Time* (1964) returns after a long absence to his native Fiddlersburg, Tennessee, which is shortly to be inundated behind an enormous dam already built downstream. His ostensible reason for being there is to make a movie about the last days of a pioneer southern town, an objective he shares with one Yasha Jones, a director who shortly joins him. Tolliver's ulterior motive in returning to his roots, however, is to find some meaning for his otherwise meaningless life—a need, he discovers, that Jones and even the people of Fiddlersburg share. If in the end he fails to find precisely what he is seeking, he does come at last to something like charity, or *caritas*, and an acceptance of a communion he does not fully understand but can somehow rejoice in. In another novel about a small Tennessee town soon to be buried under the waters of an artificial lake, *Meet Me in the Green Glen* (1971), imminent flooding has no bearing on the plot, and there is no returning native in search of meaning for his existence. Nevertheless, the emphasis here is again upon selfless love, which the principals in their preoccupation with their own loneliness fail to understand or, in the case of one of them, fail until it is too late.

An even better example of selfless love appears in the concluding portion of Warren's *A Place to Come To* (1977), where the central character, Jed Tewksbury (who in many respects resembles Warren himself), tells of returning at last to his native Dugton in Claxford Country, Alabama, and meeting for the first time his stepfather, the untutored countryman whose simple and undemanding devotion to Jed's dead mother has recently given to her final years the peace and happiness she never knew in her earlier ones. An equally noteworthy aspect of this last novel, however, is that in it Warren reverts to the autobiographical mode that had proved its usefulness in *All the King's Men* and in so doing manages to produce, perhaps inadvertently, a work that probably embodies at least as much of the mainsprings of his own life as the volumes of the more manifestly autobiographical poetry he had been writing since 1950. The narrative is wholly Jed Tewksbury's, and like that of Coleridge's Ancient Mariner whose tale served as a shaping image for some of Warren's most interesting work, it is both a confession and an exploration of the meaning of a life—in this case, one that has been spent in flight from the source of its being. Nothing in his life, however, fully satisfies until at midpoint he begins to realize that the pattern of his existence has been an unacknowledged search for something to give it meaning and recognizes that that something must be a coming to terms with the memory of his parents and the life he had abandoned in Dugton. In short, Jed Tewksbury in quiet desperation addresses the same kind of deep personal need that Warren himself spent the last half of his life satisfying in poetry and, toward the end of it, in a moving memoir.

Despite illness Warren's last few years were almost as rich and productive as the rest of his career had been. In 1986 the nation recognized his contribution to its collective life and history by naming him its first poet laureate, an honor that few if any could have questioned, although it seems to have embarrassed the recipient. He would publish no more volumes of poetry, but he had in preparation a final collection of criticism (the first had appeared in 1958), which would include his important "The Use of the Past," a lecture he had delivered in 1977, in which he gave what amounts to a rationale for all the poetry he had been writing since 1954 as well as for all the new poems now precluded by illness and age. Knowing the past in any absolute sense, he had said there, including our personal history, is an impossibility. Nevertheless, we are obligated to strive toward such knowledge even though the end of our striving can be no more than inference, a re-creation, for that striving is the process whereby we create ourselves and thus attain to an existence that elevates us above the level of a "protoplasmic swarm." *New and Selected Essays* came out in 1989, the year of Warren's death; but by that time he had written and published his *Portrait of a Father* (1988). This work had appeared a year earlier in the *Southern Review*, but he wanted a version between boards, he said, to send to friends for Christmas. Accordingly he asked the University Press of Kentucky, which in 1980 had produced a similar volume for his *Jefferson Davis Gets His Citizenship Back*, to publish it for him.

Portrait of a Father is several things. Primarily it is a beautiful tribute to a man who managed to be a lifelong support and comfort (mainly silent) to his spouse and a model of many things, including strength, to at least one of his children. It is also the reminiscence by a major poet of some of his formative experiences in a small town in rural southern Kentucky. More important, however, it is a treasury of material that the author wanted earnestly to think about and might, if time had permitted, have explored in the creation of more formal poetry. Fancifully one might call it Warren's agenda for the first years of his second life as a poet, and as such it is representative of what the best of the southern authors—Faulkner and Welty in their respective "postage stamps" of territory in Mississippi, Wolfe in mythical Altamont, Tate, Ransom, Jarrell, and Ammons in their southern kingdoms of the mind—had managed to do when circumstances stung them into activity. One might also say that Warren and all his diverse tribe of writers in the twentieth century suddenly found themselves in a strange land, a country of many counties, which they felt compelled to explore in order to discover not merely where they were but who they were. The best of them left models of what the adventurous might find, given talent, time, and dedication; but only Warren left behind as a final gesture a model for maintaining the quest. If it should turn out that younger admirers have eyes to see and a will to follow, well and good; the Southern Renaissance, or whatever one chooses to call it, may continue. If not, one renaissance may be blessing enough; and for his part in it Warren, as its best representative, more than deserves his country's designation as its first poet laureate.

Bibliographical Note

As already noted, the most valuable single work in the preparation of this review of the field has been *The History of Southern Literature*, ed. Louis D. Rubin Jr. et al. (Baton Rouge, La., 1985). In addition, two other works have proved their usefulness many times over: *Southern Writers: A Biographical Dictionary*, ed. Robert Bain, Joseph M. Flora, and Louis D. Rubin Jr. (Baton Rouge, La., 1979), and *Fifty Southern Writers after 1900: A Bio-bibliographical Sourcebook* (Westport, Conn., 1987), ed. Flora and Bain. The following anthologies have been useful: *The Literature of the South*, ed. Richmond Croom Beatty, Floyd C. Watkins, and T. Daniel Young (rev. ed., Glenview, Ill., 1968); *Southern Writing, 1585–1920*, ed. Richard Beale Davis, C. Hugh Holman, and Louis Rubin Jr. (New York, 1970); and Rubin's *The Literary South* (New York, 1979).

For general historical background I have found valuable two one-volume histories of the South: Clement Eaton's *The Growth of Southern Civilization* (New York, 1961), and Francis B. Simpkins and Charles P. Roland's *A History of the South* (New York, 1972). Roland's *The Improbable Era: The South since World War II* (Lexington, Ky., 1975) has been particularly useful for the later period. For cultural analysis of the region as it existed before the Civil War and up to World War I, I have used, sometimes with reservations and always with caution, W.J. Cash's groundbreaking *The Mind of the South* (New York, 1941) and, with less need to invoke caution, C. Vann Woodward's *The Burden of Southern History* (Baton Rouge, La., 1960). For contrast I have used Richard M. Weaver's *The Southern Tradition at Bay: A History of Postbellum Thought*, ed. George Core and M.E. Bradford (Washington, D.C., 1989), which gives an intelligent apologist's exposition of the view of southern history held by the Vanderbilt Agrarians, especially Donald Davidson. Although specifically applicable to Kentucky, Arthur K. Moore's *The Frontier Mind: A Cultural Analysis of the Kentucky Frontiersman* (Lexington, Ky., 1957) has provided a realistic appraisal of the southern frontiersman generally and of the frontiersman's contribution to the development of sensibilities characteristic of the region as a whole. For data about the Civil War, I have relied principally upon three works: Bruce Catton's *The Centennial History of the Civil War*, 3 vols. (New York, 1961–65); Charles P. Roland's authoritative and admirably succinct *An American Iliad: The Story of the Civil War* (Lexington, Ky., 1991); and, of course, Shelby Foote's *The Civil War: A Narrative*, 3 vols. (New York, 1958–74), which occupies a significant place in this account as a literary document in its own right. The present study is indebted to all the foregoing as well as to books and articles listed in the notes to individual chapters.

INTRODUCTION

Many of the generalizations here owe at least as much to the primary materials surveyed throughout the study—and to the present author's experience—as they do to academic studies of the historical and cultural background. Indebtedness of this kind is cumulative and sometimes difficult to pin down. More traceable is the indebtedness to reminiscences and astute observations in books such as Robert Bechtold Heilman's *The Southern Connection* (Baton Rouge, La., 1991), C. Vann Woodward's essay "Time and Place," which first appeared in *Southern Review* 20 (winter 1986), Andrew Lytle's last major work, the engaging and richly informative *A Wake for the Living* (New York, 1975), and, before any of these, William Alexander Percy's memorable *Lanterns on the Levee* (New York, 1941). Several miscellanies have provided valuable insights. One of the earliest and best is that edited by Louis D. Rubin Jr. and Robert D. Jacobs, *Southern Renascence: The Literature of the Modern South* (Baltimore, 1953), which contains not only the first printing of Woodward's "The Irony of Southern History" and Heilman's "The Southern Temper" but also the response by Howard W. Odum and John Maclachlan to Donald Davidson's assertion that the economically affluent Northeast could not have produced a William Faulkner. Another useful collection is Mark Royden Winchell's *The Vanderbilt Tradition: Essays in Honor of Thomas Daniel Young* (Baton Rouge, La., 1991), which contains essays about figures and activities at Vanderbilt after the Fugitives and Agrarians. In addition, I am indebted to several of the essays discussed or mentioned in the course of this study, among them Donald Davidson's "Still Rebels, Still Yankees," the pieces by Andrew Lytle and John Donald Wade in *I'll Take My Stand*, and to works by journalists such as Mississippi's Hodding Carter (1907–72) and Willie Morris (b. 1934), specifically to several chapters in the latter's autobiographical *North toward Home* (New York, 1967). I have also used several formal collections of material in such specialized studies as *The Prevailing South: Life and Politics in a Changing Culture*, ed. Dudley Clendinen (Atlanta, 1988), *A World Unsuspected: Portraits of Southern Childhood*, ed. Alex Harris (Chapel Hill, N.C., 1987), Samuel B. Hill Jr.'s *Southern Churches in Crisis* (New York, 1967), and Shirley Abbott's *Womenfolks: Growing Up Down South* (New York, 1983), which presents a broad picture that most southerners, men as well as women, will recognize and one that nonsoutherners may accept with confidence. All of these to some extent have contributed to the remarks in this chapter and the chapters that follow. Each in its way deals with significant aspects of southern life that continue to exert a shaping influence on the South's attitudes about itself and attitudes about the South outside its borders.

CHAPTER 1. THE DEVELOPMENT OF MODERN SOUTHERN FICTION

Like most studies the present one is ultimately, if not directly, indebted to Jay B. Hubbell's *The South in American Literature, 1607–1900* (Durham, N.C., 1954), but use has also been made of J.V. Ridgely's informative *Nineteenth-Century Southern*

Literature (Lexington, Ky., 1980), a companion volume in the University Press of Kentucky's *New Perspectives on the South Series*. An older study, not strictly a survey, that covers the high points of the same ground and provides useful insights about the field as a whole is Louis D. Rubin Jr.'s *Writers of the Modern South: The Faraway Country* (Seattle, 1963). A wide-ranging study of southern attempts to establish an identity, one that includes works outside the normally accepted canon, is Fred Hobson's *Tell about the South: The Southern Rage to Explain* (Baton Rouge, La., 1983). In a shorter essay Hobson concentrates on the metamorphosis of southern literature in the twentieth century: "Surveyors and Boundaries: Southern Literature and Southern Literary Scholarship after Mid-Century," *Southern Review* 27 (October 1991). An excellent, slightly earlier study that looks mainly at literary figures is Richard Gray's *Writing the South: Ideas of an American Region* (Cambridge, England, 1986), which spans the range of southern writing from Thomas Jefferson to Walker Percy and concentrates on the way in which southern authors in their literary explorations have created successive identities for the region. Another study that has proved useful, one also wide-ranging but with a narrower focus, is Robert O. Stephens's *The Family Saga in the South: Generations and Destinies* (Baton Rouge, La., 1995), which examines the exploratory use writers have made of the family saga in the changing context of southern life. Finally, there are two invaluable works by the historian and critic Lewis P. Simpson, *The Dispossessed Garden* (Athens, Ga., 1975) and *The Fable of the Southern Writer* (Baton Rouge, La., 1994), in which he focuses upon the literary imagination itself as the device by which the southern writer since the Civil War has conducted a protracted self-interpretation.

The following studies of individual authors have also proved useful: Philip Butcher, *George W. Cable: A Biography* (New York, 1962); George Garrett's "Mary Johnston: The Long Roll," in *My Silk Purse and Yours: The Publishing Scene and American Literary Art* (Columbia, Mo., 1992); Louis D. Rubin Jr., *No Place on Earth: Ellen Glasgow, James Branch Cabell, and Richmond-in-Virginia* (Austin, Tex., 1959); Louis Auchincloss, *Ellen Glasgow* (Minneapolis, 1964); Joe Lee Davis, *James Branch Cabell* (New York, 1962); Robert E. Hemenway, *Zora Neale Hurston: A Literary Biography* (Urbana, Ill., 1977); Robert Welker, "*Liebestod* with a Southern Accent" on Evelyn Scott, in *Reality and Myth: Essays in American Literature in Memory of Richmond Croom Beatty* (Nashville, 1964), 179–211. The *Southern Review* 20 (October 1984) has nine pieces on E.M. Roberts, including reminiscences and essays by William H. Slavick, Victor A. Kramer, Janet Lewis, and Lewis P. Simpson. In addition, I have used Frederick P.W. McDowell, *Elizabeth Madox Roberts* (New Haven, Conn., 1972) and William S. Ward, *A Literary History of Kentucky* (Knoxville, Tenn., 1988).

CHAPTER 2. POETRY AND POLITICS AT VANDERBILT, 1920–40

A comprehensive account of the literary and political activities of the Vanderbilt Fugitives and Agrarians, authoritative but understandably biased, is Donald Davidson's Lamar Lectures, delivered at Mercer University in 1957 and published as *Southern*

Writers in the Modern World (Athens, Ga., 1958). For the Fugitive movement, however, I have supplemented this account with Louise Cowan's *The Fugitive Group: A Literary History* (Baton Rouge, La., 1959), and Louis D. Rubin Jr.'s expanded account of the principal figures with extensive commentary, *The Wary Fugitives: Four Poets and the South* (Baton Rouge, La., 1978). For the Agrarian movement I have used Paul K. Conkin's *The Southern Agrarians* (Knoxville, Tenn., 1988), adding to this work the sympathetic reappraisals by Richard M. Weaver and Richmond Croom Beatty in *Shenandoah* (summer 1952), an issue that also contains retrospective statements by seven of the original members of the group: Ransom, Davidson, Owsley, Tate, Nixon, Lytle, and Wade. A convenient edition of *I'll Take My Stand*, published by Harper and Row in 1962, contains an introduction by Louis D. Rubin Jr. and brief but valuable biographical essays by Virginia Rock; papers presented at a symposium at Vanderbilt to commemorate the fiftieth anniversary of that volume were published as *A Band of Prophets: The Vanderbilt Agrarians after Fifty Years*, ed. William C. Havard and Walter Sullivan (Baton Rouge, La., 1982). For my remarks on Vanderbilt's part in the New Criticism I have made use of the valuable accounts included in *The Vanderbilt Tradition: Essays in Honor of Thomas Daniel Young*, ed. Mark Royden Winchell (Baton Rouge, La., 1991). The best guides to that topic, however, are primary documents: John Crowe Ransom's *The World's Body* (New York, 1938), Ransom's *The New Criticism* (New York, 1941), Allen Tate's *Essays of Four Decades* (New York, 1968), and two textbooks by Cleanth Brooks and Robert Penn Warren, *Understanding Poetry* (New York, 1938) and *Understanding Fiction* (New York, 1943). In addition I have made use of two biographical studies, Radcliffe Squires's *Allen Tate. A Literary Biography* (New York, 1971), and Thomas Daniel Young's *Gentleman in a Dustcoat: A Biography of John Crowe Ransom* (Baton Rouge, La., 1976), and the following collections of letters: *Selected Letters of John Crowe Ransom*, ed. Thomas Daniel Young and George Core (Baton Rouge, La., 1985); *The Lytle-Tate Letters: The Correspondence of Andrew Lytle and Allen Tate*, ed. Thomas Daniel Young and Elizabeth Sarcone (Oxford, Miss., 1987); *The Literary Correspondence of Donald Davidson and Allen Tate*, ed. John Tyree Fain and Thomas Daniel Young (Athens, Ga., 1974); and *The Republic of Letters in America: The Correspondence of John Peale Bishop and Allen Tate*, ed. Thomas Daniel Young and John J. Hindle (Lexington, Ky., 1981). The *Southern Review* 12 (October 1976), in celebration of Tate's seventy-fifth birthday published several valuable essays, among them the contributions by Cleanth Brooks, Denis Donoghue, Louis D. Rubin Jr., and George Core.

3. THE NEW EMPHASIS ON CRAFTSMANSHIP

The reverence for craftsmanship as practiced and zealously advocated by the Vanderbilt critics is nowhere better exemplified than in *The House of Fiction: An Anthology of the Short Story with Commentary*, ed. Caroline Gordon and Allen Tate (New York, 1950). In addition to that volume I have used the brief biographical and critical study of Caroline Gordon and her work by Frederick P.W. McDowell, *Caroline Gordon*

(Minneapolis, 1966), which lists some of the more important articles about her writing up to that time, and the only full account of Gordon's life, Ann Waldron's *Close Connections: Caroline Gordon and the Southern Renaissance* (New York, 1987). For Katherine Anne Porter, who published far less than Gordon but almost nothing that is not crafted to perfection, the standard biography, authorized by her before her death, is Joan Givner's *Katherine Anne Porter: A Life* (New York, 1982). In addition to that work I have used the one excellent collection of essays about her work, *Katherine Anne Porter: A Critical Symposium*, ed. Lodwick Hartley and George Core (Athens, Ga., 1969).

4. Two Major Novelists

For accounts of Thomas Wolfe's life and work, I have relied heavily on David Herbert Donald's definitive *Look Homeward: A Life of Thomas Wolfe* (New York, 1987), and on several of the works that Donald cites there as sources for his study: Floyd C. Watkins's *Thomas Wolfe's Characters: Portraits from Life* (Norman, Okla., 1958), Richard S. Kennedy's *The Window of Memory: The Literary Career of Thomas Wolfe* (Chapel Hill, N.C., 1962), and *Thomas Wolfe: Three Decades of Criticism*, ed. Leslie A. Field (New York, 1968). For Faulkner I have begun with Joseph Blotner's two-volume *Faulkner: A Biography* (New York, 1974) and to material from that work added data and insights found in the following: *Selected Letters of William Faulkner*, ed. Joseph Blotner (London, 1977); *Faulkner in the University*, ed. Frederick L. Gwynn and Joseph L. Blotner (New York, 1959); and three works by Cleanth Brooks, *William Faulkner: The Yoknapatawpha Country* (New Haven, Conn., 1963), *William Faulkner: Toward Yoknapatawpha and Beyond* (Baton Rouge, La., 1978), and *On the Prejudices, Predilections, and Firm Beliefs of William Faulkner* (Baton Rouge, La., 1987). I have also made extensive use of the essays by Robert Penn Warren and others in *Faulkner: A Collection of Critical Essays*, ed. Robert Penn Warren (Englewood Cliffs, N.J., 1966).

5. Southern Playwrights

As has been noted, southern writers of drama for the most part have achieved little more than the status of a footnote, the exceptions being those few who have ventured afield to find permanent success either in New York's theaters or in Hollywood. Some have achieved temporary or accidental success in this way, usually as a consequence of adaptations made of their works by others, and several of these writers have been given attention recently in a special winter/spring issue of *Southern Quarterly* 33 (1995). For biographical data about the others, in addition to the general surveys mentioned earlier, I have consulted the following: Alan S. Downer, *50 Years of American Drama: 1900–1950* (Chicago, 1941), Vincent S. Kenny, *Paul Green* (New York, 1971), Carl Rollyson, *Lillian Hellman: Her Legend and Her Legacy* (New York, 1988), and Donald Spoto, *The Kindness of Strangers: The Life of Tennessee Williams* (Boston, 1985); William S. Ward's brief account of Actors Theatre in *A Literary History of Kentucky* (Knoxville, Tenn., 1988); and Michael Bigelow Dixon and Michele Volansky, eds., *By*

Southern Playwrights: Plays from Actors Theatre (Lexington, Ky., 1996). *Conversations with Kentucky Writers*, ed. L. Elisabeth Beattie (Lexington, Ky., 1996), contains a useful interview with Marsha Norman.

6. THE BEGINNING OF RECOGNITION

The best source of information about William Alexander Percy is the book under discussion, his autobiographical *Lanterns on the Levee: Recollections of a Planter's Son* (New York, 1941). A useful complementary portrait, however, emerges from Jay Tolson's *Pilgrim in the Ruins: A Life of Walker Percy* (New York, 1992). I have used both of these sources for material in this chapter and in addition the valuable essay by James E. Rocks, "The Art of *Lanterns on the Levee*," in *Southern Review* 12 (October 1976). For the brief discussion of Warren's novel I have drawn upon James H. Justus's *The Achievement of Robert Penn Warren* (Baton Rouge, La., 1981), and essays in Robert S. Chambers's *Twentieth Century Interpretations of* All the King's Men: *A Collection of Critical Essays* (Englewood Cliffs, N.J., 1977), which contains Warren's introduction to the Modern Library Edition and contributions by Robert B. Heilman, Jonathan Baumbach, Jerome Meckier, and others. For Faulkner I have used the same references as cited for Chapter 4 but with special attention to *Faulkner in the University*, ed. Gwynn and Blotner, and Cleanth Brooks's *William Faulkner: Toward Yoknapatawpha and Beyond*. In addition, I have used Malcolm Cowley's *The Portable Faulkner*, rev. ed. (New York, 1967).

7. SOUTHERN REGIONALISM COMES OF AGE

Robert B. Heilman's "The Southern Temper," especially important to a discussion of regionalism, first appeared in *Southern Renascence*, ed. Rubin and Jacobs. For biographical data about the Kentucky authors, Jesse Stuart, Harriet Arnow, and James Still, I have used William S. Ward's *A Literary History of Kentucky*, which contains useful bibliographical entries on all three. *Conversations with Kentucky Writers*, ed. L. Elisabeth Beattie, contains an informative interview with James Still as well as valuable interviews with a number of younger authors discussed elsewhere in this study. For data on Marjorie Kinnan Rawlings, see Samuel L. Bellman, *Marjorie Kinnan Rawlings* (New York, 1974). My source for data about the early years of Peter Taylor's career is Albert J. Griffith, *Peter Taylor* (New York, 1970). More recent studies that have proved useful in other ways are Walter Sullivan's chapter in *In Praise of Blood Sports and Other Essays* (Baton Rouge, La., 1990) and Catherine Clark Graham's *Southern Accents: The Fiction of Peter Taylor* (New York, 1994). For Andrew Lytle the full-length study that has been most useful is Mark Lucas's *The Southern Vision of Andrew Lytle* (Baton Rouge, La., 1986). I have also drawn upon Walter Sullivan's "Andrew Lytle: The Mythmaker at Home," included in his *In Praise of Blood Sports*.

8. WOMEN EXTEND FICTION'S RANGE

For McCullers I have used Virginia Spencer Carr's *The Lonely Hunter: A Biography of Carson McCullers* (New York, 1975), but I have also drawn upon Louise Gossett's *Violence in Recent Southern Fiction* (Durham, N.C., 1965), and Alfred Kazin's brief comments in *Bright Book of Life: American Novelists and Storytellers from Hemingway to Mailer* (New York, 1973). My sources for material on Eudora Welty are as follows: Ruth M. Vande Kieft, *Eudora Welty* (New York, 1962), J.A. Bryant Jr., *Eudora Welty* (Minneapolis, 1968), and Michael Kreyling, *Eudora Welty's Achievement of Order* (Baton Rouge, La., 1980). For Welty's later work I have consulted essays by Robert B. Heilman, Louise Gossett, and Thomas Daniel Young, in *Eudora Welty: Critical Essays*, ed. Peggy Whitman Prenshaw (Jackson, Miss., 1979). My sources for material on Flannery O'Connor are these: Dorothy Walters, *Flannery O'Connor* (New York, 1973); Frederick Asals, *Flannery O'Connor: The Imagination of Extremity* (Athens, Ga., 1982); and essays by Frederick J. Hoffman, Louis D. Rubin Jr., and C. Hugh Holman in *The Added Dimension: The Art and Mind of Flannery O'Connor* (New York, 1977). In addition I have used *Letters of Flannery O'Connor: The Habit of Being*, ed. Sally Fitzgerald (New York, 1979).

9. THE NEW BLACK WRITERS

In addition to works by the authors themselves, notably Richard Wright's *Black Boy* and Ralph Ellison's *Invisible Man*, I have found the following sources useful: Robert A. Bone, *The Negro Novel in America*, rev. ed. (New Haven, Conn., 1965); Constance Webb, *Richard Wright: A Biography* (New York, 1968); Robert Hemenway, *Zora Neale Hurston: A Literary Biography* (Urbana, Ill., 1977); Gayle Jones, *Liberating Voices: Oral Tradition in African American Literature* (Cambridge, Mass., 1991); Ralph Ellison, *The Collected Essays of Ralph Ellison*, ed. John F. Callahan (New York, 1995); Valerie Babb, *Ernest Gaines* (Boston, 1991); and Marcia Gaudet and Carl Wooten, *Porch Talk with Ernest Gaines: Conversations on the Writer's Craft* (Baton Rouge, La., 1992).

10. THE SOUTH AFTER WORLD WAR II

For his authoritative review of economic, political, and social developments in the South during the years following World War II in succeeding chapters as well as in this one, I am indebted to Charles P. Roland's *The Improbable Era: The South since World War II* (Lexington, Ky., 1975). To George Core, I am indebted for his authoritative account of the situation that southern writers currently face, "The Literary Marketplace and the Southern Writer Today," in *Southern Review* 21 (April 1985). For biographical data on James Agee and Truman Capote, the essays by Richard R. Schramm and Helen S. Garson in *Fifty Southern Writers after 1900*, ed. Flora and Bain, have proved useful as well as convenient. Victor A. Kramer has a more detailed study of Agee, *James Agee* (New York, 1975), and Alfred Kazin has useful observations about Capote's *In Cold Blood* in his *Bright Book of Life* (New York, 1973).

11. Postwar Poetry

My remarks in this chapter on southern poets after 1960 are based mainly on familiarity with their work and reviews of it and in some cases with the poets themselves. A perceptive survey of activity during the two decades immediately following 1960 is the chapter by James Justus in *The History of Southern Literature*, ed. Rubin et al. Dabney Stuart's introduction to *The Fred Chappell Reader* (New York, 1987) is a warm and perceptive essay on the work of that poet-novelist. There is a useful appreciation of the poetry of Donald Justice by Charles Wright, "Homage to the Thin Man," *Southern Review* 30 (autumn 1994). For Randall Jarrell and his work I have used William H. Pritchard's *Randall Jarrell: A Literary Life* (New York, 1990), Suzanne Ferguson's *The Poetry of Randall Jarrell* (Baton Rouge, La., 1971), and, mainly for incidental data, my own *Understanding Randall Jarrell* (Columbia, S.C., 1986). For data about James Dickey I am indebted to Richard J. Calhoun and Robert W. Hill, *James Dickey* (Boston, 1983), and to Calhoun's more recent essay in *Fifty Southern Writers after 1900*. I am also indebted to essays by Monroe Spears: "James Dickey: Southern Visionary as Celestial Navigator," in *American Ambitions: Selected Essays on Literary and Cultural Themes* (Baltimore, 1987), "Dionysius and the Galaxy: A Reading of James Dickey's *The Zodiac*," in *The Vanderbilt Tradition*, ed. Mark Royden Winchell (Baton Rouge, La., 1991), and "James Dickey's Poetry," *Southern Review* 30 (autumn 1994); and to one by Harold Bloom: "James Dickey: From 'The Other' through *The Early Motion*," *Southern Review* 21 (January 1985). Less has been written about A.R. Ammons. The essay by William Harmon in *Fifty Southern Writers after 1900* is most useful, as are Alan Holder's *A.R. Ammons* (Boston, 1978), and Nathan Scott's "The Poetry of Ammons," *Southern Review* 24 (autumn 1988).

12. Mainstream Fiction

As with the previous chapter, some of my information here has come from encounters with the writers themselves. Fred Hobson in *The Southern Writer in the Postmodern World* (Athens, Ga., 1991) discusses a number of the writers, among them Fred Chappell, Lee Smith, and Bobbie Ann Mason. In addition to the references already cited, for Chappell I have used George Garrett's valuable short piece, "A Few Things about Fred Chappell," in *My Silk Purse and Yours: The Publishing Scene and American Literary Art* (Columbia, Mo., 1992). For Garrett himself, I have used two essays by Monroe K. Spears: "George Garrett and the Historical Novel," in *American Ambitions* (Baltimore, 1987), and "A Trilogy Complete, a Past Recaptured: George Garrett," in *Countries of the Mind: Literary Explorations* (Columbia, Mo., 1992). A full study is that by R.H.W. Dillard, *Understanding George Garrett* (Columbia, S.C., 1988). For others of these newer writers criticism is understandably less plentiful. Two useful essays on Madison Jones are Jan Nordby Gretlund's "The Last Agrarian: Madison Jones's Achievement," *Southern Review* 22 (summer 1986), and Monroe K. Spears, "A New Classic: Madison Jones, *A Cry of Absence*," in *American Ambitions* (Baltimore, 1987). In addition to an excerpt from Gurney Norman's novel in progress, *The Southern Quarterly* 34 (spring 1996) has J.D. Williamson's interview with Norman and an essay by Nancy Coman Coveney, Kakie Urch, and Lori Shenefelt, "Divine Right's Trip Redux: Feminists Read the Southern Sixties." William S. Ward discusses Norman as well as other contemporary Kentuckians, Ed McClanahan, Guy Davenport, James Baker Hall and Bobbie Ann Mason, in his *A Literary History of Kentucky*. Lee Smith has been honored with a special issue of *Southern Quarterly* 32 (winter 1994), which contains three interviews and articles on *Oral History* and *The Devil's Dream*. Ellen Douglas has been similarly honored in *Southern Quarterly* 33 (summer 1995), which contains interviews, seven essays, and a checklist of materials. Useful interviews with Doris Betts are in *South Carolina Review* 28 (spring 1996), and in *Southern Quarterly* 34 (winter 1996). The Fall 1992 issue of *Southern Quarterly* contains three essays on Anne Tyler, notably one by Barbara Harrell Carson, "Complicate, Complicate: Anne Tyler's Moral Imperative," as well as an illuminating interview with Bobbie Ann Mason by Dorothy Combs Hill. George Garrett's review, "Bobbie Ann Mason: *Love Life*" is actually a perceptive review of her work up to that point. For Mary Lee Settle the best accounts are Garrett's *Understanding Mary Lee Settle* (Columbia, S.C., 1988); Brian Rosenberg, "The Price of Freedom: An Interview with Mary Lee Settle," *Southern Review* 25 (spring 1989); and the appreciative essays by Peggy Bach, "The Searching Voice and Vision of Mary Lee Settle," *Southern Review* 20 (October 1984), and by Monroe K. Spears, "Love, Loss, and Memory in West Virginia," in *Countries of the Mind* (Columbia, Mo., 1992).

13. THE NEW MAJOR WRITERS

As a potential successor to Faulkner, William Styron attracted a fair amount of attention in the years following World War II. Afterward he became involved in controversies. Louis D. Rubin Jr.'s discussion of the early fiction, "William Styron: Notes on a Southern Writer in Our Time," is in his *Writers of the Modern South* (Seattle, 1963). Good general accounts are those by Richard Pearce, *William Styron* (Minneapolis, 1971), and Marc L. Ratner, *William Styron* (New York, 1972). Good studies of Styron's later novels are the essays by George Core, "*The Confessions of Nat Turner* and the Burden of the Past," *Southern Literary Journal* 2 (spring 1970), and Richard L. Rubenstein, "The South Encounters the Holocaust: William Styron's *Sophie's Choice*," *Michigan Quarterly Review* 20 (fall 1981). Studies on John Barth are less abundant. One of the best is Charles B. Harris's *Passionate Virtuosity: The Fiction of John Barth* (Urbana, Ill., 1983). George Garrett's review of *Giles Goat-Boy* and *Tidewater Tales* in *My Silk Purse and Yours* (Columbia, Mo., 1992) has the solid substance of an essay. Much has been written recently on Reynolds Price. I have found useful Constance Rooke's *Reynolds Price* (Boston, 1983); John W. Stevenson's "The Faces of Reynolds Price's Short Fiction," in *Studies in Short Fiction* 3 (1966); George Garrett's "Reynolds

Price: *The Tongues of Angels* and *The Foreseeable Future*," in *My Silk Purse and Yours*, and two pieces from the *Southern Review*: Ashby Bland Crowder's "Reynolds Price on Writing," 20 (spring 1986) and James A. Schiff's "Fathers and Sons in the Fiction of Reynolds Price: A Sense of Crucial Ambiguity," 29 (winter 1993). For Harry Crews, in addition to extensive comments made to me by his teacher, Andrew Lytle, I am indebted to the essay by Frank W. Shelton in *Fifty Writers after 1900*, ed. Flora and Bain, and to Shelton's "Harry Crews: Man's Search for Perfection," *Southern Literary Journal* 12 (spring 1980). For biographical data about Cormac McCarthy I am indebted mainly to Robert L. Welker's brief article in *Southern Writers: A Biographical Dictionary*, ed. Bain, Flora, and Rubin. I have also used Donald R. Noble's chapter "The Future of Southern Writing," in *A History of Southern Literature*, ed. Rubin et al., and Walter Sullivan's comments in *A Requiem for the Renascence* (Athens, Ga., 1976), pp. 70–72.

14. THREE KEY FIGURES

Comments about Shelby Foote's history that have been most helpful in addition to those in Foote's own bibliographical notes are those by James M. Cox, "Shelby Foote's Civil War," *Southern Review* 21 (spring 1985). George Garrett has an excellent short article in *My Silk Purse and Yours*. For my remarks on Wendell Berry I have relied mainly on the writing itself and my acquaintance with Berry as a colleague and friend over the years. Another former colleague, William S. Ward, discusses Berry at length in *A Literary History of Kentucky*, and L. Elisabeth Beattie has a useful interview in *Conversations with Kentucky Writers*. Comments on Walker Percy abound. I have found most useful Jay Tolson's excellent biographical study, *Pilgrim in the Ruins: A Life of Walker Percy* (New York, 1992), and two of Percy's collections of essays: *The Message in the Bottle* (New York, 1975) and *Signposts in a Strange Land*, with an introduction by Patrick Samway (New York, 1991).

15. ROBERT PENN WARREN

Like all other students of the work of Robert Penn Warren, I am deeply indebted to James H. Justus's comprehensive *The Achievement of Robert Penn Warren* (Baton Rouge, La., 1981). In addition I have found the following sources most useful: Neil Nakadate, ed., *Robert Penn Warren: Critical Perspectives* (Lexington, Ky., 1981); Victor H. Strandberg's two studies of the poetry, *A Colder Fire: The Poetry of Robert Penn Warren* (Lexington, Ky., 1965) and *The Poetic Vision of Robert Penn Warren* (Lexington, Ky., 1977); Calvin Bedient, *In the Heart's Kingdom: Robert Penn Warren's Major Poetry* (Cambridge, Mass., 1984); Joseph R. Millichap, *Robert Penn Warren: A Study of the Short Fiction* (New York, 1992); Floyd C. Watkins, *Then and Now: The Personal Past in the Poetry of Robert Penn Warren* (Lexington, Ky., 1982); and two excellent studies by Monroe K. Spears: "Robert Penn Warren as Critic," in *American Ambitions* (Baltimore, 1987), and "Robert Penn Warren and the Literary Life," in *Countries of the Mind* (Columbia, Mo., 1992).

Index

Understanding Poetry (with Cleanth Brooks), 56; *Who Speaks for the Negro,* 257; *Wilderness: A Tale of the Civil War,* 258; *World Enough and Time,* 111, 250-51, 252, 258
Warren, Rosanna, 253
Washington, George, 16
Watkins, Floyd C., 170
Waugh, Evelyn, 151, 235
Welles, Orson, 88, 156
Welty, Eudora, 6-7, 15, 62, 116, 124, 140-46, 172, 175, 199, 204, 249, 260; *The Bride of the Innisfallen,* 141, 200; *Collected Stories,* 141, 142; *A Curtain of Green,* 141, 142; *Delta Wedding,* 141, 142, 144; *The Eye of the Story,* 141; *The Golden Apples,* 141, 142, 143; *Losing Battles,* 141, 142, 144-45, 200; *One Time, One Place,* 141; *One Writer's Beginning,* 141; *The Optimist's Daughter,* 141, 144, 200; *The Ponder Heart,* 141, 143-44, 200; *The Robber Bridegroom,* 141, 142; *The Shoe Bird,* 141; *The Wide Net,* 141
Westcott, Glenway, 26-27
Whitehead, Alfred North, 55, 194
Whitman, Walt, 76, 173, 193, 244, 257
Whittier, John Greenleaf, 257
Wilbur, Richard, 187
Wilcox, James, 172
Wilkinson, Sylvia, 175, 204
Williams, Garth, 185
Williams, Jonathan, 173, 174
Williams, Tennessee, 93-97, 100; *American Blues,* 94; *Baby Doll,* 95; *Battle of Angels,* 94; *Camino Real,* 96; *Cat on a Hot Tin Roof,* 94, 96; *The Fugitive Kind,* 94; *The Glass Menagerie,* 94, 95; *Period of Adjustment,* 96; *The Roman Spring of Mrs. Stone,* 95; *Rose Tattoo,* 96; *A Streetcar Named Desire,* 95; *Suddenly Last Summer,* 96; *Summer and Smoke,* 96; *Sweet Bird of Youth,* 96; *Where I Live,* 97
Williams, William Carlos, 193, 242, 245
Willingham, Calder, 201
Wills, Jesse, 41
Wimsatt, W.K., 57
Winters, Yvor, 26-27, 58, 176
Wittgenstein, Ludwig, 173
Wolfe, Thomas, 5, 17, 21, 74-78, 88, 137, 216, 226, 260; *The Hills Beyond,* 77; *Look Homeward, Angel,* 62, 75, 76; *Of Time and the River,* 76; *The Story of a Novel,* 76; *The Web and the Rock,* 77; *You Can't Go Home Again,* 77
Wolfe, Tom (Thomas Kennerly Jr.), 173
Woodward, C. Vann, 171
Wordsworth, William, 27, 242
World War I, 4-5
Wright, James, 178
Wright, Richard, 6, 155-58; *Black Boy,* 157, 158, 159; *Eight Men,* 157; *Lawd Today,* 157; *Native Son,* 156, 157, 159; *The Outsiders,* 156; *Twelve Million Black Voices* (with Edwin Rosskam), 156

Yeats, W.B., 26, 27, 45, 60
Yerby, Frank, 196
Young, Stark, 5, 15, 35-36, 47, 87-88, 97
Young, T.D., 170

Zukofsky, Louis, 173

3